Zoltán Peterecz

Jeremiah Smith, Jr. and Hungary, 1924–1926:

the United States, the League of Nations, and the Financial Reconstruction of Hungary

VERSITA

Versita Discipline: History, Archeology

Published by Versita, Versita Ltd, 78 York Street, London W1H 1DP, Great Britain.

ISBN (paperback) 978-83-7656-006-9

ISBN (hardcover) 978-83-7656-007-6

ISBN (for electronic copy) 978-83-7656-008-3

Managing Editor: Katarzyna Ślusarska

Language Editor: Victoria Symons

Cover illustration: Jeremiah Smith, photo from 1924-1926, as appeared in Tolnai Világlapja journal, Tolnai Printing House.

www.versita.com

Contents

In loving memory of my parents.

Foreword

The present world economic situation with all its detrimental effects is said to have many common features with the Great Depression, which started in 1929 and lasted for the better part of the 1930s. That does not mean that there are not huge differences as well between the two crises. Obviously, one has to be careful with drawing too close parallels between two eras separated by 80 years of quickened globalization, still one cannot escape the feeling that history seems to repeat itself again in the sense that the root of the evil is almost identical: artificially created credit boom both in the banking and customer sector, sometimes wild gambling on the stock markets, and most importantly creating the bubble effect that was so useful a metaphor in describing the late 1920s.

If the problems are really very similar to those of the past century, the remedies should show some similarity as well. Hungary, for example, the main target of this book, had recourse both in 1924 and 2008 to outside financial help. In both instances, Hungary became a member of influential and worldwide organizations: in 1922 it joined the League of Nations, while in 1999 and 2004 it joined NATO and the European Union, respectively. The League of Nations' loan in 1924 and the International Monetary Fund's financial help in 1928 tried to serve the same end: to provide a monetary frame under which Hungary would be able to launch all sorts of fiscal reforms, achieve a stable currency and a balanced budget. Without wanting to unduly stress the point that the two actions are identical, or very similar, however, the two cases deserve attention and provide basis for a historical study. The Central European countries, historically speaking always in a weaker situation than those of the West, had to and have to once more ask for financial help outside their borders, even if reluctantly. Much has changed in Central Europe since after World War I, but many basic attitudes and the general worldview have not. An additional aim of this work is to serve a useful basis for continual studies by others in the different countries of Central Europe.

It is of importance how one wants to define Central Europe. Without going into details and controversy, for the purpose of my study I included four countries as making up Central Europe: Austria, Hungary, Germany, and Poland. Although Czechoslovakia belongs to Central Europe geographically, from the political and the monetary points of view in the years following World War I, it represented a different situation; therefore it was not included in my study. As a further refinement, I chose Austria and especially Hungary for the object of this study. Since the general topic is that of the League of Nations, Central European financial reconstruction, and the involvement of the private American sphere, it was an obvious choice that Austria and

Hungary should have the limelight in the region. Moreover, as an account of an American as the financial controller in Hungary, the bulk of the book deals with Hungary and the reconstruction there with a special emphasis on Jeremiah Smith, Jr., the American Commissioner-General. Austria is studied not in an all-out effort but rather as its role in leading up to the Hungarian reconstruction. The other two "Central European" countries, Germany and Poland, serve more as a background and as a point in comparison, both for the overall reconstruction effort in the region and the American participation in it.

However, the main emphasis of the book, which grew out of my PhD dissertation, lies on Jeremiah Smith, Jr. and Hungary. The man who oversaw the financial reconstruction of Hungary and the relationship he built and maintained with the host country. As far as I know, this is the first time that Smith has been chosen as the subject of a thorough study, therefore the book will provide some missing details about his career and personality. Hopefully, the work will serve as an addition to the already large and growing literature on American foreign policy and worldview in the 1920s. With that in mind, I will let the reader go and start on a journey back in time, which, once again, is in many ways similar to the situation today.

Acknowledgments

In collecting material about Jeremiah Smith, Jr. and his work in Hungary in the mid-1920s, I was not in an easy situation. I had to travel to many places and carry out research in various archives. In addition to the Hungarian National Archives in Budapest, I also did research at the League of Nations Archives in Geneva, Switzerland, at the National Archives in London, Great Britain, at the Bank of England Archives in London, Great Britain, and I also used material from the National Archives of the United States and other collections such as the Jeremiah Smith Papers at Phillips Exeter Academy, NH. Together with the contemporary newspapers and such primary printed sources as the Papers Relating to the Foreign Relations of the United States (FRUS), the United States Congressional Record, and the Documents on British Foreign Policy (DBFP), for example, these findings, most of which have never been used to the best of my knowledge, give the backbone of my book. Since there are many figures in the text provided in different currencies, those originally not in US dollars will be given in that currency in parentheses.

There are many people I owe debt to the successful completion of this work. Without any ranking order, I wish to list the most important persons without whom this work would not be in its present form. Professor Tibor Frank of Eötvös Loránd University (ELTE, Budapest), who was my thesis adviser, and also a mentor every student should have, provided me with good overview, a lot of constructive criticism, and a great deal of friendly advice. I hope that many of my shortcomings he pointed out over the years have been eliminated by today. Professor Tamás Magyarics of ELTE, from whom I believe I first heard the name of Jeremiah Smith, Jr., taught me much of what I know about American foreign policy and he was very influential of my choosing this field as a lifelong ambition. Professor Tibor Glant of Kossuth University of Debrecen was a true friend in advising me on some crucial points and made sure that I could read some important material. I would also like to acknowledge the professional and very helpful people at the various archives: János Kalmár at the Hungarian National Archives, Andra Crawford at Phillips Exeter, Bernhardine Pejovic and Pascal Pouillot at the League of Nations Archives, and Jeanette Sherry, Jenny Ulph, and Ben White at the Bank of England Archives. Lastly, I want to say thanks to my family, who were always patient with me when I chose to work instead of spending precious time with them.

Abbreviations

BoE	Bank of England Archives, London, Great Britain
DBFP	Documents on British Foreign Policy
FRUS	Papers Relating to the Foreign Relations of the United States
HNA	Magyar Országos Levéltár [Hungarian National Archives], Budapest, Hungary
JSAA	Jeremiah Smith Academy Archives, Phillips Exeter Academy, NH
JSP	James Speyer Papers, New York Public Library, New York, NY
LNA	League of Nations Archives, Geneva, Switzerland
LNJ	League of Nations, Official Journal
NARA	National Archives and Records Administration
TNA	The National Archives, London, Great Britain

Introduction

The International Landscape in the early 1920s

After the devastating World War I, most of Europe lay in ruin. The so far unknown destruction in both human life and material value left an indelible mark on the continent. As a consequence of the four years of bloodletting, many European countries found themselves economically and financially in dire straits. Moreover, the map of Europe was redrawn—new states were born, old empires were gone, and some defeated countries survived only at the great cost of territories and population detached. The most spectacular changes happened in Central Europe. The Austro-Hungarian Empire vanished and in its place no fewer than four new countries emerged. While Czechoslovakia or the Serb-Croat-Slovene Kingdom, for example, found in the new situation ample justification and the embodiment of Wilson's quest for nations' self-determination, Austria and Hungary were left with smaller population and territory than before. In the case of Hungary, the differences to its prewar status were dramatic: it lost two-thirds of its former territory and almost the same percentage of its population.

As time passed, it was clear that some rehabilitation would be needed. Mainly with Great Britain in the lead, Europe tried to put its house in order. The reasoning was that economic revitalization must work in parallel with financial recovery. It is little wonder that Great Britain was the main force behind the initiation of a European reconstruction. Although it had lost a lot of men too in the war, its territory was not under actual fighting, and of all the belligerent countries it remained relatively the most intact. This was of great importance since London had been the capital of the financial world for many decades. Any real organizing power with effect on a possible rebuilding of the European continent could have come only from London: the banks and financial houses here alone in Europe had the necessary resources to finance the bulk of the reconstruction. The majority of the loans could not have been raised without these institutions as the main agents.

The other reason why Great Britain had to take on the leading role was the conspicuous absence of the new number one power, the United States of America. America, after somewhat reluctantly joining the war in 1917, was on the verge of becoming a major force on the European Continent. However, Woodrow Wilson's dream of a postwar international organization to guard over the peace came into being without the United States itself. The US Senate voted against such an international commitment. Thus the League of Nations, formally established on January 10, 1920, already at the outset, suffered a great loss in terms of worldwide influence, power, credibility, and sufficiency. Moreover, other important countries were missing to give the organization more credit: Germany (becoming a member in 1926) and the Soviet Union (not a member till 1934).

The lack of the country's participation did not exclude the possibility of American contribution to financial affairs in Europe. But the subsequent Republican governments made such a course by all means more difficult. When European reconstruction became an issue in which American participation was sought, the main difficulty lay in the fact that such initiatives emanated from the League of Nations. Since the United States was not a member, the large American financial houses, the most prominent being J. P. Morgan & Co., were more careful in joining deals, even if possible profits were alluring. In addition to political differences, the relations between the Allied Powers and the United States were heavily burdened with the debt questions and reparations. The Europeans wanted to squeeze reparations out of the defeated states, mainly from Germany, and they thought to repay the American credits from this sum, a course the United States was not willing to accept. It seemed that until this problem was solved, there could be no lasting cooperation between the two sides.

Since there was no hope for official support, the League of Nations had to count on private collaboration with Americans. Next to bankers, American private citizens were working for the League, most often in an unofficial capacity, since the United States government tried to avoid any official contact with the organization. So, when the financial reconstruction of European countries came to the forefront, the League of Nations hoped to secure the support of both American bankers and private citizens. The first group was crucial for their money, the latter for their work in the schemes—a concept that was to strengthen both halves of such a vision.

The United States could not afford to turn away from Europe in an all-out fashion. If nothing else, the huge sum of debts that the European countries had accumulated during the years of war was a link that connected the two continents. Williams' famous claim that the United States' isolationism was "no more than a legend," however, needs some qualifications.[1] On the political level, isolationism did occur to a large degree: the United States withdrew from the international landscape after World War I, especially what regards Europe. Aside from small steps and the only big spectacular political event, the Washington Naval Conference in 1921–22, American official circles really showed no inclination to find themselves inside a European web they abhorred. On the financial level though, the picture is quite different. With the emergence of the United States as the new number one country with its apparently infinite capital, the American government found it to its advantage as well to let the private financial sphere to use its power and

1 William Appleman Williams, "The Legend of Isolationism in the 1920s," *Science & Society* 18, no. 1 (Winter 1954): 1.

influence all over the world. They were basically free to choose the country in which they wanted to invest in the hope of profits and hopefully establishing financial structures that would closely follow the American model. Their selection reflected their pecuniary interests above all, but it was also a reflection of the moral conviction that Europe had to be reconstructed in order to create a healthy world environment for business.

The aim of this book is threefold. First, it wants to fill a void that is conspicuous in the studies of the 1920s concerning the financial reconstruction in Europe and the role of American capital and personnel. While there are major works on many countries in English, starting from France all the way to Poland, Hungary for some reason is left out.[2] Even those works that deal with it are not comprehensive enough or focus on other aspects.[3] Therefore, the second aim is to concentrate on the Central European financial reconstruction with a special emphasis on the American participation in Hungary, which, again just like in any other case, was private and unofficial. Third, I want to add an important chapter to the growing literature of the Hungarian-American historical relations by putting Jeremiah Smith, Jr., the American Commissioner-General for Hungary from 1924 to 1926, in the limelight. Smith, who had been one of the center figures of the financial reconstruction of Hungary, and therefore one of the leading foreign personalities in the interwar years of Hungary, has conspicuously been unspoken of in works

---

2 See the following works concentrating on various aspects of the era. Carl Parrini, *Heir to Empire: United States Economic Diplomacy, 1916-1923* (Pittsburgh: University of Pittsburgh, 1969); Richard Hemmig Meyer, *Bankers' Diplomacy. Monetary Stabilization in the Twenties* (New York: Columbia University Press, 1970); Joan Hoff Wilson, *American Business & Foreign Policy, 1920–1933* (Lexington, KY: The University Press of Kentucky, 1971) and *Ideology and Economics: U.S. Relations with the Soviet Union, 1918–1933* (Columbia, Mo., 1974); Melvyn P. Leffler, *The Elusive Quest: America's Pursuit of European Stability and French Security, 1919–1933* (Chapel Hill, NC: University of North Carolina Press, 1979); Frank Costigliola, *Awkward Dominion: American Political Economic, and Cultural Relations With Europe, 1919–1933* (Ithaca, NY: Cornell University Press, 1984); Neal Pease, *Poland, the United States, and the Stabilization of Europe, 1919–1933* (New York: Oxford University Press, 1986); Michael J. Hogan, *Informal Entente. The Private Structure of Cooperation in Anglo-American Economic Diplomacy, 1918–1928* (Chicago: Imprint Publications, 1991); Philip L. Cottrell, *Rebuilding the Financial System in Central and Eastern Europe, 1918–1944* (Aldershot: Scolar Press, 1997); Aldcroft, Derek H. *The European Economy 1914-2000.* 4th ed. (London and New York: Routledge, 2002); Emily S. Rosenberg, *Financial Missionaries to the World. The Politics and Culture of Dollar Diplomacy, 1900–1930* (Durham and London: Duke University Press, 2003).

3 The major works concentrating on some aspect of the League of Nations loan to Hungary in 1924 are Ormos, Mária, *Az 1924. évi magyar államkölcsön megszerzése* [Raising the Hungarian State Loan of 1924] (Budapest: Akadémiai Kiadó, 1964); György Péteri, *Revolutionary Twenties. Essays on International Monetary and Financial Relations after World War I* (Trondheim: University of Trondheim, 1995) and *Global Monetary Regime and National Central Banking. The Case of Hungary, 1921-1929* (Boulder, Colorado: Social Science Monographs, 2002); Miklós Lojkó, *Meddling in Middle Europe* (Budapest: Central European University Press, 2006).

about the loan or the period done by other authors. It is still all the stranger, since after World War I all of Europe looked to the United States as a possible savior in the political and economic quagmire that was created after the peace treaties. Serving the League as an American in an influential position attracts attention in itself, but Smith fulfilled much more than a post under the League of Nations. He was a special "envoy," or "ambassador," who had to represent the United States even if he consciously did not want to and officially could not do so. Still, in him all Hungary saw was America, and the way he acted and carried out his duties left a lasting impression on Hungarians. By writing in detail about Smith, I hope that his role in Hungary will be both known and appreciated not only among scholars but in the public's mind as well. It is maybe time to put him next to Harry Hill Bandholtz on the pedestal the latter physically enjoys.[4]

4 Bandholtz, who helped save treasures of the National Museum in Budapest from the Romanians in 1919, has a statue commemorating this heroic deed.

Chapter 1

An American in Paris

1.1 The Last months of World War I in Europe

"This scheme is doing altogether too well. I don't know what's going to happen. But something is sure to go wrong, somewhere."[5] This quote is from Jeremiah Smith, Jr., Commissioner-General of Hungary for the League of Nations, 1924-1926, and later representative on the Financial Committee of the League, 1927-1931. As a modern embodiment of his namesake prophet of the Bible, his words became true in due course. It is impossible to know when he exactly uttered these words, but it is almost sure that it was in the second half of the financial reconstruction of Hungary. There are two very important aspects of this sentence. First, it derives from the man chosen for the supervision of the League scheme to rehabilitate Hungarian finances. Coming from such an authentic source, who presumably well understood the mechanism and currents of both the Hungarian and European financial and economic realms, it says a lot about the League-sponsored financial reconstructions in Central and Southern Europe in the 1920s. His wry observation indicates that while all was well on the surface, underlying problems were lurking. These dangers were not faced and even less met, therefore making the financial reconstruction of the region more of a chimera than a hopeful reality.

Second, Smith was an American citizen. In his capacity as League commissioner, he, whether conscious of it or not, meant a bridge between the United States and Europe. In his League post he represented his home country only unofficially, but in the problematic decade after the Paris Peace Treaties, an American being present in Europe and connected with the League of Nations and the problems of Europe inescapably carried some weight politically. The story of Jeremiah Smith, Jr. and the financial reconstruction of Hungary under the aegis of the League of Nations provide quite a few important and interesting features that bring us closer to understanding the Europe of the mid-1920s from financial and political points of view, and the significant question of American attitude toward Europe in the period.

Who was Jeremiah Smith, Jr., and how did he get to the post of Commissioner-General? These questions, together with such further ones like "How did he carry out his duties?" or "Did he embody the American mind-set concerning Europe and

5 League of Nations, *The League of Nations Reconstruction Schemes in the Inter-War Period* (Geneva: Economic, Financial and Transit Department, 1944), 152.

its problems in the 1920s?" can shed further new light on the first decade of the interwar years, when the United States was supposedly isolationist and wanted to have nothing with Europe. This was, however, also the period when America had perhaps incomparably the largest prestige in Europe, especially among the small and defeated countries. After the Paris Peace Conference the United States Senate refused to ratify the Versailles Treaty, thereby constituting to the result that the United States on the official level did not, and could not, take responsibility for Europe and for the turmoil of the continent. Through a thorough introduction to Smith's personality, and later to the political and financial undercurrents of the European surface of the 1920s, we can get a more balanced picture of the financial reconstructions in the region and their success or failure.

Jeremiah Smith, Jr. was born in 1870, in New Hampshire, in a prestigious New England family.[6] His grandfather, whose father had emigrated from Ireland, was born in 1759 also by the same name. That ancestor early showed his patriotic feelings when he voluntarily enlisted in the Revolution at the age of 17 just after he had enrolled at Harvard.[7] Later he was elected as Representative to the Second Congress in 1790 and he served three more terms in the ensuing years, but he resigned and did not serve out his fourth term and turned to practicing law instead.[8] Later he became chief justice of the Supreme Court of New Hampshire (1802–1809, 1813–1816) and was Governor of New Hampshire in the interval on the persuasion of Daniel Webster among others.[9] In 1816, political revolution moved him from office, but he was all through his life considered one of the most eminent jurists in the country. Smith's father, who was born in 1837, a very late child from a second marriage, called also Jeremiah Smith, carried on the tradition and was a judge of the New Hampshire Supreme Court at the age of 30 but resigned in 1874 due to impaired health.[10] He was appointed Story Professor of Law at Harvard in 1890, a position from which he resigned in 1910, but subsequently he was persuaded to teach on for two more years when he first

6 Smith was proud of his ancestors and as a reference to them chose to use the "Jr." as a tribute to his father. As deference to his own wish, "Jr." will be attached when his full name is cited. As a matter of fact, when Arthur Salter in one of his official reports gave Smith name only as "J. Smith," an American journalist picked up on the theme and wrote that the League of Nations felt that it had to announce a Commissioner, and simply took the most common name and initial, thus J. Smith. As a joking jibe to Slater, many months later Smith confronted Salter with the newspaper and said, "You see what happens when you don't give a man his proper name." Arthur Salter, *Personality in Politics* (London: Faber and Faber, 1947), 169–70.

7 O. W. B. P., "Morison's Life of Smith," *The Christian Examiner and Religious Miscellany* 39 (July, September, November, 1845): 173.

8 Ibid, 174–75.

9 Ibid., 175–76; *Boston Daily Globe*, May 9, 1890.

10 Joseph H. Beale, "Jeremiah Smith," *Harvard Law Review* 35 (November 1921): 1–2; *Boston Daily Globe*, May 9, 1890.

wanted to call it a day.[11] Both Smiths were known to be men with an aversion to publicity.[12]

Jeremiah, the only child, went to Exeter and Harvard, together with Thomas Lamont.[13] Leading his class at law school for three years, he was destined for a law career.[14] He served as secretary to Justice Gray of the United States Supreme Court in 1895–1896, and thereafter he practiced law in Boston in the firm of Herrick, Donald & Farley, in which he became a partner later.[15] He often dealt with local bankruptcies and was known as a person who "has held important receiverships and is prominently identified with large corporate interests."[16] He became a trustee of Exeter in 1907, a post both his father and grandfather had filled, and he even surpassed them in occupying the post of President of the Board in 1919.[17]

The big change in Smith's life came with the onset of World War I. When hostilities broke out in the summer of 1914, the United States found itself at a crucial juncture. In accord with the long-held tradition of staying out of European problems, President Woodrow Wilson was quick to reinforce neutrality. He called on Americans to be "neutral in fact as well as in name" and "impartial in thought as well as in action."[18] The majority of the Americans shared this view, Smith included. He was appointed as member of the War Relief Commission of the Rockefeller Foundation in June 1915 and visited a few European countries in this capacity. This adventure, however, did not satisfy him and, being a fervent patriot, he would have liked to participate in the thick of things. The protracted nature of the war offered a great chance to increase the United States's export dramatically. Also, dictated by ideological reasons, the United States lent huge amounts of money to Europeans, first and foremost to Great Britain. By the time

---

11 Beale, "Jeremiah Smith," 3–4; *Boston Daily Globe*, May 16, 1915.

12 *The New York Times*, June 30, 1926.

13 Thomas W. Lamont was a partner in J. P. Morgan & Co. and he played a very influential role in the loans of the house. Basically, his presence in Europe was a deciding factor throughout a loan negotiation. He was a financial advisor to President Wilson at Paris. He, and through him J. P. Morgan & Co. enjoyed tacit government backing. When he was in Japan in 1920 to negotiate a loan, Secretary of State Lansing wrote the American Ambassador in Tokyo the following instructions. "He has no connection whatsoever with the US Government, but you will please expedite and facilitate his movements in every way and cooperate with him in every respect." Lansing to Morris, February 7, 1920, FRUS: 1920 (Washington, DC: Government Printing Office, 1936), 1:497.

14 Joseph H. Beale, "Jeremiah Smith, Jr. (1870–1935)," *Proceedings of the American Academy of Arts and Sciences* 71 (Mar., 1937): 549.

15 Ibid., 549; Memorandum, 711.6412A/40, Roll 1, M. 709, (National Archives and Records Administration (hereafter cited as NARA).

16 *Boston Daily Globe*, June 23, 1907.

17 *Boston Daily Globe*, December 18, 1919.

18 Congressional Record, 63rd Congress, 2nd Session, 14042, August 20, 1914.

the United States joined the war in April 1917 as an Associated Power, Great Britain and France in particular were heavily indebted to it and this indebtedness only grew in the remainder of the war. Thanks to these loans to the European countries, United States had become from a debtor to a creditor nation in the span of four years. Naturally, this was to play a big role in the postwar years.

As for Smith, after the declaration of war on Germany he helped recruit the officers for the first Officers Training Camp at Plattsburg, which was not really what he was dreaming about as wartime activity. Naturally, his age was the determining factor. Since at the outbreak of hostilities in Europe he was well over 45, he knew he had no chance for active service. Smith's worries were put to rest when a call from Lamont freed him from his role at the Officer's Training Camp. Lamont's offer, "out of a perfectly clear sky," was that Smith go to Europe to serve in a captain's rank under Colonel Charles Dawes, after whom the Dawes Plan was named seven years later.[19] At this time Dawes was serving as General Purchasing Agent for the American Expeditionary Force in France. Since Smith did not know Dawes at the time, he would not have accepted even Lamont's offer, "but I was so crazy to get into the war somehow that I sent back word that I would come and could leave immediately." He arrived in New York City on December 30, 1917, when record cold was sweeping New England and the New York harbor was frozen, so he had to wait almost two weeks before he, and 7,000 other American soldiers, could sail to Europe on board of the *Olympic*, "the best and fastest transport on the ocean," also "well-armed." These features of the ship made it possible to avoid traveling in a convoy and instead the *Olympic* sailed alone, therefore crossing the Atlantic at a much faster pace; the voyage lasted altogether seven days.

After arriving in Liverpool and crossing to France, Smith soon found himself in Paris at the end of January, where he was going to be stationed. His first impression of the city with "a thick fog hanging over the Seine" can be read as a metaphor for the United States during the Paris Peace Conference, which commenced a year later. The next day he reported to Colonel Dawes, about whom he had mixed observations. On the one hand, Smith saw him as "no organizer, unable to make use of assistants, and rather sloppy in the way he handled business," but he also admitted that he "was a very good natured, kind hearted man, with plenty of independence and courage [...] very valuable in the Service of Supply [...] and he deserved the promotion to Brigadier General which he ultimately got." Since he preferred "something more active" instead of legal work, Smith was assigned

19 If not indicated otherwise, the information and quotations in the following are from Smith's account to his father about the Paris Peace Treaty, July 1921, Jeremiah Smith Academy Archives (hereafter cited as JSAA), Class of1945 Library, Phillips Exeter Academy, New Hampshire, USA.

to the Labor Bureau, an organization that started being organized that very day under Major John Price Jackson, under whom Smith worked almost until the end of the war. This officer, despite having spells of excellent work done, was mostly, according to Smith, "a rather dull man, who was not much respected by his own subordinates, had no knowledge at all of military matters, and was not particularly well fitted for the work of the Labor Bureau."

As assistant chief of the Labor Bureau and head of the department of contracts and relations with foreign governments, Smith was kept really busy. The main job was to do construction work for the main ports. These included docks, hospitals, warehouses, and railroad yards, among others. One of the biggest problems in connection with this was to secure labor force. Since most men had to be used on the front and the local civilians were already contracted to the French or British, or when the Americans managed to get a few, those people turned out to be not an effective workforce, and often went on strike because they were not satisfied with the allocated ration. The Bureau lacked office appliances such as desks, chairs, or typewriters. Under such circumstances, Smith and the other members of the Bureau had to be resourceful, and "by begging, borrowing, and stealing," somehow they managed things. His duties, after the problems of trying to secure enough workforce in France, took him to Spain and Italy to recruit laborers. South of the Pyrenees "it was impossible to do anything [...] without bribing the government officials," and without funds this proved a dead end street, while in Italy even food and a large loan from the American government were not enough to prod the Italian government to provide a substantial labor force. Smith learned a lesson here and made the general conclusion that "the average European considered anybody a fool who gave anything away without getting something in exchange for it at the time the gift was made." Finally, two months of "exasperating and slow" negotiations in the summer in Rome brought some result, and a contract was drawn up in which the Italians promised some labor force.

Smith returned to Paris from Italy in the middle of September and he spent the remaining of his time in Europe there. Being in Paris was a useful experience for Smith from different aspects. During the air raids and the shells of the Big Berthas, Smith was able to identify with the Parisians as he was practically one of them. He learned to see the French in a much more positive light than before, partly on account of their "splendidly" taking the hardships caused by the war. He also felt that the press was much more straightforward as far as the news of the war was concerned. Reading the French papers with their realistic rendering of what was unfolding on the front, which was sometimes geographically very close to Paris, Smith realized "how much propaganda I had swallowed from the British papers and also form the American papers, which got most of their information from British sources." Therefore, despite arriving in France with a head "full of allied propaganda," soon he started to look at things in a more balanced way. The French military actions in the summer and fall of 1918 also made a good impression on Smith, and whatever prejudices he may have had about the French in general, he put those behind him. He appreciated their war effort, both the civilian and military ones, and refused to believe it anymore that the French, the "frogs" in the American parlance then, were "an excitable, hysterical people." On the other hand, he also experienced some condescending on the part of French officers toward the American military capability. So, when a relatively small-sized American unit successfully beat the Germans back at Belleau Wood in the summer, Smith felt extremely vindicated in his admiration for his own country in almost any aspect.

After the "grand" days leading up to the Armistice on November 11th, Smith was surprised how Paris accepted what it had been waiting for so long. Contrary to the loud way that "Anglo-Saxons are accustomed to 'celebrate' with," there was no sign of any organized demonstration. There were no bands playing and the closest thing to a public celebration was when the prima donna of the Opera sang the *Marseillaise* on her balcony. Smith was really shocked at the lack of noise. "A crowd of [American] schoolboys celebrating a football victory would have made more real organized noise than everyone in Paris." Smith did feel ashamed that in the United States the victory celebrations were so loud and noisy although America was much less affected by the war than the French people and the residents of Paris.

Shortly before the war was over, Smith was assigned to the freshly organized Reciprocal Supply Bureau. Since with the Armistice there was no need for his work in this capacity, he expected to be back in the United States in a few weeks. In fact, he wanted nothing better than to go home and General Dawes knew this. Still, the latter did not do anything when another high-ranking officer pulled the wire to have Smith assigned next to him to the Judge Advocate's office in Tours. Smith's first duty in his new capacity was to travel to Spain to settle outstanding contracts. This was no easy task, since Washington had ordered a lot of different items prior to the Armistice and now, with the war suddenly over, there was no need for all these. The contractors, however, did not want to be left with raw materials and half-made pieces. Taking into consideration that the amount in question was $30,000,000, it is understandable that the Spaniards did not want to lose this source of trade income. It took three weeks for Smith and the American purchasing agent there, Sanborn, to settle the contracts, and finally they managed to strike a deal. The American party paid for one third of the contracts but did not have to pay for the remaining two thirds, which was the specific order from Washington.

After getting back to Paris just before Christmas, Smith was subjected an awkward show put on by his compatriots. A great number of Americans had travelled to Paris after the war was concluded, and their behavior did not in the least appeal to Smith's taste. Though some of it had to do with their having been "fed on propaganda and censored news" back home during the war, still Smith could find no excuse for their manners. It struck him as ridiculous that many of these Americans brought sugar and butter with them so as not to be subjected to missing their little everyday conveniences that, from the point of view of war-ravaged Europeans, were luxury. Their general state of being spoiled and ignorance angered Smith. Many of these Americans "clamored for steam heat, sleeping cars and taxi-cabs and objected to walking up and down stairs. It never seemed to enter their heads that these things weren't essentials and that millions of people had learned to go without them without suffering any great inconvenience." But Smith also had his negative opinion about those American officers who arrived from the civilian sphere. These, he thought, "lacked education, general cultivation and maturity." The men in charge of handling the business side did not escape his criticism either. Most of them were too old to be energetic and efficient on the scale the war made it necessary. Another issue that stung Smith's eyes was the way promotions were handled in the American Expeditionary Force. These were "made without any regard to the most elementary principles of justice. Combat troops got less of it than anyone else and the further you were from the front the better your chance of promotion." He was so appalled at this that he specifically refused to accept any promotion. Despite his persuading Dawes to help him in this, the only reason why he "managed to evade successfully" the widespread privilege was that with the coming of the Armistice promotions were suspended. The numerous negative characteristics that many Americans produced notwithstanding, on the whole Smith was proud of his country's war effort. He did not think that the United States had won the war, but he did believe that America was "an indispensable factor" and without the military and financial help coming from overseas, the Allies would have lost the war eventually.

1.2 Smith at the Paris Peace Conference

The Paris Peace Conference was a gigantic political gathering, one that the world had never seen before. But the scale of the war and the losses suffered by each side were also staggering by any previous standard, so it was understandable that something significant had to be born under the phrase "peace." One of the important questions was the participation of the United States. There were high hopes and great doubts as to what position the new overseas power should and would hold in international relations and specifically in Europe. One aspect was the territorial problems that were supposed to be settled upon the doctrine of "self-determination," an important element of President

Woodrow Wilson's Fourteen Points of 1918, on which he planned to build a post-war Europe.[20] He emphasized his adherence to this idealistic principle before Congress: "'Self-determination' is not a mere phrase. It is an imperative principle of action, which statesmen will henceforth ignore at their peril."[21] He stressed the significance of certain principles to be followed: "Every territorial settlement involved in this war must be made in the interest and for the benefit of the populations concerned, and not as a part of any mere adjustment or compromise of claims amongst rival states."[22] In reality, however, it served to create new states that had been fighting on the side of the Allies, and to punish the defeated parties. Great Britain and France were opposed on many points to Wilson, who they deemed as an amateur in international politics, and the final result compared unfavorably to what the American President had set out to achieve.

Fate has its twist and turns and that was what happened to Smith once more. Just as he was on the brink of returning home at last, he received another message from Thomas Lamont. Newly appointed Secretary of Treasury Carter Glass sent Albert Strauss and Lamont to Paris to act as his ears and carry out his instructions, which he did in agreement with the President.[23] Lamont in turn wrote to Smith that they were coming over to the Peace Conference soon to begin in the capacity of financial advisers to the U.S. government. Since Lamont knew Smith well both from the professional and personal aspects, he asked him to stay in Paris and work for them as their counselor. Although Smith did not have "any very clear idea what was wanted," he quickly said yes, because he figured that if Lamont wanted him to work in a job that would mean real work at last. After meeting Norman Davis, who was in Paris also as the representative of the U. S. Treasury, Smith learned that he would be European counsel for the Treasury. The title sounded a little bit mysterious but basically what "they wanted was a man whose legal training would enable him to analyze facts and draw papers which had no connection with law." The very first task was to write a memorandum for the next morning on the principles upon which the German indemnity should be fixed, which, being one of the main questions during the Peace Conference, was "quite an order." For political reasons, the American delegation was strictly forbidden to use the word "indemnity," however. To avoid the appearance of any punitive action and follow the principles of Wilson's Fourteen Points, the word "reparations" was chosen to deal with this topic in order to "secure the

---

20 For the text of the 14 Points see, Congressional Record, 65th Congress, 2nd Session, 680–681, January 8, 1918.

21 Congressional Record, 65th Congress, 2nd Session, 1937, February 11, 1918.

22 Ibid.

23 Rixey Smith and Norman Beasley, *Carter Glass: A Biography*, New York: Longmans, Green and Co., 1939), 160-62.

forbidden fruit through the permitted word." In the end, Smith's memorandum was close to the ultimate American point of view.

After this "fairly lively start" Smith became part of the Conference and his observations are very interesting and telling. He had a critical eye for the whole gathering and for the fashion in which the Peace Conference was carried out. Although the nature and scale of the event was historic in every comparison, the wrangling, jealousy, and the background practicalities were just as momentous, but unfortunately for all the wrong reason. With his New England upbringing, legal training, and a penchant for being precise, Smith understandable found many faults at the Conference.

For the first time in his life, and this was true for many Americans working in Paris, Smith had to realize the power structure of the world. The abstract notion of what it meant to be a big or small power was manifest in the very raw manner it really implicated. "Until I tackled the Peace Conference I hadn't an idea of what it meant to be a little power. They haven't a show on earth. They are treated worse than book agents. They aren't allowed in while matters vital to their existence are decided but are kept waiting in ante rooms and have to listen at the keyhole, peek over the transom or hide under the bed to find out what is going on." Perhaps stemming from their inferior position, these small powers tried to balance their lightweight status with long speeches. Their representatives "considered it a point of honor to express their views on every question and none of them had any idea of brevity," which contributed to the slow pace at which the Conference was proceeding. Smith was assigned as Strauss's assistant and the American Secretary in the Financial Drafting Committee, which was to deal with questions submitted and pertaining to financial matters and put together the list going in front of the Council of Ten.

One pending issue was the question of loans taken by the Allies during the war. The American side wanted to prevent this issue from being discussed at the Conference and believed that it should be handled separately. Wilson himself professed that there could be "no proper basis for a discussion of our foreign loans in connection with the Peace Conference."[24] Being involved with the financial questions, Smith had his share of witnessing how Europeans tried to enmesh this problem into the overall agenda. In fact, it turned out that, as far as financial questions were concerned, this was one of the thorniest issues. The different delegates kept sending proposals without a clear indication as to who was sponsoring them and "they were usually framed in the innocent sounding ambiguous language peculiar to European Diplomacy." The point of the effort was, as it turned out after a lot of cross examining, that Europeans expected the United States to forego some of the Allied war debt. Their argument was

24 Wilson to Glass, December 23, 1918, quoted in Smith, *Carter Glass*, 159.

that the goals of the war were mutual and as such every party should take the same financial burdens, especially in light of the fact that the Europeans had suffered so colossal a loss in human lives and property. Strauss, according to the clear instructions from the Treasury, refused to have this question debated in the framework of the Conference. In spite of the temperate way Strauss dressed the issue, his declaration touched a raw nerve for many present. The French Finance Minister Louis-Lucien Klotz, who became well known on account of his relentless postwar financial policy, which was embodied in his "The Boche will pay!" formula, "lost his temper completely." He questioned Strauss's authority in the first place and charged that the United States simply wanted to move the Peace Conference to Washington, which was "preposterous." After his words were translated into English, "there was dead silence for some minutes and then the meeting adjourned." Strauss chose the dignified way of not responding in kind to show the Europeans that American were indeed not "rough necks" and did not wish to add insult to injury. Not everybody tolerated the French Finance Minister's personality so delicately, however. British Prime Minister Lloyd George, for one, humiliated him in the open, and George Clemenceau, the French Premier, was similarly condescending toward him. Clemenceau, the head of the French delegation, treated him with contempt, calling him "the only Jew who knows nothing about money."[25] Smith was of low opinion of him as well and thought him to be "the weakest representative the French had."

The Council later called a Financial Commission into being to delegate some work, and Smith became the American secretary to Strauss and Lamont. Since only unanimous decisions could be adopted, few tangible results were achieved, and the Commission basically sent a summary of the varying opinions to the Council. Strauss soon returned home and since Lamont was also on the Reparations Commission, Smith started "to appear as his alternate and after a while everyone accepted it as a fact that I was the permanent American member." His being elevated so close to the center of where the question of the future of Europe was decided naturally left him with pride. He "couldn't help being amused at finding myself in one of the most magnificent rooms in the Louvre on the right hand of the Chairman as the representative of my country and rising to tell the European countries what the policy of the United States was." Still, many of the proposals that he had to sit through amazed Smith as impractical, fantastic, and much too time consuming, some of them "a violation of every principle of international law and custom for the last hundred years." Further hindrance to efficient progress, which was therefore "slower than cold molasses," was caused on another technicality. Minutes of each session had to be kept, the

---

25 Quoted in Liaquat Ahamed, *Lords of Finance. The Bankers Who Broke the World* (New York: Penguin Books, 2009), 106.

Proces-Verbal, which meant for Smith the "greatest nuisance and waste of time." He suggested that only presented proposals should be recorded but in vain. The French in particular were keen on recording every word uttered. However, as could be foreseen, the five secretaries, one for each big power, often disagreed as to what had been said. Jealousy marked these sessions and "everyone was watching to see that nothing was slipped in to the account which might come back to vex them, it was a long, wearisome and really unnecessary work."

The "awfully slow" progress finally disturbed the Big Four as well, and they decided that financial questions would be discussed in a small group of experts representing the four nominal powers, Great Britain, France, Italy, and the United States. Davies and Lamont were so busy with the reparations issue that they arranged it with Wilson that Smith should represent the United States. Within this smaller outfit it was easier to find some common ground. Firstly, the representatives were able persons, who tried to reach consensus most of the time. Moreover, the financial question caused far less acrimony than either territorial questions or the Pandora's Box of reparations. Still, some argument and disagreement did take place, and in one of those cases Smith and his fellow Commission members were summoned to the Big Four at Wilson's residence on the Place des Etats Unis, the usual meeting place for the four major heads of state. Although not so long ago Smith could not have imagined meeting with those prominent politicians at such a crucial juncture of world history, he did not "have a thrill" when the moment arrived. Wilson greeted Smith and said he had heard about him, which naturally surprised the latter. Lamont and Davis were also present, such as John Maynard Keynes on the British side, since this was before he left the Conference in disillusionment. The session consisted of going over the draft clause by clause, and when disagreement occurred, a short briefing by the experts to their respective head of state took place and the Big Four hammered out the differences in a relatively quick manner. Later Smith had the experience of having to appear before the most influential contemporary statesmen, on account of the German and Austrian treaties. The method of the session did not vary except that by that time Italian Prime Minister Vittorio Orlando had left the Conference and now it was Big Three, not Big Four. As a matter of fact, the French, British, and American leaders managed to have business done in a more practical and business-oriented fashion now.

Smith's few meetings with these heads of state and the impressions that these left on him led him to be able to describe them in his own way. Perhaps it is of interest that Keynes in his famous book painted a rather malicious picture about these men, especially about Wilson. While Clemenceau was "the most eminent member of the Council," he did not speak much, and his only goal was to weaken Germany as much as possible, Lloyd George was agile and swift, "with six or seven senses not available to ordinary men [...] perceiving what each was thinking and even what each was going to say next," Wilson was a "blind and deaf Don Quixote" who was impractical in the concrete issues at hand, with a mind "too slow and unresourceful to be ready with *any* alternatives."[26] It must be noted that Keynes was persuaded to omit some of his negative observations about Lloyd George in his book which were far from flattering: "rooted in nothing; he is void and without content... one catches in his company the flavor of final purposelessness, inner irresponsibility, existence outside or away from our Saxon good and evil, mixed with cunning, remorselessness, love of power."[27]

Smith, in his turn, perhaps because he really did see them with a little bit of more awe than Keynes, or because he was a sharper observer, or simply because he wanted to balance the picture somewhat, described the Big Four with restraint, providing both positive and negative features. Lloyd George, who Smith thought had never read a book through simply because he was "restless and impatient," received a string of praise: "clever," "adroit," or having "a great deal of humor and an attractive personality." "He had a wonderfully agile mind [and] he was always a couple of jumps ahead of everyone else and anticipated their arguments." Still, he often changed his mind on certain issues because he was careful about his political future in Great Britain, but in general "he put his country above his own political fortunes" at the Conference. Smith liked Clemenceau a lot, who "certainly looked like a formidable opponent," and the American was sorry that, since the French politician was not interested in financial questions, he hardly spoke at all. To Smith it was clear that "he cared nothing about what the Treaty contained except as it affected France." Orlando, who Smith saw only once during the conferences with the Big Four, because the Italian left the Peace Conference, "gave the impression of ineffectiveness." His own President surprised Smith. He expected him to be "pedantic, conceited, obstinate and dictatorial," but instead of "a theoretical idealist," Wilson's manner proved to be "more like that of a practical business man." He approached the questions raised in a straightforward manner, listened to his advisers, and, perhaps too much, was open for compromise. His biggest mistake was that he did not use a trained secretary and therefore put too much unnecessary work and unavoidable strain on him. Although no heroes by a long stretch, still Smith's characterizations of these men can be said favorable on the whole.

After the German Treaty was done, the Financial Commission dealt with the Austrian Treaty. All the Commission did was, as Smith described the process, that it "crossed out 'Germany' wherever it appeared and wrote 'Austria' in its place." The only issue that was a challenge, and without historic precedent, was the public debt and the currency of Austria and Hungary. The Commission decided

---

26 The quotes are from John Maynard Keynes, *The Economic Consequences of the Peace* (New York: Harcourt, Brace and Howe, 1920), 15, 21, 22.
27 Quoted in Ahamed, *Lords of Finance*, 115.

that prewar debt should be divided proportionally among the new independent states, while in the case of the currency, the Commission was of the opinion that these notes constituted war debt, since nine-tenths of them had been issued during the war. The newly created states, just like in basically any other question, were consulted in a manner in which they were clearly treated as inferior parties that had no say whatsoever in the outcome that affected them so much. Smith confessed to being partially responsible for the way these countries were treated. Although he tried to make suggestions in order to consult the affected states before the decisions on the financial clauses were made, he did not achieve anything. The reasons for these were obvious. "[N]obody would hear of it and I didn't press it, partly because I knew the clauses did them no injustice, partly because I knew they would talk forever and put forward unreasonable claims, and partly because everyone was sick to death of the Peace Conference by that time and wanted to finish."

Smith also gathered some experience about dealing with the enemy countries. He was part of the team that discussed with the Austrian financial delegation at St. Germain the way Austria would pay for the Allied food shipments. The meeting was distant and cold, and above all humiliating to the Austrians, who hoped to receive an adequate answer as to how they were going to feed their countrymen, especially in Vienna. After this episode, Smith was asked to participate in the work of the Bulgarian Reparations Commission. Despite the fact that there had been no declaration of war between Bulgaria and the United States, Wilson thought it would be useful for the U.S. delegation to take part in the proceedings, and the Allies were also keen on having the Americans on the commission. Smith was probably chosen since he had been to Bulgaria, though he was just as unfamiliar with the country as the other members of the commission. The French and British, studying some prewar figures, came up with a significant amount that the Bulgarians should pay as reparations. Smith "was staggered by the amount and tried to get them down and got some support from the Italians." Still, he did not like what the commission finally settled on, 2,250,000,000 French francs (almost $500 million) and made a few observations to persuade the others to avoid "putting a crushing burden" on the Bulgarian people. His plea did not lead to much. All he, with the help of John Foster Dulles, could achieve was to have a clause put in that stipulated that if this amount proved beyond Bulgaria's resources, the Reparations Commission's unanimous vote could reduce it. This episode is important. Partly it was a further proof to Smith about the vindictive manner of the European victorious powers, and it also showed that even facing resistance, the American was willing to raise his voice in defense of the weaker party if he thought it to be fair and just.

He defended Wilson against the usual charges of wanting to reach a peace treaty including the League of Nations at almost any price, but he also admitted that the President had committed serious errors. To his mind, "his chief defect" was his lack of training for the task he was facing. "It needed a clever negotiator, who was accustomed to trading with clever men, who knew what they wanted and didn't trust each other... He didn't know when the other fellow was bluffing or when to fight and when to compromise or how to fight." Smith thought that Wilson was only advocating "high minded" notions and "he ought to get credit instead of abuse." He also rightly assessed that the most important thing for Wilson was the League of Nations. Unfortunately for the President, the Europeans were just as sensitive in recognizing such a wish. As a consequence, "as soon as the Allies found out that Wilson had his heart set on the League of Nations, they had him at a disadvantage for they gave him that and then forced him to compromise again and again for fear of losing the League if the Conference broke up." Simply, in Smith's opinion, Wilson was not fit in character and skill for the formidable task, on account of "his lack of practical wisdom." "If he had been a better trader, he might have gotten a better trade, but that is all that can be brought against him."

The overall impression for Smith at the Paris Peace Conference was a series of disappointments. One of them was "the lack of frankness." He correctly realized that the average American could not really understand the underlying animosities that had been there for centuries as a result of more or less continual warfare. When he wrote that the "French and British didn't like or thoroughly trust each other. The Italians hated the French, who despised them. The Jugo-Slavs and the Italians hated each other, and there was no love lost between the Greeks and the Italians, while all the great powers had a positive contempt for the little ones," he managed to give an accurate picture of European relations, although the list, whether he knew or not, could have gone on. He was disenchanted not only with the diplomats he had a chance to examine first hand, the general secrecy around the proceedings, which "was unnecessary, and some of it silly," the "astonishing absence of formal dress," but also with journalism in Europe as well. He was appalled at the level of propaganda the newspapers of the Allies did, mainly France and Great Britain. When "the French newspapers started a vicious campaign against Wilson" with "diabolical ingenuity that Wilson would be to blame if Germany wasn't compelled to pay France the cost of the war," Smith became so incensed that he stopped reading French newspapers for a while. He wryly concluded that during the war, largely due to censorship and propaganda, there was no independent press in Europe in the American sense, notwithstanding the inclination of the American press "to print sensational news."

All these negative impressions he had gained during the Conference made Smith lose almost "all of the awe and veneration for Europe" he had before. "Like so many in the East, I was brought up to regard everything European, except Kings, as something superior, and to assume that if we could only be more like them we should be more civilized... I used to worry a lot about what they thought of us, [...] but I have gotten all over that and now the only thing I care about is to see the United States go ahead and do the right thing without paying any attention to 'what they will think of us.'" Not many politicians convinced him as outstanding. The biggest positive impression on Smith was made by Herbert Hoover, head of the European Relief and Rehabilitation Administration. Smith often saw him and "acquired a great admiration for his ability. He used to sit in a chair chewing a cigar and not taking a prominent part in the discussions but whenever he spoke he hit the nail on the head and I never heard anyone able to prove him wrong. Not only in economic but in political questions, he was the wisest man I saw at Paris, and if he had been allowed to write the Treaty, it would have been far better than it was." Keynes agreed with this observation and thought Hoover was "the only man who emerged from the ordeal of Paris with an enhanced reputation."[28]

As far as the Peace Treaty is concerned, Smith was not pleased. He again had a milder opinion than Keynes. The Briton considered the final result "outrageous and impossible," which would result in "nothing but misfortune," "general disorder and unrest."[29] He felt his country had no room left for the really right decision to make, because it "was left in the position of either agreeing to what it believed wrong or of being charged with pro-Germanism, and under these circumstances naturally objection was reduced to a minimum." Still, in Smith's mind there was no room for hesitancy about the quality of the signed document:

> The Treaty is a pretty poor piece of work, based as it is on national selfishness, though it does contain the first attempt to divide up territory according to the wishes of those affected, feeble though it is, and in some instances lacking entirely. The economic and reparations clauses are the worst things in it. Few believed they were workable and most felt they would have to be modified later, when some of the war feeling cooled down. The League of Nations is the best thing in it, and if Wilson had had more political sense and a better understanding of how to handle men in the mass, he could have taken the ground from under his political opponents and weakened the opposition to it tremendously. Of course, it is a great experiment and may not work, but it is the only way anyone has suggested of attempting to avoid future wars and if it doesn't work, the world will be back where it was in 1914. If the European nations approach it in the same spirit they approached the Conference, it won't work, but for the next fifteen or twenty years no one in Europe will

28 Quoted in Ahamed, *Lords of Finance*, 275.

29 Keynes to his mother, May 14, 1919, In. *The Collected Writings of John Maynard Keynes*, Vol. XVI. *Activities 1914-1919. The Treasury and Versailles*. Elizabeth Jonson ed. (London: Macmillan, 1971), 458.

> want to start a war that he has to do any serious fighting in and there is an opportunity that is worth trying of getting them accustomed to talking over their differences in conferences and settling them there instead of by fighting, and America, having no axe to grind, could have exercised great influence in the League. By entering the League, we might have become involved in European affairs though I don't think either the obligation or the danger was nearly as great as the Republicans claimed. I don't think the form of the League makes much difference; the great thing is to get the nations together to discuss their differences in common, in the hope that they will find some way of settling them without fighting.

With all the shortcomings of the Versailles Treaty, Smith showed his "internationalist" side and his commitment for some international cooperation in the political field. "Bad as the Treaty is, I would have ratified it. Ray Stannard Baker and I talked it over toward the end and while we both disliked it, we agreed that it was better to ratify it in the hope of some modification of the most objectionable parts than it was to reject the League and go it alone." Still, all the disappointment he had come across at Paris made him not attend the actual signing. Though "tickets were as scarce as hens' teeth," he was "so disgusted with the Treaty and the arrangements for its execution" that he gave his own ticket to someone else and the very next day left Paris for New York City.

Based upon his experience at the Paris Peace Conference, it is little wonder that Smith's finally "came away from Paris with a very low opinion of European diplomacy, believing that everything bad that had been said about it was true." Although the Financial Commission he was part of was largely devoid of political bickering, the overall atmosphere was almost continual clashes over French security from Germany, British postwar plans for Europe, and American ideal and practical suggestions. To Smith, the general attitude resembled "intercollegiate athletic dealings when I was in college, and men were guilty of sharp and unfair practices." Sports had improved in American higher education, but European diplomacy had not: it remained without a question "both skillful and effective but it was not an honorable performance." The greatest shock to Smith was when adherence to the Fourteen Points vanished early on in the Conference, and if anyone brought it up as a basis to a point or as a warning that the point in question was a violation of these notions, they were often treated with "impatience and ill-disguised contempt," or charged with friendliness toward Germany. Since Wilson accepted compromise rather than choosing to stand up for his principles, many of which were at contradiction with each other, and the main European powers wanted to weaken Germany regardless of what this might cause in the future, instead of the high-flying notions of Wilson's Fourteen Points, a vindictive and revengeful peace treaty was born.

Chapter 2

The United States, the League of Nations, and the Postwar Financial Scene

2.1. The New World Order after the War

After the Paris Peace Conference was concluded and the Versailles Peace Treaty was signed, many things were not clear. For example, the peace treaties with the smaller enemy states were up in the air for the time being, although it was evident that they were going to be similar to the one just written for Germany. The question of German reparations was not settled simply because this issue had a huge political load and the big powers could not come to a final compromise about it. Just as important, nobody was sure whether the United States Senate would ratify the Treaty. In the 1918 Congressional elections the Republican Party gained majority in the upper house and it was evident that Wilson was facing an uphill battle. Only one point was clear throughout the negotiations, namely that a new international organization should be set up to keep order and peace. This was the cornerstone of Wilson's postwar agenda: the League of Nations.

The new supranational organization was to aim at a high goal, namely to insure the peace after the terrible devastation of the war. It wanted to eliminate the possibility of future wars as much as possible by using open diplomacy and collective action against any country that might play the role of a provocateur or aggressor. Since most of the great and once powerful European countries joined the new organization, small countries saw in it a hope of so far unknown assurance against outside armed attack.

To the regret of European and Latin American countries though, the United States finally stayed away from the League of Nations. In wake of the carnage in Europe, the conservative side gained the upper hand in the bitter argument in American political and public circles. Based on the long ruling sentiment that the United States ought not to entangle itself with the immoral Old World, public opinion was for an independent America that was free to act if it thought appropriate. In the Senate, two groups thwarted the ratification of the Peace Treaty, which included the League of Nations. The "reservationists" led by Henry Cabot Lodge wanted to add certain conditions to the Treaty, while the "irreconcilables" were in absolute opposition to accepting the Treaty. Their antagonism in part stemmed from Wilson's blunder that he had included no prominent Republicans in the delegation to Paris. The factions in the Senate focused on the sanctity of the Monroe Doctrine. They also interpreted Article X of the Covenant, which was about collective security in the face of aggression, in a way that ensured its unacceptability to Americans. In Arthur Salter's words, the article was indeed "badly drafted and unnecessarily ambiguous" and left room for wide interpretation.[30] It was easy then for the Lodge group to argue that the Treaty would commit America to bloody fights in which it had no interest, and all this under the command of an outside body and not American leadership. Wilson's declaration that to him the controversial article seemed "to constitute the very backbone of the whole [League] Covenant" did not help either.[31] The stubborn antagonism doomed the country's participation. The League did everything though to seduce the United States into joining it: Article XXI practically gave official recognition to the Monroe Doctrine dubbing it a "regional understanding." This was hardly enough for a wary United States, where Republican isolationism reigned, a phenomenon that Averell Harriman later described as "disastrous."[32] As Eric Drummond, Secretary-General of the League of Nations, was informed in November 1919, in the United States "loud and vociferous interests shrieked hysterically against American cooperation in any international movement and apparently won the fight."[33] Nor was the media much help. William Randolph Hearst did everything in his considerable power to create a substantial anti-League atmosphere. His main concern was a potential war the United States might find itself in, because, as he put it, "I do not consider it a league to keep us out of war but a league to get us into war. A man does not keep himself free from the small pox by going to bed with four other people who have it; and we cannot keep free from war by tying ourselves up with nations like England, France, Italy and Japan, which have the war disease in its worst form."[34] The large number of readers made sure that the overall sentiment was against joining the League of Nations.

The official rejection of the Versailles Peace Treaty came from the Senate in the end, where the Treaty did not gain the required two-thirds majority on two

30 Arthur Salter, *The United States of Europe and Other Papers* (London: George Allen & Unwin Ltd., 1933), 196.

31 Ibid.

32 Quoted in Walter Isaacson and Evan Thomas, *The Wise Men. Six Friends and the World They Made* (New York: Simon & Schuster Inc., 1986), 104.

33 Raymond B. Fosdick to Eric Drummond, November 25, 1919, quoted in Anthony Adamthwaite, *The Lost Peace. International Relations in Europe, 1918 –1939* (London: Edward Arnold, 1980), 36.

34 Hearst to Harry Hay Tammen, March 29, 1919, quoted in David Nasaw, *The Chief. The Life of William Randolph Hearst* (Boston and New York: Houghton Mifflin Company, 2000), 271.

occasions.[35] In addition, the reigning foreign policy doctrine was still the Monroe Doctrine, which made it clear that Europe should keep out of the Western Hemisphere and the United States should not concern itself with European powers. Right from its birth, the League, as a key figure in of the organization put it, was facing a "grave handicap" because "America's abstention changed fundamentally the League's ability to enforce its policy."[36] Without the United States it had much lesser hope and influence to carry out a far-reaching global agenda.[37] Although the majority of Americans favored some form of American participation, many in America saw in the League rather a hindrance to the country's aims. Many Americans wanted some kind of League, mainly with the goal of perpetuating the peace; still, American interests were not to be curtailed. The United States was clearly missed from the organization. The smaller European countries, for example, thought that only the United States could provide the impartiality in politics in face of the traditional European power games. As for the Latin American states, they saw in the League of Nations a possible counterweight to American hegemony. With many members of the League of Nations coming from this region, the United States' backyard, American politicians looked at the international organization with some suspicion.

The League of Nations, from the very start, however, turned out to be a "European" League. Since Great Britain, France, and to a lesser degree Italy, were the principal members, their presence ensured that European problems would be dealt with first. There was some basis to it, since the war left most of Europe in a ravaged form. Financially and economically almost every country found itself in dire straits, and this came to be the leading agenda in the League: to restore Europe financially and economically, and parallel to this to find a way to preserve the peace on the continent. The European member states were not keen on delving into Latin American problems. The reason for this was twofold: on the one hand, they were busy trying to make Europe stand on its feet again; on the other hand, they very well knew, understood, and accepted that Latin America was in the US sphere of influence. No wonder that the request of Costa Rica that the League on Nations define the meaning and scope of the Monroe Doctrine

35 The first rejection came on November 19, 1919, while the last one on March 19, 1920, when only seven votes were missing. Congressional Record, 66th Congress, 1st Session, 8786, 8802-8803, November 19, 1919, and 66th Congress, 2nd Session, 4599, March 19, 1920.

36 Arthur Salter, *Security. Can We Retrieve it?* (London: MacMillan and Co., Ltd, 1939), 139, 145.

37 Lloyd George expressed his realistic belief in Paris in 1919, that "the only real League of Nations that we can depend upon for the long future is the action together of America and Great Britain." Thomas W. Lamont, *Across World Frontiers* (New York: 1951), 160.

led to no result.[38] Plus, in the financial restoration of Europe American capital was an essential ingredient without which it could not have been achieved. The cross-Atlantic rapport established during the war was also strained on account of the financial obligations.

The relationship between the United States and Europe was burdened with the question of debts in the first place. During the war, Great Britain especially borrowed huge amounts of money from the United States to finance its war efforts, but France and Russia were indebted to a large extent as well. Soon after America's entry into the war, Wilson told Colonel House, his confidant, "When the war is over we can force them to our way of thinking, because by that time they [the Allies] will among other things be financially in our hands."[39] Similarly to many of his postwar plans, this prophecy proved also only a half-truth. True, the Europeans accumulated a staggering amount of debt toward the United States, but they showed little deference to the wishes of the lender as to how to repay it. According to some statistics, on December 30, 1919, the net debt of foreign governments to the US government was $9,591,000,000, most of it owed by Great Britain and France.[40] Even under normal circumstances would it have meant a huge financial burden for the debtors, but after the devastating war, European countries did not have the capacity to repay it. In addition, Britain found itself in a similar situation. Many countries owed it with almost the same total amount as Europeans the United States. In Britain's case, half of it was due by France and Russia. Europeans, for both moral and practical reasons, expected the United States to cancel some, if not all, of their debt. They argued that they had lost so much money and men, partly in fighting for American values and interests as well, that they had no means to pay unless substantial reparations were extracted from the Germans. Not only did they wish to settle some of their debt from this money, but they also wanted to ensure that Germany had no resources left to start another war. In this circle, the focus point was the French-German relation. Since Northeast France had been occupied and rendered barren by Germany, France was the principle nation that wanted to squeeze out as big reparation

38 Garcia F. Calderon, "Latin America, Europe and the United States," *Foreign Affairs* 7 (January 1929): 187.

39 Quoted in Arthur Link, *Woodrow Wilson, Revolution, War and Peace* (Arlington Heights, Ill.: Harlan Davidson, 1979), 80.

40 George Soule, *Prosperity Decade. A Chapter from American Economic History, 1917-1929* (London: The Pilot Press Limited, 1947), 255. Other sources give the amount of $9,982 and $10.4 billion dollars. Cleona Lewis, *America's Stake in International Investments* (Washington, D. C.: The Brookings Institution, 1938), 447; Howard H. Quint and Robert H. Ferrel, eds., *The Talkative President. The Off-the-Record Press Conferences of Calvin Coolidge* (Amherst: The University of Massachusetts Press, 1964), 175.The value of the U.S. dollar went through little change in the 1920s after World War I. An average dollar of the era of this writing is worth approximately $12 today (2009).

from its foe as possible. France, in turn, owed huge debts to Great Britain and the United States. Until Germany paid, France was neither willing nor able to pay its debts. Great Britain found itself in the same situation: unless French debt was paid, it could not and did not pay its debts to the United States. The situation was further hampered with the American point of view that the reparation question should be totally separated from that of the debts.[41] Although Keynes clearly saw that "America will not carry through to a conclusion the collection of Allied debt, any more than the Allies will carry through the collection of their present reparation demands," the official American policy lines pursued that elusive goal.[42] Thomas Lamont's opinion was also true: "reparations caused more trouble, contention, hard feeling, and delay at the Peace Conference than any other point of the Treaty of Versailles."[43]

The Anglo-American cooperation went ahead of other relations, both politically and financially. But even this cordial relation was in a bad shape on account of the debt question. After the armistice and the Versailles Peace Treaty, the United States insisted on getting all the money it had lent. Even before the anti-League voices had gained the upper hand, the Treasury was of the opinion that "the need of Europe for financial assistance, very great and very real though it is, has been much exaggerated both here and abroad [...] We must all feel deep sympathy for the suffering in Europe today, but we must not allow our sympathy to warp our judgment."[44] When the Penrose Bill was debated in the US Congress, which would have authorized the Secretary of the Treasury to refund, convert, and extend timeframe on payment of foreign nations to the United States, isolationist senators were aghast. As the senator from Arizona said, Europe ought to work instead of hoping to live on American mercy: "I repeat that to-day, 'Let Europe go to work.' [...] We saved Europe and our Christian civilization, but that does not imply, now that the peril is past, that we should feed the Europeans and allow them in their great cities to live in idleness and sometimes in luxury."[45] Senator Kenneth Douglas McKellar from Tennessee said of the pending bill that "a more unwise, a more impolitic, a more unfair, or a more unjust, a more un-American measure to the United States could not have been devised," and it only would give "blanket authority" to the Secretary of the Treasury.[46] The epitome of short and

41 Hughes to Herrick and Boyden, October 17, 1922, Foreign Relations of the United States (hereafter cited as FRUS), 1922, vol. 2, 169; Hughes to Fletcher, August 17, 1923, FRUS: 1923, 2:66–67; and Hughes to the British Chargé (Chilton), October 15, 1923, Ibid., 70–73.

42 John Maynard Keynes, *A Revision of the Treaty Being a Sequel to the Economic Consequences of the Peace* (London: MacMillan and Co., 1922), 165.

43 Kenneth Paul Jones ed., *U.S. Diplomats in Europe, 1919-1941*, Reprinted edition. Santa Barbara, CA: ABC-Clio, 1983, 43.

44 Carter to Wilson, September 11, 1919, quoted in Smith, *Carter Glass*, 187.

45 Congressional Record, 67th Congress, 1st Session, 3016, June 24, 1921.

46 Ibid., 3021, 3023.

to-the-point sentences, President Calvin Coolidge expressed the American official point of view succinctly and unmistakably: "They hired the money, didn't they?"[47] The consecutive US governments never admitted that there was a clear connection between the reparation issue and the war debts, and this official opinion did not cease with the interwar years.[48] With time, however, the United States saw that it was really hopeless to expect the European debtors to pay all they owed. Instead, a compromise was still the better outcome than pointless bickering. Following this pragmatic principle, the United States government was willing to reduce the debts of the European states and allow lenient terms of payment. Congress in February 1922 created the World War Foreign Debt Commission, which negotiated the settlements with the interested countries with a view of a given country's ability to pay. In the five-member body, the government was to have the prevailing voice. Secretary of the Treasury Andrew Mellon was the chairman, the Secretaries of Commerce and State were also members, and the Senate and the House of Representatives could send one delegate each. In this field, as in almost any other, the number one partner was Great Britain.

Since the reparation issue hung over the whole question of cooperation, understandably this was the most tender spot for all involved. The British tried to be the initiators, but they represented the European view that the war debts should be cancelled altogether. During the summer of 1922, acting foreign secretary Lord Arthur Balfour, who was in high esteem overseas, drew up a note that created a considerable stir on both sides of the Atlantic. In the so-called Balfour Note, its author reviewed the short history of the problem and repeated that the solution lay in cancellation: "The policy favored by His Majesty's Government is [...] that of surrendering their share of German reparation and writing off through one great transaction the whole body of inter-allied indebtedness."[49] In light of the stubborn American demand that

47 It is impossible to know whether Coolidge really said the famous sentence. His wife said it sounded like her husband, a member of the President's press team believed it did happen, but it appears nowhere in the transcripts or any other source. Quint and Ferrel, eds., *The Talkative President*, 176. Coolidge, who admitted being "not gifted with intuition," saw his reticence as "the value of silence." He characterized the "pressure to speak" as "constant and intolerable," most of which he "resisted." Coolidge, *The Autobiography*, 147, 114, 164. Interestingly, Walter Lippmann found Coolidge "very loquacious" during many of their meetings at the White House. Ronald Steel, *Walter Lippmann and the American Century* (Boston Toronto: Little, Brown and Company, 1970), 204. Coolidge was also famous for not showing emotion. When told about the President's death, Dorothy Parker's comment was apt: "How can you tell?" Quoted in Isaacson and Thomas, *The Wise Men*, 107.

48 The State Department claimed as late as 1975 that "The United States has never recognized a link between payments of the debts owed us and German reparations." Department of State, Bureau of Public Affairs, "Foreign Indebtedness to U.S." *GIST* (May 1975), par 6. Quoted in Costigliola, *Awkward Dominion*, 104.

49 The whole text can be read in *The New York Times*, August 2, 1922.

debts ought to be repaid, however, Great Britain was left with no other choice but collect money from its own debtors, but only to the extent Britain was able to meet its obligations toward the United States. The Note was the object of fierce criticism both in Europe and the United States, even in some circles of Great Britain, with the sole exception of Germany.[50] Despite the efforts to the contrary, Great Britain sized up the possibilities and gave in, because it knew it could lose much more by alienating the most powerful and influential country by antagonizing to the bitter end. The United States also wanted to preserve the relatively good rapport with Britain and believed that certain concessions were possible.

The manifestation of such attitudes, both political and financial, was the debt agreement between the two countries on June 19, 1923. The settlement was to refund the British debt at the rate of 3% for the first ten years, then 3.5% for 52 years, which altogether meant a reduction of about 30%.[51] Thus, compared to the beginning $187 million as annual payments, Prime Minister Stanley Baldwin and Montagu Norman, Governor of the Bank of England, managed to reach a more favorable $161 million for the first ten years and $184 million for the remaining fifty-two years. Not everybody had the same level of satisfaction at the end of the day. Baldwin, while representing the Agreement to the British cabinet, met some resistance first, and later recalled, "I never felt so miserable in all my life."[52] Norman on his part welcomed the news and said already during the debt negotiations: "I now seem to see a light at the end of the tunnel!"[53] The Republican Party Platform of 1924 hailed the settlement as "the greatest international financial transaction in the history of the world."[54] Other European countries followed suit with the same time frame but at a varying rate. Hungary, for example, signed a debt agreement on basically the same terms on April 25, 1924.[55] France, probably the most difficult partner, settled the question with the United States on April 29, 1926. The aggregate effective cancellation was just over half of the original amounts.[56]

---

50 Sydney Henry Zebel, *Balfour: A Political Biography* (Cambridge: Cambridge University Press, 1973), 275–76.
51 Soule, *Prosperity Decade*, 263. The original interest rate was 5%.
52 Quoted in Costigliola, *Awkward Dominion*, 107.
53 Norman to Blackett, February 26, 1923, quoted in Sir Henry Clay, *Lord Norman* (London: Macmillan & Co. Ltd., 1957), 179. On the settlement of the British war debt to the US, also see, Ahamed, *Lords of Finance*, 139-44.
54 Republican Party Platform, June 10, 1924. Kirk H. Porter and Donald Bruce Johnson, eds., *National Party Platforms, 1840-1968* (Urbana: University of Illinois Press, 1972), 259.
55 Congressional Record, 68th Congress, 1st Session, 7149, 7204, April 25, 1924, 8391–96, May 12, 1924, and 8775–76, 8800, May 17, 1924.
56 Soule, *Prosperity Decade*, 263. The first country to sign the debt settlement with the US was Finland on May 1, 1923, the last one was Yugoslavia on May 3, 1926. Lewis, *America's Stake*, 365–66.

As long as reparation was not paid, however, the debt settlement was practically inconceivable. To channel the reparation question into a legal and official form, the League of Nations had a special group of experts, called the Reparation Commission, to deal with such issues. Its members were representatives of nine governments, including France, Great Britain, Italy, and the so-called Successor states.[57] The rivalry between the two biggest nations, France and Great Britain, and their respective allies, ensured a highly political underpinning to the Commission's work. The Italians often hesitated and the Belgians almost always sided with the French. As a contemporary British diplomat noted, "[i]nstead therefore of becoming, as had been intended, an impartial, judicial and independent body, the Reparations Commission became a body sensitive to French political pressure."[58] To insure that the United States could keep a close eye on the League, the government had an unofficial representative on the Commission. Roland Boyden, who was chosen by Wilson for the post, had no right to vote, but took part in the proceedings and his very status made his opinion count to a large extent, and, as he said, the title was "a distinction without much practical difference, for I do just the same as the others do."[59] Thus, the American government was following closely how the reparation question was unfolding, but wanted no official connection with it. Still, Secretary of State Charles Evan Hughes's belief that such persons as Boyden "represent[ed] the government as 'completely'" as official ones sheds light on the American attitude.[60]

The United States entered the 1920s under the era of successive Republican administrations. President Harding declared in his first address to Congress, "In the existing League of Nations, world-governing with its superpowers, this republic will have no part;" a sentence that was greeted with "enthusiastic applause."[61] The official policy line was that of "a return to normalcy," under whose banner the country was leading a supposedly isolationist decade. It is an oversimplification

---

57 These were Czechoslovakia, Romania, and the Serb-Croat-Slovene Kingdom, called Yugoslavia from 1928. Later these states formed the Little Entente.

58 Harold Nicolson, *Curzon: The Last Phase* (London: Constable & Co., 1934), 219.

59 *In Memory of Roland William Boyden* (Boston: Commonwealth of Massachusetts, 1933), 10; Boyden succeeded Albert Rathbone on April 1, 1920, as American unofficial representative on the Reparation Commission. Although Boyden was withdrawn from the Commission in February, 1921, due to his "anomalous" position, he was reinstated in May by President Harding. *The New York Times*, February 19, May 7, and May 11, 1921.

60 Jones, *U.S. Diplomats in Europe, 1919-1941*, 64. The United States was represented in such form till February 1, 1927, when the American unofficial representative was withdrawn and a staff member of the embassy at Paris took over the task of close observation. FRUS: 1926 (Washington, DC: Government Printing Office, 1941), 1 :120–25.

61 Congressional Record, 67th Congress, 1st Session, 172, April 12, 1921. Harding meant what he said. For almost a year, the US State Department did not even answer mails coming from the League. Clarence A. Berdahl, "The United States and the League of Nations," *Michigan Law Review* 27 (April 1929): 622.

of what really happened, but there is no denying that the crusading liberal internationalism of Wilson took a setback and America did not wish to have really close ties with Europe, in the best tradition of George Washington.[62] Calvin Coolidge, Harding's successor, thought that the United States was "better off out of the League."[63] That does not mean the United States did not monitor very closely the events both in the world and in the League of Nations.

While in its traditional spheres of interests, Latin America and the Far East, it followed its earlier policy to a large degree, in the case of the League of Nations, US representatives were a constant feature in its work. To avoid the appearance of close connections though, most of these Americans served as unofficial observers or simply private citizens not in an official capacity. Hughes defined their status as "official representatives acting in an unofficial capacity."[64] The United States rarely moved to an official basis with the League. If it was so, it was only with the committees or conferences touching upon the question of opium, double taxation, abolition of import and export prohibitions and restrictions, and, mainly, disarmament.[65] Even if the United States showed signs of detachment, it was only common diplomatic sense and national interest that in some issues America must cooperate with the League. Since Secretary Hughes recognized this fact, he instructed Joseph Grew, ambassador to Switzerland, to establish contacts with League representatives, collect material, and be an unofficial messenger. Since such activity would have been highly controversial and gone against the official line of Washington, Grew had to carry out his task in the most clandestine way.[66] This line of attitude mirrored well the public opinion of the country, which was highly isolationist.

However isolationist the Harding and Coolidge administrations may have been, they were also tainted with a touch of international outlook following the Wilson era. It manifested in the sense that these people sought to expand private marketplaces and were opposed to most kinds of state regulation. Naturally, this was not a really new concept. It was articulated in the belief that one of the most important outcomes of the war, namely that the United States had become the biggest creditor nation in the world, created the possibility of practicing financial

62 The most significant international undertaking by the US government was the Washington Naval Conference, 1921–2, in which different treaties were signed concerning naval armaments and upholding the Open Door principle in the Far East.

63 Calvin Coolidge, *The Autobiography of Calvin Coolidge* (New York: Cosmopolitan Book Corporation, 1929), 150.

64 Berdahl, "The United States," 629.

65 Congressional Record, 71st Congress, 1st Session, 2599–2601, June 10, 1929; Berdahl, "The United States," 630.

66 Waldo H. Heinrichs, *American Ambassador. Joseph C. Grew and the Development of the United States Diplomatic Tradition* (Boston and Toronto: Little Brown and Company, 1966), 52–53.

influence, even if many saw it as financial imperialism. The notion that the position of the United States had shifted was not new to some. Secretary of State John Hay, the emblematic figure of the Republican Party, twenty years earlier had already claimed in an address commemorating William McKinley that "The 'debtor nation' has become the chief creditor nation. The financial center of the world, which required thousands of years to journey from the Euphrates to the Thames and the Seine, seems passing to the Hudson between daybreak and dark."[67] These words coming from the man who was a key architect of spreading American financial and military influence around the globe contributed that this attitude was labeled by many contemporary and future observers imperialistic in nature.

Whatever it may be called, the huge accumulation of capital in the United States was welcome and needed everywhere. American bankers became increasingly eager to take part in the booming business cycle and hoped that American diplomacy would take the lead in reconstructing Europe. In this they were frustrated, because the official line tried to avoid any form of taking responsibility and believed in taking the lead only if that was unofficial and depoliticized. Instead, American foreign policy, in many ways, was embodied in foreign loans in this period. There was basically no European country that did not borrow money from the United States in the decade.[68] This fact, however, was not due to the government's efforts. Most of the loans during the war were government loans, and this was what already the Wilson government wanted to do away with. Wilson's financial advisers, including Thomas Lamont and Norman Davis, suggested taking an active role in the European reconstruction, but the US Treasury opposed this and other banker initiatives later.[69] President Wilson accepted the Treasury's view and government funds were largely reduced. The main goal of the United States became that the debts be repaid without touching the issue of reparations. Nonetheless, they wanted the Europeans to have money to spend on American goods, so they encouraged the private bankers to give loans.[70] As John McCloy later remembered, "back then the rehabilitation of Europe was done in a private capacity. Practically every merchant bank and Wall Street firm, from J. P. Morgan and Brown Brothers on down, was over there picking up loans. We were all very European in our outlook, and our goal was to see it rebuilt."[71] The Harding and Coolidge governments, in this sense, but in this sense only, followed Wilson's policy.

---

67 Congressional Record, 57th Congress, 1st Session, 2201, February 27, 1902.
68 Lewis, *America's Stake*, 619–23.
69 Ibid., 576–81.
70 Paul P. Abrahams, "American Bankers and the Economic Tactics of Peace: 1919," *Journal of American History* 56 (December 1969): 572–74.
71 Quoted in Isaacson and Thomas, *The Wise Men*, 122. McCloy was a Wall Street lawyer first, later he worked in the War Department and was president of the World Bank.

2.2. The US and the Financial Advisory System

Although the United States was presented with a historic moment to take over Great Britain's traditional leading role in many ways, the young empire failed to convert its economic and financial dominance into working political capital. It is clear that the American governments following World War I did not want to play an integral part on the political level of making the world regain its sound form. They wished to leave it more or less to the private financial sphere: the American capital and bankers. On the one hand, the foreign policy elite believed in financial and economic expansion in the true fashion of laissez-faire; on the other hand, they wished to separate diplomacy from economic foreign policy. This was only possible on the surface naturally, and big business was acting in concord with the government. The huge capital in the United States was useful, because by spreading in the forms of loans and charity it was also a helpful tool in opposing the Bolshevik ideology.[72] Indeed, one of the main political goals of the United States administrations in the postwar era was to contain the new and hostile ideology.

Bolshevism, which started in the Soviet Union, this new and hardly apprehensible dogma, was an anathema in Washington's eye. The red doctrine basically denied everything that the United States was established upon and believed in. Due to its nature of the wish to spread and the postwar situation, Central and Eastern Europe were especially in danger, which the events in Germany and Hungary right after World War I seemed to eloquently prove. Former secretary of state Elihu Root characterized this region as "filled with turbulent masses without stable government [...] There can be no settled peace until these masses are reduced to order. Order must be restored."[73] Other members of the US political elite shared this view and they saw in feeding these hungry peoples a way to curb the possible spread of the dangerous ideology. Secretary of State Robert Lansing phrased it perhaps best, "full stomachs mean no Bolsheviks." Joseph C. Grew, diplomat to various European countries in the 1920s and undersecretary of state for three years, 1924–1927, came to the same conclusion that "if you fight it with arms it will grow; if you fight it with food it will die a natural death." Herbert Hoover, Secretary of Commerce in the 1920s and earlier head of the American Relief Agency, did perhaps the most in order to achieve such a goal.[74] His organization focused first and foremost on Central and Eastern Europe and his charity work was clearly aiming at political

72 Wilson, *American Business & Foreign Policy*, 17–19.

73 Costigliola, *Awkward Dominion*, 31.

74 On the politically motivated role of the ARA under Hoover, such as working for broader American interests, like creating stability and working against Bolshevism and any other revolutionary ideas, see Costigliola, *Awkward Dominion*, 39–54.

ends. He asserted that the main policy program was "to prevent Europe from going Bolshevik," because in case it gained the upper hand on the European continent, he warned, it would "attack our own institutions." Future secretary of State Frank B. Kellogg thought the ratification of the peace treaties would be valuable in the struggle against Bolshevism, or otherwise "the flame of revolution and anarchy which lights the skies of Russia today [...] may sweep westward to the Atlantic and [...] the Western Hemisphere."[75] The freshly appointed American Ambassador to Germany, Alanson B. Houghton, reminded the State Department that

> the only people who possess the power to give the necessary impulse are the people of the United States. They can give the impulse that will lead to prosperity by giving the peoples of Europe the opportunity to choose the peace that leads to prosperity... Anything less is, I believe, a moral duty either neglected or refused. But the time is short. If we mean to do our part, we must not delay. Already the conditions are dangerous. Already the Bolshevist tide is beating against the barriers of European civilization. And if once those barriers go down, if the German people, in despair, believing that sympathy and help and understanding of their position are denied them, turn, for relief, to the East, the time is past. The tide will sweep resistlessly [sic] to the Atlantic.[76]

Therefore, the fight against Bolshevism coming from the east met with the wish to achieve stability in the whole of Europe, but mainly in Germany. The principal defeated country, with its vast potential in a few years' time, both in the economic and military sense, was seen as the most endangered and most important country for the United States. As the previous thoughts well show, the US government believed that by feeding Germany and the other starving countries, the stability of Europe, from economic and financial chaos on the one hand, and the Bolshevist menace on the other, would be solved. The basic pillar of that strategy was the economic and financial restoration in many weakened states. This had to be achieved, however, without official undertaking on the part of the US governments. They sized up well the ruling American sentiment and saw that it would not have allowed such a course. The government chose to urge the private sphere behind the scenes to take the steps necessary, but it refused to take any responsibility for the actions. This limited and two-dimensional approach appeared to serve American interests

75 The quotes in the paragraph come from Costigliola, *Awkward Dominion*, 31, 41, and 80.
76 Houghton to Hughes. October 23, 1922, FRUS: 1922 (Washington, DC: Government Printing Office, 1938), 2:173.

best in the 1920s. As long as this private, unofficial, mainly financial-economic approach produced results, there was no need to change it.

Hoover, who was for the spreading of American hegemony and stemming the Bolshevik tide, was also cautious of easy money lending: "We are morally and selfishly interested in the economic and political recovery of all the world. America is practically the final reservoir of international capital. Unless this capital is to be employed for reproductive purposes there is little hope of economic recovery."[77] He believed that loans should be given only in the case if the borrower country was not wasting it away and proved that such American money would be used to productive goals in the long run. He also wanted that the proceeds of a certain loan to be spent in the US, but this idea failed to gain widespread backing.[78] The government kept reiterating that it was not a party to foreign loans and such a financial undertaking was strictly for private business. Still, largely attributed to Hoover, the State Department wished to retain the right to pass judgment on foreign loans. This is all the more understandable in the light of the data that in 1920 foreign loans issued in the United States amounted to about $100 million per quarter-year, which sum doubled in 1921.[79] What he wanted to achieve was that foreign bonds issued in the United States should represent only those loans that were used for productive purposes, and such loans should be made on behalf of countries that might be deemed as unlikely to default.[80] Actually, this practical notion should have been maintained and used in order to avoid later problems. But in the early 1920s all appeared fine on the surface.

That does not mean that Hoover's efforts were all in vain. The first step was made on May 25, 1921, when the Harding cabinet met with investment bankers and asked to be informed of all public flotation of foreign bonds, so that the government "might express itself regarding them."[81] The participating investment bankers were to inform the State Department of any loans about to be issued on the American money market, because it "believe[d] that in view of the possible national interests involved it should have the opportunity of saying to the underwriters concerned, should it appear advisable to do so, that there [wa]s

77 Herbert Clark Hoover, *The Memoirs of Herbert Hoover*, vol. 2 (New York: The Macmillan Company, 1952), 87.
78 Priscilla Roberts, "Benjamin Strong, the Federal Reserve, and the Limits to Interwar American Nationalism," *Economic Quarterly* 86 (Spring 2006): 80.
79 Robert L. Sammons, "Capital Movements," In *The United States in the World Economy*, ed. Hal. B. Lary, (Washington, D. C.: Government Printing Office, 1943), 94. Although in 1923 it went back to the 1920 level, from the middle of 1924 a foreign lending boom started and reached its peak in mid-1928.
80 Hoover, *Memoirs*, vol. 2, 89.
81 Murray N. Rothbard, *America's Great Depression* (Auburn: The Ludwig von Mises Institute, 2000), 141.

or [wa]s not an objection to any particular issue."[82] Secretary of State Charles Hughes made up his mind only in December that the statement should be made, apparently due to a large number of fresh loans floated by American bankers without informing the State Department.[83] Benjamin Strong, the powerful Governor of the Federal Reserve Bank of New York, agreed with Hoover in 1921 that American capital was needed in revitalizing Central, Eastern, and Southeastern Europe. Hoover idea was bank cooperation "of purely private character that would embrace essentially: (a) rehabilitation of currencies (b) provision for initial raw materials (c) conditional to the above such proper cooperation of each of the eastern European governments in the inauguration and maintenance of such economic policies as would give promise of economic stability."[84] Strong liked Hoover's idea of a "purely private character," but he made the cooperation with other central banks a condition of the support of the Administration, which never came.[85] The successive administrations were determined not to be allied with big business in an open way. The above-mentioned note came out in March 1922 and, following Thomas Lamont's grumbling letter to Hoover, Strong filed a protest in April, arguing that there should be no such control.[86] His protest was important because he was probably the most influential man concerning the financial policy of the country. He was a dedicated if not "the most dedicated advocate of Europe's recovery," whom Hoover, who from 1922 was on unfriendly terms with Strong, labeled as a "mental axis" to Europe.[87] From the duel of the two the latter emerged as the winner, clearly backed by Harding and Secretary of Treasury Andrew Mellon, and, succeeding Harding upon his death, President

82 Press Release Issued by the Department of State, March 3, 1922, FRUS: 1922 (Washington, DC: Government Printing Office, 1938), 1:557–58. This policy was somewhat lessened although maintained a few years later. The Secretary of State to Diplomatic Officers and Certain Consular Officers, December 28, 1297, FRUS: 1927 (Washington, DC: Government Printing Office, 1942), 1:312–15. See also Coolidge's statement on October 14, 1927: "our country doesn't undertake to make any suggestion about the desirability of a loan, or the financial soundness of it, or whether it is worthy or unworthy of investment in its bonds by investors in this country.... our interest in it is chiefly a determination as to whether a loan made would interfere in any way in the foreign relations, the relations that exist between this country and the country proposing to make a loan." Quint and Ferrel, eds., *The Talkative President*, 197.

83 Silvano A. Wueschner, *Charting Twentieth-Century Monetary Policy. Herbert Hoover and Benjamin Strong, 1917–1927* (Westport, Connecticut: Greenwood Press, 1999), 33.

84 Hoover to Strong, August 30, 1921, quoted in Lester V. Chandler, *Benjamin Strong, Central banker* (Washington, D. C.: The Brookings Institution, 1958), 253–54.

85 Wueschner, *Charting Twentieth-Century Monetary Policy*, 30.

86 Michael J. Hogan, *Informal Entente* (Chicago: Imprint Publications, 1991), 100; Hoover, *The Memoirs of Herbert Hoover*, vol. 2, 86.

87 Roberts, "Benjamin Strong," 66; Hoover, *Memoirs* Vol. 3, 9; According to Hoover's desk calendar, in the four years following their fall out in 1922, they had only one official meeting. Wueschner, *Charting Twentieth-Century Monetary Policy*, 42.

basically took part in every significant loan in Europe, and the success or the failure of any issue might have depended on their coming in or staying away.

It is also important to note that the non-official control of loans by the American State Department was aimed mainly at Latin American issues.[96] This is understandable in light of the United States' efforts previously. One of the main goals had always been to secure the Western Hemisphere as an American sphere of interest and exclude European powers from it. The State Department did not want to see such loans that could have easily led to default and later, as a consequence, to political problems, not to mention intervention. Latin American countries had been in the past two decades often occupied by American troops. The government, in line with the General Loan Policy, never lost an occasion to repeat that they had nothing to do with loans politically. Coolidge said in 1924 that "American investors receive no assurances that their loans or agreements will be supported by American arms. It is not, it has not been, the policy of this Government to collect debts by force of arms."[97] In order to ensure that the United States did not need to take steps in that direction, they had to find the method by which they managed to avoid such a course. A possible tool to prevent such a scenario was the "institution" of financial advisers.

Dollar diplomacy introduced under President William Howard Taft was aiming at the dual purpose of keeping European creditors out of Latin America and thus making good on the Monroe Doctrine, and ensuring that these countries would become financially stable. The grand strategy was that in the wake of such trends these states that were notorious for local revolutions would show progress and politically stability as well. With this motive achieved, the United States would secure Latin America as its sole sphere of influence, plus it did not have to send marines from time to time to quell riots and petty revolutions that would endanger American citizens and interests on the ground. This American policy opened the way for professional monetary experts, who went to work in these Latin American countries as financial advisers. The emergence of the private sphere was also needed in order to lessen the governmental role that in 1911, for example, in the cases of Honduras and Nicaragua, was significant and, in the end, detrimental to State Department schemes.[98] The appearing method of hiring American financial experts thus diffused the political edge of the issue and cloaked the troublesome relationship between the United States and mainly Central American countries in the omnipotent expertise of these persons.

96 European issues were examined more closely when it came to the question of armament.
97 William Smith Culberstone, *International Economic Policies* (New York: D. Appleton and Company, 1925), 374.
98 In more detail, see Rosenberg, *Financial Missionaries*, 61–76.

The system of financial advisers as such was never a clearly formulated set of principles, either in its theoretical framework or by the governmental support it received. However, already during World War I, and in all likelihood seen as a strategic necessity, the economic advisory system started to take shape by Congressional blessing in Nicaragua and Haiti.[99] Such a strategy brought the administration and investment bankers to a close rapport. Financial control was introduced in Haiti, the Dominican Republic, Nicaragua, and Liberia throughout World War I, and the financial advisory system was also set up in Cuba and Panama before 1920.[100] Therefore, it is safe to say that President Wilson was also an advocate of dollar diplomacy, even if he repudiated it on the surface, because he saw in it a tool of achieving his foreign policy aims, that is, to stabilize Latin American countries in order to spread American-type democracy in that region as well. The State Department made successful efforts to work together with investment bankers in placing controlled loans in Central American countries in order to create stability and financial dependency. Obviously, this created problems as well, but the overarching aim was achieved: the dependent relation between the United States and Latin American countries was firmly established.[101]

The question is why Latin American countries, so desperately seeking a helping hand against US hegemony, not only accepted but also outright wished to have these financial experts. The answer is evident: once a financial expert, or group of experts, visited any of the Latin American countries, the chances of raising a loan in the United States grew substantially. The financial advisers carried with them an aura of technical and theoretical superiority together with the know-how of healthy financial reforms, and their simple presence was enough to create trust in a proposed loan, or to give renewed support for countries in pecuniary needs. Moreover, these experts, at least on the surface, were not attached to the American government, so their position was seen as more liberal and independent, and they were easily accepted as honest brokers for the given country. Still, until the

99 Norman L. Rosenberg, "From Colonialism to Professionalism: The Public-Private Dynamic in United States Foreign Financial Advising, 1898–1929," *The Journal of American History* 74 (June 1987): 64.

100 In relation to the work of the various Financial Advisers to Haiti, see FRUS, 1917 (Washington, DC: Government Printing Office, 1926), 802–33; 1919 (Washington, DC: Government Printing Office, 1934), 2:303–73; 1920, 2:760–853; 1921(Washington, DC: Government Printing Office, 1936), 2:188–232; 1922 (Washington, DC: Government Printing Office, 1938), 2:471–553; 1923 (Washington, DC: Government Printing Office, 1938), 2:385–423. Obviously, Cuba was one of the most important Latin American countries to the United States. The financial adviser's (Albert Rathbone) work in detail see FRUS, 1920, vol. 2, 49–57; the loan negotiations with Cuba and the special envoy's (General E. H. Crowder) work on it in detail see FRUS, 1921: 1:734–73; 1923: 1:837–43; N. Rosenberg, "From Colonialism to Professionalism," 64–65.

101 E. Rosenberg, *Financial Missionaries*, 105–121. Rosenberg labeled this controlling system as "professional-managerial" throughout her book.

fall of 1924, the governments of Colombia, Cuba, Guatemala, Honduras, Liberia, Panama, Persia, and Peru engaged American experts by the assistance of the US government. In the same period, American financial experts were hired without governmental assistance by the governments of Bolivia, China, Ecuador, Hungary, Mexico, and Paraguay.[102] As can be seen, the phenomenon of American financial experts was not limited to Latin America alone.

Thus Latin American countries were eager to employ these persons. The most accomplished person in trying to rectify financial problems in Latin American countries after the First World War was Edwin Walter Kemmerer, the "international money doctor." It is worth taking a closer look at his work to see how widespread American unofficial involvement worked. In 1919, a trip that can be considered as the trial of his methods, Kemmerer visited Guatemala. As he confessed to Strong, although it was a "most interesting experience", "the problems there presented were quite different in many respects from any I have come in direct contact before."[103] This was his way of saying that he ran into opposition, and indeed, the country's fierce resistance to foreign control in money matters made his work largely a failure.[104] Later he was in Peru, where he was offered to manage the new reserve bank, but the unstable political situation made him decline the offer.[105] His third post was Colombia in 1923. After the United States and Colombia settled the claims arising form the Panama Canal with a $25,000,000 indemnity to the Latin American country, Colombia asked the State Department for financial advisory help.[106] For the US it was crucial that Latin American countries function financially and economically soundly, therefore they selected Kemmerer. The "doctor" worked very efficiently and successfully and returned to Colombia to help Colombia receive further loans in 1931. Kemmerer's next stop was Chile in 1925, again with the approval of the State Department. If subsequent investments are a measure of success, then the work of Kemmerer and his team bore fruit: from 1925 to 1929 investments reached almost $200,000,000, while between 1919

102 Text of address of Dr. Arthur N. Young, at the Institute of Politics, Williamston, Massachusetts, August 26, 1924. "The Department of State and Foreign Loans." No. 14. 21. United States policy regarding foreign loans, Economic and Financial Section, S. 118, Salter Papers, League of Nations Archives (hereafter cited as LNA).

103 Kemmerer to Strong, October 9, 1919, Box 16, Folder 5: Strong, Benjamin, 1916-1928, Edwin W. Kemmerer Papers (MC # 146), Princeton University Library (hereafter cited as Kemmerer Papers).

104 N. Rosenberg, "From Colonialism to Professionalism," 68–70.

105 Kemmerer to Strong, September 16, 1922, Box 16, Folder 5: Strong, Benjamin, 1916-1928, Kemmerer Papers.

106 The subsequent appointments of and information on Kemmerer are from Seidel's work if not indicated otherwise. Robert N. Seidel, "American Reformers Abroad: The Kemmerer Missions in South America, 1923–1931," *The Journal of Economic History* 32 (June 1972): 527, 533, 535–39, 541. See also N. Rosenberg, "From Colonialism to Professionalism," 68–70, and E. Rosenberg, *Financial Missionaries*, 155–65.

and 1925 they were 30% of that sum. Ecuador also had the privilege to have Kemmerer after he accepted an invitation in 1926, and although Kemmerer's view did not meet that of the State Department, it is attributed to his financial reforms in the country that Ecuador earned *de jure* recognition in 1928. Bolivia was the next patient on the list. After two years of courtship, Kemmerer said yes to the request that he should try to help put the financial matters in order. The final stop on Kemmerer's grand tour was Peru in 1930, where he was also able to make the Peruvian government, basically a dictatorship, accept and implement some financial reforms. Kemmerer also tried to work his magic in Poland and China. Kemmerer, whose opinion carried weight, attributed the demand for American financial advisers to three reasons: the relative lack on American side of political aggrandizement, the economic and financial prosperity of the US, and countries' desire to attract American capital.[107] The rhetorical skill also helped achieve this: the word "scientific" was an often recurring one in Kemmerer's repertoire, which also strengthened his politics-free stance and his professionalism.[108] His success only gave substantial basis to the belief that American advisors can do miracles. In addition, he worked a lot, sometimes twelve hours a day, but also charged a lot for his activities, thus further magnifying the technical knowledge he alone could provide.[109]

Kemmerer's main goals were to set up central banks, issue new gold-back currencies, and bring the involved nations onto to the gold, or gold-exchange, system. It is important to note that these monetary goals were basically the same as in Europe in the 1920s.[110] A major difference was that Kemmerer, in comparison to his American colleagues working in Europe, enjoyed a much freer hand. While, for example, Jeremiah Smith, Jr. in Hungary had to follow the path laid down by the League of Nations and Montagu Norman, Kemmerer had no such restrictions. The goals were the same however: to make sure that there would be financially stable countries. Wherever the "doctor" and other American financial advisers went, they were greeted with high hopes to which they usually lived up to. All the countries these persons visited benefited from their being there either in the form of financial reforms or American loans, sometimes both.

American financial advisers covered the whole globe. A long list of other Americans were involved in similar undertakings, and not only in Latin America

107 E. W. Kemmerer, "Economic Advisory Work for Governments," *The American Economic Review* 17 (March 1927): 2–4.

108 E. Rosenberg, *Financial Missionaries*, 29.

109 Ibid., 194.

110 There are critics who say that this system was too inflexible and during the time of crisis in the 1930s it did not allow for countercyclical lending, which was one of the main reasons for the depression. See, Barry Eichengreen, *Golden Fetters: The Gold Standard and the Great Depression, 1919–1939* (New York: Oxford University Press, 1992).

but around the world: Thomas William Lamont in Japan, China, Mexico, Austria, France, and Italy, Charles Dawes in Germany and the Dominican Republic, Owen Young in Germany, Seymour Parker Gilbert also in Germany, Jeremiah Smith, Jr. and Royall Tyler in Hungary, Dwight Whitney Morrow in Cuba, Arthur Chester Millspaugh in Persia and Haiti, William Wilson Cumberland, Kemmerer's student, in Armenia, Turkey, Peru, Haiti, and Nicaragua, Charles Schuveldt Dewey in Poland, and Henry Parker Willis in the Philippines and Ireland. They embodied much of the American interests in foreign policy as far as the 1920s went. Quite a few of these men, Millspaugh, Dewey, and Gilbert, for example, left their governmental positions to function in an advisory capacity. Therefore, it would be hard to assume that the American administration had no contact with them, and in many cases they in fact did because the US government had a stake in these people's work. Naturally, at least on the surface, these men performed their duties in an unofficial capacity, rarely in a semi-official status. Even if a financial expert performed under the aegis of the League of Nations in Europe, of which Jeremiah Smith, Jr. is the best example, he acted as a private American citizen and not as an American government representative. As a historian put it, this "had the virtue of depoliticizing issues, avoiding government responsibility, and maximizing American financial leverage."[111] This was a continuation of the dollar diplomacy of the prewar decade of the century: this time though not only financial penetration took place, but, adding a touch of Wilsonianism, also help in such monetary issues as budget and currency.

It is important to note that the functions these advisers carried out were very different in Latin America and Europe. In Latin America, they were often in very close connection with the US government and enjoyed quite large freedom how they did their job. In Europe, however, the picture was different. American financial experts were also welcomed here but their role was not as defining and far from a freelancer. These people followed the same path of financial reforms as their colleagues in Latin America: stable currency based on the gold standard and an independent central bank under whose leadership all this can be achieved. Although they also brought with them the hope of the prosperity of the new world, in most cases it remained just like that: hope.[112]

---

111 Melvyn P. Leffler, "American Policy Making and European Stability, 1921–1933," *The Pacific Historical Review* 46 (May 1977): 220.

112 American private capital did not flow exclusively to Europe and Latin America. American banks took part in the Australian Rehabilitation Loan in 1923, and the next year the loan to Japan had an American participation of $150 million. Culberstone, *International Economic Policies*, 354. As always, J. P. Morgan & Co. played the leading part here and had all the hope of securing the Japanese government as "a permanent client of the house." E. Lamont, *The Ambassador from Wall Street*, 196.

With such an advisory system, the United States could without much effort ensure its hegemony, especially in Latin America. When it came to the League of Nations to show its commitment to Latin America, it shamelessly withdrew in the face of American resistance. The United States had its way when League observers were excluded from the Pan-American Conferences in 1923 and 1928.[113] Under the cloak of Pan-Americanism, the North-American powerhouse thwarted any chance of the League coming to the help of Latin American countries. When disputes arose in the 1920s, such as between Panama and Costa Rica or Peru and Chile, the countries involved opted for Pan-Americanism, which, in effect, meant American arbitration, instead of the League's help.[114] This attitude changed only in the 1930s, when the US finally allowed the League to take part in Latin American disputes, although this cooperation was "subject to certain conditions" that were not clarified.[115] But by then a major shift had happened: US investments in Latin America took over the first place from Europe.[116] So, when President Franklin Roosevelt announced the Good Neighbor Policy in 1933, a continuation of Hoover's work to a large degree, financial dominance had been established.

113 David, D. Burks, "The United States and the Geneva Protocol of 1924: 'A New Holy Alliance'?," *The American Historical Review* 64 (July 1959): 891.
114 Wilson, *American Business & Foreign Policy, 1920–1933*, 163; Percy Alvin Martin, "Latin America and the League of Nations," *The American Political Science Review* 20 (February 1926): 27.
115 The case was the dispute between Colombia and Peru in 1933. League of Nations, Official Journal, (hereafter cited as LNJ), 14th year, No. 4, April 1933 (Part I), 614.
116 Wilson, *American Business & Foreign Policy, 1920–1933*, 168.

Chapter 3

The Beginning of the European Financial Rehabilitation

3.1. The First Steps

After the conclusion of World War I in late 1918, Europe was in a devastated condition. The four years of continuous fighting had taken their toll: not only the soldiers and many civilians were victims of the killings, but certain economies in some countries came close to a nonexistent state. The bulk of the misery in wake of the war appeared in Central and Southern Europe, where large-scale hunger reared its ugly head. The Allied Powers soon understood that it was in their best interest not to leave these countries in the hold of bitter hopelessness, because it might lead to social disorder. The German example already in 1918 and the short-lived communist coup in Hungary in 1919 were clear signs that economic instability made political volatility and disturbance a likely scenario. The Western powers decided to provide relief to these countries, mostly in the form of food.

Despite its unofficial status in the relief efforts, the United States also played a big role in Europe. Driven mainly by humanitarian considerations, American capital was coming to the continent and was crucial if any success was to be achieved. As can be expected, the United States provided the largest sum of the total coming from all participating countries. Aside from money, food and raw material were the most needed in Central and Eastern Europe. Wilson first seemed to be a committed supporter of the reconstruction of Europe even if he had some reservations about the Allies' aims.[117] But contrary to his early enthusiasm, he started to speak more and more only in general terms about helping Europe and later avoided the question entirely.[118] It was a sign of things to come from the American official circles. In January 1920, Congress reduced relief for Europe from $150,000,000 to its one third.[119] In the presidential election of 1920, Harding clearly represented the view that Europe would be left

117 Michael J. Hogan, "The United States and the Problem of International Economic Control: American Attitudes toward European Reconstruction, 1918-1920. *The Pacific Historical Review* 44 (February 1975): 96.
118 Anne Orde, *British Policy and European Reconstruction after the First World War* (Cambridge: Cambridge University Press, 1990), 73.
119 Lansing to the Ambassador in France (Wallace), February 6, 1920, FRUS, 1920:1:254–55.

on her own despite the call that the United States should come to the rescue.[120] It meant a fatal blow to those British politicians who thought that only a strong Anglo-American cooperation could solve the political and financial problems on the old continent.

The British initiative in reconstructing Europe was not only political. The only traditional power that was still strong enough after the war wanted to resuscitate the European trade for no unselfish reasons. They argued that especially South-Eastern Europe must be strengthened economically since this region was in the most terrible conditions. But the stabilization of these countries was to be part of an overall European reconstruction effort.[121] Since the volume of trade compared to before the war had been reduced, Great Britain had a vital stake in making it larger again, because it promised an outlet for British money and finished articles. As a Treasury memorandum formulated it in 1920: "The United States can do without Europe; we cannot."[122] At the same time, London wanted to remain the financial center of the world and was not willing to pass this status over to New York.[123] With the traditional financial channels existing in Europe, and the hesitant American attitude, for the time being this goal seemed achievable. Thus a duality was present. Great Britain wanted cooperation with the United States, both in the political and financial fields, but with possibly retaining its dominant status on the continent. But by the end of 1920 it became clear that the United States would not take part in the political difficulties of Europe. Warren G. Harding won on the slogan "a return to normalcy," which was to mean a renewed isolationist policy, leaving Europe in its lurch.

In lieu of politicians then, it was left to the private sphere to carry on the possible collaboration between the two countries. In the decade following World War I, this task fell mainly in the hands of the two defining characters of the banking world, Benjamin Strong and Montagu Norman.[124] Strong, Governor

---

120 T. Lamont, *Across World Frontiers*, 218.

121 György Ránki, *Gazdaság és külpolitika. A nagyhatalmak harca a délkelet-európai gazdasági hegemóniáért (1919–1939)* [Economy and Foreign Policy. The Fight of the Great Powers for Economic Hegemony in South-Central Europe] (Budapest: Magvető Kiadó, 1981), 50–51.

122 Quoted in Lojkó, *Meddling in Middle Europe*, 65.

123 Ibid., 64. Both views are from Ralph G. Hawtrey, the Director of Financial Enquiries. Norman, who had his opinion about everyone, said that Hawtrey was a "leading light" of the Treasury, but later added: "He seems to me to treat his subjects as if they existed in a vacuum." Norman to Strong, February 24, 1922, and October 31, 1922, G35/3, Bank of England Archives (hereafter cited as BoE).

124 The two bankers first met in March 1916, and held a close rapport till Strong's death in 1928. On the close relationship between the two men, see Sir Henry Clay, *Lord Norman* (London: Macmillan & Co. Ltd., 1957), 121–24, 132–33, 138–43, 149–58, 163–64, 172–74, 181–85, 196–212, 221–22, 233–37, 256–66, 282–86, 300–04; Chandler, *Benjamin Strong*, chapters 7–11; and Cottrell, *Rebuilding the Financial System*, 27–107.

of the Federal Reserve Bank of New York since 1914, had an aim to have an Anglo-American post-war economic cooperation, as part of the international order, and this was the mission and purpose that was the dominant theme in his life.[125] Even before the United States joined the World War, Strong expressed his wish to participate in central bank cooperation with European counterparts.[126] When the United States was finally on the brink of entering the war in the spring of 1917, he wrote to Norman about his happiness, and when a larger loan of $200 million of J. P. Morgan & Co. to Britain was concluded shortly afterward, he characterized his feelings with the terms "joy and satisfaction."[127] Strong was a good friend of Lamont, and the worldview of the Governor of the Federal Reserve Bank and J. P. Morgan & Co. was largely the same.[128] Right after the end of the war, Strong feared the main danger lay in the economic field. He was convinced that the United States and Great Britain must work together to prevent "a period of economic barbarism."[129] To avoid this, there was a great need for Anglo-American cooperation in the financial sphere. "There is no doubt," Strong wrote to Norman, "that much of the world's happiness in the future will depend upon the relations now being established between your country and ours."[130] After the war he characterized the American noninvolvement in Europe as "an act of cowardice."[131]

Montagu Norman, who became Governor of the Bank of England in 1920, was international in outlook and knew that a restored world economy was to the advantage of Great Britain.[132] He was a firm believer of central banks and their cooperation, and held the notion that central banks ought to be free of government interference and this sovereign position carried the promise of a rewarding collaboration among the fellow banks.[133] One of his main goals was to create the financial system in the world on the gold standard. Together with many of his contemporaries, he saw this as a crucial key to financial stability. Lloyd George characterized him as "the high priest of the golden calf" whose "main preoccupation was to keep his idol burnished and supreme in the Panthéon of commerce. In his honest view it was the only god to lead the nation out of the

---

125 Roberts, "Benjamin Strong," 63, 65.

126 Chandler, *Benjamin Strong*, 93.

127 Strong to Norman, April 2, 1917, and May 16, 1917, G35/1, BoE.

128 Strong and Lamont were neighbors and friends. Strong succeeded Lamont as secretary of the Bankers in 1904, and as Vice President of the Bankers Trust in 1909. Chandler, *Benjamin Strong*, 26, 30–31.

129 Strong to Norman, May 16, 1917, G35/1, BoE.

130 Strong to Norman, November 22, 1918, G35/1, BoE.

131 Quoted in Chandler, *Benjamin Strong*, 146.

132 Clay, *Lord Norman*, 169–70.

133 Clay, *Lord Norman*, 169; György Péteri, *Revolutionary Twenties*, 60.

wilderness."[134] He was against any political influence in the financial world and saw war debts and reparations as especially harmful for international trade.[135] As a French contemporary characterized him:

> In his view politicians and political institutions are in no fit state to direct with the necessary competence and continuity this task of organization which he would like to see undertaken by central banks, independent at once of government and of private finance... [It is important to take] out of the political realm those problems which are essential for the development and prosperity of the nations: financial security, distribution of credit, movement of prices.[136]

He was rather conservative, and innovations were only to serve the goal of securing Great Britain as the leading power in financial matters on the continent.[137] He nonetheless knew too well that without American support, many of his plans for a reinvigorated Europe would be unmanageable. This was one of the reasons why he wholeheartedly agreed with Strong in the necessity of a strong Anglo-American financial cooperation.[138] It stemmed from his apolitical attitude that he did not approach the Foreign Office on his own initiative and thought it best to leave foreign policy questions to the Treasury.[139] Nonetheless, his views in the political domain tended to be the same as that of the Foreign Office, but this was not due to his close connection to the political leadership, rather the result of his upbringing and sharing the same core belief as to what was best for the country.[140]

Both men distrusted politicians and were mindful of their countries' interests. They also needed each other, since both held such influence in their own country with which they could provide needed assistance the other. This does not mean that Strong was necessarily a great friend of Norman's or the latter's country. Rather, he saw the relevant potential for cooperation with Norman for certain issues. Later, if it did not suit him, he was not so friendly. However, both men saw the path leading to the financial stability of a country upon the same prerequisites: balanced budgets, stable currencies, gold standard, and a well-managed bank of issue were the main fundamentals. Next to J. P. Morgan, these two bankers' opinion was the determining factor in the possibility of a successful

134 Lloyd George, *The Truth about Reparations and War-debts* (London: William Heinemann Ltd., 1932), 116.
135 Clay, *Lord Norman*, 169; Péteri, *Revolutionary Twenties*, 56.
136 Pierre Quesnay to Emile Moreau, quoted in Péteri, *Revolutionary Twenties*, 61–62.
137 Péteri, *Global Monetary Regime*, 28.
138 Norman to Strong, December 11, 1918, G35/1, BoE.
139 Clay, *Lord Norman*, 286.
140 Meyer, *Bankers' Diplomacy*, 10.

floating of any loan. For example, J. P. Morgan & Co. would never float any loan without Strong's informal approval, and in turn, without Morgan there was no real chance of a loan to be floated in the United States.[141] Norman was acting in the same capacity and his word meant a "yes" or "no" to a country seeking a loan in the City. Thus from 1920, the Strong-Norman pair would define to a large degree what was done in order to rehabilitate Europe financially, and it also depended on their opinion in what fashion any loan would be carried out.

Naturally, there were cooperative endeavors by others to deal with the European problems collectively, first and foremost, by the League of Nations. As was mentioned, next to trying to insure a lasting peace, the main task for the organization was to achieve the economic and financial reconstruction of Europe, and the two were possible only together. It was evident that efforts by single countries were not sufficient. Without some collective measure, the manifold problems of the continent would become an ongoing obstacle to prosperity.

But before the League of Nations could commence its work, financial experts and bankers tried to organize strictly informal meetings in order to arrive at a possible solution for the financial problems of Europe. One of the main minds behind this was Gerard Vissering, president of the Netherlands bank, who invited various leading financiers from the United States and Europe to discuss the challenges at hand. These talks in themselves were only a starting point at best though, and it was clear that the idea had to be elevated on the formal international scene.

The first big step was the Brussels Conference between September 24 and October 8, 1920. Although the conference raised one of the most burning questions, that of reparations, this proved premature, since no countries wanted to give up their claims. To make things worse, although thirty-nine countries were represented, including defeated states such as Germany, Austria, and Hungary, for example, at the conference, the United States was not.[142] Since the conference was convened by the League of Nations, the American government felt that not being a member it ought not to be officially represented. The person chosen for the task of unofficial representation was Roland Boyden, the American unofficial representative on the Reparation Commission.[143] Obviously, Boyden was not to speak for his country in an official capacity, but his address at the conference was clearly the manifestation of the official American opinion. In this speech he emphasized the greater cooperation of Europeans to be done in order to create American confidence in Europe.[144] In view of the US Treasury, "further

141 Chandler, *Benjamin Strong*, 286.

142 The correspondence concerning the Brussels Conference, the League invitation, and the US refusal to it, see FRUS: 1920, 1:88–107.

143 FRUS: 1920, 1:95–96.

144 Abrahams, "American Bankers," 581–82.

governmental loans by the US, cancellation of some or all of obligations of European governments held by the US Government, and deferring of obligations of foreign governments held by the US to liens created in favor of loans subsequently made for reconstruction purposes, are clearly not appropriate for consideration of conference."[145] The other reason why the United States did not find the conference satisfactory was that the American opinion strictly held that government-to-government lending should cease and the private sector should take over that role. Besides, the conference was crucially close to the presidential elections in the United States. A few weeks prior to a domestic political showdown, it was hardly surprising that the government practiced restraint. Examined from the reparation aspect and its notorious partner, the debt question, the meeting was not successful and could not bring the European scene closer to the overall solution.

It is important to emphasize that the conference was still a positive event and the principles the conference laid down in the field of finance and economy were central to the next decade in Europe. Since many of the participating countries had budget deficit, it is little surprise that budget equilibrium with reduced government expenditures was one such principle. An important element of the Conference was the ter Meulen plan, named after Dutch banker Carel Eliza ter Meulen. This plan suggested that in a to-be-reconstructed country the main tasks were: budget equilibrium, a halt to inflation, setting up a central bank of issue, and providing external credits in the form of bonds to be secured out of the revenues of the assigned assets.[146] This idea, which in some measure resembled John Maynard Keynes' proposal back in 1919 at the Peace Conference, proved to be the main stepping-stone on which League of Nations loans were established later.[147] Resolution No. 5. actually prodded the League to help those countries that were incapable of solving their own economic problems.[148] This decision foreshadowed the future stabilization schemes by the League, so an important consequence of the conference was that it inspired the League's efforts in the financial field. Soon both the Financial Committee and the Economic Committee of the League of Nations were born, which comprised impartial advisers instead of state representatives, a sharp contrast to the Reparation Commission. As

145 Houston to Boyden, September 17, 1920, FRUS: 1920, 1:95–96.
146 League of Nations, *The League of Nations Reconstruction Schemes in the Inter-war Period* (Geneva, 1944), 8.
147 Keynes's idea in was that enemy states should issue bonds secured by the Associated Powers, and from the proceeds these countries could finance reparation payments or reconstruction. The Allies could have used such purchased bonds for paying debts. Keynes, "Scheme for the Rehabilitation of European Credit and for Financing Relief and Reconstruction," In. *The Collected Writings of Keynes*, Vol. XVI., 429-431. The American side refused to deal with the bond proposal.
148 Péteri, *Global Monetary Regime*, 9.

its head noted, the report of the conference "had an enormous influence in transforming national financial policies."[149] Boyden thought the ter Meulen scheme was "neither very useful nor very objectionable," but later added that it might provide a little help in the stabilization effort.[150] Notwithstanding the lack of tangible results, the conference was clearly a first step toward finding the right path to reconstruct Europe.

Despite the efforts at Brussels, however, not much was done in practice. As always, the political considerations overrode the economic ones, and the victors were hardly disposed to help ex-enemy states. Any effort to try to achieve some kind of reconstruction in Austria, for instance, was stalling and the general picture, especially in other countries of Central and Southern Europe, was not rosy either. Month after month, desperate signals were sent about famine and lack of vital raw materials from the Danubian countries. Finally, the Western powers had concluded it was necessary to take a further step. They knew that they could not afford to lose almost half of Europe to long-term poverty. Both political and economic considerations made them want to find a solution to the acute crisis.

One and a half years after Brussels another conference was called into being by the Allied Powers, this time in Genoa, Italy, from April 10 to May 19, 1922.[151] In sharp contrast to the previous talks in Belgium, the Italian city welcomed not only all the European states but also one of the most important players, the Soviet Union, which understandably accepted the invitation to the Conference with enthusiasm. The total number of states participating reached thirty-four. This was the first time that all these countries had participated and met on "equal terms," although clearly the biggest powers carried much more prestige and influence, while the Eastern European countries, similarly to Smith's observation at the Paris Peace Conference, were simply bystanders.[152] Nor can one fail to note that the League of Nations was not invited to the conference in its own right; it was only "trusted" with carrying out the implementation work after the conference. This was a clear manifestation of the envy and suspicion of the great powers

149 Sir Arthur Salter, *World Trade and Its Future* (London: Oxford University Press, 1936), 43.

150 Boyden to Davis, September 30, and October 6, 1920, and Boyden to Davis and Houston, October 9, 1920, FRUS: 1920, 1:100–03.

151 On the antecedents of the conference, the political strife among the chief players, the postponement, see Carole Fink, *The Genoa Conference: European Diplomacy, 1921-1922* (Chapel Hill: University of North Carolina Press, 1984), 3–142.

152 Lloyd George's term. Minutes of the First Plenary Session of the Genoa Conference, held at the Palazzo San Giorgio, April 10, 1922, at 3 p. m., Documents on British Foreign Policy (hereafter cited as DBFP), First Series, 19: 340.

toward the international body.[153] Especially Great Britain wanted to follow its own course without any hindrance the League might have meant. Therefore, Lloyd George calling the conference "the greatest gathering of European nations which has ever been assembled in this continent" and predicting that "the results of the conference will be far-reaching in their effects" showed undue optimism and somewhat dishonest commitment.[154] Still, on the whole, the nature of this conference was much more promising at the outset.

The gathering was supposed to be a financial and economic conference with such questions as central banks and the securing of foreign credits and capital for reconstruction, and in this sense it was a clear continuation of the Brussels Conference.[155] However, the question of the relations to the Soviet Union was also on the agenda, and it stood out disproportionately as the main issue. This latter point was the main reason why the American government thought the conference assumed too much political character and it did not accept the invitation.[156] According to Strong, besides the Soviet issue, the United States did not want to discuss inter-allied debts, and wanted to avoid possible obligations following economic discussions.[157] Lamont believed that the US government would be soon ready for such a conference, but in order to achieve any success, it should be held in Washington.[158] In the end, the American government only went as far as allowing James Addison Logan, Assistant U.S. unofficial delegate to Reparation Commission, and the new Ambassador to Italy Richard W. Child to take part unofficially at the conference and inform the government about what transpired there.[159] Besides them, two more Americans attended the conference. William B. Causey and Alvin B. Barber were technical advisors of the American Relief Administration to Austria and Poland, respectively.[160] According to one

---

153 The League of Nations, which was to follow up on the recommendations reached at the Genoa Conference, represented itself with a delegate but found itself basically as a second-rank group. H. R Cummings, head of the League of Nations' information section, wrote after five weeks in Genoa: "I found it a salutary experience to move.... in a distinctly non-League atmosphere and to realize, painfully, close at hand, that in the really first-class problems of the world, the League has not taken its proper place." (Ibid., 257) On the League of Nations at Genoa in detail, see Ibid., 252–57.

154 Minutes of the First Plenary Session of the Genoa Conference, DBFP, First Series, 19:340.

155 In more detail about the events during the conference, see Fink, *The Genoa Conference*, 143–280.

156 The correspondence about the attitude of the US toward the conference and its refusal to take part in it, see FRUS: 1922, 1:384–96. See also Fink, *The Genoa Conference*, 47–49, 97–98.

157 Norman to Strong, February 24, 1922, G35/3, BoE.

158 Orde, *British Policy and European Reconstruction*, 193–94.

159 Hughes to Child, March 24 and 31, 1922, and Hughes to Herrick, April 8, 1922, FRUS: 1922, 1:394–96.

160 Wueschner, *Charting Twentieth-Century Monetary Policy*, 43.

observer, the four-man delegation was "both helpful and conciliatory in the background."[161] Still, in all likelihood, the lack of an official American delegation at Genoa did not help the outcome, though this fact alone should not have caused failure. The unsuccessful result was rather due to the disagreement between the Western powers and the Soviet Union.[162] The latter country came to Italy with the aim of settling its relations with the Allied Powers, but especially in the question of reparations and debts the two sides could not find a mutually satisfactory answer. The British came to the conference seeing the Soviet Union as a possible key to the economic recovery in Europe, but they soon switched over to achieving political results, while the French prevented the raising of the German problem and the question of reparations, the real key to Europe.[163] As a result of the selfish attitude of these powers, it was only logical that Germany and the Soviet Union tried to achieve some tangible result that was advantageous for them and they concluded the Rapallo Treaty in April, during the Conference.[164] This was a sharp rebuke to the Allied powers who should have understood that the rehabilitation and some political consolidation were necessary in the future.

The reparation and debt questions were a clear obstacle why the United States was not willing to take part in talks that might have helped bring Europe closer to a more prosperous period. The United States sensed early in the British initiation the effort to try to evade paying their financial obligation. As George Harvey, American ambassador to London, reported well before the Conference opened, the British initiation stemmed from the wish to "put the United States under tacit obligations to make pecuniary sacrifices through cancellation of debts in full or in part [... and its] underlying purpose is to obtain great reduction of English indebtedness to the United States. "[165] Indeed, Lloyd George, the British Prime Minister was arguing in the same sense as the soon to be written Balfour Note when he was meeting with Louis Barthou, who led the French delegation to Genoa during the conference.[166] The British prime minister knew that everything depended on the American participation or staying away. In

---

161 Harold Nicolson, *Curzon: The Last Phase* (London: Constable & Co., 1934), 296, note 1.
162 In more detail about this side of the Genoa conference, see FRUS: 1922, 2:770–813.
163 Lloyd George, *The Truth about Reparations and War-debts*. London: William Heinemann Ltd., 1932), 69; Nicolson, *Curzon*, 243; Orde, *British Policy and European Reconstruction*, 195; Fink, *The Genoa Conference*, 82–84.
164 Fink, *The Genoa Conference*, 126–33.
165 Harvey to State Department, December 13, 1921, quoted in Stephen A. Schuker, "American Policy Toward Debts and Reconstruction at Genoa, 1922," In *Genoa, Rapallo, and European reconstruction in 1922*, Carole Fink, Axel Frohn, and Jürgen Heideking, eds, (Cambridge: Cambridge University Press, 2002), 102.
166 As a good indication of the crux of the French postwar policy, Barthou already in his opening speech declared that revision of existing treaties was out of the question. Fink, *The Genoa Conference*, 153.

Calvin Coolidge reduced the governmental authority in question.[88] This so-called control, the General Loan Policy, however, did not mean a strict scrutiny on the part of the State Department; it was more of a gesture than a real policy. Indeed, it was rather an expression of an informational measure and it did not address the financial soundness of a loan. In fact, the only exception may have been the case of the State of Sao Paulo, Brazil, when the State Department did express its disagreement with a proposed loan twice in 1925. The reason, apparently, was "the policy of coffee valorization" by that state.[89] Three years later the approval was granted though.[90] In the case of the Dominican Republic in 1926, only after some wrangling and specific condition was the State Department willing to approve a $10,000,000 loan.[91] Therefore, approval of a loan did not really mean approval of its financial soundness but rather was a political point of view.

In Europe, Strong had a counterpart, who shared much of the same ideology, but from a British perspective. Montagu Norman, the Governor of the Bank of England since 1920, wanted European financial reconstruction seen, which he knew very well was a necessary prerequisite of a healthy circulation of currency and trade of which Great Britain should be the prominent beneficiary. He had the plan for leading back the pound to the gold standard and in this scheme Strong was an indispensable ally. Next to the Strong-Norman pair,[92] the most powerful and influential name in the financial business was that of J. P. Morgan & Co. *The New York Times* characterized the personality of J. P. Morgan as an "indefinite conception in the public mind," who seemed "more an institution than a human being with likes and dislikes, habits, abilities."[93] Already during World War I, the company established itself as the chief creditor of the Allied Powers. Despite Wilson's call to be neutral, the Morgan house, in Lamont's words, "had never for one moment been neutral; we didn't know how to be. From the very start we did everything we could to contribute to the cause of the Allies."[94] This situation did not change later and the Morgan house played a key role in the financial side of the European reconstruction. The ambivalent attitude of the US government led to the official aloofness despite Hughes' informal interest in the reconstruction effort.[95] The vacuum this situation created was filled by J. P. Morgan & Co. They

88 Hoover, *Memoirs* Vol. 2, 88.
89 FRUS:1925 (Washington, DC: Government Printing Office, 1940), 1:533–35.
90 FRUS: 1928 (Washington, DC: Government Printing Office, 1942), 1:1022–25.
91 FRUS: 1926, 2:40–50.
92 In more detail about Strong and Norman, see Chapter 2.
93 *The New York Times*, September 24, 1923.
94 Edward M. Lamont, *The Ambassador from Wall Street. The Story of Thomas W. Lamont, J. P. Morgan's Chief Executive* (Lanham, Maryland: Madison Books, 1994), 68.
95 Stephen V. O. Clarke, *Central Bank Cooperation: 1934–1931* (New York: Federal Reserve Bank of New York, 1967), 47.

his opening remarks at the Conference he sounded optimistic and claimed, "if we can set these things right at this conference, I feel sure that America will not merely come in, but come in gladly."[167] As he later said to Barthou, "it was essential to get the confidence of the United States of America" in the pending questions, and the participant powers should come to terms favorable by the US government, "America was awaiting the result of this conference to deal with the question of debts, and that their first condition was that peace should be established in Europe. If this conference failed to re-establish European peace, such a project would be hopeless, as America would in that case turn her back on Europe."[168] The conference simply assumed too much politics for the United States. Secretary of State Hughes would have rather seen a meeting of private financial experts to discuss the reparation issue.[169] As he informed the British Ambassador in December 1922, "there was no prospect of a loan of any sort until the reparation question was adjusted."[170] Keynes also thought that only an international loan could alleviate Europe's actual problems. He held the belief that "the burden of finding the immediate resources must inevitably fall in major part upon the United States."[171] At this stage, the United States still insisted on being fully paid by its debtors, which was only imaginable if the European countries came to terms over the reparations. That was unlikely at that time and it affected the whole picture. To the possibility of any loan, reparations were the major impediment, since countries entitled to reparations wanted such claims to form a first charge on liens of any borrowing country. Keynes thought he had the solution in technical points. As he said, the securities of a possible loan "should rank, both for payment of interest and discharge of capital, in front of all Reparation claims, all Inter-Allied Debt, all internal war loans, and all other Government indebtedness of any kind."[172] Unfortunately, the liberal views of Keynes were not shared by the overwhelming majority of the politicians at that moment. It can be safely stated that the timing of both conferences was premature due to the reparation question and it was clear that it was going to be the major hurdle in the future too.

In the end, the Genoa Conference passed a number of resolutions concerning financial, economic, and trade issues, thus creating a basis to further international

167 Minutes of the First Plenary Session of the Genoa Conference, DBFP, First Series, 19:342.

168 Notes of a Meeting between Prime Minister (who was accompanied by Sir Maurice Hankey) and M. Barthou (who was accompanied by M. Camerlynck), at the Hotel Miramare, Genoa, on Saturday, April 29, 1922, DBFP, First Series, vol. XIX, 625–26.

169 Hogan, *Informal Entente*, 44-45.

170 Memorandum by the Secretary of State of an Interview with the British Ambassador (Geddes) December 18, 1922, FRUS:1922, 2:193.

171 Keynes, *The Economic Consequences of the Peace*, 163.

172 Ibid., 165.

cooperation, which work was carried on by the League of Nations.[173] For example, the gold exchange system was such one idea, but most central bankers refused it at the time, except Norman.[174] The nonbinding recommendations also spoke of balanced budgets, currency stabilization, possibly based on a gold standard, central bank cooperation, and one of the resolutions passed said that in order to achieve stability in most of the countries, foreign loans were needed in the near future, especially where taxation could not grow and expenditure had reached the reasonable maximum.[175] In a letter to Hoover during the conference, Strong drew up a six-point plan of stabilization that showed similarity to the resolutions of Genoa.[176]Although it was left to the League to try to carry out the recommendations, it was left most of time in the cold during the conference.

Though economic in its name, the Genoa Conference was clearly political. The opinions of the two American observers were telling. Child characterized the conference with the label "confusion," while Logan left the conference with an even firmer certainty that the US government acted wisely in staying away terming Genoa a "cess-pool of Machiavellian political intrigue and machinations."[177] As the United States government noted, the conference attempted to lessen antagonism between nations and to create a lasting peace, but partly it contributed to sharpening differences as well.[178] The Americans were not the only one being skeptical about the event. Arthur Salter, the principal man of the League's financial and economic section, looking back on the conference gave it low grades. As he formulated his assessment, he opined that the conference "failed completely [... because] each official was the prisoner of his own national

173 As a sign, however, how enormous a task the different sections faced, it is enough to quote Maurice Colrat, president of the Economic Commission: "The economic problems of the present day are of so wide and complicated a nature that the commission of which I had the honour to be president might well have found in its title an excuse for ambitious resolutions. [The people composing it] have not judged it necessary, or even useful, to offer to a still-bruised and suffering Europe the cold comfort of those high-flown resolutions which fall from the lips of theorists with an air of oracular solemnity." Minutes of the Third Plenary Session of the Genoa Conference, held at the Palazzo San Giorgio, May 19, 1922, at 9 a. m., DBFP, First Series, 19:1004.

174 Meyer, *Bankers' Diplomacy*, 6.

175 Second Plenary Session of the Genoa Conference, held at the Palazzo San Giorgio, May 3, 1922, at 10 a. m., DBFP, 19:705–10; Tamás Bácskai ed., *A Magyar Nemzeti Bank története* [The History of the National Bank of Hungary]., Vol. 1, 501. n. 2; Péteri, *Global Monetary Regime*, 10.

176 Strong to Hoover, April 22, 1922, quoted in Chandler, *Benjamin Strong*, 278.

177 Quoted in Fink, *The Genoa Conference*, 207. As a sign of British antagonism toward the United States, and perhaps what was seen as its amateurism, Curzon often times made the pun during the conference that Child came up with "childish" notions. Nicolson, *Curzon*, 320.

178 Ibid., 303.

system."[179] He added the result was "rather to endorse and consolidate a system of trade barriers [...] and those passages in them which recommended reductions remained as merely pious hopes without practical effect."[180] Its dubious outcome notwithstanding, the Genoa Conference was another step in the right direction, especially in the financial field. Basically, the cooperation urged by financial and economic experts in Brussels was elevated onto the political level in Genoa. Now there was a blueprint how to achieve a more stable financial condition, which was a clear prerequisite of a more vigorous European economic life.

Despite the lack of official American recognition and endorsement of acute European problems, the private sphere kept up its interest. It is well worth looking at how the diplomatic and financial policy of the United States had evolved in connection with the European scene and reconstruction efforts after World War I. Particularly, it is crucial to see what course the United States chose, both on the governmental and the private banking level, in relation to the deep Central European financial reconstruction. In other words, what if any role America had in the Austrian, Hungarian, German, and Polish reconstruction schemes in the 1920s. The Europeans, although would have preferred to see the US government participate, were still satisfied with the amount of attention they received from American financial circles. With the possibility of American capital coming in, the long due work on the continent could commence. Indeed, from 1922 the continent was witness to a chain of reconstructions, as if a row of dominos had been set off. After so much preparatory work, the time had surely come to put all these ideas of financial reconstruction into practice. The first patient was Austria, which had been on the agenda since the spring of 1920.

3.2. The Austrian Reconstruction

It is worth outlining the main features of the Austrian financial reconstruction with a main stress on the commissioner-general. The reason is that Hungary came on the heels of the seemingly successful Austrian model, plus Jeremiah Smith, Jr.'s situation and work can be much better understood if a comparison is provided. Moreover, the two neighboring countries had many similar characteristics, politically and financially alike, and both needed some outside help that the League of Nations provided.

Austria, the remnant of the once powerful Habsburg Empire, found itself under devastating circumstances in the wake of World War I. The territory of the country became a fraction of what it had been and it meant the loss of agricultural

179 Salter, *World Trade and Its Future*, 39.
180 Ibid., 41.

products, raw materials, and finished products. The fact that most of these had been produced in its former provinces, now new and independent states and understandably on unfriendly terms with Austria, further aggravated the situation. The population of approximately 6 million in the country was always in lack of sufficient food supply and, as in such conditions it is inevitable, the social tension within the country was high. Part of it was that after the war great migration started and Vienna became swollen with people from everywhere. In the capital, where lack of food caused starvation, a concentrated population of about two million tried to make ends meet. With a large population but insufficient resources, the once happy capital reflected a gloomy picture. The political landscape was not promising either. On November 12, 1918, a republic was declared and Austria showed political polarization that was to be the norm for the next 15 years. In the country the Christian Democrats enjoyed a majority, whereas in Vienna the Social Democrats ruled. The most crucial question of the day was that of the *Anschluss*[181], which led to further ruptures within the society.

The most defining event for Austria was the peace treaty. The country had to accept the Treaty of Saint-Germain-en-Laye, which was signed on September 10, 1919. As in the case of Germany, the Treaty contained the Covenant of the League of Nations, of which Austria was not yet a member.[182] Article 88 forbade Austria to try to join Germany, without referring to the country by name, thus the *Anschluss* was officially outlawed as a possibility.[183] The territorial changes were almost always negative for Austria and the economic and financial clauses of the Treaty were strict too. They contained the war guilt clause and, as a consequence, Austria was liable to pay reparation for loss and damage done during the war. The amount of the sum to be paid was to be determined by the Reparation Commission.[184] The country also had to accept its new name, Austria, instead of German-Austria, its self-chosen name.

The economic situation was terrible and it led to riots and looting in Vienna in December 1921. The government managed to control the situation but when two weeks later it signed the Lana Treaty, in which the final border between Czechoslovakia and Austria was ratified, its fate was sealed. Although there was simply no other choice but to sign it, and in return a Czechoslovak loan was promised, the fact that many compatriots officially

181 Political or economic union, typically used for the union of Germany and Austria in the twentieth century.

182 This clause was the reason why the United States did not ratify the Treaty, just like in the case of Germany, and a separate peace treaty was signed between the two countries on August 24, 1921.

183 The text can be found in H. W. V. Temperley, ed. *A History of the Peace Conference of Paris*, Vol. 5 (London: Henry Frowde and Hodder & Stoughton, 1921), 201.

184 For the text of the relevant clauses, see, Temperley, *Peace Conference*, 219–20.

became foreigners was too much for a lot of Austrians.[185] The government proved far too unpopular. Obviously, such open-ended questions of social identity, political turmoil, and economic ruins made the first years of the new republic painful at best.

The first three years after the armistice were characterized by international charity in the form of food and public loans, the bulk of which was provided by Great Britain and the United States.[186] These measures, however, proved inadequate to alleviate the mounting troubles. The economy came to a virtual standstill and there was rampant inflation. But Austria, in the middle of Europe, could not have been left to pass into social upheaval. Fears were especially high in the wake of the Hungarian Bolshevik coup in 1919, which amply proved that unstable political setting would create stumbling blocks in the path of achieving lasting peace. Economic instability, with a worthless currency,[187] it was feared, would lead to revolution, a concept the Austrians tried to emphasize.[188] On the other hand, there was a theoretical possibility that social and economic dissatisfaction might lead to the *Anschluss* with Germany. With such apprehensions in mind, the British leadership set into motion to solve the Austrian problem through the League of Nations.

The British already in 1919 came at the conclusion that Austria was "economically and financially bankrupt unless assisted from without," and "unable to stand alone."[189] The British were also the most popular foreign power in Austria and Austrians, in general, hoped that help would come from there.[190] Moreover, the British saw in Austria the key to the South-Eastern European trade with all its possible profits. The British initiative was also more significant because the United States did not want to take any responsibility for the region. Although the American Administration was aware of the "hopeless" situation in

185 Erich Zöllner, *Ausztria története* [The History of Austria] (Budapest: Osiris Kiadó, 1998), 379.

186 League of Nations, *The Financial Reconstruction of Austria. General Survey and Principal Documents.* (Geneva, 1926,) 11; The Austrian Chargé (Prochnik) to Hughes, February 23, 1922, FRUS:1922, 1:615–16; Ránki, *Gazdaság és külpolitika,* 40. Berger gives somewhat different numbers and claims the American part to have been $44 million. Peter Berger, "Rebuilding Economies after External Shocks," *Development and Finance* 1 (2003): 66.

187 Clerks in Vienna tended to use the back of crown notes as scribbling paper, simply because it was the cheapest paper available. Sir Arthur Salter, *Memoirs of a Public Servant* (London: Faber and Faber, 1961), 175.

188 See, for example, the first Austrian Counter Reply to the Treaty in Box 6, Folder 2, Austria, 1918-1951, Series 1, Correspondence, Allen W. Dulles Papers, Princeton University Library, Princeton, New Jersey.

189 Sir Francis Oppenheimer's memorandums, June 3 and June 20, 1919, DBFP, Series I, 6:40, 48–49.

190 Curzon to Balfour, July 9, 1919, DBFP, Series I, 6:50. See also, FO Memo by C. Howard Smith, August 15, 1919, Ibid., 153–56.

the Austrian capital, that the country was on "the verge of a reign of anarchy," and "rumors of bolshevist plots [we]re rife," it still believed the problem should be solved by the Europeans.[191] The lack of willingness from the United States persuaded the British that the only possibility was the League of Nations. This was no easy task either, since the undertaking was a first of such a character, and without clear precedents, the outcome was dubious at best.

The Financial Committee of the League of Nations met on April 4, 1921, and defined the principal conditions concerning Austrian reconstruction in the spring of 1921, and in the fall of the same year the League Assembly drew up a draft agreement based on the ter Meulen plan.[192] For more than a year, however, no progress was made, because the question of reparations proved to be a huge stumbling block.

Without any chance of official cooperation, it was left to private enterprise between Great Britain and the United States to form some collaboration nonetheless. Already in 1921, Norman had already approached Strong with the Austrian case. He understood that without American help the weak economic and volatile political situation could not be helped. If the United States stayed away, any scheme would be more political in character than economic. Things had not proved much since the armistice, especially in Central and Eastern Europe, and Norman feared "the whole position in those parts must go from bad to worse."[193] Strong, sympathetic to Norman's cause, asked for Herbert Hoover's help and even met with Hughes in order to gain State Department backing, but achieved little positive result.[194] This American rebuff made the Bank of England Governor leave the case alone for some time, because he believed that without American participation no concerted European effort was possible. When Norman broached the issue again to Strong three months later, the latter was not able to express any optimism, partly because US domestic politics.[195] Nonetheless, the US Congress in the early spring of 1922 passed legislation authorizing the release of assets pledged to America, and President Harding

---

191 Lansing to Crane, January 23, 1920, FRUS:1920, 1:248–49. Also see, Franz Adlgasser, "The Roots of Communist Containment: American Food Aid in Austria and Hungary after World War I," in *Austria in the Nineteen Fifties, Contemporary Austrian Studies* 3 (1995): 171–88.

192 League of Nations, *The Financial Reconstruction of Austria*, 12; League of Nations. *Reconstruction Schemes*, 9.

193 Quoted in Clay, *Lord Norman*, 183.

194 Wueschner, *Charting Twentieth-Century Monetary Policy*, 31. This action is also interesting in light of Strong's emotional claim: "Politics is no part of our business!" It seems that both Strong and Norman did make politics a part of their business if their interests needed such a course. Strong to Norman, March 4, 1922, G35/3, BoE.

195 Norman to Strong, February 6 and 20, 1922, and Strong to Norman, March 4, 1922, G35/3, BoE. It must be noted that this was the time when the State Department note about loan control came out.

approved and signed it, thus removing one of the big stumbling blocks from the way.[196] This way the Austrians could exercise their right to secure some loan on the international money market. But all this was in vain unless someone was willing to provide money.

Contrary to hopes, J. P. Morgan & Co., the primary creditors, be it governmental or private loan, found itself first unable to issue an Austrian loan. Most probably to Strong's persuasion, however, Morgan changed his mind in a few weeks, and in late June Strong happily informed Norman that the American banking house after all would be interested in handling an Austrian loan in New York.[197] Only a few days after the good news from J. P. Morgan & Co., however, the bankers in Britain and the United States once again found that Austria was not a good investment. Morgan, Grenfell & Co., the British affiliate of J. P. Morgan & Co., also informed the Austrian government that at present they could not issue a loan to Austria.[198] As Norman informed Strong, the British government had simply had enough of financing Austria and decided that "no more good money is going to be thrown after the bad which has already been doled out."[199] A few days later, he told Strong again that conditions kept deteriorating in Austria.[200] The dictator of Threadneedle Street expected the Austrians to appeal to the Allied Powers, which soon took place.

The relative stability on the Austrian domestic scene came with Ignaz Seipel's chancellery from May 1922. Originally a Roman Catholic priest, Seipel was the most gifted politician of the right in Austria, and he was the most defining Austrian person in the decade. The British chargé d'affaires in Vienna characterized Seipel as "a man of intelligence, tact and moderation [...] confident and determined [...] not sit[ting] with crossed hands waiting for something to happen."[201] Otto Niemeyer found him "the only force in the country."[202] His dynamic leadership received a big boost when the Reparations Commission made the decision on July 31, 1922, that certain revenues should be released for 20 years, so that they might serve as security for the National Bank and the proposed loan.

---

196 Congressional Record, 67th Congress, 2nd Session, 3997, March 16, 1922, and 5095, April 6, 1922. The text was as follows: "the extension for a period of not to exceed 25 years of the time for the payment of the principal and interest of the debt incurred by Austria for the purchase of wheat from the United States Grain Corporation, and for other purposes." Ibid.

197 Clay, *Lord Norman*, 183.

198 Morgan, Grenfell & Co. to Franckenstein, July 8, 1922, F. 2073/020/1. Austria, T160/64, TNA.

199 Norman to Strong, July 6, 1922, G35/3, BoE.

200 Norman to Strong, July 15, 1922, G35/3, BoE.

201 Akers-Douglas to Curzon, June 1, 1922, C8134/396/3, 7349, FO371, TNA.

202 Memorandum by Niemeyer respecting the results of his visit to Vienna, November 10, 1922, DBFP, First Series, 24:400.

The new Chancellor had no other choice and, just as Norman had predicted, appealed in the name of the Austrian government to the Allied Powers in August, 1922, asking for political guarantee for a loan of £15 million ($69 million), since international bankers would not otherwise raise it.[203] The Supreme Council made the decision to refer the Austrian case to the League of Nations. Norman interpreted this decision that the Allies would not do anything more for Austria.[204] This might not have been so bad news to him after all. Earlier he had written to Strong that he had apprehensions about the League scheme. He was of the opinion that "if financed and controlled by the Entente [it] would inevitably be more political in the long run than economic."[205] His apolitical views and the indirect power he held gave him a useful leverage to achieve that the first reconstruction scheme in Europe would not be victim to immoral politics.

The Austrian government officially pleaded to the League for help on August 23, 1922.[206] The powers showed lukewarm interest and it was only due to a British request that the Austrian question was put on the agenda at the next session of the Council.[207] On September 6, Seipel appealed to the League Council, and officially declared Austria would accept control, but at the same time the Chancellor also used the ongoing political and economic situation in his country as blackmail.[208] The Austrian situation was in fact so infused with the possibility of social disturbance that now Europe as a whole started to consider it to be of vital importance that a solution be reached. Furthermore, the prestige of the League was on the line: if they failed in their very first undertaking, what would the future hold?

In the meantime, Czechoslovakia had wanted to raise a loan for some time, and the first part of it was issued in London, Amsterdam, and New York in early 1922. As an extra guarantee, the creditors wanted some kind of control over the Czechs. First the principal successor state did not want to hear about it, but finally it accepted the League of Nations as an arbiter if any problem arose in the future. This deal was very significant from the point of view of the Austrian and Hungarian reconstructions, where this method was further developed into full-fledged League of Nations control. This was the control to which Austria finally was willing to submit itself. It must be seen that after having failed to raise

---

203 League of Nations, *The Financial Reconstruction of Austria*, 14–5; Lajos Kerekes, *Ausztria története, 1918–1955* [The History of Austria, 1918–1955] (Budapest: Akadémiai Kiadó, 1966), 41.

204 Norman to Strong, August 17, 1922, G35/3, BoE.

205 R. S. Sayers, *The Bank of England, 1891-1944*, vol. 1 (Cambridge: Cambridge University Press, 1976), 165.

206 Seipel to the League Council, August 23, 1922, C12652/74/3, 7340, FO371, TNA.

207 British Cabinet to the Secretary-General, August 25, 1922, C12838/74/3, 7340, FO371, TNA.

208 League of Nations, *Reconstruction Schemes*, 29.

money through the private sphere, Austria clearly had no other choice than to accept both political obligations and outside financial control. The first meant the disavowal of the *Anschluss*, the latter the acceptance of the League of Nations' Commissioner-General as the controller of the Austrian financial matters.

Upon the recommendations of the Financial Committee, three Protocols were signed by Great Britain, France, Italy, Czechoslovakia, and Austria on October 4, 1922. In the first mutual assurance of political independence and territorial integrity was given to and by Austria; the second stated the conditions of the guarantee of the loan not exceeding 650 million gold crowns ($125 million); the third was about Austria's obligation and the functions of the Commissioner-General, a person working in Vienna as an agent of the League and controlling the loan proceeds and the reconstruction.[209] A Bank of Issue was also to be set up that was to be independent of the government with the sole authority to issue any money. These steps were to insure the arrest of the fall of the crown and stop the inflation. Although Norman first thought the League of Nations plan and the Protocols the guarantor countries signed together with Austria were "practically unworkable," when most of his wishes had been included, he agreed to take on the case.

Protocol No. III drew up the Commissioner-General's rights and authority. It stated that it was his duty to make sure the reform programs were carried out. He had to supervise the whole scheme and any funds or proceeds derived from the loan were only available by his authorization. He had sole control over a special account to which the yield of the gross revenues had to be paid.[210] His unique position was the sieve through which the League and Austria were able to communicate with each other. With such a wide range of powers, it was understandably of great importance who would fill such a position. Right after the signing of the Protocols, the search for the would-be Commissioner-General started in earnest. Time was a crucial factor. A League delegation was to visit Vienna in the first days of November, and the League wanted by then to find a suitable person for the position.

As a starting point, he was not to represent any of the guaranteeing powers. Nor was he to come from any neighboring countries. These were sound political considerations, since such a case would have compromised the possible execution of the reconstruction scheme. Therefore, a person was needed with impeccable credentials, who represented a country economically, historically, and politically as detached as was possible. Austrians then would not feel sheer domination; it was enough to put their country under League control. Anyone filling the post also needed to be able to work with the political tension prevailing in Austria between the two main parties.

209 League of Nations, *The Financial Reconstruction of Austria*, 137–50.
210 Ibid., 147-48.

Soon it was clear that the person was to be either an American or a Dutchman, both belonging to the neutral zone, but, even more importantly, also to the circle of agreement of Norman.[211] The Governor of the Bank of England, sensing the difficulties of securing an American, pushed slightly for the Dutch Alfred Zimmerman. In addition to a few prominent League officials, Norman also tried to influence the Foreign Office, which is a further proof that his apolitical views notwithstanding, when it came to raw interests, Norman was not shy to use his heavyweight status. He wrote Arthur Balfour that "Mr. Zimmerman is a first-class man in every respect and especially fitted for the post."[212] This Dutch lobby became so strong that there was a scheme that another Dutch person could fill the position of the adviser to the National Bank of Austria. The French, however, were much against such a possible Dutch hegemony. Obviously, the reason was political, since the excellent British-Dutch relation did not facilitate French hegemonic schemes in Central Europe.

As a consequence, the search quickly settled on an American, Roland William Boyden, who quickly became a very serious candidate. He had been an unofficial delegate on the Reparation Committee since 1920, he had also represented his country unofficially at the Brussels conference, and his name was well known and liked all over the continent. For instance, when Eric Drummond, Secretary-General of the League, broached the idea of securing Boyden as Commissioner-General to Lord Balfour, "the idea of appointing an American, intimately acquainted with the problems at issue, greatly appealed" to the latter.[213] Roland Boyden seemed to hold the qualities needed from the political point of view as well, and the League wanted the American. Boyden was willing to accept the job and wrote the State Department and asked whether they had any objection to his holding such a position. A quick and short answer came giving the State Department's consent, but Boyden was slow in notifying the League, which caused significant problems for the organization. The young world organization rightfully thought that its prestige was at stake. With every single day, not only was the situation of Austria deteriorating, but also the international status of the League was weakening. If it was impotent to launch a reconstruction scheme in a tiny Central European state, how would it be able to cope with much more ambitious plans? Also, the securing of an American for the job would have meant some kind of cooperation between the League and the United States, even if it was to be of the most informal character. The State Department, however, did not

211 Wallenberg to Monnet, October 14, 1922, No. 6. Austria. 2/4/1. Appointment of Commissioner General, S. 109. Salter Papers. LNA; Norman to Vissering, October 14, 1922, OV28/53, BoE.

212 Norman to Balfour, October 21, 1922, OV28/53, BoE.

213 Monnet to Hankey, November 2, 1922, Financial Reconstruction of Austria. Appointment of a Commissioner General for Austria, Doc. No. 24510, Registry Files, R. 519, LNA.

come to the rescue. It seemed to have misunderstood the message of Boyden concerning the Austrian position, and in a later telegram asked him not to accept it.[214] Afterwards, League officials had no other choice but to move forward with Zimmerman and started serious negotiations with him.

Alfred Zimmerman, Burgomaster of Dordrecht from 1899, then of Rotterdam since 1906, was characterized as a high-quality administrator with good organizing ability. He took part in the Brussels Conference in 1920 as a member of the Dutch delegation. He had a considerable knowledge of Central Europe and in particular Austria, since he had been President of the Austro-Hungarian Arbitration Tribunal, which tried to find a solution for part of the Burgenland Frontier Problem. He also spoke German, a feature that was to be crucial in his daily work. Perhaps most importantly, he had had to face Socialist opposition in Rotterdam after the war, which he handled well—a good sign as far as the political situation in Austria was concerned.[215] All the members of the Austrian sub-committee accepted Zimmerman and an official invitation was sent out duly to which Zimmerman was supposed to reply as soon as possible.[216] Now it was all depending on the Burgomaster to help the League.

Zimmerman gave up his home position with regrets and was somewhat reluctant to fill the offered position. Maybe this was the reason why he proved not an easy one to deal with. He was simply not enthusiastic about the job and always came up with certain requirements to create easier circumstances for himself once in Vienna. For example, he was not willing to go to Geneva to discuss details of his position on account of his daughter's wedding and rather expected League officials to travel to the Netherlands.[217] He also made a demand of six months preliminary appointment with indemnity payable if for any reason

---

214 Boyden to Monnet and Salter, November 8, 1922, No. 3. Austria. Correspondence concerning appointment of Commissioner General. Telegrams despatched and received, S. 106, Salter Papers, LNA. What really happened was a fatal twist of history. Someone in the State Department saw the first, consenting message and found it too curt in light of the service Boyden had given his country. So, in another telegram, they expressed their reluctance at losing Boyden to another post. It was not meant to prevent him from taking the new post, but he interpreted it that way. Salter, *Personality*, 167; *In Memory of Roland William Boyden*, 14.

215 All this bibliographical information is in "Note as to Zimmerman," October 31, 1922, No. 6. Austria. 2/4/1, S. 109, Salter Papers, LNA, and Pelt to Nixon, February 18, 1922, C2708/74/3, 7336, FO371, TNA.

216 Drummond to Tufton, November 20, 1922, C15903/74/3, 7343, FO371, TNA; Drummond to Zimmerman, November 20, 1922, Doc. No. 24510, Registry Files, R. 519. LNA.

217 Zimmerman to Drummond, November 26, 1922, No. 6. Austria. 2/4/1, S. 109, Salter Papers, LNA.

he lost the job, a situation not comforting to the League.[218] Moreover, he was not keen to take part in a venture that might fail. He was not satisfied with £6,000 ($28,0000) a month for expenses either and wanted some increase, next to the £1,000 ($4,600) indemnity in case his duties would be terminated.[219] While he was granted £6,500 ($30,000) finally, it is interesting to note that Boyden would have been satisfied with £2,000 ($9,230) a month.[220] Zimmerman had some leverage over the League of Nations, however. In February 1922, the Austrian government was looking for a new financial adviser and Zimmerman's name was mentioned as a possibility. Nothing came of it, but Zimmerman might have borne some grudge and decided to make life a little bit difficult for the League of Nations. The other factor was time. The League simply could not delay the issue; they needed a man for the post, whatever the demands. Zimmerman's overall good qualifications for the post and the decreasing time available worked in his favor: the League accepted Zimmerman's conditions, as they ultimately caused no significant changes to the overall scheme.[221] Even with his demands met, Zimmerman accepted the post only provisionally until April 1, 1923.[222] As the preceding paragraphs show, it was a long and arduous process to find the right and available man, hence the time difference between signing the protocols and the announcement of the Commissioner-General on December 12, 1922. Alfred Zimmerman finally took up his duties in Vienna on December 15. His deputy was also a Dutch man, Rost van Tonningent.

Therefore, in the first League-sponsored reconstruction effort, one of the most important goals, that is, to secure an American in an official post, was not successful. Although a major underpinning of the scheme was to make sure that there was some connection between European reconstruction and the United States, the work had not been in vain. First of all, as it turned out, the US government would not have been against Boyden taking up the post in Austria. Second, even if the first attempt was not all that triumphant, the reconstruction plan was launched and that in itself accounted for measured success. Plus, there was the floatation of the Austrian loan ahead in which American private participation was counted on.

218 Drummond to Niemeyer, November 30, 1922, and Drummond and Monnet to Salter, December 8, 1922, Ibid. This must have been in connection to the fact that the Dutch government gave him leave of absence till April 1, 1923. Zimmerman to Drummond, December 6, 1922, Ibid.

219 Drummond to Tufton, November 17, 1922, F. 2073/021/3, Austrian Reconstruction, T160/584, TNA; Doc. No. 24510, Registry Files, R. 519. LNA.

220 Commissioner-General: Note as to Action, No. 6. Austria. 2/4/1, S. 109, Salter Papers, LNA.

221 Drummond to Zimmerman, December 10, 1922, No. 3. Austria, S. 106, Salter Papers, LNA.

222 Drummond to Balfour, December 11, 1922, C17107/74/3, 7344, FO371, TNA.

Despite the fact that at last the League of Nations secured a Commissioner-General, the problems of the Austrian reconstruction scheme were far from over. Although in November inflation was stopped and in the first days of December both the Reconstruction Law and the Geneva Protocols were ratified by a majority vote in the Austrian Parliament, during November and December unemployment doubled from 58,000 to 117,000.[223] Although the person of control was chosen, the soon-to-open National Bank had no president, and the loan itself was a remote fact. The newly established National Bank was to open in January 1923, so an anxious search began for a suitable bank president. After much acrimonious wrangling, in the end, former Austrian Minister of Finance Richard Reisch was nominated to the post with the condition that a foreign adviser would be attached as well with large powers.[224] This compromise was acceptable for everyone, especially because Reisch was well known both in London and Paris. The British then blackmailed the Austrians that there might not be further loans if the Austrians were stubborn in the question of the bank adviser.[225] The Adviser finally was nominated by the Commissioner-General and was appointed by the Chancellor. Zimmerman nominated the Swiss Charles Schnyder de Wartensee, who was accepted by the League and duly appointed by the Chancellor; he arrived in Vienna on June 5.[226] This train of events coincided with the actual raising of the loan. After securing a short-term loan of the amount of £3,500,000 ($16,100,000) in February 1923, the focus shifted to the more monumental task of securing a long-term loan.[227]

It was important from the political point of view that private American capital be involved. The League saw in American participation a possible "precedent involving far-reaching consequences," even if the money raised in the United States was a small one.[228] Norman was asked to try to lay the groundwork in America for the Austrian loan, but J. P. Morgan & Co. signaled that at present

223 League of Nations, *The Financial Reconstruction of Austria*, 36.
224 Keeling to Curzon, December 8, 1922, DBFP, First Series, 24:436–37; Keeling to Curzon, December 21, 1922, TNA, FO371/7344 C17515/74/3; Keeling to Curzon, December 21, 1922, C17603/74/3, 7344, FO371, TNA; Foreign Office to Keeling, December 22, 1922, C17537/74/3, 7344, FO371, TNA. This contention over the leadership of the National Bank led to the first major change in the original agreements. Though not provided for in the original Protocols, an amendment was passed by the legislation in April as to send an adviser to the new bank. League of Nations, *The Financial Reconstruction of Austria*, 44.
225 FO to Keeling, April 6, 1923, F. 2073/020/2. Austria. Bank of Issue, T160/64, TNA.
226 Zimmerman's 5th and 6th Reports. OV28/64, BoE. In the next few years, there were more advisers, namely Anton van Gijn of the Netherlands (1924–5) and Charles Robert Kay of Great Britain (1926).
227 League of Nations, *The Financial Reconstruction of Austria*, 38–39.
228 De Bordes' memorandum, April 27, 1923, C. 6. 4–8c. Dr. Zimmermann's mission to the U.S.A, Financial Reconstruction of Austria, LNA.

there was no chance of issuing an Austrian loan in the US.[229] This was partly due to the fact that Secretary of State Hughes was not willing to give official endorsement to the loan, although he urged Lamont to float it.[230] This was another typical manifestation of the American decision making circles' wish for politics to be carried out by unofficial agents. The American government, at least on the surface, gave first priority to the British debt settlement. In April Norman got further information from a New York banker that the loan in its present form had not much chance in the United States.[231] In spite of such unfavorable news, Norman now used all his powers to ensure the success of the loan to Austria. He reassured a worrying Zimmerman that despite the great financial and political problems, he was doing everything possible.[232] His efforts might have been too little but help came from J. P. Morgan in the end. Contrary to their earlier views, J. P. Morgan & Co., who now considered the Austrian loan a "public duty," decided to take up the Austrian case, in cooperation with Kuehn, Loeb & Co.[233] This was despite the efforts of the banking house to secure American governmental assistance in the loan.[234] In May, Thomas Lamont, came over to Europe to deal with a tranche to be floated later in New York. The sheer weight of his presence meant that now the scheme had a realistic chance of becoming a reality. Norman did the lion's share of the background work. He had almost daily conversations with Lamont, and Norman himself gave an interview to American reporters, despite the fact that he avoided publicity as much as he could.[235]

The effort paid off and the London issue of the Austrian Loan was made on June 11, and the American tranche was launched on the same day. Only fifteen minutes after opening, the American subscription totaled five times the $25 million the banks were committed to, and Jack Morgan found the "oversubscription almost bewildering."[236] Most of the bankers agreed that the Austrian loan could be regarded as a test case of a possible future German loan. Since Germany was the most important piece in the European puzzle for the United States, it was of immense importance what the outcome of the first League loan would be. Throughout the summer the long-term loan of a net total of 613,000,000 gold

---

229 Strakosch to Norman, December 30, 1922, and J. P. Morgan to Morgan, Grenfell & Co., January 17, 1923, OV28/54, BoE.

230 Costigliola, *Awkward Dominion*, 113.

231 Norman to Bark, April 25, 1923, G3/179, BoE.

232 Norman to Zimmerman, May 16, 1923, G3/179, BoE.

233 Quoted in *U.S. Diplomats in Europe, 1919-1941*, 14.

234 Hogan, *Informal Entente*, 65.

235 Norman's Diary Entries, May 30, June 1, June 4, and June 8, 1923, ADM 34/12, BoE.

236 *The New York Times*, June 12, 1922; Hogan, *Informal Entente*, 66; J. P. Morgan to Morgan, Grenfell & Co., June 11, 1923, OV28/56, BoE.

crowns ($125 million) was floated in several countries. Great Britain stood out with subscribing more than 300,000,000 gold crowns ($58,310,000), while the United States' share was about 123,000,000 gold crowns ($25,000,000). The remainder of the loan was provided by Belgium, France, the Netherlands, Italy, Sweden, Switzerland, Czechoslovakia, Spain, and Austria. The price of issue was typically in the 76-8 % range, while the nominal rate of interest was 6%; in the United States it was 85.625% and 7% respectively.[237] The numbers reflected well that the loan was not judged as a great investment. Moreover, about 20% of the received loan had to be paid to France, Britain, and Czechoslovakia for earlier credits. But what the League of Nations had set out to achieve was completed despite the many obstacles placed in its path. After all, the League made sure that a country in the heart of Europe would be helped collectively. Only a few years after the war, a former enemy country received the help it so badly needed.

The Austria reconstruction scheme got off to a promising start. Revenues kept rising from the second half of 1923, while the budget deficit kept declining and in 1925 there appeared a surplus of 76.45 million crowns ($15.5 millions).[238] It was a clear sign that the introduced reforms did achieve some positive results. The Austrian crown became so stable that it was often referred to as the "Alpine dollar."[239] Obviously, the dry budget figures did not reveal the whole story and while on paper the picture was becoming rosier, there remained many fields in which the reconstruction period was not able to alleviate major problems. The administrative reforms, for example, meant one of the dynamic features of the reconstruction plan. The number of state officials, even too numerous for the former empire, had to be drastically curtailed. The ambitious reforms, however, were lagging and instead of the promised 100,000 only 68,300 officials were dismissed by July 1924.[240] The high unemployment rate led to an almost continuous series of strikes and the government was all along walking a tightrope.

The financial picture was not as smooth either. Already in his first report, Zimmerman warned that despite "a remarkable growth in public confidence" due to the League's presence in Vienna, there was "an increase in speculation on the exchange."[241] After a false boom in the fall, the average index of the stocks fell from 2,167 to 1,774 between March 15 and April 15, 1924, which led to a

237 For the statistical data concerning the Austrian loan see, League of Nations, *The Financial Reconstruction of Austria*, 41–42. The detailed subscriptions by the different countries can be seen in Appendix 1.
238 Zimmerman's 42nd Report, OV28/66, BoE.
239 Kurt Wilhelm Rothschild, *Austria's Economic Development between the Two Wars* (London: Frederick Muller Ltd., 1947), 33. In 1925 a new unit, the schilling was introduced.
240 League of Nations, *The Financial Reconstruction of Austria*, 52.
241 Zimmerman's 1st Report, OV28/64, BoE.

panic.[242] The official bank rate was increased from 9% to 15% and the financial crisis led to the withdrawal of a large amount of foreign credits. All these bad symptoms convinced the Financial Committee that League control in the form of the Commissioner-General should not cease by the end of 1924, which was the original plan, but rather be continued.[243] After a League committee studied the situation in Vienna together with Zimmerman, even the original Protocol was altered on September 16, 1924. It was now the Financial Committee that could recommend the Council to declare that financial stability had been achieved, on condition that budget equilibrium had been sustained, reforms had been carried out, and the economic situation looked promising.[244] The Austrians were very disappointed but understood that they had no other choice but cooperate. Toward the end of the critical year of 1924, things went back to normal in the first months of 1925, foreign capital started to come back, and the bank rate went down again.

By early 1925, the picture was somewhat mixed. On the one hand, there were high unemployment, bankruptcies, and trade balance deficit.[245] On the other hand, throughout the first half of the year, signs of improvement were evident. To see more clearly, in the summer the League asked two prominent economists to carry out an investigation into the economic and financial situation of Austria. The Layton-Rist Report, optimistic in its overall view, said that as soon as the financial criteria were satisfied, economic life might become normal, but a "new commercial policy based on the ideal of economic cooperation" was needed.[246] What the report said was nothing new. It was obvious that without healthy financial frame, no economy can be positively sustainable. Moreover, the Central European region was anything but a friendly economic and trade block. The neighboring countries followed a highly protectionist trade policy and without markets no small country was able to ensure the necessary balance between imports and exports. Still, the report was optimistic and strengthened the belief that the League action was a viable one and would achieve success.

With strict adherence to a sound fiscal policy on the Austrian side and the recommendations from the Financial Committee, the situation became so steady that Zimmerman himself recommended the relaxation of control in August

242 Siegfried Pressburger, *Oesterreichische Notenbank, 1816–1966* [The Austrian Bank of Issue] (Wien: Oesterreichische Nationalbank Hausdruckerei, 1966), 392.

243 League of Nations, *The Financial Reconstruction of Austria*, 213.

244 FO Memorandum on the League of Nations Control, and General Economic Situation in Austria. February 24, 1926, C2375/246/3, 11212, FO371, TNA.

245 League of Nations, *The Financial Reconstruction of Austria*, 64.

246 LNA, Report on the Economic Situation of Austria. C.440(1). M.362(1). 1925. II. W. T. Layton was editor of the London *Economist*, Charles Rist was a French expert of economics.

1925.[247] Effectively from January 1, 1926, control of the budget ceased, but control of the assigned revenues and of the balance of the reconstruction loan remained in Zimmerman's hands, although he was not required to live in Vienna any longer.[248] This came at a price. The Austrian Parliament had to pass a bill that an Adviser to the National Bank would be in Austria for three more years once decontrol was accomplished, and the Council could reestablish control in case the budget equilibrium or the service of the loan was in danger.[249] In light of the increasingly better circumstances, the National Bank rate went down to 7½% in March 1926, and the Financial Committee recommended that the Council declare that "the financial stability of Austria is assured, and to terminate the office of the Commissioner-General as on June 30th, 1926, subject to the re-establishment of his office if it should become necessary under the conditions specified in the resolution of the Council of December 9th, 1925."[250] Zimmerman was congratulated on his "indefatigable efforts" that he "rendered to the League and Austria," but the general Austrian sentiment was sheer antipathy toward the Commissioner-General.[251]

Partly as opposition to the system of control, partly as hostility toward the figure of control, Alfred Zimmerman was a constant target of criticism. He was simply "one of the best hated men in Austria."[252] Austrians used cynicism when they referred to the post of the Dutchman as the "financial dictatorship" of the League of Nations, and their bitter sense of humor led to the "*Wir sind zu Tode saniert*" (we are cured to death) attitude.[253] Feelings were strong especially in Vienna, where Zimmerman resided and where the League control was really manifest. Only a few months after Zimmerman took up the post, the Socialists drew up a resolution that wanted to prevent the League Commissioner from carrying out private negotiations and getting any information from Austrians, by labeling such an act High Treason against the State.[254] The motion died a quick death, but the anti-Zimmerman sentiment remained. The Socialist urged Zimmerman's leave from Austria in the spring of 1924, but Seipel defended him

---

247 LNJ, 6th Year, No. 10, October 1925, 35th Session, 1356.
248 FO Memorandum on the League of Nations Control, and General Economic Situation in Austria. February 24, 1926, C2375/246/3, 11212, FO371, TNA.
249 Ibid.
250 League of Nations, *Reconstruction Schemes*, 35; Work of the Financial Committee during Its twenty-Second Session, June 3-9, 1926, C.359. M.127. 1926. II., LNA. Also in LNJ, 7th Year, No. 7, July 1926, 916.
251 League of Nations, *The Financial Reconstruction of Austria*, 279.
252 *Time*, July 12, 1926.
253 *The New York Times*, June 27, 1926.
254 Keeling to Curzon, March 29, 1923, F. 2073/021/4. Austrian Reconstruction, T160/584, TNA; Kerekes, *Ausztria története*, 46.

in the Parliament.[255] The average opinion was well summed up in the saying that "even the locomotives will whistle cheerfully when they carry Zimmerman back to Holland."[256] This extreme dislike was not confined to the Socialists but was an overall sentiment, largely due to the Austrian opinion about the Dutchman as having too rigid an attitude and manner and being impatient with everybody.[257] Even foreigners sensed that Zimmerman was out of touch with the locals. Hamilton Fish Armstrong of *Foreign Affairs* referred to him as "that severe Dutchman."[258] Zimmerman was resented for his presumptuous lifestyle in Vienna, because he went by car everywhere and lived in a palace.[259] For example, when he published parts of his Nineteenth report without informing the government beforehand, and these parts contained criticism of the government, the Minister for Foreign Affairs described Zimmerman's treatment of the Austrian people "intolerable."[260] The Commissioner-General got his share of antipathy from the government also because he pushed for new taxes when Austrians found the existing taxation too high.[261] *The New York Times* summed up his tenure in Vienna correctly in the following way: "Dr. Zimmerman's three-year regime in Austria was an uninterrupted series of frictions between the League's representative and the Austrian Government."[262] In Zimmerman's defense it must be admitted that he was working under unfavorable circumstances and he was only devoted to the successful conclusion of his task. Still, one wonders how it is possible that his counterpart in Hungary, Jeremiah Smith, Jr. enjoyed immense popularity while carrying out the same job.

When at last decontrol was within sight, the Austrians did not hide their joy. The sheer psychological value of regaining independence was enormous. The Council, on June 9, terminated the office of the Commissioner-General as of June 30, 1926. Alfred Zimmerman was not wholly satisfied with the achieved results and held the feeling that the scheme was not fully accomplished.[263] There was a farewell luncheon before his departure in his honor given by the President of the Confederation, and he got the Grand Cordon of the Decoration of Honor of the Republic for his distinguished services to Austria. The Austrian Assembly praised the Dutchman when his office was terminated: "For the lucky conclusion, in the greatest part, Dr. Zimmerman's and his colleagues' untiring effort is to be

255 *Magyarország*, May 14, 1924. XXXI/91.
256 *The New York Times*, December 10, 1925.
257 Akers-Douglas to MacDonald, June 28, 1924, DBFP, First Series, 26:265.
258 *The New York Times*, April 29, 1925.
259 *The New York Times*, December 10, 1925, and June 27, 1926.
260 Akers-Douglas to MacDonald, August 29, 1924, DBFP, First Series, 26:318.
261 *Az Est*, September 10, 1924. XV/187.
262 *The New York Times*, June 27, 1926.
263 Bark to Norman, May 20, 1926, OV/28/62, BoE.

thanked."[264] On the official level, especially at the happy conclusion of affairs, Alfred Zimmerman was a friend now. As Chancellor Ramek put it, "You came to us as a stranger, now you leave us as a friend, as one of us. Austria will never forget you, our heartiest good wishes accompany you."[265] By all means, this kind of good bye could not wholly hide the general dislike Zimmerman had generated for himself during his stay.

By any analysis at the conclusion of the plan, the financial reconstruction of Austria was a success. In addition to the balancing of the budget and stabilizing the currency, the two most conspicuous accomplishments, the standard of living of the working class became much higher than it had been only a few years earlier, and public health also showed a remarkable improvement. From all angles, the reconstruction period was very advantageous for Austria. It escaped an absolute breakdown. The weak economic and financial situation would have, in all likelihood, driven the country into total social chaos, and such an event might have meant outside interference. Czechoslovakia and Italy in particular were eager to play a dominant role in post-war Austria. Also, a possible *Anschluss* with Germany was not a remote possibility and in Austria many people were for such an outcome. Great Britain and France were determined to make sure that no such course would happen. Great Britain, relying largely on its financial background, its influence in the League of Nations, and its good relations with the United States, wanted an independent and functioning Austria in the heart of Europe, because they saw in it the possibility of achieving the grand vision of turning Central Europe into a more or less working economic block that would provide peace, stability, and an economic outlet for Great Britain and the whole of Europe. However, Austria was only an important start. Soon after that the Austrian reconstruction scheme was set into motion, the attention turned toward the next country, Austria's eastern neighbor, Hungary.

264 Pressburger, *Oesterreichische Notenbank*, 414.
265 Chilston to Chamberlain, July 6, 1926, C7753/246/3, 11213, FO371, TNA.

Chapter 4

Hungary's Appeal to the League of Nations

4.1. The Postwar Situation

Hungary, part of the Austro-Hungarian Monarchy, was naturally fighting alongside the Central Powers and ended the war in defeat. After the conclusion of the war, it found itself among the newly created successor states, Czechoslovakia, Romania, and Yugoslavia, whose main aim was "a common policy against Hungary," which "must be merely part of a broader political conception."[266] To make things worse, on March 21, 1919, a bolshevist coup led by Béla Kun established communist rule in Hungary, which, from a political point of view, was a disaster for the country. The surrealistic aims of the bolshevist regime, spurred by the successful communist takeover in Russia in 1917, were never in accord with the domestic or international possibilities.

The Western powers obviously saw a grave danger in the new regime, the United States being no exception. Nicholas Roosevelt right after the communist takeover reported that the new situation represented the risk of spreading, first and foremost to Germany, the most important country in Europe for the United States:

> The great significance of this revolution is that [...] the precedent set by this action will offer an encouragement to the Germans which may be disastrous. [...] The conclusion of the matter is that unless immediate and vigorous action is taken the Allies will be met with a disastrous state of affairs in Central Europe which it may take years to straighten out. Hungary has defied the Peace Conference and allied herself with the Bolsheviki. It is Germany's turn next.[267]

266 Eduard Beneš, "The Little Entente," *Foreign Affairs* 1, no. 1 (September 1922): 69. Later on, these three countries formed the Alliance called Little Entente. The treaties, in chronological order, were the following: convention between Czechoslovakia and the Kingdom of Serbs, Croats and Slovenes, signed on August 14, 1920, fully blown into a treaty two years later; treaty between Czechoslovakia and Romania signed on April 23, 1921; and treaty between Kingdom of Serbs, Croats and Slovenes and Romania signed on June 7, 1921.Beneš called the first of these treaties a "'*defensive convention*' against the Hungarian menace." Ibid., 68. Emphasis in the original text. See also, Thomas Garrigue Masaryk, *The Making of a State. Memories and Observations, 1914–1918* (New York: Frederick A. Stokes Co., 1927).

267 Captain Nicholas Roosevelt to the Commission to Negotiate Peace, March 26, 1919, FRUS:1919, PPC (Washington, DC: Government Printing Office, 1947), 12:,418–419. Substance of this report was transmitted to President Wilson by Secretary Lansing the next day.

Herbert Hoover recalled later that the United States could not "even remotely recognize this murderous tyranny," for the danger it would represent for the whole of Europe.[268] The American minister in Prague was of the opinion "that the Bolshevist revolution in Budapest in the interest of any stability in this country must be suppressed and suppressed soon."[269] The general sentiment in the West that the regime should be met by force was finally refused by Wilson and instead a blockade was established. While the principal powers hesitated in Paris, Romania attacked Hungary on the basis that Hungary had a larger army than the 35,000 stipulated in the armistice. This led to the collapse and defeat of the Bolshevist regime and Romanian occupation of half of the country.[270] The threat of communism played against Hungary to a large degree in the international landscape and this sentiment was manifest at the wording of the peace treaty.

The Treaty of Trianon, signed on June 4, 1920, was a fatal blow to Hungary and sealed its fate for a long time to come.[271] Although the country expected harsh terms and more or less accepted the new realities of Central Europe, Hungarians all the way through had hoped and believed that Wilsonian principles would prevail and territories with Hungarian majorities would not be lost. To the shock of the whole nation, the treaty detached huge Hungarian ethnic blocs, which was due to nothing else but serving the wishes of the neighboring Slavic countries. Both the territory and population of Hungary was reduced to one third of its prewar size, and 3,000,000 ethnically pure Hungarian remained in the Successor States. Such losses had further consequences. Hungary was much weakened from an economic point of view having lost most of its raw

---

268 Quoted in Costigliola, *Awkward Dominion*, 51.

269 King to Allen Dulles, March 28, 1919, Series 1, Correspondence, Box 15, Folder 14, Czechoslovakia, 1919-1955, Allen W. Dulles Papers.

270 About the Romanian occupation and life during that period in general, see, Harry Hill Bandholtz, *An Undiplomatic Diary* (Safety Harbor, FL: Simon Publications, 2000).

271 About the Treaty of Trianon, see, for example, H. W. V. Temperley, ed. *A History of the Peace Conference of Paris*, vol. 5. (London: Henry Frowde and Hodder & Stoughton, 1921); Sándor Taraszovics, "American Peace Preparations during World War I and the Shaping of the New Hungary." In Ignác Romsics, ed. *20th Century Hungary and the Great Powers* (Boulder, Colorado: Social Science Monographs, Atlantic Research and Publications Inc., 1994), 73-97; Deák, Francis. *Hungary at the Paris Peace Conference. The Diplomatic History of the Treaty of Trianon* (New York: Columbia University Press, 1942). The literature of the Peace Treaties is abundant and seemingly never ending. The two latest works of value are Margaret MacMillan, *Peacemakers: The Paris Peace Conference of 1919 and Its Attempt to End War* (New York: Random House, 2002) and, from Hungarian perspectives, Bryan Cartledge, *Mihály Károlyi & István Bethlen: Hungary* (London: Haus Publishing Ltd., 2009).

material and industry.[272] The devastated circumstances were furthered by the flood of refugees of Hungarians from the territory of old Hungary. Until the end of 1920 about 350,000-400,000 of them arrived, and this large extra population meant an enormous extra burden to the state. Moreover, based upon the German peace treaty, Hungary was guilty for the war and it was expected that financial obligations would also burden the country. The text declared that Hungary would have to pay reparations for a period of thirty years starting from May 1, 1921, although the sum of it was not specified.[273] By the Financial Agreement of March 11, 1920, the Reparations Commission was to fix the amount of the reparation debt of Hungary. Article 180 declared that "the first charge upon all the assets and revenues of Hungary shall be the cost of reparation."[274] This in practice rendered any chance of borrowing money from abroad impossible and was a major source of runaway inflation in the coming years. The Hungarian Assembly reluctantly ratified the Treaty on November 13, 1920, but the wording expressed the whole nation's sentiment: "it considers the peace document as being based on false data, unjust and contrary to the interests of humanity [...] the National Assembly assents to its ratification solely because of [...] irresistible pressure."[275] In fact, the next two decades of Hungarian foreign policy was riveted around the question of revision of the Trianon Treaty. For the next eighteen years, all flags were flown at half-mast.[276]

When the Romanian occupation in the wake of the Kun regime came to an end, Admiral Miklós Horthy entered the capital and the National Assembly elected him overwhelmingly to be Regent on March 1, 1920, a position in which he remained until 1944. Judgment on Horthy was mixed. Harry Hill Bandholtz, the American member of the Inter-Allied Military Mission to Hungary, for example, characterized him as "a fine-appearing, intelligent-looking officer," believed he

272 See, for example, Joseph Rothschild, *East Central Europe between the Two World Wars* (Seattle: University of Washington Press, 1974), 156, 167; C. A. McCartney, *Hungary and Her Successors. The Treaty of Trianon and Its Consequences, 1919–1937* (London: Oxford University Press, 1937), 463; Derek H. Aldcroft, *From Versailles to Wall Street, 1919–1929* (London: Allen Lane, Penguin Books Ltd., 1977), 28; Kaser, M. C. and Radice, E. A., eds. *The Economic History of Eastern Europe, 1919-1975*. vol. 1. (Oxford: Clarendon Press, 1985), 227. The American delegation at Paris tried to achieve some more favorable settlement for Hungary, but in the end, on almost all points the final decisions were against Hungary. As an interesting document concerning the territorial question of Hungary and its neighbors, see, Memorandum by Archibald Coolidge: The New Frontiers in Former Austria-Hungary. Without date (but probably toward the end of 1919), Box 15, Folder 14, Czechoslovakia, 1919-1955, Series 1, Correspondence, Allen W. Dulles Papers (MC#019).

273 Temperley, *Peace Conference*, 219.

274 Ibid., 235.

275 Deák, *Hungary at the Paris Peace Conference*, 337. The Treaty came into force on July 26, 1921.

276 Nicholas Horthy, *Memoirs* (Safety Harbor, FL: Simon Publications, 2000), 136.

was "sincere in his desire and intention to do everything for the best," and he had "great confidence in his ability and good sense."[277] Ulysses Grant-Smith, who was appointed Commissioner to Hungary on December 4, 1919, and who often met with Horthy, liked him as a person, but was very disappointed and critical about Horthy's responsibility on account of the ruling "White terror," and thought that Horthy was lacking certain abilities.[278] A few years later, the British Consul General in Budapest described him as follows:

> Admiral Horthy is a man of sterling honesty but of no great cleverness: he has no suppleness of mind, and when he gets hold of an idea, it crystallizes within him into a principle. He has [...] the views of an English country squire or naval officer of the sixties or seventies, and change and innovation are abhorrent to him. [...] I would limit myself to saying that he is incapable of adjusting himself to the new conditions in which the world finds itself today.[279]

With a strong man at the helm, who for some time turned a blind eye to the white terror, Hungary's problems were still grave. Under such circumstances Hungary had to rely on outside charity to a large degree.

Similarly to Austria and other Central and Eastern European countries, Hungary was provided with relief.[280] In all likelihood due to the Bolshevik takeover, however, the country got only a fraction of what other recipient countries were given. Especially Austria was an exception. It received more than ten times more than Hungary between 1919 and 1923, and it was little wonder that children in Austria were, according to an American officer, "conscious of two factors today: 'Food'-'America'."[281] While the whole region received relief to the extent of

277 Bandholtz, *An Undiplomatic Diary*, 172; General Bandholtz to the Commission to Negotiate Peace, November 19, 1919, FRUS: 1919, PPC, 12:724.

278 Zsuzsa L. Nagy, "Amerikai diplomaták Horthy Miklósról, 1920-1944," [American Diplomats on Miklós Horthy] *Történelmi Szemle* 33, nos 3-4, (1990): 175-77. Grant-Smith served in various American legations during his illustrious career. Allen Dulles, who provided Grant-Smith with some facts about Hungary, wrote that "You certainly deserved it and no one is better able to take on the job than you." Dulles to Grant-Smith, December 20, 1919, Box 29, Folder 19, Grant-Smith, U., 1917-1958, Series 1, Correspondence, Allen W. Dulles Papers.

279 Hohler to Curzon, January 3, 1924, DBFP, First Series, 26:9. On Hungarian opinion about Horthy during and after his Regency, see, Ignác Romsics, "Changing Images of Miklós Horthy," *Cultic Revelations:* Studies in Modern Historical Cult Personalities and Phenomena. Ed. By Anssi Halmesvirta. Helsinki: The Finnish Literature Society, 2008), 127-48.

280 In more detail about the ARA's work in Hungary, see Tibor Glant, "Herbert Hoover and Hungary, 1918-1923," *Hungarian Journal of English and American Studies* 8, no. 2 (2002): 95–109. On the general Central and Eastern European relief work, which in the greatest part was provided by American sources, see Hoover, *Memoirs*, vol. 1, 282–430.

281 Ibid., 99–101; "The Roots of Communist Containment," 180.

almost $500 million, the sum given to Hungary was a meager $9.3 million.[282] Not surprisingly, the main share of the relief was financed by the United States. When the issue of repatriation came to the fore, relief was also largely needed. When about 13,000 men were successfully brought back from the Soviet Union, the $1,200,000 needed for the enterprise was also largely provided by American sources.[283] American relief was not restricted to material questions only. In 1922, when the worst was over, the United American Lines Inc. decided to give 1 million crowns (*korona*)[284] to a Hungarian cultural institution.[285] The Hungarian Historical Society was chosen as the beneficiary. With these outside efforts, Hungary slowly climbed back to a healthier status, but it was clear that without political consolidation the country would stand no chance of rehabilitation of any kind.

The real change came with István Bethlen becoming Hungary's new Prime Minister on April 14, 1921.[286] The son of a traditional noble Transylvanian family had been always close to the political events of the country, had studied in the best schools, and was destined to become one day the leading politician in Hungary. His political approach was very practical and realistic. As he put it, "What I say and what I do depend on the requirements of foreign and domestic policy. My policies are shaped by the circumstances."[287] Miklós Horthy, the Regent, found him "a man of outstanding mental power and of fine character."[288] An American diplomat characterized him as "a man of very unusual intellectual ability," besides being "quite forceful and farseeing," while the American minister in Budapest described him as "the real political pivot and barometer of political life."[289] When William Lampson, the head of the Central European Division in the British Foreign Office, visited Budapest in late 1922, he characterized Bethlen as "a serious and sensible statesman, fully conscious of the very difficult tasks," who was "prepared to do his best to pull his country through present times of stress."[290]

---

282 Kaser and Radice, eds. *The Economic History of Eastern Europe*, 387. Glant gives the worth of supplies as $220 million and Hungary's share as 1.3%. He adds that this small amount was still seventy times as much as what Hungary was given in the armistice period. Glant, "Herbert Hoover and Hungary," 99.

283 Grant-Smith to Hughes, December 10, 1921, 864.00/482, Roll 6, M. 708, NARA.

284 *Korona* (crown) was the currency of the new monetary system created in Hungary in March 1920. It was succeed by the *pengő* from January 1, 1927.

285 Doroghi to Bethlen, July 11, 1922, 7/37, K 468, Bethlen Papers, HNA.

286 The latest and best biography on Bethlen is Ignác Romsics, *István Bethlen: A Great Conservative Statesman of Hungary, 1874–1946*, Boulder, Colorado: Social Science Monographs, 1995.

287 Romsics, *István Bethlen*, 156.

288 Horthy, *Memoirs*, 153.

289 Unidentified person to Lansing, November 3, 1920, 864.00/564, Roll 6, M. 708, NARA; Memorandum on Hungary in Brentano to Hughes, October 1, 1922, 864.00/517, Ibid.

290 Quoted in Romsics, *István Bethlen*, 188.

Bethlen already after the war tried to establish good relations with Great Britain, because he saw in that country the possibility of securing a counterweight against the successor countries, but despite the general good impressions he made on foreigners, his move got a "no action" from Foreign Office officers.[291] His main reason for this policy was that he clearly perceived that France was trying to achieve hegemony in the Danubian basin, something that Great Britain would not let become a reality. Although right after the war the British diplomacy did not support him, after his becoming the prime minister of Hungary, the British minister in Budapest sent a report in which he praised Bethlen's program speech for its liberal and realist character and wrote that "every effort should be made to help in the consolidation of the country."[292] Early in his premiership, he sent Count Pál Teleki, former and future Prime Minister and renowned cartographer, to Paris to size up the sentiment toward Hungary. The negative reception met there made Teleki conclude that the French orientation was no alternative and he traveled on to London to seek support.[293] Here he also met with prominent figures and the idea of an Anglo-American loan was born in the City.[294] This kind of attitude was what Hungary counted on. If Great Britain once decided that Hungary should be helped, it practically meant that help was within reach. Therefore, it was no coincidence that Hungary was trying to put emphasis on the Anglo-Saxon orientation. Naturally, Bethlen needed to deal with domestic problems in order to strengthen the sympathy he had earned.

His accession closely followed Charles IV's first failed endeavor to regain the throne of Hungary. A second attempt in October the same year was similarly unsuccessful, because both Horthy and Bethlen opposed such a move.[295] Bethlen tried to calm the international waters with the enactment of the dethronement in November 1921, which officially excluded the possibility of having a Habsburg king in Hungary again. The act made Hungary presentable to the western democracies, a fact that was crucial in achieving the consolidation with their help, but in order to enjoy British backing, Hungary first needed to become a member of the League of Nations. When the League of Nations was born in 1919, quite logically it was the victorious nations, their allies, and some

291 Ibid., 93–94.

292 Quoted in Romsics, *István Bethlen*, 153.

293 In Teleki's words: "The overall picture is unfavorable. No matter ho much we expose ourselves, with French orientation we cannot in a short time achieve that French policy should be openly pro-Hungarian.... We will not get decisive help." See Teleki's report about his Paris trip in Teleki to Bánffy, June 12, 1926, 38/1921–266, K 58, The Cabinet of the Minister, HNA. His report about his stay in London is in Teleki to Bánffy, June 14, 1926, Ibid.

294 Ibid.

295 In more detail about the events and diplomacy of the Karlist coup attempts, in Magda Ádám, *A Kisantant és Európa, 1920–1929* [The Little Entente and Europe 1920–1929] (Budapest: Akadémiai Kiadó, 1989), 39–112, and Horthy, *Memoirs*, 139–52.

neutral countries that became members—the enemy states were not invited to the organization. Shortly after the peace treaties, when the Allies thought that the continent was ensured against a similar conflict like in 1914, the door of the League slowly opened to the defeated countries as well. The order in which these states were admitted reflected how much the principles members, or their involved allies, were satisfied with the attitude of such a country, and whether these states might have meant any political disturbance in the new Europe. According to this opinion, Austria and Bulgaria were admitted to the League already in December 1920. It seemed only a matter of time before both Hungary and Germany could also qualify for membership. When the question of Hungary's possible admittance was on the agenda in the fall session of 1922, the situation was favorable. Out of the three members of the Little Entente, it was Yugoslavia that was the most opposed to the Hungarian membership. But the unofficial leader of the alliance, Eduard Beneš, the Czechoslovakian foreign minister, an influential diplomat in western countries, was against such an idea, because he knew that supposedly Hungary's place was already assured.[296] Beneš must have been informed from British sources that Great Britain wanted to see Hungary in the family of the League of Nations and would have taken issue if due to petty fussing Hungary had remained outside. So, on September 18, 1922, the Assembly voted unanimously to admit Hungary to the League.[297] This was an important step from the point of view of Hungary's political status. With becoming a member of the most important international political body of the day, Hungary stepped out of the political isolation it had been subjected to since the end of the war. This change was the key to significant possibilities: it meant an automatic protection against the Little Entente and Hungary could keep the minority question on the agenda.[298]

Also, with belonging to the League, the door opened for Hungary to have the chance to try to find allies for its plans and causes. First of all, the Hungarian government sought British political backing on the continent. It was well known that within the League of Nations Great Britain and France vied for leadership.

---

296 Árpád Hornyák, *Magyar-jugoszláv diplomáciai kapcsolatok, 1918–1927.* [Hungarian-Yugoslav Diplomatic Relations, 1918–1927] (Újvidék: Forum Könyvkiadó, 2004), 115–16.

297 In more detail about Hungary's entry into the League of Nations, see, Mária Ormos, "Magyarország belépése a Nemzetek Szövetségébe," [Hungary's Entry to the League of Nations] *Századok* 91, no. 1 (1957): 235–49.

298 Hungary brought up already the question of the Hungarian minorities in the successor states during the Genoa Conference. Bethlen sent an urgent plea to the Conference to pass the Hungarian problem onto the League, which, thanks to the opposition of France and the Little Entente, led to no result. Meeting of the First Session of the First (Political) Commission held on April 11, 1922, at 10.30 a. m., DBFP, First Series, 19:360–61; Meeting of the Inviting Powers to the Genoa Conference held on May 10, 1922, at 11 a. m., at the Palazzo Reale, Annex N, Ibid., 836–37.

France was the principal supporter of the Little Entente, so it was also a necessity for Hungary to be on the best possible terms with the French. However, Hungary knew that if there was one country on the continent that could have sway over its antagonistic neighbors even more than France it was Great Britain. On the whole, the British must be said to have had the bigger influence, so it was all natural for Hungary to be attracted to Great Britain. In addition, Britain was of the opinion that it could not allow Hungary to "go under financially."[299] Naturally, Hungary was well aware of the fact that in the changing postwar world the most influential country was outside Europe. Thus it was only logical that Hungary tried to develop a good relationship with the United States.[300]

Since during World War I Hungary and the United States found themselves on the opposite sides of the belligerent camps, it was important to put their relations on a normal footing in the hope of future cooperation. Charity came from the United States and American prestige was high in Hungary. Trade and communication were again authorized between the parties beginning September 2, 1919, and shortly after Ulysses Grant-Smith was appointed to Hungary.[301] He was not accredited as a diplomatic representative since no peace treaty had been concluded between the two countries, but his main task was not altered by this lack of formality as he was to do everything in his power to help a representative government take root in Hungary.[302] This was important for the United States after the bolshevist rule. Since the United State Senate refused to ratify the Paris Peace Treaty, America neither became part of the League of Nations, nor concluded peace treaties with its ex-enemies, that is why it was important to sign a separate peace treaty.[303] As in other cases, the German treaty served as the basis for the other two countries. The United States made clear that it was willing to talk with Hungary concerning peace only if it was based on a similar peace treaty with Germany.[304] The American government basically blackmailed Hungary, coated in nice diplomatic terms, that acceptance of the terms agreed to by Germany was the condition necessary reestablishing diplomatic relations

---

299 Lampson's note on February 22, 1923, C3081/942/21, 8861, FO371, TNA.

300 Both Horthy and Bethlen were Protestant, or rather Calvinist. This fact, at least on the subconscious level, must have helped their case in connection with the United States.

301 Notice Issued by the War Trade Board Section of the Department of State, September 2, 1919, FRUS: 1919 (Washington, DC: Governemnt Printing Office, 1934), 2:410.

302 The Secretary of State to the Commissioner at Vienna (Grant-Smith), December 10, 1919, Ibid., 410–12.

303 The clear signal that the United States treated these countries as one group was evident when it concluded separate peace treaties with these states within a few days: on August 24, 1921, with Germany, on August 25, 1921, with Austria, and on August 29, 1921, with Hungary. The treaties came into force on November 8, November 11, and December 17, 1921, respectively.

304 Hughes to Grant-Smith, July 9, 1921, 711.64119/1, Roll 1, M. 709, NARA.

again.[305] Grant-Smith pointed this out to the Hungarians, but he also alluded to "the advantages which would accrue to Hungary, both of political and economic nature, by their acceptance of the stipulations of the Peace Resolution, and the subsequent negotiation of an agreement with the United States."[306] Hungary had no real choice but to accept the offered treaty without reservations. The Hungarian Parliament passed the resolution on August 12, 1921, while the US Congress ratified the treaty on October 18, 1921, and ratifications were exchanged on December 17, 1921, when the treaty came into force.[307] Finally, diplomatic relations were resumed, and Grant-Smith was replaced by Theodore Brentano in April 1922, who arrived as minister. As for the Hungarian side, Count László Széchenyi presented his credentials in January 1922 and became the first Hungarian Minister to Washington.

It is little wonder that Hungary sought Anglo-Saxon goodwill. Both from political and financial perspectives, the United States and Great Britain were the two countries that Hungary could expect the most help from. Obviously, Hungary needed to find help far from its geographical position, because its neighbors were its enemies, France was their quasi ally, Germany was burdened with its own problems, Soviet Russia was an ideological enemy, and Italy had not yet shown its interest in Central Europe. This meant that only Great Britain and the United States remained; both were far enough away to be friendly and powerful enough to help. And Hungary, despite the political consolidation after regulating its relations with the United States and becoming a full member of the League of Nations, was in need of effective help.

4.2. The Economic Situation and Attempts for a Loan

Hungary could not shake off the depressing conditions it found itself after the war and this long unhealthy financial and economic period started to maim the country more and more, both psychologically and physically. Prices kept rising relentlessly and compared to the prewar years showed scary differences. At the end of 1921, for instance, the price of first class pastry flour cost two hundred times its peacetime price, and similar ratio was true for potatoes and eggs.[308] In October 1922 alone, prices in Budapest increased on an average of 23.8%, while the index number was 328.69 compared to prewar prices.[309] The production of

305 Hughes to Grant-Smith, July 23, and July 28, 1921, 711.64119/1 and /2, Ibid.
306 Grant-Smith to Hughes, August 3, 1921, 711.64119/15, Ibid.
307 Grant-Smith to Hughes, August 12, and December 14, 1921, 711.64119/8 and /36, Ibid.; FRUS: 1921, 2:258–59. The text of the treaty is in FRUS: 1921, 2:255–58.
308 Grant-Smith to Hughes, December 3, 1921, 864.00/472, Roll 6, M. 708, NARA.
309 Kemp to Hughes, December 5, 1922, 864.00/524, Ibid.

almost all of the industries sharply fell back. In the 1922/23 financial year, the production of sugar was 30%, of beer it was 15%, of alcohol it was 40%, and of coal it was 45% compared to ten years earlier.[310] Since agricultural production was down, the volume in foreign trade was negative as well, between 200 and 300 million gold crowns ($40-60 million).[311] The financial leverage of the state was diminishing year by year as well and the budget deficit was substantial.[312] The new American minister to Hungary informed the State Department about the "gloomy" economic situation, the "alarming rate of increase in the cost of living," and the general depression "in the hearts of most people."[313] Under such circumstances it was inevitable that Hungary needed to do something significant to abort the negative projectile it had been following. Although Hungary was in a better condition than Austria, to many it was clear that the remedy should take the form of a foreign loan.[314] As Bethlen put it in a speech in Hungary, "Our financial situation is serious. From our revenues we cannot cover our expenditures. It will be a long time before we achieve this goal with hard work. In this work without foreign help we cannot reach the goal."[315] The Prime Minister knew exactly that the unsettled question of reparations would render such a course almost insurmountable. In fact, he hoped to avoid paying reparations somehow while enjoying a foreign loan.

The first tentative moves had been carried out already. The Hungarians tried to secure a British loan on various occasions, but the question of reparations made it impossible to deal with the issue in detail.[316] Obviously, there was no

---

310 9/VIII/2/Appendix 12, Various Data on the Output of Hungary's Industries, 56, K 275, The Semi-official Papers of Finance Minister Kállay Tibor (hereafter cited as Kállay Papers), 1901-1941, HNA.

311 6/V/7, The Volume of Foreign Trade, and the Industrial and Agricultural Output of Hungary, 1920–1923/1, Ibid.

312 "Annual Report on Hungary" in Balfour to MacDonald, May 23, 1924, C8423/8423/21, 9914, FO371, TNA.

313 "Memorandum on Hungary" in Brentano to Hughes, October 1, 1922, 864.00/517, Roll 6, M. 708, NARA.

314 The first comprehensive work of the surrounding of the loan, albeit with a political angle and chiefly relying on the sources available in Hungary at the time, was György Magos, *Az amerikai imperialisták szerepe a Horthy fasizmus stabilizásában, 1924–1929.* [The Role of the American Imperialists in the Stabilization of the Horthy Fascism, 1924–1929] Budapest: Akadémiai Kaidó, 1952. A decade later a somewhat more balanced work came out, Ormos, *Az 1924. évi magyar államkölcsön megszerzése.* The latest study on the League loan to Hungary with an emphasis on the British role is Lojkó, *Meddling in Middle Europe*, 81–126. The most comprehensive studies from the technical point of view are those of Péteri, *Revolutionary Twenties and Global Monetary Regime.*

315 *Magyar Hírlap*, March 28, 1922.

316 Lojkó, *Meddling in Middle Europe*, 73-74, 77-78; Péter Sipos, "Teleki Pál párizsi és londoni útja 1921-ben és a magyar külpolitikai orientáció," [Pál Teleki's Journey to Paris and London] In. *A hosszú tizenkilencedik és a rövid huszadik század* [The Long Nineteenth and the Short Twentieth Centuries] Ed. Gergely Jenő, (Budapest: ELTE BTK, 2000), 496–97.

one in the world who would have been willing to lend money to a country that had obligation to pay first to someone else. With the question of reparations pending and a major block in the way of any possible loan, the Hungarian government first thought they would try to raise a loan outside the League of Nations through private channels. The notion of a private loan was clearly shaped in a Hungarian government memorandum in late 1922: "A favorable trend in our balance of foreign trade, therefore, can only be expected when, in the shape of advantageous loans, foreign capital starts flowing into this country making it possible for us to make investments inevitably needed for a powerful development of agriculture and industry alike."[317] With refusal on the continent, further attempts were made for outside money, this time in the United States. Several attempts resulted in only warm-toned replies making clear that there was no possibility for a Hungarian loan in the United States due to the budget deficit, the unsettled situation of Hungary's foreign debts, the passive trade balance, the low price of any possible Hungarian loan, and the lack of understanding in the question of reparations.[318]This list contained all the ills of Hungary, but everyone concerned was well aware of the impossibility of changing all these prerequisites in a very short time.

After the disappointments in America, Hungary knocked once more on British doors. In Great Britain, financial and political circles alike emphasized again that without the reassuring solution of the reparation issue there was simply no way for a long-term loan for Hungary, but these people also realized that Hungary's situation needed to be tackled. Thomas Hohler, the British minister in Budapest, warned of a possible crisis on account of the tragic economic situation and thought that a loan would be "the only remedy," because "it is certain that prevention is better than cure."[319] Even Beneš thought that Hungary was on the verge of bankruptcy.[320] If Great Britain once thought that Hungary should be helped, they also believed that such aid ought to come through the League of Nations.[321] This was the only forum at which the reparation question could have been solved and that was the precondition of a possible loan from either British or American financial circles. For some time, the idea of turning

317 Quoted in Péteri, *Revolutionary Twenties*, 144. The memorandum was written by Alajos Szabóky, who was at this time the director of the Central Statistical Office.

318 Max Warburg to Schossberger, November 23, 1922, 9/X./232, K 275, Kállay Papers, HNA. Also quoted in Péteri, *Global Monetary Regime*, 17; Joy to Schossberger, December 1, 1922, Ibid., X./233.; Széchenyi to Daruváry, February 4, 1923, 9/VIII/5 Plan for a foreign (Swiss, British, American, and French) loan, 3-4, Ibid.; Steiger to Kállay, January 15, 1923, Ibid./5.

319 Hohler to Curzon, March 2, 1923, DBFP, First Series, 24:531–32.

320 Salter, "Notes on the Present Financial & Economic Position of Hungary," March 26, 1923, Doc. No. 27435, Registry Files, R. 296, LNA.

321 Szapáry to Daruváry, March 28, 1923, 9/VIII/5/11, K 275, Kállay Papers, HNA.

to the League was unwelcome for the Hungarian government. Hungary did not want to submit its finances under any kind of supervision. After the Treaty of Trianon the ruling mood of the country was that of revision and not further weakening Hungarian sovereignty. Since a League loan would have meant strict outside control, Hungary wanted to see some other solution. As Bethlen said, "the Austrian recipe is good for reparation but not for a loan. Strong wailing is not good."[322] But the country was not in a position to dictate and was anxious to have any help that might be offered. Since it seemed that only Great Britain took up the Hungarian problem, and British dominance was tangible in both the Financial Committee of the League and in the whole organization, it was therefore crucial for Hungary to have British backing.

It would be misleading to believe that the British were head over heels working for the Hungarian cause, but their overall policy needed a stabilized Central Europe of which Hungary was a key country. Otto Niemeyer, Controller of Finance at the British Treasury and member of the Financial Committee of the League of Nations, produced a since then often quoted line in connection with this policy that illuminates the British thinking very well: "If we could tie up another loose end in this way [League loan to Hungary along the lines of the Austrian scheme] we should I believe, extend and increase our consolidation in South East Europe. I hope the Foreign Office approve these notions and if so that you will do anything you can to push them."[323] The Foreign Office and the Treasury agreed that without assistance Hungary would "fall into hopeless collapse."[324] In the light of this it is not surprising that they were "prepared to support the scheme" and "genuinely anxious to set [Hungary] upon the right rails."[325] The British recommended Hungary to turn to the League for advice, to be ready to accept a similar scenario to what had been going on in the case of Austria, and to go to the Reparations Commission first, since it was the key to freeing the liens for a possible loan.[326] Hungary had no room for much maneuvering and by mid-April the Bethlen government was ready to accept League control if none of the Little Entente countries performed such a role; they also made it clear that they would not take any steps contrary to Britain's wish.[327] With this new attitude taken, the possibility of a loan was a realistic expectation, but first

322 Quoted in Ormos, *Az 1924. évi magyar államkölcsön megszerzése*, 22.
323 Niemeyer to Lampson, March 16, 1923, OV33/70, BoE. Also quoted in Péteri, *Global Monetary Regime*, 51; Péteri, *Revolutionary Twenties*, 168; Lojkó, *Meddling in Middle Europe*, 83.
324 Note on Hungary by Niemeyer, April 26, 1923, C7514/942/21, 8861, FO371, TNA.
325 Butler's minute, March 21, 1923, C4996/942/21, Ibid; Curzon to Hohler, April 13, 1923, DBFP, First Series, 24:583.
326 Summary of conversation between Lampson and Ruttkay, April 6, 1923, C6281/942/21, 8861, FO371, TNA; Curzon to Hohler, April 13, 1923, DBFP, First Series, 24:583.
327 Hohler to Curzon, April 17, 1923, DBFP, First Series, 24:591–93.

the Reparations Commission had to be convinced that Hungary should not pay reparation for the period of a loan.

According to this new course, Bethlen and Frigyes Korányi, future finance minister, representing Hungary appeared before the Reparations Commission on May 5, 1923. They tried to convince the Commission using statistical data that since the war Hungary had been in awful conditions, it was now near bankruptcy, and urgent financial help was needed. Bethlen emphasized that Hungary was in need of all sorts of raw materials and finished products but the country had an adverse balance of foreign payments. To give a good impression to the Commission and show that Hungary had already done what it had been able, he informed the Commission that in 1922 over 11,000 state employees were discharged and a further 20% was among the plans. All this culminated in the real point of the report: he asked the Reparations Commission to suspend the treaty charges and help Hungary financially by virtue of a loan in which case Hungary would be happy to follow the advice of the Financial Committee.[328] With this step, Hungary handed over the decision to the League of Nations. Since in the Reparations Commission France and the Little Entente were in majority, it was little wonder that they did not assent to the Hungarian plea. William Goode, the unofficial financial adviser to Hungary, had done everything in his power to make the Commission agree to refer the question to the Financial Committee, but he predicted that the scheme was in all likelihood going "to prove an even more difficult situation than that of Austria."[329] Unfortunately for Hungary, the American unofficial representative had no right to vote. In all likelihood, Boyden would have cast his vote in favor of a positive decision for Hungary. He suggested conferring with bankers who were likely to be interested in a Hungarian loan as to what they thought the best method would be for Hungary to raise a loan.[330] He also was of the opinion that the League should have the control, not the Reparation Commission. However, without the American, Chairman of the Commission Louis Barthou's casting vote was needed to reach a decision and he helped the Little Entente. The following resolution was born: "Not to oppose, in principle, the request of the Hungarian Government that the charge be temporarily raised for certain revenues of Hungary, which may be needed as security for authorised loans, but [...] a fixed part of which would be assigned to reparation."[331] Aside from political considerations on the part of the

328 Speech of Count Bethlen before the Reparation Commission, May 5, 1293, Communiqués from Kallay and Bethlen. Doc. No. 28903, Registry Files, R. 296, LNA.

329 Goode to Salter, May 16, 1923, Release of Hungarian liens by the Reparations Commission. Doc. No. 28362, Ibid.

330 Reparation Commission Minutes, May 23, 1923, OV9/430, BoE.

331 Reparation Commission Minutes, May 23, 1923, Ibid. The text of the resolution of the Reparation Commission of May 23, 1923, can also be found in 122/ 6/706–707, K 69, Economic Policy Department, HNA.

Little Entente, another possible reason why the Reparations Commission did not want to go ahead with the plan was the fact that at this point the Austrian loan had not been issued yet and they might have feared to acquiesce with a shaky scheme. Whatever the cause, the Commission's condition that part of the loan should go to reparations would have rendered the whole plan undoable, which was obviously what the successor countries wanted to achieve.

Bethlen and the government found themselves in a difficult situation. With the Reparation Commission's decision, a possible loan became suddenly very distant. Although the Hungarian government issued a note in June to the governments that were represented on the Commission urging them to reconsider their decision, the only place they could count on help concerning the future was London.[332] Here, as was mentioned earlier, both the political and financial spheres were inclined to help Hungary. Norman stood behind the Hungarian case and even before Bethlen appeared before the Reparation Commission, Norman had expressed to the British political elite what he thought about the Hungarian situation:

> I do indeed think that the position of Hungary needs to be tackled without delay. Czechoslovakia is more or less standing on her own legs; great efforts are being made to arrange for the Austrian Loan to be issued in a month or so, after which Austria should be able to regain stability; so Hungary is the next country to tackle both from the standpoint of her geographical position and her needs. I do not suppose that her condition is as serious as that of Austria, but I daresay some sort of foreign control will be essential in addition to a release of all Liens. Will you give this business a push in the right direction, and we will then try to get the question taken up by the League or through some other channel.[333]

Since the British influence proved insufficient this time, they started to use their financial clout too in order to achieve the desired outcome. All the successor countries needed financial help and this could be only provided by Great Britain, which would be no stranger to using hardball tactics with them. The key to the Little Entente was Czechoslovakia and its foreign minister, Beneš.

---

332 As a sign of how much Hungary was trying to involve the United States, it is important to note that the Hungarian Government also sent a letter to American embassy in Budapest on June 18, 1923, which was identical to the letter sent to the governments represented on the Reparation Commission. Shoecraft to Daruváry, June 20, 1923, 122/ 6/780, K 69, Economic Policy Department, HNA.

333 Norman to John Bradbury, April 28, 1923, G3/179, BoE. Also quoted in Péteri, *Global Monetary Regime*, 78. After his appearance before the Reparation Commission, Bethlen went to London, where he met not only the representatives of Rothschilds, Baring Brothers, and Schröder & Co, bit Norman as well.

Since the Czechs wanted to raise a loan in the City, the British knew they had "some sort of a hold over him" and through him over the other two members.[334] The very diplomatic terms the British used notwithstanding, the Czechs, the Romanians, and the Yugoslavs were blackmailed by the British to support the Hungarian scheme.[335] Norman made clear what these states had in store: "There is no money for the Czechs (or Roumanians) till Hungary has release from reparation—which was prevented last month by Little Entente. Beneš is free to come to London, but the City takes no part in his domestic politics and is not ready to talk future loans."[336] His confidence had been boosted by Sir Eyre Crowe's letter that assured the Governor that the political leadership agreed with this line of policy.[337] In fact, the British foreign policy establishment sent an ill-disguised message to the countries concerned when Lord Curzon said in the House of Lords on July 25, 1923:

> We are giving our full support to the appeal of Hungary. [...] We desire to prevent the financial collapse of Hungary, with its incalculable consequences. We desire to see in force a complete scheme of reconstruction. [...] We earnestly hope, therefore, that the Reparations Commission will reconsider their decision of May last and will refer the question without delay to the League of Nations.[338]

The pressure on the Little Entente worked to some extent and the three countries held a meeting at Sinaia, Romania, at the end of July. Here they agreed to raise the liens, but they still held to the belief that part of the long-term loan should be devoted to reparations.[339]

---

334 Record by Cadogan of a visit to the FO by Goode and Niemeyer, May 24, 1923, DBFP, First Series, 24:668; Lampson to Sargent, June 26, 1923, Ibid., 737.

335 Foreign Office Memorandum on Hungary, August, 24, 1923, C14677/942/21, 8865, FO371, TNA; Dering to Curzon, October 18, 1923, and Treasury to Foreign office, November 13, 1923, DBFP, First Series, 24:884; Memo of conversation between M. Milojevics, Yugoslav minister at Budapest and Sir William Goode at the S. H. S. Legation, Budapest, June 30, 1923, 9/VIII/5/95, K 275, Kállay Papers, HNA.

336 Norman's Diary Entries, July 5, 1923, ADM34/12, BoE. See also Norman to Gaspard Farrer, May 25, 1923, OV33/70, BoE; Norman to Niemeyer, June 7, 1923, Norman to Eyre Crowe, June 27, 1923, and Norman to Niemeyer, July 5, 1923, G3/179, BoE.

337 Crowe to Norman, June 28, 1923, OV112/1, BoE.

338 British Parliament Diaries, 32nd Parliament, 2nd Session, vol. 54, House of Lords, London: His Majesty's Stationery Office, 1922, 1364–65. Curzon also warned Hungary to follow a more reconciliatory policy toward its neighbors. Ibid., 1365–66.

339 Curzon to Clerk, July 20, 1923, DBFP, First Series, 24:776; Millington-Drake to Curzon, July 30, and August 1, 1923, Ibid., 782–85, and Howe to Curzon, August 2, 1923, Ibid., 786; Clerk to Curzon, August 4, 1923, Ibid., 794. In more detail about the Sinaia Conference, see 122/ 6/82430–85457, K 69, Economic Policy Department, HNA.

After some wrangling, Beneš agreed to meet Bethlen in early September in Geneva, and at the headquarters of the League of Nations agreement was hammered out. The most important element was that Bethlen accepted the idea of a reduced time of reconstruction and money, and of a controller of the League, while the Little Entente became more cooperative in the questions of reparations.[340] Naturally, the other two members were being convinced by the British to help the Hungarian cause.[341] All this ended in the favorable decision of the Council on September 29th that the Financial Committee should start working out a plan for the Hungarian financial reconstruction after hearing from the Reparation Commission. The latter body itself made the decision on October 17th that it agreed in principle later to raise the charges on reparation and invited the League to draw up a plan.[342] Despite the fact that the reparation question was not closed, this represented a major positive result for Hungary, because in the Financial Committee it was the British view that prevailed, and from this point on it seemed that the scheme could be drawn up and carried out with little difficulty.

In November, a League delegation arrived in Budapest for ten days to study the local situation before making any final suggestion regarding the loan. Despite the efforts of Bethlen and Tibor Kállay, Finance Minster of Hungary, the League was not inclined to give either as much time or as much money as in the case of Austria.[343] The Hungarian government had to swallow this bitter pill. Upon the work of the delegation, the Financial Committee submitted its report to the League Council in which they suggested the following: inflation must be stopped, a point of which was achievable with the setting up an independent Bank of Issue; balance of the budget must be reached by June 30, 1926; and all this by the help of a reconstruction loan of 250 million gold crowns ($50million), the control of which would be practiced through a Commissioner-General as

340 Goode to Niemeyer, September 26, 1923, 8/VII. The Material of the Negotiations of the League Loan. VII/3/20, K 275, Kállay Papers, HNA; Ormos, *Az 1924. évi magyar államkölcsön megszerzése*, 71–81.

341 Salter to Niemeyer, September 15 and 22, 1923, No. 12. Correspondence Letter-Book. 1923-1930, No. 1. 23. Correspondence 1923, S. 115, Salter Papers, LNA.

342 Török to Daruváry, September 29, 1923, 8/VII/3/31, K 275, Kállay Papers, HNA; LNJ, 4th Year, No. 11, November 1923, 26th Session, 1356; Decision No. 2665, October 17, 1923, Doc. No. 28362, Registry Files, R. 296, LNA.

343 Notes from conversation between the Delegation, and Count Bethlen and M. Kallay in the afternoon of November 13, 1923, Various Conversations between the League of Nations Delegation and Hungarian officials. Budapest, November 1923, Doc. No. 32496, Registry Files, R. 297, LNA; Conversation between Delegation and Count Bethlen and M. Kallay, November 14, 1923, Ibid; November 22, 1923, Press Reviews. Doc. No. 32459, Registry Files, R. 296, LNA.

in the case of Austria.[344] One of the most important suggestions was that the loan should enjoy priority over Relief Bonds and reparation. With this list of recommendations the final outcome was not at all insured despite the hopes of the Hungarians, and Salter was realistic when he thought that failure was still possible.[345] On December 10, the Council created the Hungarian Sub-Committee with representatives of Great Britain, France, Italy, Hungary, Czechoslovakia, Romania, and the Kingdom of Serbs, Croats and Slovenes. This small body was to decide on the final points of the scheme of the Hungarian reconstruction. The five meetings in December produced the two Protocols to be signed later. Instead of reparations, Treaty Charges got in the wording, which was not to exceed 10 million gold crowns ($2 million) on an annual average during the amortization of the loan, and in the first 5 years after 1926 was to be substantially less.[346] However, the idea of reparations was not eliminated, and France and the Little Entente countries kept pushing for such a course under which some reparations would be paid from the loan. The British were quite upset about the French and Little Entente demands for reparation. Niemeyer's anger was aimed at the French: "We should certainly resist any Gallic attempt to go further. Apart from legal and practical impossibilities a further parade of Reparation nonsense would put the lid finally on any loan."[347] The main fear of the French was that if Hungary got out of the reparation hold, the same might happen in Germany's case. Since they proved adamant on this point, Great Britain needed to assure them that the Hungarian case would not be cited as a model in the German case.[348]

In the meantime, the Hungarian domestic situation did not provide much basis for hope. Besides the continuous depreciation of the crown, which may have been intentional on the part of the government, there was a crash in the stock exchange in August and only slight recovery followed.[349] Moreover, the cost of living started

344 Report of the Financial Committee to the Council, November 30, 1923, Report to the Council on the 12th Session of the Financial Committee. Doc. No. 32475, Registry Files, R. 297, LNA.

345 Salter to Niemeyer, December 6, 1923, Economic and Financial Section. No. 12. Correspondence Letter-Book. 1923–1930, No. 1. 23. Correspondence 1923, S. 115, Salter Papers, LNA.

346 1st Session of the Committee of the Council, Paris. December 1923. Doc. No. 32636, Registry Files, R. 297, LNA.

347 Niemeyer to Kemball Cook, January 2, 1924, OV9/430, BoE.

348 Memorandum by Cadogan respecting the meeting of the Hungarian Committee of the Council of the League of Nations on February 9. February 11, 1924, DBFP, First Series, 26:77; FO Memorandum, February 4, 1924, Ibid., 73; Crewe to MacDonald, and MacDonald to Crewe, February 22, 1924, Ibid., 100–01;

349 Ormos states it as a fact that Bethlen was behind a deliberate devaluation of the crown. In any way, the numbers are curious. From the end of 1923, the crown suffered almost 300% devaluation in two months' time. Ormos, *Az 1924. évi magyar államkölcsön megszerzése*, 104-07.

to approach that of the United States.[350] Officials were hardly able to live on their salaries and there was "an amazing increase of corruption."[351] In addition, there was a sizeable opposition to the loan. These voices lamented the allegations that such a small amount the domestic arena could have provided and with foreign borrowing the Little Entente would have a controlling role in Hungary's internal affairs.[352] Still, Bethlen was successful overall in having the concept accepted that only a foreign loan could help the country, and the opposition shrunk to a narrow political segment that antagonized the government on principle. This was very important, because his government might have fallen on this issue, an opinion Hohler shared.[353] The British feared such a course, because in their view Bethlen's fall would mean the rise of "the most undesirable extremists [...] If this forecast should be true it would portend a period of inexpert adventure and experiment, which would be full of danger to the peace of Europe."[354] Thus for the British the battle was one regarding the future of the whole continent. Without the Hungarian piece, the Austrian scheme was almost useless. They used all of their influence to win this fight and they were not moved by certain Hungarians, such as Gyula Peidl, Ernő Garami, Rusztem Vámbéry, and former prime minister Mihály Károlyi, who tried to undermine the possibility of the loan and asked the British government to force the Hungarian government to ensure liberal civil rights, most prominently a general election and the repeal of the *numerus clausus* law.[355]

After varying hardball tactics and friendly discourse, the British were finally triumphant. The decision on February 21 was a victory of diplomatic skill and perseverance. The compromise reached declared that certain specified assets for the Hungarian loan were released, and the reparation question was agreed. According to the decision by the Reparation Commission, Hungary was to pay a sum of annually 10 million gold crowns in a twenty-year period starting after the reconstruction period. For the time being, this prospect was acceptable for the Bethlen government as well, which hoped that eventually they would be able to avoid paying reparations. The timetable of the reparation payments was drawn up in the progressive fashion, starting with 5 million gold crowns ($1,000,000) in 1927 and reaching 14 million gold crowns ($2.8 million) in the last two years each, 1942 and 1943.[356] The now finalized Protocols also said that financial control would be reestablished if Hungary did not pay according to the scheme.

---

350 Brentano to Hughes, January 2, 1924, 864.00/568, Roll 6, M. 708, NARA.
351 Hohler to Curzon, January 3, 1924, DBFP, First Series, 26:9.
352 Ibid., 8; Brentano to Hughes, January 2, 1924, 864.00/568, Roll 6, M. 708, NARA.
353 Hohler to MacDonald, January 21, 1924, DBFP, First Series, 26:98.
354 Hohler to Curzon, January 3, 1924, Ibid., 10.
355 Romsics, *István Bethlen*, 235.
356 For the detailed timetable, see Appendix 2.

This formula seemed at last to satisfy every party and it was only a matter of time before all the signatures were given. The British was the first to sign it on March 5, while typically it was the Little Entente that was the last party to put its signature on the Protocols on March 14, 1924.[357]

The two Protocols provided for every possible aspect of the loan. Protocol No. I. was a political one in which the parties undertook to "respect the political independence, the territorial integrity and the sovereignty of Hungary," while Hungary undertook "strictly and loyally to fulfil the obligations contained in the said Treaty, and in particular the military clauses, as also the other international agreements."[358] Protocol No. II. contained the technical details. The fifteen Articles touched upon every important aspect of the reconstruction period: the amount of the loan; the required minimum sum to be reached by taxation, the maximum possible expenditure and deficit in every half year; concluding commercial agreement especially with the neighboring states; the powers of the Commissioner-General, the Committee of Control, and the Trustees; the possible reestablishment of control if the balance of the budget or the revenues assigned to the loan were in danger; the gross revenues from the customs, the sugar tax, and the tobacco monopoly, and the net revenue from the salt monopoly served as first charge for the service of the loan, and all these, together with the yield of the loan, would be paid into a special account under the control of the Commissioner-General; and a new Central Bank of Issue must be opened with such statutes that would ensure its independence from the government.[359] In March another League delegation visited Hungary, which talked to all political parties and they approved of the reconstruction law, the bank act, and six monthly budgets that were to come before the Hungarian National Assembly.[360]

All that remained now was the necessary legal act of the National Assembly passing the reconstruction bill, which contained the bill for the new National Bank, too. On March 27, Bethlen submitted the package to the National Assembly, where debate, sometimes fierce in tone, lasted three weeks often in 16-hour sessions before it was passed on April 18.[361] The package contained six separate bills: 1. to balance the state budget; 2. to establish the Hungarian National Bank; 3. issuing a domestic loan; 4. postponing the Hungarian debt concurred

357 Minutes of the meeting on March 14, 1924. Doc. No. 34921, Registry Files, R. 299, LNA.
358 League of Nations, *The Financial Reconstruction of Hungary*, 80–81.
359 Ibid., 81–92.
360 The delegation consisted of Henry Strakosch as Chairman, Avenol, Giuseppe Bianchini, C. E. ter Meulen, Vilem Pospíšil, and Marcus Wallenberg. Janssen and Salter, who had also been appointed, could not visit Budapest on account of other duties. Ibid., 25.
361 National Assembly Diary, 1922–27, Budapest: Athenaeum Nyomda, 1924, vol. 22: 60–68, 237, 268–89, 299–315, 317–41, 343–97, 399–452; 23:1–153, 163–241, 243–333, 335–426, 437–510.

toward French creditors; 5. financial and debt agreement with Czechoslovakia; and financial agreement with Italy. The political opposition criticized the whole scheme. A recurrent point during the debate was that the government would have powers that the National Assembly had been titled to. Another was that Hungary allowed foreign countries to interfere with Hungary's domestic policy. A further point was the question of control and that it could be reestablished. Since the phrase was not absolutely clear this point might have been understood in a wide arrange of interpretations and could be harmful to the country. Despite such voices, the passing was never in danger due to the majority of Bethlen's Unified Party. With the Protocols signed and the reconstruction bill passed, three outstanding issues were on the agenda. One of them was to find the right person for the position of the Commission-General.

Chapter 5

The Selection of Jeremiah Smith, Jr.

5.1. Search for the Commissioner-General

The financial reconstruction of Hungary had thus reached an important phase. The slow negotiations, often filled with acrimonious bickering over reparations and burdened with the unavoidable political underpinning of the whole situation, finally led to the signed Protocols which were, in a similar fashion to the Austrian reconstruction, the blueprint of the next two and a half years. This successful step seemed to guarantee that a long-term loan would be a realistic undertaking even without state guarantees, a conspicuously different feature compared to the case of Austria. However, before this still momentous task could begin, the Commissioner-General for Hungary had to be found and appointed. Without such an official, both the loan negotiations and the subsequent reconstruction work in Hungary could not have started in earnest. Almost two years earlier in Austria, it became apparent that finding a suitable candidate was far from easy. This time around the League of Nations wanted to avoid facing a similar situation again, where the lack of a Commissioner-General might have wrecked the entire scheme. The search had already begun in the last weeks of 1923, since "even a slight delay at any point would render the completion of the task by the terminal date impossible."[362]

From the very beginning, there were no clear favorites or settled nationalities. The Italians, for example, wanted an Italian to fill the post. J. Nathan, the London representative of the Banca d'Italia, had already approached Norman in November 1923 with the goal of ensuring that the League Commissioner would be an Italian, but was met with refusal.[363] The Italians thought that their support of the Hungarian case throughout proceedings would entitle them to such a job. This view was vehemently opposed by the British, whose preference for a neutral person necessarily excluded an Italian.[364] The first names raised as possibilities were Arnold Christopher Ræstad, ex-Foreign Minister of Norway, J. Akerman, a Swede who spoke both German and French, and a Spanish ex-Finance Minister,

362 Reconstruction of Hungary, Proposed calendar of action required before external loans can be issued, December 18, 1923, C./S. C. H. /5. F.114, LNA.

363 Cottrell, *Rebuilding the Financial System*, 47.

364 Memorandum by Butler on Hungarian Reconstruction, December 7, 1923, DBFP, First Series, 24:909.

Francisco Cambo, who, however, did not enjoy any support.[365] Originally, the Commissioner-General was to be chosen by February 1, 1924 but, as with other stages in the process, it seemed sure to be delayed. To avoid the bitter quarrel that could have occurred if someone had been chosen from the continent, even if they represented a neutral country, the principal actors looked to the United States once again, since the United States was perhaps the only country that could count on friendly feelings throughout Europe, and could boast of being genuinely neutral. No wonder that at the time of the Austrian reconstruction the League wanted to secure the American Roland Boyden as Commissioner.

Once again, after the initial failure to find a suitable candidate on the continent, the organization put its hope in the United States. Hungary itself was also in favor of having a person from overseas. In addition to the expected political goodwill of an American, the Bethlen government supposedly had information that the American money market would be willing to participate only if an American were chosen for the post.[366] Bethlen also calculated shrewdly that "in case an American specialist were sent to be the controller of the Hungarian loan, this would so much please the vanity of the Americans that the placing of our loan there would be much easier."[367] László Széchenyi, the Hungarian minister in Washington, was of the opinion that "from the point of view of placing the loan in America, in my view, it would be advantageous if we managed to entrust an American with the role of the controller."[368] The nationality of the future financial supervisor was one thing, however; his powers were a different issue, one with which the Hungarian government was quite concerned.

Simply put, Hungary wanted to avoid giving the financial supervisor an Austria-like level control, which they judged far too strict and wide-reaching. During a dinner in September 1923 hosted by Joseph Avenol, Deputy Secretary General of the League, where the topic of discussion was the Hungarian case, Bethlen raised the question of the future Commissioner and said his powers should be more limited than Zimmerman's in Austria, which, in his view, amounted to those of a foreign dictator.[369] A memorandum by the president of the future National Bank of Hungary, Sándor Popovics, called for harmonious cooperation between the Commissioner-General and the Hungarian government, which, in turn, could

365 Niemeyer to Salter and Lampson, December 8, 1923, OV9/433, BoE; Wallenberg to Salter, December 16, 1923, and Note, December 27, 1923, Ibid.; Niemeyer to Salter, January 3, 1924, OV9/430, BoE.

366 Magos, *Az amerikai imperialisták szerepe*, 16; Ormos, *Az 1924. évi magyar államkölcsön megszerzése*, 115.

367 Bethlen to Daruváry and Khuen-Héderváry, November 27, 1923, 123–6–54200/96618, K 69, Economic Policy Department, HNA.

368 Széchenyi to Daruváry, December 31, 1923, 123–6–54200/162110, Ibid.

369 Lojkó, *Meddling in Middle Europe*, 94.

lead to a more simplified level of control.[370] As the Hungarian finance minister saw it, "The position in Austria has evolved on this basis that the controller plays, so to speak, the role of the Finance Minister with dictatorial power [...] therefore, without the knowledge or contrary to his views, hardly anything can happen in Austria."[371] He also emphasized the importance of cooperation. The Hungarians hoped that this might be easier to achieve if an American were appointed. In light of this belief, the Hungarian government had already started to make steps toward securing a prominent American for the role. The reasoning was that if they managed to convince a high-standing American to accept the post, it would automatically create the needed confidence on the money markets. The United States took part in the Austrian reconstruction and it was no secret that the Americans were following the British lead there. It seemed that if an American were named Commissioner, the doors of the private American banks would open and the United States would play a large role in securing the needed loan. The first person approached was William Procter Gould Harding, Governor of the Federal Reserve Bank of Boston.[372] Without question, such a figure was very prominent. Bethlen was informed in December that Harding, who had received all the important documents concerning the future loan, had indicated that he would accept the post and asked for details concerning the work and salary, but wanted to avoid any publicity.[373] Samuel Reading Bertron, the Hungarian government's American link, also conferred with Dwight Morrow of J. P. Morgan & Co. and asked him to use their influence in order for Harding to be accepted.[374] Not much pressure was needed.

In Great Britain and the League of Nations the secret news that Harding might accept the post was met with general enthusiasm. Niemeyer was also in favor of having an American for the post and promised to do his best.[375] The appointment was backed by other influential men. The most well known of them was Edward M. "Colonel" House, President Wilson's one-time friend and adviser, who told Eric Drummond that he thought Harding's nomination would "be [the] best

370 Popovics's memorandum, October 24, 1923, 123–6–54200/92852, K 69, Economic Policy Department, HNA.

371 Kállay to Daruváry, October 26, 1923, Ibid.

372 Harding was a member of the Federal Reserve Board from 1914 to 1922, and its Governor, 1916–1922. He opposed President Harding when the latter wanted to put political nominees at several Reserve Banks. In retaliation, the President did not reappoint him in 1922. In 1923 he became the Governor of the Boston Federal Reserve Bank. Chandler, *Benjamin Strong*, 44.

373 Széchenyi to Bertron, December 15, 1923, 209/123, Economic Negotiations. 10–1390/135, K 69, Economic Policy Department, HNA; Széchenyi to Daruváry, December 31, 1923, 123–6–54200/162110, Ibid.

374 Bertron to Szechenyi, December 17, 1923, 10–1390/136, Ibid.

375 Goode to Bethlen, January 4, 1924, 264/113, Reparation and Social Issues. 50052–50263/1077–1078, K 69, Economic Policy Department, HNA.

possible way of insuring American cooperation financially in Central Europe. I would strongly recommend his selection."[376] The official line was somewhat different. The Financial Committee, in reply to the request of the Hungarian Committee, named the following nationalities as desired for the post: British, Czechoslovak, French, Hungarian, Italian, Romanian, and Serbian.[377] This was an incomprehensible and unrealistic list since, due to political reasons, there was no way that either a Hungarian or a person from the successor countries would be accepted. True, the Committee added that they "did not intend to exclude a national of a country such as America," thus possibly paving the way for hopes and realities later on.[378] The list may well have been merely a show for the countries mentioned within because in fact, in a secret meeting only a few days later, the Hungarian Committee agreed to the choice of Harding in principle, although no concrete steps were taken.[379] On the one hand, all the governments' approvals were needed; on the other hand, there were three other European candidates, Campboo Catalan, Ræstad, and De la Croix, out of which only the first was serious.[380] The overall strategy was to keep all possible nominees secret.

Behind the scenes, Harding was not so universally favored. When Norman, for example, gently warned Benjamin Strong that under the prevailing conditions of reparations still burdening the proposed scheme, the issue of a loan was not possible, Strong replied that he would not inform Harding about it, because the latter should find out himself whether the circumstances promised success.[381] This is somewhat strange, because in the case of Kemmerer, for instance, Strong shared all the information he had. Not all of the British officials welcomed Harding either. A Foreign Office paper characterized Harding as "an odd retiring sort of person, ugly, silent and gauche," but added that "his reputation for honesty is above reproach."[382] By the end of January, the picture was therefore mixed at best. There was no clear favorite, although Harding, largely because of his nationality and earlier posts, enjoyed the biggest support. The Hungarians, parallel to trying to secure Harding, were also actively looking for other suitable

376 House to Drummond, January 15, 1924, Appointment of a Commissioner General by the League. Doc. No. 33315, Financial Reconstruction of Hungary, Registry Files, R. 298, LNA.

377 Financial reconstruction of Hungary, Hungarian Committee of the Council, January 18, 1924, C./S.C.H./8. F.127, LNA.

378 Ibid.

379 Memorandum by Cadogan respecting the decisions of the Hungarian Committee of the Council of the L. of N. for Hungarian Reconstruction, January 22, 1924, DBFP, First Series, 26:53.

380 Szapáry to Daruváry, January 22, 1924, 209/123, 10–1390/1480, K 69, Economic Policy Department, HNA.

381 Norman to Strong, January 24, 1924, 2A165/ and OV33/70, BoE; Strong to Norman, January 30, 1924, OV33/70, BoE.

382 FO Minute by Sir A. Willert, January 24, 1924, C1447/37/21, 9904, FO371, TNA.

candidates. It was urgent for both the Hungarian government and the League of Nations to select the Commissioner as soon as possible. This sense of urgency left no time to go through the selection process at a comfortable pace, but necessitated the reaching of an acceptable decision quickly.

Due to the prevailing circumstances, the decisive voices were in favor of Harding, if for nothing else but the fact that his name did carry some weight in financial circles, especially in the United States. Therefore, the French government agreed with the British proposal to nominate Harding.[383] A few days later at an informal meeting of the Hungarian Committee, all seven members accepted Harding's nomination with a possible annual salary of $15,000-20,000.[384] *The New York Times* first claimed that an American would be the nominee, then narrowed the race down to either Charles G. Dawes or Harding, and finally declared that Harding was unofficially nominated and that he would accept if he was officially designated.[385] Harding claimed that he did not know any more than what he was reading in the newspapers. Unfortunately, in the zeal for secrecy, which was not warranted, the League sent an invitation to Harding as late as February 11, and only through Colonel House, which the former, for unknown reasons, never received.[386] This obviously hurt Harding's pride and the League tried to make amends by sending an official invitation directly to him on February 28. The news that Harding was sailing for Paris very soon afterward was interpreted by everyone as a confirmation of his accepting the job, but in reality it was only the adherence to the orders of his doctors, who strongly advised him to take a European vacation for his shaken health.[387]

The Hungarian public was informed of the "secret" negotiations by the newspapers. First, the readers gathered that the Commissioner would be either Swedish or Dutch.[388] Soon enough rumors spread that Alfred Zimmerman would fill the Hungarian post as well, and failing that baron Theodor Adelswärd, a Swedish ex-finance minister, would be picked as Commissioner.[389] Different newspapers relied on different sources. *Budapesti Hírlap* wrote that there was every indication that the post would be offered to an American.[390] The Hungarian minister in Stockholm wrote that Marcus Wallenberg, managing director and later chairman of Stockholms Enskilda Bank, was inclined to accept the post, which would mean

383 Clauzel to Lord Cecil, February 2, 1924, C2424/37/21, 9905, FO371, TNA.
384 Lord Cecil to House, February 11, 1924, C2521/37/21, Ibid.
385 *The New York Times*, January 30, February 9, 19, 1924.
386 FO Minute by P. J. Baker, February 28, 1924, C3418/37/21, 9905, FO371, TNA.
387 Ibid.
388 *Magyarország*, January 22, 1924. XXXI/18.
389 *Magyarország*, January 23, 1924. XXXI/19.
390 *Budapesti Hírlap*, January 23, 1924. XLIV/19.

a well-qualified expert instead of the incompetent Adelswärd.[391] When toward the end of February it came to light that Harding seemed in fact to be the chosen one, the papers in Hungary were enthusiastic. They noted that this would involve the neutrality the United States represented and American participation in the loan, while Harding's name would induce all interested foreign financial circles to take part in the Hungarian reconstruction.[392] *Magyarország* had information that the Hungarian government was already preparing Harding's office in Budapest.[393] Hungarians, politicians and the public alike had reason to be cheerful. After all, in a reasonably short time they had managed to secure the Commissioner they wanted. The League was also pleased with such a development. It came as a heavy blow, then, that Harding finally refused to accept the job.

Harding had been ill for some time and came to Europe on his doctors' advice. How deeply he was interested in the Hungarian post is not clear; he might have been disillusioned with his job back in the United States and have been content to find a fresh start in his life. The only sure thing is that he never committed himself to the cause, he only signaled his interest. In the end, it seems that his illness was a significant consideration. Soon after he arrived in Paris, his doctors suggested that further rest would be desirable, and such a post as Commissioner-General in Hungary could prove too detrimental to his unstable health. Accordingly, he signaled in early March that due to his state of health he would not be able to accept the post.[394] In an interview he gave the *New York Herald* in Paris, he said he was only in Europe for the sake of his health and he did not have the slightest intention to accept such a position as Zimmerman's in Austria.[395] Besides physical illness and hurt pride, pecuniary considerations might have played a role as well. As Governor of the Federal Reserve Bank in Boston, he had made $30,000-40,000 a year. In this job he would have made half of that sum in an alien surrounding and Bethlen heard "from a private reliable source" that this was the true reason.[396] On March 8, Harding informed Hevesy, the Hungarian minister in Paris, that he had not made up his mind yet, but in the course of the next week he finally refused to be considered for the job.[397] With this turn of events, the reconstruction scheme suffered a setback.

---

391 Bornemissza to Daruváry, January 22, 1924, 209/123, 10–1390/1476, K 69, Economic Policy Department, HNA.
392 *Budapesti Hírlap*, February 23, 1924. XLIV/45; *Magyarország*, February 24, 1924. XXXI/46.
393 *Magyarország*, March 5, 1924. XXXI/54.
394 Harding to Salter, March 7, 1924, C4678/37/21, 9907, FO371, TNA.
395 *Magyarország*, March 11, 1924. XXXI/59.
396 Goode to Niemeyer, March 16, 1924, C4408/37/21, 9906, FO371, TNA.
397 Hevesy to Daruváry, March 8, 1924, 209/123, 10–1390/1449, K 69, Economic Policy Department, HNA.

On the eve of the Protocols being ratified by the final signatory, the Hungarian reconstruction plan was in serious danger of stalling. Without a Commissioner-General there was no prospect of efficient work being accomplished in Hungary, and raising the long-term loan would be simply untenable. The League had to find a suitable person in the shortest time possible. Norman Davies and Owen Young recommended Boyden without hesitation, Jeremiah Smith, Jr. as second best, and Walker Dower Hines as a third possibility for the job, who was a favorite by Logan too.[398] Harding warmly recommended, if Boyden could not be secured, an old colleague of his, Frederick Adrian Delano, who was Vice-Governor of the Federal Reserve Board from 1914-1918, had worked in Europe, and spoke French.[399] The chances that Boyden would accept were not great after the events a year and a half earlier, when he was virtually assured the position of the Austrian Commissioner-General, only to lose it at the last moment. Besides, his wife was very sick, which would have made it doubly difficult for him to accept the appointment.[400] At the March 15 meeting of the Hungarian Committee, the body decided that an official invitation would be sent to Boyden and, if he refused, the other candidates, Smith, Hines, and Delano would be approached.[401]

In the following three days, Delano seems to have become a favorite. Owen Young praised him warmly, and Morgan Harjes of Paris, who was of the same opinion, added that Delano would be from every point of view better than Smith.[402] The British started to see him as the best candidate, probably due to his knowledge of French and some German.[403] They officially informed the League of Nations that "H. M. Government [...] are inclined to look on Delano as probably the most suitable candidate."[404] Bertron, who had been so active in securing Harding from the beginning, also recommended Delano for the Hungarian position, with the indication that Delano would accept.[405] The prospect of securing another prominent American seemed, despite the short time period, to be settled. But within a few days all that changed once again.

---

398 Salter to Niemeyer, March 11, 1924, C4124/3721, 9906, FO371, TNA. Both Boyden and Hines had visited Hungary in 1921, when they were studying the changed river commerce. *The New York Times*, March 29, 1921.

399 Telephone message from Salter to Drummond, March 14, 1924, Financial Reconstruction of Hungary, Appointment of a Commissioner General by the League. Doc. No. 33315, Registry Files, R. 298, LNA.

400 Hevesy to Daruváry, March 15, 1924, 209/123, 10–1390/1437, K 69, Economic Policy Department, HNA.

401 Cadogan to FO, March 15, 1924, C4542/37/21, 9907, FO371, TNA.

402 Telephone message from Salter, March 17, 1924, Doc. No. 33315, Registry Files, R. 298, LNA.

403 Niemeyer to Lampson, March 18, 1924, C4766/37/21, 9907, FO371, TNA.

404 Foreign Office to Secretary General of League of Nations, March 20, 1924, Doc. No. 33315, Registry Files, R. 298, LNA.

405 Bertron to Mikes, March 21, 1924, 209/123, 10–1390/1457, K 69, Economic Policy Department, HNA.

5.2. Enter Mr. Smith

As was expected, Roland Boyden did indeed refuse the position of Commissioner-General to Hungary, citing personal reasons. He did, however, recommend Jeremiah Smith, Jr. for the job.[406] This flew in the face of the recent support built around Delano. Even more momentous than Boyden's recommendation was when Drummond informed the Hungarian Committee that the "highest financial circles [in] America strongly take [the] same view," and it was "clearly of greatest importance obtaining [a] person acceptable [to] financial circles best qualified."[407] Since the League expected that a third of the loan would be subscribed in the United States, they needed someone for the post who enjoyed the favor of the American financial circles. If they had to choose between two American candidates, they would certainly pick the one that promised an easier and more generous American participation. Both the British Foreign Office and the Treasury were of the opinion that the decisive factor was that the person should be an American citizen.[408] By April it was clear that Smith's candidacy had attracted an overwhelming backing.. In addition to Boyden and Davis, both Pierre Jay, chairman of the Board of Directors of the Federal Reserve Bank of New York, and Thomas Lamont of J. P. Morgan & Co. supported him, with the latter three "definitely adverse to Delano."[409] As Lamont wrote to Salter in a confidential letter "quite aside from personal liking for the two men last mentioned (Mr. Hines and Mr. Delano) [I] would regard neither one as fully equipped for the job; Smith would be better than either."[410] In all probability, it was Lamont's opinion that proved decisive in the end. It was he who arranged the American portion of the Austrian loan, so it was understandable that the League was sensitive to his recommendation. Yet Smith was, at that point, an obscure and low-profile figure.

Jeremiah Smith, Jr. as a person was at the time, and has since remained, something of an enigma.[411] He rarely appeared in newspapers, a medium that he shunned, and he almost never allowed his picture to be taken. He led a reserved life, never married, and had only a younger sister with whom he lived in Boston. Salter described him as having "impeccable and transparent rectitude" in addition to being "shy, inexpressive and with a misleading appearance of

406 Telephone message from Drummond to Walters, March 24, 1924, Doc. No. 33315, Registry Files, R. 298, LNA.

407 Drummond to Members, March 24, 1924, C5039/37/21, 9907, FO371, TNA.

408 Lampson's minute, March 24, 1924, Ibid.

409 Memorandum, April 2, 1924, Doc. No. 33315, Registry Files, R. 298, LNA.

410 Lamont to Salter, March 22, 1924, quoted in Salter to Bethlen, April 11, 1924, Ibid.

411 This is true for the Hungarian historian György Magos, who claimed that J. P. Morgan had "sent Smith to Hungary." György Magos, "The Role of the British and American Imperialists in the Stabilisation of Horthy Fascism," *Acta Historica. Academiae Scientarium*, 2, no. 1–2, E. Nadics, ed., (Budapest: Magyar Tudományos Akadémia, 1953), 202.

diffidence which concealed a shrewd judgement and a firm will."[412] Lamont, his good friend and loyal advocate, characterized him as "the most entertaining man I think that I ever met [...] intensely patriotic [...] a man whose simplicity carries him through all barriers."[413] Lord Robert Cecil during his stay in America gathered the impression that Smith was "a nice, straight fellow."[414] The leading newspaper of his home city had this to say about Smith: He possessed a "capacity to come down to brass tacks on a complicated situation, stick to the issue and win his point, and still keep the confidence and good will of the other fellow."[415] The editor of the *Christian Science Monitor* believed that Smith possessed "both a shrewd and winning personality," that he was reticent with a "frank, vigorous and open" voice, and that he "would seem to be an ideal conciliator, or man for a position where one of his chief duties would be to hold the confidence."[416] These sympathetic opinions give a good impression and, in fact, Smith could always boast of being liked on account of his personality.

With the Paris Peace Conference, Smith's international career had begun. After Paris, he accompanied Lamont to Japan and China as an aide, and later to Mexico in the capacity of counselor in the Mexican debt settlement.[417] Largely thanks to Lamont's unwavering help, Smith gained immense experience in international negotiations pertaining to financial questions and problems. His prominent place in the daily news led his local Democratic branch to try to convince him to run for representative to Congress in 1922, but he refused.[418] Although the international expertise Smith had accrued was clearly a key aspect in his appointment to the post of Commissioner-General of the League of Nations, it seems that Lamont's recommendation was the decisive factor. In the spring of 1924, Bethlen and his government knew virtually nothing about Jeremiah Smith, Jr., and greeted his selection for the position with disbelief.

The Hungarians had put so much energy into securing Harding that they were almost blind to any other possibilities. Moreover, they believed that Harding's standing would prove a useful asset in promoting optimism within American financial circles toward the Hungarian reconstruction. When Harding finally

412 Salter, *Personality in Politics*, 168.
413 Lamont, *Across World Frontiers*, 82.
414 Hevesy to Daruváry, April 5, 1924, 209/123, 10–1390/1399, K 69, Economic Policy Department, HNA.
415 *Boston Daily Globe*, April 13, 1924.
416 Rácz to the Press Department of the Foreign Ministry, May 13, 1924, 209/123, 10–1390/1229-30, K 69, Economic Policy Department, HNA.
417 For the work in Japan and China, and the negotiations for the organization of a new financial Consortium for China, see FRUS: 1920, 1:497, 575–89. In connection with his work in the Mexican debt settlement in 1922, see E. Lamont, *The Ambassador from Wall Street*, 175–86, and *The New York Times*, January 2, 1924.
418 *Boston Daily Globe*, July 30, 1922.

refused the job on account of his health, Hungarian officials were left at a loss. But Harding, who visited Budapest toward the end of March to show his support for the Hungarian cause, quickly suggested Frank Delano as an alternative, and the Hungarians felt reassured that they would get a similarly significant person. So, when the news reached them that the League had picked Smith, they were astounded. Their surprise was compounded by worrying reports concerning Smith's reputation, most significantly from Harding, Bertron, George Murnane, Vice-President of the New York Trust Company, Ivy Lee, who was hired by J. P. Morgan and Co. to help advertise the Austrian loan, and Professor Jenks, an American economist. From these people, Hungarian officials were led to believe that Smith would carry no weight at all in the United States and was no fit for the job.[419] The League tried to reassure the Hungarians that this was not the case. Niemeyer, at Salter's request, instructed Miles Lampson of the Foreign Office to send a telegram to the Hungarian Prime Minister with the words: "Smith is most strongly recommended in important quarters in America."[420] They pointed out that Great Britain, Italy, and France had already consented to the appointment, together with two of the Little Entente countries, and argued that Hungary should agree with the majority decision.[421] The League also gently warned Hungary that any balking on its part would "inevitably lead to further and undesirable delay which it is obviously in Hungarian interests to avoid."[422]

In addition to concerns about Smith's standing, his name created some confusion in Hungary, leading to further problems. Not well versed in New England local culture, the Hungarian leaders suspected that Smith might be a Jew. Under Hungary's prevailing anti-Semitic sentiment, it would have been unacceptable to the Bethlen government for a Jew to control the country's finances. It is enough to mention that only a few years earlier, the Hungarian Parliament passed a special bill, the infamous *Numerus Clausus*, which limited the number of Jews who were allowed to study in the highest education, and there were also many atrocities committed against Jews.[423] Bethlen's flexible pragmatism was evident in the Jewish question, which he admitted existed. As freshly appointed Prime Minister, he stated in his program speech on April 19, 1921, that the problem of the middle class was that

---

419 Goode to Niemeyer, April 2, 1924, C5503/37/21, 9907, FO371, TNA and 209/1231, K 69, Economic Policy Department, HNA; Goode to Niemeyer, April 4, 1924, OV9/433, BoE.
420 Telephone message from Salter to Niemeyer, April 2, 1924, and Wilkinson to Lampson, April 2, 1924, C5526/37/21, 9907, FO371, TNA.
421 Interview with Mr. Baranyai, April 3, 1924, Doc. No. 33315, Registry Files, R. 298, LNA.
422 Drummond to Stoppani, April 4, 1924, Ibid.
423 The text of the bill is in Magyar Törvénytár, 1920. évi törvénycikkek [Hungarian Law Collection, Law Bills of 1920] (Budapest, 1921), 145–46. See also, Gergely Egressy, "A Statistical Overview of the Hungarian Numerus Clausus Law of 1920—A Historical Necessity or the First Step Toward the Holocaust?" *Eastern European Quarterly* 34 (January 2001): 447–64.

> instead of looking for a new development for its life in trade, industry, and entrepreneurship, it went into the office. The result of this was that trade, entrepreneurship, and finance got in the hands of those who were not, and perhaps are not even today, welded to the feeling of the nation to the extent it would be right and desirable.[424]

Despite this clear reference to the Hungarian Jewry as not true Hungarians, he also said that "I am against all kinds of noisy anti-Semitism. We will under all circumstances make the law prevail."[425] Still, he made no efforts to change or withdraw the anti-Semitic bill. This was obviously attributable to his personal, albeit moderate, anti-Semitism. As leader of the Unified Party, Bethlen had to make compromises. As a result, his party admitted the openly anti-Semitist Gyula Gömbös and his followers, alongside members of the Jewish elite. As Bethlen pointed out, he approved of "Christian policies, but these policies should not be manifest in anti-Semitism but must be made pro-Christian."[426] With such prevailing attitudes restricting the freedom of Jewish people, in part because they were used as scapegoats for the Bolshevik coup of 1919, it would have been a political impossibility for Bethlen to accept a Jew as a League Commissioner. Only after being convinced that Smith was not of Jewish descent did the Hungarian government finally approve of his nomination, a fact that the British Consul General happily conveyed to London.[427]

The League officially invited Jeremiah Smith, Jr. to become Commissioner-General for Hungary until June 1926, with an $18,000 a year salary.[428] In light

---

424 István Bethlen, *Bethlen István gróf beszédei és írásai* [The Writings and Speeches of Count István Bethlen] vol. 1, (Budapest: Genius Könyvkiadó Rt., 1933), 157. The whole program speech is in Ibid., 154–68. Although Jews represented about 6% of the total population, they were dominant in medicine, law, journalism, engineering, and music. See, Ezra Mendelsohn, *The Jews of East Central Europe between the World Wars* (Bloomington: University of Indiana, 1983), 100–02.

425 Ibid., 161. Also see Romsics, *István Bethlen*, 151.

426 *Magyarság*, October 19, 1922, III/238.

427 Hohler to MacDonald, April 5, 1924, C5704/37/21, 9907, FO371, TNA. In more detail about anti-Semitism in Hungary in the interwar period, see, Nathaniel Katzburg, *Hungary and the Jews. Policy and Legislation 1920-1943* (Ramat-Gan: Bar-Ilan University, 1981).

428 Salter to Smith, April 5, 1924, Doc. No. 33315, Registry Files, R. 298, LNA. This was a handsome amount. American financial advisers were also paid lavishly in Latin America. The Collector-General in Nicaragua had a yearly salary of $15,000 with other benefits. Arthur Young, for example, received from the Honduran government in 1922 $1,000 a month, almost double what the president of that country earned. Smith's salary was even above these cases, although it came not even close to Kemmerer's, who made between $70,000 and $100,000 a mission. As a comparison, the salary of Seymour Parker Gilbert, Agent General for Reparations Payments in Germany under the Dawes Plan from the fall of 1924, was $50,000 a year. E. Rosenberg, *Financial Missionaries*, 224–25; Ron Chernow, *The House of Morgan* (New York: Atlantic Monthly Press), 402.

of the drawn-out process of securing a Commissioner-General, they asked him to give an answer as soon as possible. The League strictly ordered that no communiqué be given out to the press before his affirmative answer arrived.[429] In what Montagu Norman, who during these weeks regarded the success of the Hungarian loan with reservations, described as "a moment of enthusiasm," Smith accepted the offer.[430] The State Department officials deemed it an event that called for no action and, as was typical in almost every case, the Department assumed no responsibility.[431] With this step, the previously established protocol was repeated: the United States did not officially assume any responsibility for the country; still an American was in charge of sensitive financial supervision, which fact undeniably gave an accent of American influence nonetheless. It must be noted that this is the most that can be said in the case of Hungary, since the United States was simply not interested in the country. The Bolshevik danger seemed to have dissipated and in economic terms Hungary had little to offer the giant overseas power. The possibility of future American investments was also of marginal interest in relation to their volume.

As with later events, virtually nothing is known about Smith's personal reasons for accepting the role in Hungary. It is probable that, to a large degree, his decision must have stemmed from his commitment to the League's ideals.[432] As a Democrat, he supported President Wilson's dream, and all through his life he was an advocate of the League of Nations. Under the Republican leadership there was no chance to make good on his wish, so the job in Hungary offered Smith the opportunity to become an earnest participant in that organization. Although he considered himself "neither a pacifist nor an internationalist," he admitted being "a strong believer in what the League of Nations is trying to do."[433] His affirmative answer lifted a heavy burden off the League officials' shoulders and they were delighted to announce that "the League of Nations has appointed Mr. J. Smith of Boston U.S.A. as Commissioner General under the League scheme for the Financial reconstruction of Hungary."[434] In addition, the Reparations Commission named a Committee of Control, which could not interfere with or block action, and was to communicate only with the Commissioner-General and not with

429 Hevesy to Daruváry, April 5, 1924, 209/123, 10–1390/1399, K 69, Economic Policy Department, HNA.
430 Norman to Blackett, May 21, 1924, G3/180, BoE.
431 E. Rosenberg, e-mail message to author, January 6, 2009.
432 For Smith's thoughts about the League of Nations, see Jeremiah Smith, *The Preservation of the Peace* (Cambridge, MA: Harvard Law School, 1927).
433 Ibid., 1, 11.
434 Official League communiqué, April 8, 1924, 1924-1929, P.III. Press communiqués, C. 117, Financial Reconstruction of Hungary, LNA.

the Hungarian Government.[435] To represent the interests of the bondholders, three Trustees were appointed by the Council of the League.[436] With these three elements, total control over the loan was assured.

Three days after Smith's nomination, Salter undertook the job of clearing the air with Bethlen. This was needed because in the preceding few weeks so many names and so much misunderstanding had accrued around the appointment. It was essential that the Hungarian government, which had been so keen on securing either Harding or Delano but not Smith, should understand that they were not cheated or left out in the cold, and that all steps that had been taken, even if contradictory at times, with a view to achieving the best possible outcome for Hungary and the long-term loan. Salter's long letter gave a step-by-step description of the events leading to the nomination of Smith.[437] The Hungarians had no real r grounds for complaint, and in the event Smith's nomination was "greeted by commercial, financial and political circles with the greatest satisfaction."[438] What mattered most to the Hungarians was the candidate's ability to create as much confidence in the Hungarian loan as possible, which was clearly aided by the appointment of an American, and with the reassurance of Lamont and other prominent financial figures this seemed easy to achieve. As Prime Minister Bethlen declared, there were three reasons to celebrate the nomination:

> Only an American could exert influence of quite the same independent and authoritative quality and could secure us against any external attempts which might be made to gain undue influence in Hungarian affairs [...] without American co-operation and active assistance, Europe can hardly hope to put itself on a stable basis [...] now we can hope that the confidence created by the appointment of Mr. Smith will attract to Hungary the private capital from America and elsewhere we need so much for our complete recovery.[439]

Bethlen concisely summarized what Hungary really expected from the League endeavor with an American as Commissioner-General: political protection against mainly the Little Entente, and a flood of American capital. He saw in the future

435 League of Nations, *The Financial Reconstruction of Hungary*, 86–87. The Reparation Commission appointed the members on September 4, 1924. These were representatives of Great Britain, Czechoslovakia, France, Italy, Romania, and the Kingdom of Serbs, Croats and Slovenes. Ibid., 220.

436 Giuseppe Bianchini of Italy, Henry Strakosch of South Africa, and E. C. ter Meulen of Holland were appointed as Trustees on September 13, 1924. Ibid., 220.

437 Salter to Bethlen, April 11, 1924, Doc. No. 33315, Registry Files, R. 298, LNA.

438 *The New York Times*, April 10, 1924.

439 *Christian Science Monitor*, April 10, 1924.

ensured in these two elements, at least in the short run. Naturally, reparations were still to be paid, but if the country regained its financial and economic stability, its financial and later economic health, then a realistic revision of the Trianon Treaty might be on the agenda. Consequently, the Hungarian political leadership was left satisfied for the time being.

In order to give Smith a more sizeable credibility, Boyden wrote a letter in which he praised Smith, his friend, and congratulated both the League and Hungary on securing him as the Commissioner, and Széchenyi, the Hungarian minister to Washington, had it published on both sides of the Atlantic.[440] Smith called on Széchenyi in Washington to gather some preliminary information about the country he had never visited. He made a very good impression on the Hungarian diplomat, who expressed his confidence "that Mr. Smith with his ability and charming personality will very soon gain an understanding of the Hungarian people and obtain the complete confidence and cooperation so necessary to a successful conclusion of his task."[441] Indeed, this was a crucial part of Smith's pending job. He would arrive as a total stranger in a country with strange customs and with different concepts about the world. He knew that the country would count on him as the link to both the League, the organization that had taken up the Hungarian cause, and the United States, the country from which Hungary expected about one third of the loan.

The American's position was also delicate from the Hungarian domestic political point of view. Throughout the general debate of the reconstruction package in the Hungarian National Assembly, the very fact that Hungary would be subject to the strict control of a foreigner engendered strong feelings. Bethlen tried to play down this point when he introduced the bill by saying that it was a great achievement that the control had passed from the Reparations Commission to the League of Nations, and would be practiced through a neutral person.[442] This was not enough to calm the opposition. A major charge against the Commissioner-General was that he was entitled to interfere with the financial and economic questions of Hungary. Many speakers raised the issue that in their opinion the League Commissioner would enjoy too wide a range of powers. Count Gyula Andrássy, a renowned member of the body, said concerning the control, "The largest control, the financial dictatorship, is in the authority of the Commissioner-General [...] a step toward dependency."[443] Another member of the opposition claimed,

440 Boyden to Széchenyi, April 9, 1924, and Széchenyi to Boyden, April 12, 1924, 264/113, 50052–50263/929, 931, K 69, Economic Policy Department, HNA.
441 Széchenyi to Boyden, April 12, 1924, 264/113, 50052–50263/929, 931, Ibid.
442 National Assembly Diary (Budapest: Athenaeum nyomda, 1926), 22:280.
443 Ibid., 334.

falsely, that in the Austrian bill there were only six lines about the powers of the Commissioner whereas in the case of Hungary three columns were needed, and, as he concluded, "here the Commissioner-General is given the right to do everything."[444] János Zsirkay did not mince his words: "If this bill is passed, it will be the last nail in the coffin for the independent, free Hungary."[445] Only a few years after Trianon, the heightened emotions about the independence of the country were understandable. A further problem was that the termination of the control was left somewhat vague, and there was no clear-cut end to the pending control.

Naturally, there were voices in favor of the in-coming Commissioner, too. Endre Zsilinszky said that the three layers of control was far too complicated, but "I admit that of the three types of control I take that of the Commissioner-General as the most sympathetic, so to say, because it is for only two and a half years for the time being."[446] The Finance Minister played on the general positive sentiment held for Americans:

> We can even have more faith in the fact that the Commissioner sent here by the League of Nations will be an American. I think this was a very fortunate choice, because nobody believes about an American that he can be influenced by political lobby or in the interests of other countries. The son of an independent, great nation, that of North America, will come here, which provides all the guarantee that he will be independent. And the main guarantee that the control will be for our benefit: our interests are the same [...] An advantage of this control is that the Commissioner will live among us and so, if needed, he can be our advocate and protector, and his words will always be heeded at the League of Nations.[447]

Bethlen also emphasized that precisely due to the fact that Smith was American, no interference with Hungarian domestic policy would take place. He tried to shoot down the points raised by the opposition one by one and, in the end, the bills passed easily thanks to the majority of Bethlen's party.

It is true that Smith, as Commissioner-General of Hungary for the League of Nations, was indeed provided with wide ranging powers. These were spelled out in detail in Article VI. of Protocol No. II. It is indicative of the importance of the post that this article was the longest in the two Protocols. The main points were as follows: supervising the whole reconstruction program; all information

444 Ibid., 377–79.
445 National Assembly Diary, 23:76.
446 Ibid., 395.
447 Ibid., 424.

requested by him to be provided by the Hungarian government; he could, in case of the program being in danger, require the Hungarian Government to increase money from taxation; only with his consent was the government allowed to take up new loans; he would reside in Budapest and would provide the Council with monthly reports on the reconstruction program; and, most importantly from the government's point of view, he would remain in Hungary until the League Council decided that Hungary's financial stability was assured.[448] In addition, he was to have total authority over the special account into which the yield of the securities was paid, and over any amount payable on annuity of the loan.[449] In light of the tight supervision that Smith could exercise in Hungary, it was evident that Hungarians were somewhat afraid lest they should get a dictator, similar to what the Austrian people experienced in the appointment of Zimmerman; on the other hand, Smith's nationality provided a basis for hope. The Hungarian public was awaiting the coming of the Commission-General between these two modes of anticipation.

Jeremiah Smith, Jr. arrived in Hungary on May 1, 1924. His deputy was another American, Royall Tyler, whose presence on the staff was desired early on because he "would be invaluable."[450] There were ample reasons for Tyler to be included. He had served on the American delegation during the Paris Peace Conference and later on the Reparation Commission. Besides his qualifications and American nationality, he also spoke the major European languages, German included, and was needed to help Smith in daily conferences. He had already been to both Vienna and Budapest. Although he was not enthusiastic about leaving Paris, he felt "I must take it."[451] Tyler immediately took a liking to Smith. He found his compatriot "exceedingly attractive," and "liked him from the first moment."[452] Smith was also assisted by the British Harry Siepmann, the Frenchman René Charron, and a Belgian called Livio Licen.[453] The newly appointed controller wanted to be clear at the outset about what his post required and what he considered his duty; he did not want to leave any room for misunderstanding. His press release the very next day was unambiguous:

448 League of Nations, *The Financial Reconstruction of Hungary*, 84–86. The whole article can be read in Appendix 4.
449 Ibid., 84, 89–90.
450 Lord Cecil to House, February 11, 1924, C2521/37/21, 9905, FO371, TNA.
451 Tyler to Mildred Bliss, April 9, 1924, Box 2, Papers of Royall Tyler (1902–1967), Harvard University Archives, Cambridge, Massachusetts (hereafter cited as Tyler Papers).
452 Tyler to Mildred Bliss, April 26, 1924, Ibid.
453 This latter person was also well-known by the Hungarian government. He worked for the Reparation Commission and watched over the advance of reparations in kind to Greece, Italy, and Yugoslavia in 1923 and 1924. 161/17, 84564/1278–1303. K 69, Economic Policy Department, HNA.

> I wish to say first that I consider it a great honour to be asked to assist the Hungarian Government and people in carrying out this plan [...] I have one personal statement to make. My duties are financial, not political, and to them I shall devote all my energy, hoping to assist a people for which my country has always had a great admiration, to establish the conditions which are so necessary for their comfort and happiness.[454]

With this note he wanted to strike both a cordial tone and issue a warning to those who would expect him to fight for the country's political causes. He met not only with the press but with all the political parties as well. The newspapers unanimously greeted the arrival of the American. *Pesti Hírlap* called Smith, hyperbolically, "the most prestigious financial man of the United States."[455] Regardless of its truth value, this sentence described the reigning mood of optimism that greeted Smith's arrival in Hungary. Another newspaper saw the fact that Hungary's Commissioner was an American as invoking enormous publicity, in the wake of which American tourists would appear, and Smith's work was thought to be seen as a national cause in the United States.[456] Whatever the future held, the mood in Hungary had become calmer with Smith's arrival.[457] Brentano reported that Smith had seemingly won "the general admiration of the Hungarian Government and people, due especially to his assiduity, modesty and courtesy."[458] Everything was set for work to begin on the loan, except for one thing.

A serious problem was that Hungary needed all the involved countries to waive their priority of relief bonds in favor of the reconstruction. Somewhat interestingly, the United States proved to be one of the most difficult partners in this question. Hungary asked the US government to give priority to the loan over charges of the relief bonds, and also of reparations from other countries.[459] It was willing only to do so if all the other countries concerned did the same, a line of policy mirroring the British one.[460] After the signing of the Protocols, the Dutch, Danish, Swiss, and British Governments agreed to give the reconstruction loan priority, but the United States, Norway, France, and Sweden remained to waive

454 Smith's press release in Budapest, May 2, 1924, P.III. Press communiqués, C. 117, Financial Reconstruction of Hungary, LNA.

455 *Pesti Hírlap*, May 6, 1924, XLVI/84.

456 *Pesti Napló*, May 6, 1924, 75/84.

457 Balfour to MacDonald, May 16, 1924, DBFP, First Series, 26:201.

458 Brentano to Hughes, June 11, 1924, 864.00/583, Roll 6, M. 708, NARA.

459 Daruváry to Brentano, February 4, 1924, Release of charges from Hungarian Relief Bonds. Doc. No. 35072, Registry Files, R. 299, LNA.

460 Niemeyer to FO, January 26, 1924, C1480/37/21, 9904, FO371, TNA; Hughes to Pelényi, February 16, 1924, FRUS: 1924 (Washington, DC: Government Printing Office, 1939), 2:325–27.

their right over the Relief Bonds.[461] So, Hungary asked the US government again to waive priority over the relief bonds for the sake of an international loan and a debt settlement along the lines of the Finnish agreement.[462] The latter point was obviously important for America, if not for the value, but for the principle and precedent it was to strengthen. On April 25, 1924, the debt funding agreement was signed, and now the United States was willing to suspend priority charges over relief bonds for the sake of a loan for Hungary, still provided that all other countries in the same position did so too. The House of Representatives passed the agreement on May 12, with the Senate following on May 17, 1924.[463] After some final niggling on the part of the United States the US Treasury, on May 29, 1924, officially declared that the United States had waived its priority of liens for the sake of the reconstruction loan, a fact of which Jeremiah Smith, Jr. was notified immediately.[464] By the end of May, then, all countries had waived their priority on behalf of the reconstruction loan.[465] With the protocols signed, the countries waiving their priorities for a loan, and the Commissioner-General staying in the country, the most arduous phase of the scheme was set to begin: to raise the loan for the Hungarian reconstruction scheme .

461 Hungarian Foreign Ministry to Széchenyi, March 16, 1924, Release of charges from Hungarian Relief Bonds. Doc. No. 35072, Registry Files, R. 299, LNA; Hohler to MacDonald, March 21, 1924, C4883/37/21, 9907, FO371, TNA.

462 Széchenyi to Hughes, March 27, 1924, FRUS: 1924, 2:327–28.

463 Congressional Record, 68th Congress, 1st Session, 7149, 7204, April 25, 1924; 8391–96, May 12, 1924; and 8775–76, 8800, May 17, 1924.

464 The US government wanted to see all the original and certified copies of the other countries before it consented. Logan to Bordes, May 14, 1924, and Salter to Logan, May 20, 1924. Release of charges from Hungarian Relief Bonds. Doc. No. 35072, Registry Files, R. 299, LNA; Felkin to Tyler, May 22, 1924, and Felkin to Smith, May 31, 1924, T.II, Incoming Telegrams, May-June, 1924, C. 120, Financial Reconstruction of Hungary, LNA; Hughes to Logan, May 29, 1924, FRUS: 1924, 2:331–332.

465 The chronological order was the following: Great Britain: January 31, 1924, Holland: February 16, 1924, Denmark: February 23, 1924, Sweden: March 27, 1924, Norway: April 25, 1924, France: May 15, 1924, and the United States: May 29, 1924. Note on the Postponement of the Charge in Favour of Relief Bonds by Felkin, May, 1294, Release of charges from Hungarian Relief Bonds. Doc. No. 35072, Registry Files, R. 299, LNA.

Chapter 6

Raising the Hungarian Loan

6.1. The Unsuccessful Attempts

With finding a suitable person for the job of Commissioner-General, the Hungarian reconstruction needed one final piece before the actual work could begin. This was the most important one to which all the problematic preliminary events were a necessary prelude. In order to launch the financial rehabilitation of the country, it was essential to secure the money for it. After all, the Protocols and the Commissioner were just stops along the way to the main task: to raise the long-term loan for Hungary on the international money market. Since most of the scheme to raise a loan for Hungary was similar to the Austrian case, the main participants expected that it would be no extraordinary task to find the money. As it will be seen, they were wrong, and just as in the case of the reparations, raising the liens, signing the Protocols, and picking the Commissioner, raising the international loan for the financial reconstruction for Hungary also proved immensely difficult.

Hungary had already tried to secure a loan in the early 1920s, but all of these efforts failed. Now with the backing of the League of Nations and the successful launch of the Austrian reconstruction, the prospects were much better. Two things were given from the start. Great Britain was the most important possible lender on the continent. Without British help it was no possible to raise enough money. Politically they were the most influential European country, in and out of the League, and the Bank of England was the financial center of the continent. The other crucial thing was to somehow make sure that the United States would participate. Just as in the case of Austria, both Hungary and the League of Nations hoped that American banking houses, most notably J. P. Morgan & Co., would take part in a loan to Hungary. Although, contrary to the Austrian case, the Hungarian loan was not guaranteed by other countries, the sheer eminence of the scheme and Hungary's better situation than Austria was thought sufficient to attract British, American, and other financial circles. The reports concerning the possibility of an American loan, however, were sobering. Confidential news gained from the Morgan house made it clear that at present there was no chance for Hungary to secure a loan overseas.[466]

466 Steiger to Kállay, January 15, 1923, and Széchenyi to Daruváry, February 4, 1923, 9/VIII/5/3–5, K 275, Kállay Papers, HNA. The prospects were equally dim in London. Smith to Hajdu, March 28, 1923, and Schober to Kállay, April 4, 1923, 9/VIII/5/12–13, Ibid.

When Count Albert Apponyi, the most well-known and respected Hungarian politician gave a series of lectures in the United States in the fall of 1923, one of his chief tasks was to turn the attention of the United States toward Hungary in the hope of a future loan.[467] As a prelude for his stay, he was given a dinner where all the leading bankers of New York were present. Thomas Lamont sat at the same table as Apponyi and said to him the following in connection with a possible loan to Hungary:

> There is something in it what you say about the peace treaties. But try to put on my shoe, as a banker, when it comes to loans. Well now, for example, if a poor widow from Nebraska comes to me with trust and asks me whether she should invest her little saving into Hungarian bonds, what should I tell her? As a conscientious man, can I advise her to buy the bonds of a country that, according to its own admission, is dissatisfied with its international standing and would like to change it? Answer me sincerely as an honest man: what advice can I give to this old lady?[468]

Apponyi's answer was this: "Mr. Lamont, you could very well advise that widow to buy Hungarian bonds and I will tell you why... Since we act openly and we do not want to make anybody believe something that does not and can not exist, we deserve to be treated as honest people and turned to with trust."[469] Obviously, this reasoning was not too persuasive and the prospects for a substantial American loan were more in the realm of wishful thinking than realistic expectations. J. P. Morgan & Co. was very cautious in committing itself to a tiny and insignificant country in deep Central Europe. They well represented the American investment houses whose overall sentiment was that if loans should be placed in any country that was first and foremost Germany. To make things more difficult, Oszkár Jászi, former member of the Károlyi government, led a campaign against the Hungarian government and its attempts to raise a loan in the United States.[470] Arthur Salter received the same information that at present no issue was possible in America.[471] Goode informed Bethlen that on account of

467 In more detail about Apponyi's tour, see Count Albert Apponyi, *The Memoirs of Count Apponyi* (London; William Heinemann Ltd., 1935), 195–214; and Tamás Magyarics, "Count Teleky's and Count Albert Apponyi's Missions in the USA in the First Half of the 1920s," (In: *Americana and Hungarica*, ed. Charlotte Kretzoi. Budapest: 1989), 69–77.

468 Apponyi, *Memoirs*, 203–04.

469 Ibid., 204.

470 In more detail about the Apponyi-Jászi feud in the American press in the fall of 1923, see Tibor Glant, "Apponyi Albert és Jászi Oszkár amerikai vitája a népszövetségi kölcsönről 1923 őszén," [The American Debate of Albert Apponyi and Oszkár Jászi over the League Loan in the Fall of 1923] *Vasváry Collection Newsletter* 17, no. 1 (1997): 3-5.

471 Bartlew to Salter, December 4, 1923, Publicity in connection with the Hungarian Loan. Doc. No. 32508, Registry Files, R. 297, LNA.

the presidential election at the moment not much could be expected, but added that unless Norman declined to support the plan, the present tendency would change.[472] Indeed, the Governor's "yes" or "no" could mean all the difference.

Everybody knew that the most important figure in the whole loan business would be Montagu Norman. He was, almost single-handedly, the key to the success of the Austrian loan and the Hungarian case was to be no different. When the Hungarians asked Seipel's advice in the question, he without hesitation put Norman on top of the list to whom Hungary should turn. He added that if Hungary sought Norman's help, it should turn to no other, because the Bank of England Governor would not like it.[473] Norman had his own design in Central Europe. As was mentioned, his political views agreed with that of the Foreign Office, and he also thought of the region surrounding Hungary as one unit. In his often quoted letter to Strong in April 1923, shortly before the international loan for Austria was launched, he spelled out his vision:

> If we can thus set up Austria, we must tackle Hungary next, so as to establish one by one the new parts of Old Austria. & then perhaps the Balkan Countries. Only by thus making the various parts economically sound & independent shall we reach what I believe to be the ultimate solution for Eastern Europe viz an Economic federation to include half a dozen countries on or near the Danube free of customs barriers &c.[474]

This passage is good evidence that Norman was dedicated to the Hungarian reconstruction early on. It was, however, not because he was so sympathetic to the Bethlen government or felt some missionary zeal to do justice to Hungary after the Treaty of Trianon. His considerations rested on his conviction alone that only a unified part of the Central and Southeastern region of Europe would serve both British interests and those of the Bank of England. In contrast to Strong's country-by-country effort, Norman did not really believe in this method but preferred regional thinking. As he wrote to Strong, otherwise these undertakings were "non-rationalistic & almost altruistic ventures."[475] Only a comprehensive plan relating to the whole region was promising. But Norman also had to realize that only the Strong method was achievable at the moment.

---

472 Goode to Bethlen, January 4, 1924, 264/113. 50052–50263/1076, K 69, Economic Policy Department, HNA.

473 List without date. 9/VIII/1, "To Whom Can Hungary Turn in a Loan?" K 275, Kállay Papers, HNA.

474 Norman to Strong, April 9, 1923, G35/4, BoE. Also quoted in Clay, *Lord Norman*. 189–190; Péteri, Global Monetary Regime, 51; Péteri, Revolutionary Twenties, 168; Lojkó, *Meddling in Middle Europe*, 71.

475 Norman to Strong, October 8, 1923, G35/4, BoE.

After the initial support to the Hungarian scheme notwithstanding, by early January Norman had changed his mind. He made clear that unless reparation charges were eliminated from the plan as payable from the reconstruction loan, the Bank of England would have no hand in it.[476] Norman also reiterated this to Salter, who was "surprised, indeed aghast" at such view that was "considered unalterable" at the moment.[477] This was a huge blow for the League. Now that they thought they were on the brink of settling the few remaining points with the French and the Little Entente, their very backbone to the scheme had turned his back on them. Strakosch also came to plead with Norman "for support and assistance in raising loan for Hungary," but the Governor was adamant and remained opposed.[478] The very same day Bethlen and Kállay called on Norman to learn the prospects of a loan to Hungary. Norman explained that under the present scheme no loan was possible due to the reparation payments, the exclusion of which was a question of principle for both London and New York.[479] He added that the question was even more important than in the case of Austria because the Hungarian loan would not be guaranteed by other countries. The loan would be launched in his fashion or it would not be issued at all.

To secure his participation, the highest political circles in Britain started to try to persuade him that it was essential that the League scheme go ahead according to the plans. Norman was offered that the British government would distinctly say that it desired to see the Hungarian reconstruction plan go through if the Governor wanted so.[480] Norman was well aware of the situation. He knew that British diplomacy had invested so much energy and prestige into this second League undertaking that it was basically a moral obligation to carry it to fulfillment. Indeed, the Foreign Office asked the Treasury "to exert influence on the City bankers in order to meet the expectations and London should be able to raise enough money, almost as a responsibility, having shown interest before and pressured the Little Entente to accept it."[481] Almost ridiculous as it was, it all came down to the all-powerful Governor's nod for the loan to be issued. Norman wanted the loan seen raised, but maybe due to his ego or unwillingness to move without political backing, he expected some incentive to set him in motion. Finally, with Chancellor of the Exchequer Philip Snowden's letter requesting him to help the Hungarian scheme, the awaited communication from the proper place had arrived.[482] Parallel to this political game, the reconstruction plan advanced along

476 January 9, 1924, Extract from Minutes of the Committee of the Treasury, G14/108, BoE; Norman to Niemeyer, January 10, 1924, G3/180, BoE.
477 Norman's Diary Entries, January 11, 1924, ADM34/13, BoE.
478 Norman's Diary Entries, January 23, 1924, ADM34/13, BoE.
479 Memorandum, January 23, 1924, G14/108, BoE.
480 Niemeyer to Norman, April 26, 1924, OV33/71, BoE.
481 FO to Treasury, May 5, 1924, DBFP, First Series, 26:198.
482 Snowden to Norman, May 7, 1924, G14/108, BoE.

the lines of Norman's thinking. As a believer of central bank cooperation, it was also important for Norman that the subscription of the shares of the new Hungarian National Bank took place between April 28 and May 7, with a capital of 30 million gold crowns ($6.08 million), of which the state had to subscribe 11.85 million ($2.4 million), a result more favorable than in the case of the new Austrian Bank of Issue.[483] On the closing day of the subscription, the all-important message arrived to the Commissioner: "Ground prepared. Suggest you advise Government send Loan Delegation immediately."[484] With definite political support in the domestic field and promising events in Hungary, Norman set out to arrange the loan.

In the international banking world Norman's word counted as no one else's. When he pushed for some results, those would soon come. Now in total control of the situation, the Bank of England Governor began what he was best at. Although he still had some reservations about the plan as it stood, he had promised to support it wholeheartedly.[485] In the course of the next five weeks, he basically requested every central banker that mattered to help and join the proposed loan for Hungary.[486] He directed the Hungarian loan delegation to visit the Rothschilds in London, from whom a large part was hoped.[487] As the Governor informed Rothschild, League representatives had already contacted the Morgan house.[488] Obviously, the possible participation of J. P. Morgan & Co. had a very positive effect on any loan. It was crucial that the American market take up as big a share as possible, since there was little free money on the continent and every penny counted. Also, both financially and politically, the presence of American banking houses in the Hungarian reconstruction would boost its chances for success. When anyone spoke of Americans, it was J. P. Morgan & Co. that was really meant. The most influential banking house had been busy investing money in many loans, one of which was the Austrian reconstruction loan. Now the League of Nations hoped that a very similar scenario would be repeated and a part of the loan would be subscribed in the United States. There were rumors already in March that Morgan would take over $20 million with 7.5% interests.[489]

483 Annual Report on Hungary, Barclay to Chamberlain, March 25, 1925, C4508/4508/21, 10778, FO371, TNA.
484 Strakosch to Smith, May 7, 1924, T.II, Incoming Telegrams, May–June, 1924, C. 120, Financial Reconstruction of Hungary, LNA. Also quoted in Péteri, *Global Monetary Regime*, 85.
485 Norman to Vissering, May 12, 1924, G3/180, BoE.
486 Norman to Leese, May 15, 1924; Norman to Robineau, May 19, 1924; Norman to Moll, June 5, 1924; and Norman to Vissering, June 12, 1924, Ibid.
487 Norman's Diary Entries, May 12, 1924, ADM34/13, BoE. The Hungarian delegation consisted of two members, János Teleszky, a former Hungarian Finance Minister, and Peter Bark, the last Finance Minister of imperial Russia, also a confidant of Norman.
488 Norman to Niemeyer, May 8, 1924, Miscellaneous correspondence. Doc. No. 35939, Registry Files, R. 413, LNA.
489 *Budapesti Hírlap*, March 18, 1924, XLIV/65.

Two months later when things started to heat up, the League tried to use every tool possible to convince the mammoth American house to come in. Niemeyer asked Smith to write to Morgan, where his advice was supposed to matter, and urge them to give "support."[490] Accordingly, Smith, whom many saw as the link to a successful American participation in the Hungarian reconstruction, cabled Lamont and provided him with his favorable impressions of the Hungarian situation.[491] In the meantime, J. P. Morgan & Co. had already told the loan delegation that they would in no case take over more than London, which was no more than £3 million ($13,000,000).[492] One reason was that the Austrian loan stood at a lower price than in London. J. P. Morgan & Co. simply played careful and finally they decided that they would not come in.

On May 21 everything still looked rosy. Strakosch optimistically informed Smith that Hungary should not prepare to issue a short-term domestic loan, because "the negotiations for the long-term loan" seemed to be "completed within a reasonable period."[493] It was a sobering experience for everyone when two days later he had to cable that J. P. Morgan & Co. had changed their mind and was definitely out.[494] Lamont had informed Britain and Smith a day earlier. He said the Dutch and Czechoslovak issues had been poor and the American public was not ready for a new bond issue, an argument Niemeyer found "part of the usual American poltroonery when asked to take concrete action."[495] An ideologically driven Hungarian historian attributed Morgan's staying away to the Hungarian-Americans opposition to Horthy![496] To be sure, J. P. Morgan & Co. was already busy laying the groundwork for the big prize, the German loan in the upcoming fall.[497] Smith was understandably disappointed. He knew that the public in Hungary looked at him as somewhat of a Messiah, who would roll out the red carpet for American money. Despite this fiasco, he faced the future with optimism and had "no regrets at having undertaken this work."[498]

---

490 Niemeyer to Smith, May 15, 1924, T.II, Incoming Telegrams, May–June, 1924, C. 120, Financial Reconstruction of Hungary, LNA.

491 Smith to Strakosch, May 17, 1924, C.III (4) Correspondence - Sir Henry Strakosch, C. 111, Financial Reconstruction of Hungary, LNA.

492 Szapáry to Daruváry, May 15, 1924, 209/123, 10–1390/1323, Economic Policy Department, K 69, HNA; Norman's Diary Entries, May 20, 1924, ADM34/13, BoE.

493 Strakosch to Smith, May 21, 1924, C.III (4) Correspondence - Sir Henry Strakosch, C. 111, Financial Reconstruction of Hungary, LNA.

494 Strakosch to Smith, May 23, 1924, OV9/434, BoE.

495 Lamont to Smith, May 22, 1924, C9203/37/21, 9908, FO371, TNA; Niemeyer's memo on Hungary in Treasury to FO, June 5, 1924, DBFP, First Series, 26:226.

496 Magos, *Az amerikai imperialisták*, 59.

497 Frank Costigliola, "The United States and the Reconstruction of Germany in the 1920s," *The Business History Review* 50 (Winter 1976): 490–92.

498 Smith to Salter, May 24, 1924, OV9/434, BoE.

6.2. Flotation of the Reconstruction Loan

The main figures tried to overcome this latest blow quickly. Since the flotation of the Hungarian loan was the main ingredient of the financial plan and without it there was no chance of reconstruction, it was essential for both the League of Nations and Hungary that in the shortest time possible another American banking house come in the place of J. P. Morgan & Co., even if no other company could compete with Morgan in terms of prestige and influence. The time factor was as critical as ever, therefore a limited set of possibilities was the most that was to be hoped for. There were a few American names out there, but the most likely candidate after J. P. Morgan & Co.'s retreat was Speyer & Co.

The Speyer family was an old Jewish banker family of German origins, but Gustavus Speyer moved to the United States and Speyer & Co. was founded in Manhattan in 1837. After being educated in Frankfort, Germany, and a tour of apprenticeship in the London and Paris Speyer banks, the 24 year-old James Speyer joined the company in New York City in 1885 and later became its head. He was trying to be very active mainly in the foreign loan business and railroads, first of all in Latin America, and, for example, he was the first to float a Cuban loan. Parallel, Speyer was also an active philanthropist. He was closely associated with the founding of the University Settlement Society, the Provident Loan Society, the Economic Club of New York, the Speyer School at Columbia University, the Ellin Prince Speyer Hospital for Animals, the United Hospital Fund, the salvation Army and the New York World's Fair Finance Committee, and he was the initiator and founder of the Museum of the City of New York.[499] James Speyer believed in the cooperation of the United States and Europe. Naturally, he meant financial and economic collaboration along well established private lines. As he saw, "the granting of credit by our banks and bankers, and the purchase of foreign securities by investors [was] a practical business... It would add to our contribution towards European recovery."[500] Whistling a similar tune to that of the State Department's Note, he warned that this was only possible in case of well-examined securities, balanced budgets, increased taxes, and avoidance of large standing armies.[501] Not surprisingly, Speyer & Co. had signaled more than once that they wanted to come in for the Hungarian loan.[502] According to an American businessman, Speyer & Co. was "anxious to occupy the place in any Hungarian

499 The data are from *Biographical Note*, James Speyer Papers, Rare Books and Manuscript Division, The New York Public Library, (hereafter cited as Speyer Papers).

500 James Speyer, "America's Cooperation in European Rehabilitation Primarily Dependent on Europe," *Annals of the American Academy of Political and Social Science* 102 (July 1922): 176–77.

501 Ibid., 177.

502 Norman to Strong, April 9, 1923, G35/4, BoE.

loan that J. P. Morgan & Co. hold in the Austrian loan, and are preparing, they tell us, to underwrite $25/30,000,000 of such Hungarian loan."[503] There was one problem with Speyer & Co. though. The company did not enjoy popularity and was disliked by other banking houses and investment bankers, above all by John Pierpont Morgan.

The overall antipathy toward James Speyer originated from J. P. Morgan's dislike for his business rival. It was one thing that Speyer was of German origin, a nation Morgan came to dislike very much on account of World War I. The War was quite damaging for the Speyer house on account of their close relations to Germany. The English branch suffered most, which was closed down and Edgar Speyer, James Speyer's brother and the head of that branch, was deprived of his nobility.[504] To make things worse, James Speyer, despite having been born in Manhattan, had a heavy German accent.[505] Aside from the fact that the aristocratic Morgan was, in his own words, "not very enthusiastic about Jews" and did not want to see business in their hands, business incidents had burdened their relation.[506] The anti-Semitic trait ran in the family. The senior J. P. Morgan, according to one of his first biographers, "had a deep-seated anti-Semitic prejudice and on more than one occasion needlessly antagonized great Jewish banking firms."[507] The older Morgan also referred to Jacob H. Schiff, also a German-born Jew, head of archrival Kuehn, Loeb & Co., simply as "that foreigner," and declared already in the nineteenth century that he did not wish to see "business largely in the hands of Speyer & Co. & similar houses."[508] Already before World War I, J. P. Morgan & Co. tried to outmaneuver Speyer and was not shy to use its status. James Speyer often filed complaints to the State Department about governmental favoritism toward the Morgan house and its close collaborating banking houses, obviously to no avail.[509] During the Mexican debt settlement, for instance, J. P. Morgan & Co. made sure that Speyer & Co. did not have a seat on the ICBM, presumably

---

503 Caldwell to Beneš, August 10, 1923, in Wheeler to Hughes, August 22, 1923, 864.00/547, Roll 6, M. 708, NARA.

504 See H. W. Brown and Gordon Leith's letter written to the English press on January 6, 1922, Box 1, Speyer Papers.

505 *Time*, June 13, 1938.

506 Quoted in E. Lamont, *The Ambassador from Wall Street*, 210-211. Also, there was the factor of envy and rivalry. At the turn of the century, James Speyer was the second richest New York banker after J.P. Morgan. Steven C. Topik, "When Mexico Had the Blues: A Transatlantic Tale of Bonds, Bankers, and Nationalists, 1862–1910," *The American Historical Review* 105 (June 2000): 734.

507 John Kennedy, Winkler, *Morgan, the Magnificent: The Life of J. Pierpont Morgan* (Vanguard Press, New York, 1930), 10.

508 Chernow, *The House of Morgan*, 90.

509 Rosenberg, *Financial Missionaries*, 65, 94.

because of Speyer's business tactics in Mexico.[510] J. P. Morgan's anti-Semitism was quite active sometimes. Naturally, the younger Morgan followed his father both in his business practices and anti-Semitic worldview. In 1920, when a vacancy occurred on the board of Harvard, he warned of what he saw as a great danger of nominating a Jew for the post. As he put it, "the Jew is always a Jew first and an American second."[511] With Morgan's prestige and connections it was not surprising that other firms were not enthusiastic about Speyer either.

In Great Britain, the anti-Semitic sentiment was strong as well. Although constitutionally it was solved in the second half of the 19th century, it did not disappear.[512] For example, Montagu Norman, the powerful Governor of the Bank of England, according to Émile Moreau, his French counterpart, seemed "full of contempt for the Jews about whom he spoke in very bad terms," and described Speyer & Co. as "Jews, with great ambitions."[513] The main London house, Rothschild, would have been willing to work in cooperation with Hallgarten, Dillon, or Chase National, for example, but not with Speyer & Co.[514] In light of the fact that the Rothschild family was of the same German Jewish origins as Speyer and was conspicuous in fighting for equal rights for Jews in Great Britain in the 19th century and elsewhere in the 20th century, one arrives at the conclusion that religious and racial ties were secondary to those of connections of wealth, once the opposition to one's race was overcome.[515] Smith, in all likelihood to his ties to the House of Morgan, also thought that the Speyer house, though not insignificant, was speculative and its participation was to be avoided.[516] It is important to emphasize, therefore, that the anti-Semitic feeling of the era was not

510 Stephen N. Kane, "Bankers and Diplomats: The Diplomacy of the Dollar in Mexico, 1921-1924," *The Business History Review* 47 (Autumn 1973): 343; Also, E. Lamont, *The Ambassador from Wall Street*, 210–11. The bitter rivalry led to the exclusion of Speyer & Co. from the American part of the Dawes loan. Ibid. Also, Chernow, *The House of Morgan*, 74.

511 Chernow, *The House of Morgan*, 214–15; J. P. Morgan, Sr. to J. S. Morgan & Co., February 1, 1895, quoted in Chernow, *The House of Morgan*, 74. Morgan partners referred to Speyer as "Jimmie." While as a historian believed it was a belittling term, in reality James Speyer went by this name in a wide circle of friendly people as well, which suggests that it was not used as derogatory by the Morgan partners. Costigliola, *Awkward Dominion*, 124.

512 In more detail about the subject see, Colin Holmes, *Anti-Semitism in British Society, 1876-1939* (London: Edward Arnold, Ltd., 1979) and Gisela C. Lebzelter, *Political Anti-Semitism in England, 1918-1939* (Oxford: Macmillan, in association with St. Anthony's College, 1978).

513 Quoted in Ahamed, *Lords of Finance*, 260; Norman to Siepmann, May 15, 1925, OV33/73, BoE.

514 Szapáry to Daruváry, May 28, 1924, 209/123, 10–1390/1282, K 69, Economic Policy Department, HNA.

515 It is also interesting to note here that allegedly, up until the rise of the Rothschilds, at the end of the eighteenth century, the Speyer house was the richest Jewish bank in Frankfurt. Topik, "When Mexico Had the Blues," 734.

516 Korányi to Teleszky, May 17, 1924, 209/123, 10–1390/1339, K 69, Economic Policy Department, HNA.

limited to Hungary. On both sides of the Atlantic, many in the privileged sphere looked down on the Jewish people. This was true for the financial world perhaps even more, because this was a field where Jews thrived and were successful.[517]

In any case, the personal views had to be put on the backburner, because the task at hand proved difficult enough. J. P. Morgan was out by the end of May and for Norman it was crucial that somebody else should fill the vacuum. For the League of Nations its prestige was on the line, while for Hungary it was almost a question of life or death to have an American firm among the lenders. In such a crisis the highest authorities had no one else to turn to than Montagu Norman. Although he was "viciously anti-Semitic," his goal to consolidate Central Europe tied closely to Great Britain and the pound overrode other considerations.[518] The Chancellor of the Exchequer also appealed to the Governor. He cloaked his request "in the interests of European reconstruction," and reasoned in the following language: "The League is so deeply committed to the scheme that I fear its prestige, on which its power for every purpose depends, would be fatally injured by a failure."[519] Norman was without doubt very pleased by this turn of the events. Since he had in the meantime already committed himself to the Hungarian cause in order to achieve his Central European plans, he quickly put aside whatever prejudices he may have had and set out to arrange the loan business that had many other difficulties without taking into consideration racial biases.

Norman immediately set to working out a detour that would insure that adequate money was at hand. Through Smith he asked Sándor Popovics[520], the president of the newly established Hungarian National Bank, to come to London to talk about an advance to bridge the gap in wake of American disinterest.[521] On June 3rd, Norman made with Popovics the draft agreement about a £4-million ($18 million) advance from the Bank of England to the Hungarian National

517 In more detail about anti-Semitism in the United States in the era, see, Leonard Dinnerstein, *Anti-Semitism in America* (Oxford University Press, New York/Oxford, 1994), Leo P. Ribuffo, "Henry Ford and 'The International Jew,'" *American Jewish History* 69 (June 1980): 437–77, Oliver B. Pollak, "Antisemitism, the Harvard Plan, and the Roots of Reverse Discrimination," *Jewish Social Studies* 45 (Spring, 1983): 113–22, and Tamar Buchsbaum, "A Note on Antisemitism in Admissions at Dartmouth," *Jewish Social Studies* 49 (Winter, 1987): 79–84.

518 Chernow, *The House of Morgan*, 245.

519 Snowden to Norman, May 29, 1924, G14/108, BoE. Also quoted in Lojkó, *Meddling in Middle Europe*, 109; Péteri, *Global Monetary Regime*, 84; and Péteri, *Revolutionary Twenties*, 158.

520 Due to his widely known experience, both the League of Nations and Norman wanted Popovics to become the president. Péteri, *Global Monetary Regime*, 89.

521 Strakosch to Smith, May 30, 1924, Box 3. 1924–1930. No. 1. 24. Financial Negotiations, S. 56. M. De Bordes Files, LNA.

Bank.[522] The agreement became official the next day, though not open. Using the uncomfortable situation and the often uneasy experience with the Austrian National Bank, Norman secured special privileges for himself. First of all, the pound became the standard value of the stabilization, a sharp contrast to the Austrian case, where it was the US dollar. Secondly, Norman claimed to have the right to demand a higher Hungarian discount rate if he thought it proper.[523] On June 14, two secret further agreements were concluded between Norman and Popovics, which spelled out the strategy that Norman wanted to see as the basic elements of central bank cooperation.[524] With the signed agreements, the Hungarian National Bank lay at the mercy of the Bank of England Governor, but as soon adviser to the Hungarian National Bank Siepmann realistically phrased: "Still, beggars cannot be choosers; and we [the Bank] simply must have the money. Pride is a sentimental luxury—like hatred of Jews & Czechs and pro-agrarianism—which these people will have to learn that they cannot afford."[525] As for Bethlen, he was booming with joy and gratitude for Norman for the agreement.[526] On the other hand, Siepmann thought the conditions laid down in the agreement "stiff," while Niemeyer called the transaction "a wholly abnormal arrangement."[527] Nevertheless, this step proved to be necessary and the Hungarian loan seemed insured if the remaining four million pounds could be raised on the continent.

The agreement between the two central banks was highly needed, because in the early days of June, in the light of the American retreat, the prospects were not good for a long-term loan for Hungary. The Dutch and Swiss loan issues were languid, the French part looked to be between half a million and 1 million pounds, while Spain was promising little.[528] Signals arrived that no more than

---

522 Norman's Diary Entries, June 3, 1924, ADM 34/13, BoE. The amount of the advance was to enjoy one percent higher interest than the prevailing bank rate, but minimum 5 percent. Lojkó, *Meddling in Middle Europe*, 113.

523 Péteri, *Global Monetary Regime*, 92.

524 Ibid., 94-95; Siepmann to Strakosch, June 4, 1924, 1/1924. May-June, K 304, H. A. Siepmann Papers. HNA.

525 Siepmann to Norman, June 3, 1924, OV33/71, BoE. Also quoted in Péteri, Global Monetary, 117; Péteri, Revolutionary Twenties, 171; and Lojkó, *Meddling in Middle Europe*, 116.

526 Bethlen to Norman, June 13, 1924, OV33/71, BoE.

527 Siepmann to Norman, June 3, 1924, OV33/71, BoE; Treasury to FO, June 5, 1924, DBFP, First Series, 26:225. The £4-million advance was finally made on June 20th, and first it was transferred to an account at the Note Institute then transferred to a blocked account at the National Bank. Norman to Strakosch, June 19, 1924, OV33/72, BoE. The whole advance was paid back by June 11, 1925. Péteri, *Revolutionary Twenties*, 167.

528 Széchenyi to Daruváry, May 17, 1924, 209/123, 10–1390/1204, K 69, Economic Policy Department, HNA; Salter to Strakosch, June 2, 1924, Miscellaneous correspondence. Doc. No. 35939, Registry Files, R. 413, LNA; Treasury to FO, June 5, 1924, DBFP, First Series, 26:225.

a cautious sum of quarter of a million could be expected from Sweden.[529] In addition to these tepid and unpromising countries, Italy meant further trouble. Using the halfhearted interest from other countries, the Italians used the situation as a pretext of offering little money, plus blackmailing the League and Hungary for special bonuses, such as an Italian trustee, an Italian on the Board of the Hungarian National Bank, and an Italian tobacco expert to be nominated.[530] The British considered such blackmail antagonistic and were determined to oppose it, in which they were successful.

By the middle of June in Hungary, an internal loan had been raised to the sum of 26 million gold crowns ($5.2 million).[531] This amount was needed to bridge over the time until the delayed long-term loan on the international money market was realized. But the lack of American participation was still hanging over the whole project. With each passing day it was more important to find someone to fill the gap J. P. Morgan & Co. had left. With pressing time, there was no playing fastidious and the earlier refused possibility of Speyer & Co. came back. In addition, Speyer, together with Chase Securities Company, reiterated their willingness to take part despite the initial refusals.[532] On June 16th, a representative of Speyer, who sought directly the Hungarian delegation, met with Teleszky and Bark in Paris.[533] The amount they would be willing to take up was varying between $4.25 million and $10 million.[534] Despite a renewed interest on the part of J. P. Morgan & Co., when Lamont wrote that they were after all interested in issuing the American tranche of the Hungarian loan, the League did not want to burn its fingers again.[535] Although Speyer's offer was two percent worse than the English one, the Hungarian loan delegation and Strakosch were in favor of accepting it and asked quick consent from Budapest, which duly arrived.[536] Speyer declared the next day that he would take only $5 million instead of $10 due to the very short time available. Norman felt relief even at this reduced sum from Speyer. In many ways he considered the project

529 Felkin to de Bordes, June 5, 1924, Dossier concerning the Swedish tranche. Doc. No. 36735, Registry Files, R. 413, LNA.
530 Nemes to Daruváry, May 30 and 31, 1924, 209/123, 10–1390/1244, 1250, K 69, Economic Policy Department, HNA.
531 Statement by Hungarian Finance Minister, June 17, 1294, Press Reviews. Doc. No. 32459, Registry Files, R. 296, LNA; Ormos, *Az 1924 .évi magyar államkölcsön megszerzése*, 116–18.
532 Bergmann to Salter, June 5, 1924, Miscellaneous correspondence. Doc. No. 35939, Registry Files, R. 413, LNA.
533 Teleszky and Bark to Bergmann, June 12, 1924, Ibid.
534 Norman's Diary Entries, June 18 and 20, 1924, ADM34/13, BoE.
535 Lamont to Salter, June 23, 1924, and Salter to Lamont, June 25, 1924, Dossier concerning the American tranche. Doc. No. 37289, Registry Files, R. 413, LNA.
536 Strakosch to Smith, June 24, 1924, T.II, Incoming...May–June, 1924, C. 120, Financial Reconstruction of Hungary, LNA.

his own, and he confessed that no matter what happened, "in one way or another I must provide for the National Bank of Hungary a sum to make up the total to G. K. 250,000,000."[537] Thus even without American participation, Montagu Norman would have made sure that the Hungarian loan would be launched as planned. He somehow would have found the missing sum, but naturally it was all the best with an American house coming in.

With Speyer & Co. taking up $5 million should have automatically ensured other countries raising their parts. On the contrary, however, some of them had become even less enthusiastic. Although the Dutch part increased to £360,000 ($1.6 million), almost a 40% plus, and the contract was ready to be signed, Belgian participation was impossible, while Czechoslovakia and France remained silent.[538] Both these two latter countries finally clarified their situations with different results. While the Czechs on June 26th signaled their participation to a moderate sum, the French refused to come in. Maybe surprisingly, it was not due to political considerations. Simply, the financial situation of France did not allow the country to take part in the reconstruction efforts of an ex-enemy country, when France needed all its resources to heal the franc.[539] By the end of June, the participating countries were ready to issue the tranches of the Hungarian loan.

Speyer was stirring waters till the very last moment. He wanted to make the most out of this loan business. On the one hand, he tried to secure governmental backing for the deal. He asked the State Department to issue a statement saying that American bankers do intend to take part in the pending loan. The Department decided that such action would constitute a bad precedent, since it was private banks that were doing the lending and a statement of that nature might imply US government involvement, which was inconceivable. First, Speyer tried to threaten that he would not participate if the required State Department statement was not made, but he did make the loan anyway in the end.[540] James Speyer also asked Smith to give out a publication to the American public, so that the loan would become popular.[541] All Smith was willing to do was to give an interview to the Associated Press on June 29th, but that proved "of considerable value" to Speyer.[542] Despite this help, James Speyer later recalled in a Senate Hearing that to issue the Hungarian tranche of the League loan "was a most

537 Norman to Vissering, June 25, 1924, OV33/72, BoE.

538 Felkin to Salter, June 24, 1924, and Drummond to Salter, June 25, 1924, Dossier concerning the American tranche. Doc. No. 37289, Registry Files, R. 413, LNA.

539 Moreau to Salter, June 25, 1924, Correspondence with the French government. Doc. No. 37288, Registry Files, R. 413, LNA.

540 E. Rosenberg, e-mail message to author, January 6, 2009.

541 Speyer to Smith, June 28, 1924, L. V. c–1, June 24–30, 1924, C. 114, Financial Reconstruction of Hungary, LNA.

542 Speyer to Smith, July 21, 1924, Ibid.

difficult business because a good many people in our country did not know where Hungary was. We published books with pictures [...] we had a regular campaign in order to let the public know the circumstances. We got some men to make speeches and to explain to the people what the purpose of the loan was. It was quite a campaign."[543] Looking ahead, Speyer raised his participation to $7.5 million, but wanted exclusive right to do other Hungarian business in New York during the period of the loan, which was vehemently refused by both the British and Hungarians.[544] Finally, on June 30th he signed the loan contract without the exclusive clause.[545] After so much work and negotiations, which sometimes were burdened with hopelessness and bitter desperation, the moment at last arrived and the different countries started to launch their respective tranches.

The subscription began in London by Baring Brothers & Co., Rothschild and Son, and J. Henry Schroder & Co. on July 2, 1924, and the very next day in New York by the consortium led by Speyer & Co. After so much worry, the news was more than welcome that in the two most important places the loan was a huge success. In London, lists had to be closed before noon, and the sum offered was oversubscribed many times.[546] In New York, the subscription was a similar success. Brentano, the American Minister in Hungary, attributed the oversubscription to American sympathy to and belief in Hungary.[547] Speyer sent the reassuring cable that the whole block was subscribed and the lists were closed.[548] Naturally, Smith was "very much pleased that there was an American participation," and so was Bethlen, who confidently stated: "Now the American bankers have also decided that Hungary is a good, safe investment."[549] In retrospect, this statement contained an element of hubris and self-deception. The Hungarian government did not seem to mind that the American bank was in the hand of a Jewish family, let alone that the Rothschilds were Jewish as well. "Money has no smell," and

543 Quoted in Ilse Mintz, *Deterioration in the Quality of Foreign Bonds Issued in the United States 1920–1930* (New York: National Bureau of Economic Research, Inc., 1951), 64. Parallel to the efforts of Speyer & Co., Arthur Salter did similar fieldwork of advertising the Hungarian loan in Europe. Lee to Salter, June 27, 1924, and Salter to Lee, June 28, 1924, Publicity in connection with the Hungarian Loan. Doc. No. 32508, Registry Files, R. 297, LNA.

544 Norman's Diary Entries, June 28, 1924, ADM34/13, BoE; Felkin to Salter, June 28, 1924, 1924, Dossier concerning the American tranche. Doc. No. 37289, Registry Files, R. 413, LNA.

545 Felkin to Salter, June 30, 1924, 1924, LNA, Registry Files, R. 413. Dossier concerning the American tranche. Doc. No. 37289. The text of the contract is in 9/VIII/5/62–66, K 275, Kállay Papers, HNA.

546 Strakosch to Smith, July 2, 1924, C.III (4) Correspondence - Sir Henry Strakosch, C. 111, Financial Reconstruction of Hungary, LNA.

547 *Az Est*, July 25, 1924, XV/150.

548 Felkin to Salter, July 4, 1924, 1924, Dossier concerning the American tranche. Doc. No. 37289, Registry Files, R. 413, LNA.

549 Smith's report to Speyer & Co. in *The New York Times*, July 6, 1924; *Time*, July 7, 1924.

all that mattered for Hungary was that the United States be represented among the lender countries. Next to an American controller, it was reassuring to Bethlen that the United States chose active participation in Hungary's matters, even if in the private sphere. In the course of the next week, the Dutch, the Swedish, and the Italian tranches scored great successes as well. The *Vienna Tageblatt* gave the credit to Smith for the successful flotation of the loan and said he had made wonders during his time so far in Hungary.[550] The subscription in Switzerland was on July 29th, in Hungary between August 1st and 9th. The government did everything it could to make sure that the Hungarian tranche would be fully subscribed. In order to call as much attention as possible, "Budapest ha[d] been placarded with orange-and-black posters depicting a large dollar sign – the currency in which the loan is to be offered."[551] In case of the Czech issue in mid-August, no public subscription took place. The Hungarian government had been against a Czech tranche, but the League emphatically warned the Hungarians that from political considerations it was very important.[552] The whole amount of 83,620,000 Czech crowns ($2.45 million), which was in effect equal to the Czech demand of 10 million gold crowns stemming from the state railways trade, were taken over by the *Böhmische Industrie- und Landwirtschaftliche Bank*.[553] For the Czechs it was crucial to take part somehow in the Hungarian loan, because they wanted money in London. Their effort bore fruit and as soon as they had made clear that they would participate, Norman gave the green light for a second Czech loan in the City.[554] If not without obstacles, the League of Nations achieved what it had set out to do. This satisfaction was reflected in Strakosch's message when the London issue had started: "The League has done its duty, and now it rests with the Hungarians to make a real success of the plan of Reconstruction."[555]

6.3. The Adviser to the New National Bank

Under the passed reconstruction bill, a new National Bank had to be set up as part of the reconstruction scheme. The subscription of the shares of the new Bank started on April 28th and was closed on May 7th. The institution formally was

550 *The New York Times*, July 11, 1924.
551 Brentano to Hughes, August 16, 1924, 864.00/586, Roll 6, M. 708, NARA.
552 Szapáry to Daruváry, May 16, 1924, 209/123, 10–1390/1335, K 69, Economic Policy Department, HNA.
553 *Az Est*, July 26, 1924, XV/151.
554 Norman's Diary Entries, May 14, 1924, ADM34/13, BoE.
555 Strakosch to Smith, July 2, 1924, C.III (4) Correspondence - Sir Henry Strakosch, C. 111, Financial Reconstruction of Hungary, LNA. The overall picture of the Hungarian loan looked similar to the Austria case and the data can be seen in Appendix 3.

established on May 24th, its president was Sándor Popovics, and the institution enjoyed total freedom from the government, at least on paper. With a capital of 30 million gold crowns, of which the state had to subscribe 11.85 million, the Bank started its operation on June 24th, in the wake of which the inflation disappeared. The new rate of the crown, which was tied to the British pound, was the following: 1 pound=346,000 paper crowns; 1 dollar was 4.935 gold crowns. With the opening of the National Bank, the *Devisenzentrale* was to be closed and the business of foreign currencies fell under the competence of the Bank.[556]

One of the first big obstacles for Smith was to find a suitable adviser to the Bank as it was laid down in the Protocols. Just like in any other position of the League schemes, finding the right person here was far from easy. The first name that appeared in early May was that of Anton van Gijn of the Netherlands, offered for consideration by Popovics.[557] Largely due to the selfish disposition of Zimmerman, who wanted to secure his countryman to himself in Vienna, the Dutchman refused the post.[558] One of the next two possible men put forward was Calmes of Luxembourg, but he was utterly unsuitable on account of his lack of experience in central banking. The other was Vanderzypen of the Belgian National Bank, who did not seem independent enough, but the prevailing sentiment was that if no better candidate was found, he would do, because it was "extremely difficult to find a more suitable candidate."[559] Again, after the first round of possible candidates, the outcome was at best doubtful.

Montagu Norman was highly interested in this post. Being one of the most enthusiastic advocates of central bank cooperation, he needed someone trustworthy and competent as a link between the Bank of England and the Hungarian National Bank. As always, he sounded Benjamin Strong whether he could offer any names for the post.[560] One of the reasons why Norman was asking Strong's help may have very well been that he wanted an American for the post.[561] Strong replied that he thought the financial rewards would not be enough to lure good names, nonetheless he listed about a dozen persons, the two most notable ones being Edward Kemmerer and Norman Davis.[562] The

556 Smith's First Report, LNJ, 5th Year, No. 7, July 1924, 974–981; Berend and Ránki, *Magyarország gazdasága, 149.*
557 Strakosch to Smith, May 10, 1924, C.III (4) Correspondence - Sir Henry Strakosch, C. 111, Financial Reconstruction of Hungary, LNA.
558 Ter Meulen to Strakosch, May 9, 1924, Confidential Correspondence concerning the appointment of a foreign adviser to the proposed Bank of Issue. Doc. No. 33088, Registry Files, R. 298, LNA.
559 Strakosch to ter Meulen, May 10, 1924, and Ter Meulen to Strakosch, May 12, 1294, Ibid.
560 Norman to Strong, May 16, 1924, 2A165/1, BoE.
561 Lojkó, *Meddling in Middle Europe*, 115.
562 Strong to Norman, May 29, 1924, 2A165/1, BoE.

Governor passed three names on to Strakosch, those of Aiken, Voorhees, and Davis.[563] Moll, whom Norman had also asked for names, advised a certain Modig for the post, and Norman passed his name for consideration as well.[564] In early June, therefore, there were quite a few names for the job but none of them was either convincing enough or believable to accept the job for so little money. The man they finally picked had been all along working in Budapest.

When Smith arrived in Hungary, he found himself in an alien surrounding. Although he had widely traveled around the world, and some of those tours had taken place in Europe, the Hungary of 1924 was a place to him like none before. The unique situation the country was in and the nagging language problem made the transition all the more difficult. He had a great asset in a special financial adviser attached to him, Harry Arthur Siepmann of Great Britain. It was Strakosch who, after the first few unsuccessful rounds of trying to find someone, broached the subject of nominating Siepmann for the job of the adviser.[565] Smith was somewhat reluctant to lose Siepmann. First he suggested that the Briton serve parallel in both advisory positions, to himself as well as the National Bank, but in the end, on Siepmann's wish to have a permanent appointment and the expertise he provided, Smith agreed with the transfer.[566] When the official nomination had not materialized until the opening day of the new Bank, it was Smith who urged the appointment in order to ensure the smoothest beginning for the institution.[567] The official appointment finally took place after the positive feedback of the loan subscriptions in early July, especially the Italian tranche, so that there was no fear of Italian demands for the post.[568] Siepmann's salary was £2,500 a year ($11,400, equal to Popovics's salary), free of Hungarian taxes, paid in practice by the Hungarian government.[569] He basically became a member of a triumvirate with Popovics and Dusán Tabakovics, the director of the banking and exchange department, and these three people governed the Bank.[570] Smith had lost a good work force in Siepmann, which caused him "considerable inconvenience," and

563 Norman to Strakosch, May 30, 1924, OV33/71, BoE.
564 Norman to V. Moll, June 2, 1924, G3/180, BoE.
565 Strakosch to Smith, May 31, 1924, C.III (4) Correspondence - Sir Henry Strakosch, C. 111, Financial Reconstruction of Hungary, LNA.
566 Smith to Strakosch, June 3 and 4, 1924, Ibid.
567 Smith to Strakosch, June 24, 1924, Ibid.
568 Smith to Bethlen, July 10, 1924, B. II (1) National Bank of Hungary, May, 1924–October, 1925, C. 107, Financial Reconstruction of Hungary, LNA; Strakosch to Siepmann, July 9, 1924, 1/1924. May–June, K 304, Siepmann Papers, HNA.
569 Smith to Korányi, July 10, 1924, B. II (1) National Bank of Hungary, May, 1924–October, 1925, C. 107, Financial Reconstruction of Hungary, LNA.
570 Lojkó, *Meddling in Middle Europe*, 120; Péteri, *Global Monetary Regime*, 97–98.

he was "on the hunt for an economist and statistician to take his place."[571] After Frére refused the post on account of family and business interests, in the end René Charron, a Frenchman, became Smith's adviser.[572]

Siepmann joined the Treasury in 1912, and after the outbreak of World War I he volunteered for active service during which he was promoted to the rank of captain. He was a gifted administrator, someone who was against complicated bureaucracy. As a sign of things to come, his phrasing of why he liked to build dug-outs and other work on the front line showed characteristics he would later try to put in practice in the financial world. As he wrote to his mother during the war, "I love working out a scheme of my own, and working it out on large, ample lines, and then, before anything is even begun, submitting the completed idea to the Major for his approval, for execution in weeks or even months of work.." He added how he liked "the 'economy' of building: thinking out the best way of adapting local conditions, making sure of the standing walls, the material lying about, and so on, and combining everything so as to kill several birds with one stone."[573] After he took a short part in the occupation of Germany, he was involved in the Paris Peace Conference as a Treasury delegate under Keynes. He served as Secretary of the Financial Committee of the Supreme Economic Council, of which the General Secretary happened to be Arthur Salter, thus a further link was reestablished with Siepmann becoming part of the League effort in Hungary. His experiences in the Army during the war years and the bickering political atmosphere in the postwar diplomacy also created another side to the young man's characteristic. As he put it, "I went back to England before Keynes did, with some ideas about the conduct of world affairs which enthusiast for the League of Nations might have called cynical."[574] This cynicism, which marriage problems did not help to soothe, became a standard basic trait of the Briton, sometimes coupled with moods of depression.

Though Siepmann resigned from the Treasury in 1919, he shortly found himself again working for the government. Before taking up the office in Hungary, he had returned from India only in April, where he was an Assistant to Blackett, the man responsible for the financial affairs of the Viceroy's Council, and after a few days went off straight to Budapest.[575] In fact, it was Salter who first tried to convince Siepmann to go to Hungary when the latter was in Paris. It was not successful, but a few days later, when Siepmann met with Smith, he could not help but accept the

571 Smith to Felkin, July 30, 1924, LNA, C.III (6) Correspondence - M. A.E. Felkin, C. 111, Financial Reconstruction of Hungary, LNA.

572 Smith to Felkin, August 7, 1924, Ibid.

573 Siepmann to his mother, October 13, 1917, in Harry Siepmann, *Echo of the Guns. Recollections of an Artillery Officer, 1914-18* (London: Robert Hale, 1987), 74.

574 Siepmann's Diary, Ibid., 182.

575 Lojkó, *Meddling in Middle Europe*, 115, 150; Péteri, *Global Monetary Regime*, 97.

offer, because the American had "won my heart."[576]. After studying the situation in Hungary from early May, he first seemed to form a positive opinion about the future and started "to see something of the wood instead of the trees."[577] But as soon as the National Bank had opened and Siepmann had begun to work there, a shift started to take place in his opinion. In a letter on July 4th, he poured out his misgivings to Strakosch in a mordant fashion:

> [T]he Bank is making a bad start, which I wish I were in a position to correct. Anyone can see for himself what sort of a start the Bank is making, by simply walking in and looking around, or, better still, by trying to do business there. It is more like Billing's gate fish market than a Central Bank. The whole internal organization is wretched beyond description [...] Whether such things are meant to be any concern of the Adviser's I cannot say. I gather that Popovics is of the opinion that the less the Adviser interferes the better. Popovics is a strong man and obviously competent; but he will have nothing at all to do with details, and he seems to delight in surrounding himself with colourless, incompetent people who are content to take his orders and be his tools. I hope he does not look forward to my falling with the rest of them. The truth is, if I am not utterly mistaken, that the general policy of the Bank in its very broadest outlines will be safely looked after by Popovics. But his subordinates are starting the Bank on altogether slack and slovenly lines. It is all a question of personalities. Schober, the General Manager, is as pleasant a man as ever I hope to meet; but he is much weaker than milk and water. Maday, the Chief Accountant, is so stupid that [he will not] give a fig for the whole book keeping of the Bank. He had entered up a loss of several milliards in the first week on exchange deals, on the ground that when we buy from a Bank we allow them a turn of ½ %.[578]

Siepmann had great trust in Norman, and he considered their relation as that of "mentor" and "pupil."[579] The two had a correspondence that, typically on Siepmann's part, regularly ran into many pages. A busy Norman found it hard to catch up with the torrent of words and rather wanted to talk to Siepmann in person. The Governor urged the young adviser to travel to London, and Smith welcomed the idea of close collaboration between the two English men.[580] On

576 Siepmann's *Memoir* written in 1944 and held in the Siepmann family archive of private papers of H. A. Siepmann, in the possession of his son, H. R. Siepmann (hereafter cited as Siepmann Papers), 35.
577 Siepmann to Strakosch, June 4, 1924, 1/1924. May–July, K 304, Siepmann Papers, HNA.
578 Siepmann to Strakosch, July 4, 1924, Ibid.
579 Quoted in Péteri, *Global Monetary Regime*, 98.
580 Norman to Siepmann, September 26, 1924, OV33/37, BoE.

account of travel cost and the amount of work in Budapest, however, Siepmann rarely managed to meet Norman in London though.

Now everything had fallen in place to start the work: all the major tranches had been issued with usual oversubscription; the persons of control had been chosen and appointed; and the Hungarian political leadership accepted that under the aegis of the League of Nations the country's financial rehabilitation would commence. With this phase, the real work of Jeremiah Smith, Jr. had also commenced to a hopefully successful conclusion.

Chapter 7

The Technical Side of the Hungarian Reconstruction

7.1. The First Year

The work of Jeremiah Smith, Jr. in Hungary is a tale of a foreigner who worked hard for results that in the beginning seemed hard to reach, and whose manner and positive perseverance gained so many friends in the country for the benefit of which he labored so much. He accepted a challenge in a country that a leading New England daily described as "the country of all Europe least touched by democracy and Western civilization [...] selfish nationalism in impulsive, haughty Hungary now overrun by a defiant Ku Klux Klan of Jew-baiting, Fascisti [sic] terrorist."[581] Despite such opinions in his home state, from the very moment that he undertook the job, he put all his energies into the work and he believed he was going to succeed. His internationally open-minded personality was fitting for such a task as controlling the Hungarian financial matters, especially that it was under the aegis of the League of Nations, an organization Smith had faith in right from its very conception. Although the time he spent in Hungary was not really long, a little bit over two years, he left an indelible mark on the Hungarian financial and human landscape. His competent but rational individuality made it possible that he and the Hungarian government would work in harmony.

There are really two ways of looking at and assessing Smith's work in Hungary. One is the official side; the other is the private sphere. Thanks to the official duties of Smith, he was required to send a report every month to the League of Nations. In these reports one is able to follow the program of the financial reconstruction of Hungary. Step by step, Smith gave a meticulously detailed survey of the evolution of the state finances and the additional information that concerned daily life and possible outlook. With his reports not only did he cover a given month but also tried to send messages, sometimes well-disguised ones, sometimes hardly so. In sharp contrast, his personal life remained highly elusive. In Hungary he naturally did not change his semi-retired lifestyle; on the contrary, he was even more restrained and tried not to occupy a prominent place in public life. Due to his devotion to work and spending most of his time at his workplace in Budapest or in Geneva, and on account of lack of personal

581 *Boston Daily Globe*, April 13, 1924.

correspondence, not much can be learned about the man firsthand. Still, relying on others' memories about him and opinions in the period, a good sketch can be made about the character of the New Englander. It is only logical to start to study his time in Hungary through his reports, because they cover and present most of the Hungarian financial reconstruction program.

Exactly in the same fashion as in the Austrian case, the Commissioner-General for Hungary was required to send monthly reports to the League of Nations concerning the reconstruction plan. Naturally, other information that fell under the scope of finance was possible to include as well. In this respect, Smith had the possibility to study Zimmerman's reports and decided to follow a similar outline. When the two met in early June in Vienna in the shape of a courtesy call from Smith, they discussed besides the two reconstruction programs such questions as well.[582] A characteristic difference between the two men was that Smith sent the press advance copies of his reports for future release—a distinctly American innovation that Zimmerman declined to practice because of lack of confidence in the Austrian press.[583] Smith's reports alone, however, would give only a one-sided picture of the time he spent in Hungary. With adding ample other information from a score of different sources, the whole picture of the more than two years of financial reconstruction can be studied.

The first more than two months of his job was consumed mostly by two things. One was the raising of the international loan for Hungary, discussed in detail in the previous chapter. The other was to ensure and watch over the transition phase before the loan was launched. After his arrival on May 1st, Smith immediately flung himself into the thick of things in Budapest. The very same day he visited the members of the Cabinet and heads of the diplomatic missions, and started work on Monday, May 5th.[584] He also met with the representatives of the press the first week. He emphasized that he thought the main job of the newspapers lay "in reassuring the Hungarian public opinion, whose faith and trust were in great need."[585] He naturally met with Bethlen but was quick to reiterate his independent and unbiased status when the leaders of the Kossuth Party made a courtesy call at his office.[586] He believed that he must remain above local politics if he wanted to achieve positive results. His popularity, which was tangible from the first day, was mounting each week. This was largely attributed to his modest and sympathetic personality and behavior. His office was in the building of the Finance Ministry, with a desk originally used by Lajos Kossuth.

582 *The New York Times*, June 4, 1924; *Magyarország*, June 3, 1924, XXXI/107.
583 *The New York Times*, September 2, 1926.
584 Balfour to MacDonald, May 9, 1924, C7751/21/21, 9902, FO371, TNA; *Magyarország*, May 6, 7, 1924, XXXI/84, 85.
585 *Magyarország*, May 10, 1924, XXXI/88; *Budapesti Hírlap*, May 10, 1924, XLIV/88.
586 *Pesti Napló*, June 6, 1924, 75/110.

His quarters were very modest. He refused accommodations in the Royal Palace or a luxury suite in Hotel Hungaria, and rather moved to the top floor of the hotel in a single bedroom.[587] With such steps, the Commissioner-General managed to make a very good first impression in Hungary.

In early June, duty called Smith to Geneva, Switzerland, headquarters of the League of Nations. It was the time of the summer session and Smith was to present in person his first report of the reconstruction. Obviously, close attention was following this second League-initiative and many officials and observers were keen on hearing the American Commissioner-General's first impressions. He divided his reports into small parts touching upon the subjects of inflation, assigned revenues, measures of reform, financial, and statistical tables in the appendix, but these were often changed later due to the pending issues. On June 14th, Jeremiah Smith, Jr. appeared before the League Council for the first time in his official capacity and explained his first report.

In this report covering the month of May, the American described the major events of the first month concerning the reconstruction program. After outlining the subscription of the National Bank's shares, he stated that compared to the Austrian subscription the picture was satisfactory.[588] Since the flotation of the international loan was still weeks away, the interim time had to be bridged financially. For this reason, the Hungarian government secured in April a 20-million Swiss franc loan, and a domestic forced loan to cover the deficits. In May, the Vienna stock exchange speculation caused some anxiety, and "the natural consequences in a country which since the war has become accustomed to feel disillusioned was that the difficulties of the moment overshadowed everything else in the public estimation, and faith in the prospects of the reconstruction programme could only be won at the price of concrete evidence which it was not possible to furnish immediately." This unfavorable situation was furthered by a general increase in prices, and it caused an almost 30% drop in the currency. Although Smith was satisfied that most prohibitions on exports (wheat, rye, barley, hay, and meat) had been abolished since the League delegation's visit in March, he criticized the pending tariff bill as one that does not follow the suggestion of the Financial Committee. In conclusion, despite that "the mentality of the country was not altogether favourable at the outset," he asserted that "generally speaking, the conditions appear fundamentally sound

587 *Boston Daily Globe*, May 22, 1924.

588 Smith's First Report, LNJ, 5th Year, No. 7, July 1924, 974–981. Subsequently, Smith's reports will be given with the LNJ as source in the first footnote, thereafter they will be referred to only according to their number. Smith's reports can also be found in BoE, OV9/434 and /436. The whole First Report can be found in the Appendix. A short summary of Smith's reports usually appeared in the *Wall Street Journal*, *The New York Times*, and *The Times*.

[...] There is no reason apparent why the execution of the Reconstruction plan should not produce the expected results."[589] This sentence was what Goode later described as "a good deal of courage."[590] Smith's optimism partly stemmed from the fact that he already in May established that the revenues from the assigned assets would exceed the League estimates.[591] Also, he was an optimist by nature.

Still it cannot be said that Smith was satisfied with everything. One thing that bothered him was the late time that budget plans, actual budgets, and closed accounts reached him. He laid stress on it that "preliminary budgets should not be furnished at the last possible moment but should be submitted to the Commissioner-General a sufficient length of time in advance to permit careful examination of their details." He was of the opinion that in other fashion they would lose their value. He also requested "that accurate statements of debts concentrated and remaining unpaid should be furnished monthly, and the success of the plan depends in no small degree upon establishing a practice which will insure these results." But it was not only the lack of data that created problems; he also had to cope with a strange environment: "So much time has been spent during the first month in organization of the control and in becoming acquainted generally with the economic, financial and administrative conditions that it has not been possible to prepare statistical tables for the first report."[592] In his verbal summary in Geneva, Smith praised both the Financial Committee and the Hungarian government, the first for the preparation of the plan, the latter for its cooperation.[593] With this successful and sanguine performance both the League and Hungary could rest assured that the process of rehabilitation had commenced satisfactorily.

In Geneva decision was also made about the Commission-General's expenses. As Smith's detailed calculation showed, he and his staff would need $4,642 a month.[594] This covered besides Smith's salary the salaries of Tyler, Siepmann, Charron, and Licen, the work of the clerical staff, and expenses relating to translations and traveling.[595] At the meeting in Geneva, the Council authorized Smith's total expenses at $5,000 a month.[596] A Hungarian historian, in all likelihood driven by ideological consideration, wrote, in addition to Smith's being sent by J. P. Morgan personally, that

---

589 Smith's First Report.
590 *The Times*. May 23, 1925.
591 Balfour to MacDonald, May 16, 1924, C8073/37/21, 9908, FO371, TNA.
592 Smith's First Report.
593 LNJ, 5th Year, No. 7, July 1924, 910.
594 LNA, C. 267, 1924. II.
595 9/VII/6/183. The second Budapest negotiation in March 1924 and its antecedents. The first report of the Commission-General in Geneva, K 275, Kállay Papers, HNA.
596 LNJ, 5th Year, No. 7, July 1924, 911.

> The incredible sum which J. Smith [...] pocketed each month as his salary expresses the unscrupulous exploitation of the country more clearly than anything else. J. Smith was given 5,000 dollars monthly as honorarium and office expenses [...] which sum was almost three times the pay of the head of the Hungarian State, Regent Horthy [...] at this time.[597]

Naturally, the 5,000 dollars were provided for Smith and the whole staff, not for Smith alone. The staff included three typist secretaries and a male messenger clerk as well, and there were expenses related to translations and traveling.[598] This was a typical manifestation of how post World War II Hungarian historiography changed or tilted certain facts in the interwar period and presented them in a falsified way.

In light of this distorted interpretation and later events, it is important to quote the note attached to the above decision: "The Commissioner-General does not intend to draw upon the amount provided for his salary for more than his actual living expenses at Budapest and travelling expenses for the purpose of his work. As far as he can judge at present, his expenses may amount to some $8,000 yearly."[599] So, Jeremiah Smith, Jr. already in the beginning decided not to spend or accept any extra money save for his actual living expenses and this move basically meant that he forwent his salary. This noble act was followed by exasperation on Smith's part when the question of expenses was brought to public.[600] The root of his anger was that the resolution was read at a private meeting in order not to get out to the press, but it still leaked out. In the given situation he wanted to avoid even the possibility of the Hungarian public discussing how much money the foreign controllers received when the population had to endure extra burdens. He was quick to reassure to the Hungarian press that the sum was a maximum and he was not going to spend a cent more than necessary.[601] He naturally did not want his precarious situation to be attacked on the ground of such banal things. He wanted to evoke confidence toward his own self and the work of the reconstruction.

---

597 Magos, "The Role of the British and American Imperialists," 202.

598 9/VII/6/183. The second Budapest negotiation in March 1924 and its antecedents. The first report of the Commission-General in Geneva, K 275, Kállay Papers, HNA.

599 E. I. Expenses of the Office of the Commissioner General, C. 113, Financial Reconstruction of Hungary, LNA; 9/VII/6/183. The second Budapest negotiation in March 1924 and its antecedents. The first report of the Commission-General in Geneva, K 275, Kállay Papers, HNA.

600 Smith to Salter, June 16, 1924, Dossier concerning the departure of the Commissioner General from Budapest. Doc. No. 36545, Registry Files 300, R. 300, LNA.

601 *Budapesti Hírlap*, June 17, 1924, XLIV/118; *Magyarország*, June 17, 1924, XXXI/118.

The second report of Smith covered the month of June. Due to some lapse between the period covered in these reports and the necessary time needed to work on the data, it came out on July 22nd. Of the various issues he touched upon three deserves mentioning. One was the state of finances. The revenues from customs and tobacco had increased immensely since May, but the estimated deficit for July was almost 5 million gold crowns more ($1 million) than in the Reconstruction Program. He quickly added that this was no basis for worry, because July was a weak month in terms of revenues, under the monthly average, plus tax collection of direct taxes fell on the months of February, May, August, and November, thus the weak results. The overall good news was that it was clear that by the end of June there would be already a surplus compared to what the League had estimated. Smith, however, was quick to add that it did not mean the possibility of any changes in budget limits. As he put it, "in approving the [July] budget, I have called the attention of the Government to the fact that the monthly deficits during the balance of the calendar year must be reduced below the monthly average, in order that the total deficit for the six-months period shall not exceed the deficit for that period fixed in the reconstruction budget, and that I shall be governed by this consideration in making future releases."[602]

Another point was the problem of the state employees. It was a rather difficult one that was to haunt the program all throughout, therefore giving credence to Smith's prediction that "the question of the State employees is a difficult one and likely to remain so." The disproportionally high number of state officials meant a very big financial burden on the budget; roughly 60% of the annual expenditure was for pay for personnel and pensions. In addition, the government granted an increase in their pay from July 1st instead of October 1st, which nonetheless was acceptable in the light of the fact that their salary was very low and hardly enough to make ends meet. The third interesting point was Smith's practicality that he advanced money for the government when the proceeds of the loan were not on hand yet in June. It would have made little sense to play rigid and endanger the smooth run of the program over technical points. In conclusion, Smith professed careful optimism when he wrote, "The successful issue of the loan cannot of itself effect miracles; the execution of the plan is the only way of establishing a firm foundation for the future; this requires time and will require sacrifices in addition to those already made, but I have every confidence they will be made when necessary and that the Hungarian people will take full advantage of this opportunity."[603]

This positive attitude and practical approach shown by the Commissioner-General found resonance in Hungary. Bethlen praised Smith's decency and

---

602 Smith's Second Report, LNJ, 5th Year, No. 9, September 1924, 1228–38.
603 Ibid.

knowledge and said that he had won the love and respect of not only those who had official contact with him but the whole population.[604] Smith also had a very good opinion about his relation with the government and he described their discussions about budget issues "amicable."[605] These discussions at present mainly focused on the July budget, which the Commissioner took issue with because it stepped over the limits of the budget Law. Finally, the two sides found a middle ground and Smith accepted the reasoning of the government about the installments of the forced loan that was not included in the reconstruction budget, and he approved the July budget.[606] To take further steps in the smooth cooperation of both sides, Smith was willing to take part in rare public events. One was the 4th of July commemoration in the City Park at the statue of George Washington organized by the Hungarian-American Society. Both Smith and Brentano appeared and all the speakers praised Smith and he got a cheer from the people present.[607] All these signs showed that the American controller had been accepted and so far his work had been successful. Naturally, with the successful flotation of the loan in the first two weeks of July, which made it seem assured that the necessary money would be on hand to carry out the program, his status became even more respected in Hungary.

July was a very important month not only because of the international loan. Most significantly, an early agreement was made about the official multiplier. This was the number stating the ratio between a gold crown and paper crowns. It was fixed at 17,600 in July, though the real value should have been 16,000. Despite the fact that still in July it was reduced to 17,000, Smith was not satisfied with this state of affairs, and in the future wanted to see it reduced, because in this form it caused a net loss. The estimated August budget deficit was again largely in excess of the planned deficit, so Smith asked the government to reduce it by 2 million gold crowns. In the wake of this problem, agreement was reached that the departments would submit their budget plans to the Finance Ministry till the 15th of each month, while the Finance Ministry would submit the whole monthly budget plan for the state to Smith till the 20th. This way the parties could avoid having such arguments in the future.[608]

---

604 *Budapesti Hírlap*, July 2, 1924, XLIV/131.

605 Smith to Salter, June 28, 1924, Miscellaneous correspondence. Doc. No. 35939, Registry Files, R. 413, LNA.

606 Smith to Korányi, July 10, 1924, C.III. (7) Correspondence - Hungarian Ministers, 1924, C. 111, Financial Reconstruction of Hungary, LNA.

607 Brentano to Hughes, August 16, 1924, 864.00/586, Roll 6, M. 708, NARA; *Budapesti Hírlap*, July 7, 1924, XLIV/135.

608 All the information in the paragraph is from Smith's Third Report, LNJ, 5thYear, No. 10, October 1924, 1447–58.

The administrative reforms had begun as well. The total number of officials dismissed on June 30th was 6,991.[609] In connection with this, the Commissioner-general made the following observation:

> Present Hungary, which has approximately one-third of the geographical area and 40 per cent of the population of the country as it existed before the War, has about 60 per cent of the pre-war number of State employees and that the classified personnel of the Civil Administrations (excluding the State undertakings) has actually at the present time more *functionnaires de classe* than there were in 1913. This is due partly to the War. Many Hungarian civil servants, who were employed in those parts of Hungary annexed to other countries by the Treaty of Trianon, returned to Hungary. They had claims upon the Hungarian Government for retention in the Civil Service which could not be ignored, and naturally resulted in a very large establishment which, in turn, results in an underpaid Civil Service, the total expense of which is nevertheless a heavy drain on the Government Treasury. Other changes were made soon after the end of the War which contributed to the increase rather than to the decrease of the staff of the Civil Administrations. The Reconstruction plan makes no attempt to deal with this situation other than providing for the discharge of 15,000 employees [...] It is apparent that, so long as a large proportion of the State revenues must be spent on the payment of its employees, the amount available for other purposes will be correspondingly limited.

Still, it was the pensioners who suffered the greatest cutbacks in the new fiscal policy with a decrease of 40% as of July 1, 1924.[610]

As far as state finance went, however, things looked surprisingly good. The assigned revenues kept coming in neatly. The highest of them was that of tobacco, which the British minister attributed to the new regulation that forbade shops selling tobacco to close their doors during "an indefinitely long luncheon hour!"[611] In Smith's view the most important thing was the step toward "the establishment of confidence, both internally and externally, in the permanence of the conditions within Hungary created by the operation of the Reconstruction plan [and] a normal and healthy market has been re-established in Hungarian crowns."[612] But confidence worked toward his direction too. Smith seemed, in the American minister's words, "to retain the entire confidence of Hungary and

---

609 Ibid.
610 Romsics, *István Bethlen*, 238.
611 Barclay to MacDonald, July 19, 1924, 11764/21/21, 9903, FO371, TNA.
612 Smith's Third Report.

to maintain the popularity with which he was first received."[613] In July, none other than Boyden came to call on Smith to get firsthand information about the execution of the program in Hungary.[614] Naturally, Smith was happy to see a compatriot who was also a good friend. Such a visit meant a high point in his otherwise hermit-like lifestyle. As one paper wrote, he started at his workplace at nine and never left before six, but often stayed late and carried home with him big folders to study.[615] He was really in the thick of things concerning his duty.

On August 1st, Smith had been in Hungary for three months and he reiterated his optimism concerning the reconstruction work.[616] He had really won the confidence of the Hungarians and was not seen at all as "the financial czar of Hungary," a label that foreign newspapers tagged him with.[617] The most momentous event of the month was James Speyer's visit to Budapest.[618] The American banker, whose Company led the way in issuing the American tranche of the Hungarian reconstruction loan, came to the Hungarian capital to conclude further business. Speyer, who was provided with Smith's monthly reports directly by the Commissioner-General, wanted to achieve his business objective that was frustrated in June. His stay was marked by generous Hungarian hospitality, led by the government. A dinner was given in his honor in the prestigious Gerbaud by József Vass, deputy prime minister, where all the foreign notables and a Hungarian who's who were invited.[619] The next day it was finance minister Frigyes Korányi, who gave a smaller dinner for Speyer and his team.[620] The lavish reception was the result of the fact that Speyer & Co. did manage to take over $1.5 million from the Hungarian tranche, 80% of the domestically raised total amount, increasing the American participation to $9 million, while at the same time reducing the Hungarian participation to $850,000.[621] The real cause behind that move was that the American issue stood at a premium of 2 ½ in New York, and Speyer hoped to include the Hungarian part under the same condition.[622]

613 Brentano to Hughes, August 16, 1924, 864.00/586, Roll 6, M. 708, NARA.

614 Boyden to Smith, July 12, 1924, T.II., Incoming Telegrams, July–August, 1924, C. 120, Financial Reconstruction of Hungary, LNA.

615 *Pesti Hírlap*, July 13, 1924, XLVI/140.

616 *Budapesti Hírlap*, August 1, 1924, XLIV/156.

617 *The New York Times*, August 3, 1924.

618 Speyer arrived together with K. W. Krech, President of the Equitable Trust Company, the house Speyer & Co. launched the Hungarian tranche together, but in all measures it was Speyer's personality that mattered.

619 Daily News, Daily Reports (1920-1944), August 13, 1924, K. 428. a, HNA.

620 Daily News, Daily Reports (1920-1944), August 14, 1924, K. 428. a, HNA.

621 Smith to ter Meulen, August 21, 1924, L.V. c–1, Jun 24–Jun 30, 1924, C. 114, Financial Reconstruction of Hungary, LNA; Korányi to Smith, August 22, 1924, and ter Meulen to Smith, August 23, 1924, C.III. (7) Correspondence - Hun Minister, and C.III. (11) Correspondence - Mr. C. E. ter Meulen, C. 111, Financial Reconstruction of Hungary, LNA.

622 Barclay to MacDonald, August 15, 1924, C13283/37/21, 9909, FO371, TNA.

The transaction was largely a result of the successful negotiations between Fülöp Weiss, President of the Hungarian Commercial Bank of Pest, the agents of Speyer, and Speyer & Co.[623] Smith approved of the deal, but asked official approval, which the Trustees duly gave.[624] The contract was signed in Geneva on September 3rd, and it was amended compared to the earlier contract in a fashion favorable to Speyer & Co.[625] The business aim that Speyer & Co. should enjoy exclusive rights in case of future Hungarian loans in the United States now was achieved. Hungarian Finance Minister Korányi signed the relevant contract with the Americans:

> As you have declared your willingness to purchase out of the Hungarian tranche of the State Loan of the Kingdom of Hungary 1924 obligations to the amount of 1 ½ million dollar of nominal value, I undertake on behalf of the Hungarian Government, according to your wish the engagement that the Hungarian Government will not make arrangements with any American financial concern as to the issue or purchase of a direct or indirect Hungarian Government loan or a similar financial transaction in New-York U.S.A. for which the negotiations would commence after the conclusion of the purchase of the additional $ 1.500.000 bonds, without inviting the offer of Messrs. Speyer & Co. and that in such future transactions the Hungarian Government will, in the case of equal conditions, give preference at all times to the offer of Messrs. Speyer & Co.[626]

This was also a sure sign that the two parties would work together in the future again, which was the undisguised aim of the American banking house. On the other hand, the Hungarian government was equally happy to have an American banking house to count on.

Smith began his fourth report with the following statement: "The fact that I have little to report with regard to purely financial conditions may be taken as a satisfactory symptom." The actual deficits for July and August showed a much favorable picture than estimated and the revenues, for the summer months covered comfortably the annual service of the loan, which were 31 million gold crowns. The bigger than estimated revenues were welcomed because the first

623 "Report on the Work of the Savings Banks and Banks in 1924," 16. 5/1923-1928 B/3, K 468, Bethlen Papers, HNA. Later on this Hungarian Bank represented the interests of Speyer & Co. in Hungary.
624 Smith to ter Meulen, August 21, 1924, and Smith to Speyer, August 22, 1924, L. V. c–1, June 24–30, 1924, C. 114, Financial Reconstruction of Hungary, LNA.
625 The text of the new contract is in 9/VIII/5/68–73, K 275, Kállay Papers, HNA.
626 Hungarian Royal Minister of Finance to Speyer & Co., September 3, 1924, 332 /116, K 269, Finance Ministry, General Papers, HNA.

quarter of the financial year was always the worst in terms of deficit and the data provided by the Treasury showed that the next quarter would be even better. Retail prices, though still high, had started to fall, and there were signs that the country had adjusted itself to the new conditions. In addition to the increasing revenues, speculation on the stock exchange had largely ceased, and deposits in the banks began to show an increase. Naturally, this was only one side of the equation. Smith put in perspective that only long-term capital could alleviate the problem of a country that was notoriously poor in capital. "But the genuine shortage of capital which exists in Hungary will not be relieved by offers of money for a few months at a time. Such relief can come only if foreign capital seeks out the opportunities which undoubtedly exist for relatively long-term investment in productive Hungarian enterprises, or if sufficient savings can be accumulated gradually in Hungary for re-investment in the enterprises of the country".[627]

As a closing act to the summer, on August 30th Smith appeared again in front of the Council in Geneva to give a summary of his work so far. He gave a succinct but accurate picture of the past four months and how the reconstruction had advanced since his arrival. He repeated the satisfactory amount of the revenues and further indicated that Hungary had become a healthily functioning country by giving the example of the stock exchange, whose volume had increased by a factor of 90 since the opening of the National Bank back in June.[628] Smith praised the League and the Financial Committee for "a striking illustration of international cooperation," and he also had warm words for the "faithful cooperation of the Hungarian Government and people."[629] He declared that the first stage had been passed, the second stage could begin, and he was optimistic that the work would be successful.[630] As he said, the main task now would be that of reducing the budget expenditure to the level fixed in the reconstruction program and to conclude commercial treaties. Korányi also spoke and praised the League and Smith, while the League congratulated the Hungarian government and Smith.[631] The meeting at Geneva also decided about the three trustees, who were Giuseppe Bianchini, Henry Strakosch, and Carel Eliza ter Meulen.[632] When the American returned to Budapest in mid-September, he was pleased to declare in an interview that at Geneva the question of the Hungarian reconstruction got

---

627 All the information in the paragraph is from Smith's Fourth Report, LNJ, 5th Year, No. 11, November 1924, 1741–48.

628 8/35, K 78, Népszövetségi Kiadványgyűjtemény [Collection of League of Nations Publications], HNA.

629 Ibid., 36–37.

630 Ibid., 37.

631 LNJ, 5th Year, No. 10, October 1924, 1289–1291.

632 Ter Meulen represented Hope & Co., Amsterdam, Bianchini was President of the United Bank of Italy, while Strakosch was member of the Financial Committee of the League of Nations.

the biggest attention, aside from that of disarmament, and he received positive feedback from everywhere.[633]

In his report for September, the Commission-General could once again provide the news the officials hoped to hear in Geneva: revenues pledged as security kept growing; prohibitions on export were almost totally removed and requirements of import licenses were largely abolished, though there was the new tariff law; the volume of total trade was increasing significantly; wholesale prices had diminished by 2.3% in August for the first time; the number of unemployed went down since July (from 31,134 to 20,026) among the members of the Union of Socialist Workers. Naturally, Smith did not allow the government or the Hungarian people to believe that the worst was over. "In order to avoid misapprehension, it should be realised that the gain in actual over estimated receipts, and the consequent reduction of the estimated deficit for these three months [July, August, September], does not mean that the Government is in a position to spend more money than the amounts fixed in the reconstruction programme." Besides, on September 17th the National Bank raised the discount rate from 10 to 12 ½ %, but Smith quickly concluded that it was part of a normal seasonal fluctuation.[634] In his home country, Hungary also got in the focus a little bit because of Smith's favorable report.[635]

Not everyone involved in the execution of the reform program was automatically optimistic about the results. Harry Siepmann, the foreign adviser at the National Bank, was one. In his frequent letters to Norman, he often gave voice to criticism if he thought it justified. In a letter written on the same day as the raise of the discount rate, Siepmann formulated his opinion in a striking fashion when he said there was "a fundamental mistake in the reconstruction plan."[636] The basis for this statement was that only putting the state finances in order would be less than what was needed. According to Siepmann, Popovics agreed with the Briton, and asserted that in a country where foreign capital had always been and would be a primary asset, automatic reconstruction would not be achieved just by making budget deficit disappear.[637] This small episode is a good example how difficult the situation was. The numbers told only one side of the story, but future prospects might not depend on present figures alone. Still, this observation, however true it might have been, did not render those good numbers valueless. On the contrary, what Hungary had been able to produce in the short time span since late spring was more than what could have been expected. Maybe a slight indication that foreign trust had returned

633 *Budapesti Hírlap*, September 16, 1924, XLIV/192.
634 All the information in the paragraph is from Smith's Fifth Report, LNJ, 5th Year, No. 11, November 1924, 1749–58.
635 28/1924 I-5. Washington/788, K 66, Press and Cultural Department, HNA.
636 Siepmann to Norman, September 17, 1924, OV 33/37, BoE.
637 Ibid.

toward Hungary was that Charles E. Mitchell and Paul Grosjean, President and Vice-President of the National City Bank of New York, came to Budapest to study local conditions and the possibility of investing in form of a loan.[638]

The next month again produced a favorable report from Smith. Thanks to the high customs revenues, assigned revenues were the largest so far. For the first time, the estimated budget for November showed a small surplus and wholesale price index showed a slight decrease again. Despite the surplus of 2 million gold crowns in October, Smith was careful because state expenditure was still higher than estimated: "The conclusion should not be drawn that the State is in a position to incur additional expenditures." Smith dealt with the Hungarian State Railways in detail, which was the most important state enterprise. The obvious reason for this was that the surpluses or deficits created by the various state enterprises had a significant bearing on the state budget. From a financial point of view, everything seemed all right with the State Railways; the preliminary numbers even showed a little surplus. But there was more to the numbers than first met the eye, and it also caught Smith's attention. The problem was that 16.7% of the operating expenses was eaten up by pensions, while in the pre-war years this figure was only 3-4%. In addition, compared to the numbers of active employees, in 1913 pensioners represented 16%, while in 1924 this was 90%, and further increase was expected. The number of people employed at this time was around 60,000. The expenditure on coal showed again a curios picture. The Railways now spent on coal 94% of what it had before the war, although the railway system had only 40% of the number of kilometers, and rise in coal prices could be only a partial explanation. According to Smith's observations, small cuts should be practiced in basically every field in the enterprise over a longer period, which must not affect wages, because they were already very low.[639]

The government continued to use the multiplier of 17,000 paper crowns to one gold crown, which was 10% above the real value. As a result of this, state officials were overpaid with 10%, which meant deficit for the state, but agreement was reached with the Financial Committee that till the end of the calendar year this should be upheld. This was doubtless a fundamental question, but common sense dictated that it was well worth losing some money on these inflated payrolls in order to keep the many officials financially afloat, especially when all the figures indicated that deficit had disappeared and soon surplus would be realized. Still, Smith found it prudent to attach his mild warning: "The conclusion should not be drawn that the State is in a position to incur additional expenditures."[640]

---

638 Curtis to Hughes, October 7, 1924, 864.00/590, Roll 7, M. 708, NARA.

639 All the information in the paragraph is from Smith's Sixth Report, LNJ, 5th Year, No. 12, December 1924, 1835–45.

640 Ibid.

Despite the good numbers, the month of October witnessed the first problems of the reconstruction. There was a continuation of general business depression and economic stagnation, with many bankruptcies. In the first half of the month there was a panic on the stock exchange with 15-25% drop in quotations, but the government solved the situation providing 100 billion paper crowns.[641] Smith himself had his moments of uncertainty because of the situation. Aside from the budget issue and despite the good overall picture, he had the sensation of "wandering about in a pretty thick fog."[642] One of his complaints was that there were too many banks in the country and he was sure that many of them ought to be simply closed.[643] The leading banks, on the other hand, thrived. There is statistical data only for the fourteen most important banks at that time, but these numbers showed a steady increase in savings. Smith included this table in his reports and the numbers reflected a trusting public inasmuch the amount of savings kept growing.[644]

In November revenues once more reached the peak so far, largely thanks to the customs receipts. Smith did not necessarily think that high customs receipts were a good thing. As he noted, it meant that those who brought the goods into the country paying high customs duty would want to sell them at a high price as well, thus the price index would remain high. If the prices did fall, however, it would mean that the trader, who had paid a large customs duty, had to suffer a substantial loss—neither scenario was very encouraging. The Hungarian Treasury wanted to spend the surplus on hand immediately, but Smith resisted such ideas and wanted a longer period to pass before he authorized any such action. The Hungarian currency had gained strength thanks to the pound becoming stronger against the dollar.[645] This was thanks to the movement to bring back the pound to gold parity, even if about 10% overrated. In the scheme the main actors were Strong and Norman: their cooperation made it to a great degree possible for the pound to reach the magic number in the spring of 1925.[646] For the first time, there was a slight surplus in foreign trade, and compared to 1923 the increase in volume was 63.8%. Still, as Smith noted, it was "substantially 20% of the foreign trade of pre-war Hungary for the same period of time, and about 50% of the estimated normal volume of trade of present Hungary."[647] Somewhat shocking

641 Curtis to Hughes, November 8, 1924, 864.00/597, Roll 7, M. 708, NARA.
642 Smith to Strakosch, October 20, 1924, OV9/434, BoE.
643 Ibid.
644 Smith's Seventh Report, LNJ, 6th Year, No. 3, March 1925, 388–96.
645 Smith's Seventh Report.
646 In more detail about this subject, see Clay, *Lord Norman*, 134–171; Chandler, *Benjamin Strong*, 291–331; Clarke, *Central Bank Cooperation*, 71–104; and Ahamed, *Lords of Finance*, 224 –40.
647 Smith's Seventh Report.

was the revelation in the November report that the retail price of many textile articles was 50-100% more than in the United States, Great Britain, and France, a phenomenon with no clear explanation.[648]

The month also produced some strange news. A certain Feldman of Belgium appeared on the scene and was trying to act as a coordinator of the Hungarian government in raising a loan for the Hungarian Railways. Norman and Niemeyer were upset about this non-official route and Smith promptly let them know that no one had ever heard about Feldman in Hungary.[649] Norman's irritation stemmed from the fact that similar attempts had in fact been made by Hungary's neighbors. He warned the Hungarians not to fall in the same trap as the Austrians and Czechs, who had become known to "make a habit of injuring their credit by semi-official loanmongering."[650] There were genuine channels working as well. Speyer asked Smith about the chances of another government loan for Hungary. Smith replied that neither he, probably nor the Reparations Commission would agree to such a plan.[651]

In Britain, where interest obviously was big toward both the Austrian and Hungarian reconstructions, an article in *The Times* gave a mixed picture about the results in Hungary. Despite admitting that businessmen were "looking confidently to the future," the author did not mince his words when he described the daily situation: "Business is dead and is bound to become deader still [...] Many shops are shut, and the centre of the city after dark is like the grave. Now and for some time to come there will be little money to spend."[652] As for Smith, the article went on to say: "He is credited with extreme broad-mindedness and impartiality, and his personality is surrounded by a sort of nimbus of dollars."[653] Both sides of this analysis were fair. On the one hand, the expected depression had set in, however promising the fiscal

648 Ibid.

649 Smith to Norman and Niemeyer, November 12, 1294, and Norman to Smith, November 18, 1924, S. III. a. 1, C. 119, Financial Reconstruction of Hungary, LNA.

650 Norman to Smith, November 4, 1924, Ibid.

651 Smith to Speyer, November 19, 1924, Ibid. For some time, therefore, Speyer & Co. had to wait for another possibility to invest in the Hungarian market. It does not mean that the company was not active elsewhere. It was particularly true in Germany, where despite the fact that Speyer & Co. was prevented from taking part in issuing the Dawes loan due to J. P. Morgan, they made up for it in the following years. As a matter of fact, the Company issued altogether $ 53.8 million, mainly in city and railway loans. Speyer & Co. issued $10 million for the German Railway Co. in November 1924, $15 million for the City of Berlin in July 1925, $3,750,000 for the City of Dresden and $2,800,000 for the City of Frankfort, both in November 1925, $6,500,000 for the Hamburg-American Line in December 1925, $3,750,000 for the City of Leipzig in March 1926, and $12,000,000 for the Berlin Electric Elevated and Underground Railways Co. in November 1926. Robert R. Kuczynski, *American Loans to Germany* (New York: The Macmillan Company, 1927), 20, 44, 46, 48, 51.

652 *The Times*, November 24, 1924.

653 Ibid.

numbers may have been; as far as Smith went, he was really liked for his modest and unbiased behavior.

December meant the end of the first half of the 1924/25 fiscal year, so the results so far were important and indicative of future prospects. Smith's monthly report for this month emphasized the good news that payments from the loan for monthly deficits and providing working capital had to be made only in the first four months (July–October) and there was a surplus of 2.1 million gold crowns ($420,000) after the first six months. Receipts for pledged revenues were again higher than in the previous month. Although expenditures were 10% higher than fixed in the reconstruction program and also higher than provided at the end of the reconstruction period, revenues were about 40% higher than estimated. Deposits in the banks and the number of the unemployed kept growing. The multiplier used for converting gold into paper money had been reduced from 17,000 to its true ratio of 15,100, which was another indication of healthier circumstances. This fact was important because importers, on account of the too high multiplier, had to pay an extra tax in essence, which now with the real value of the multiplier had disappeared. Despite all the favorable results, Smith still warned against "premature conclusions," because he was of the opinion that the pledged revenues would not be able to produce as much in the second half of the financial year. As he noted, in this case any extra expenditure on the part of the government would either make budget deficit permanent or would render a future tax reduction impossible. He knew very well that the program was far from its successful conclusions and there would be many obstacles along the road, but he was as optimistic as he had been in the beginning. One such issue was the state officials. On December 31st, 2,780 state employees got their notice, in addition to the 6,991 who had received it on June 30th. About 1,000 posts had been abolished since June 30th. But as Smith noted, this was nothing compared to what should be done, but such reduction could only come over a much longer period.[654] As far as treaty charges were concerned, Hungary had paid the counter value of the daily 880 tons of coal to Yugoslavia, and Smith told the Hungarian government that it should suspend such daily deliveries to its southern neighbor for December.[655] The British minister reported that Smith confirmed to him in person that the general financial situation was healthy and hopeful, and he had "great faith in the in the capacity and intentions" of the new Finance Minister, János Bud.[656]

654 All the information in the paragraph is from Smith's Eighth Report, LNJ, 6th Year, No. 3, March 1925, 397–408.
655 Smith to the Reparation Commission, December 15, 1924, OV9/437, BoE.
656 Barclay to Chamberlain, December 19, 1924, C19232/37/21, 9909, FO371, TNA. Bud assumed the post on November 25, 1924, and held it until September 5, 1928.

7.2. The Year of 1925

The first month of January brought news not closely related to the reconstruction program. As far as this was concerned, Smith's ninth report informed everyone interested that in Hungary the multiplier was further reduced reaching 14,800 paper crowns on February 1st. This was finally on roughly par with its real value. Gross receipts showed a record so far and deposits in the banks kept growing. Expenditures were 20% in excess of what planned originally, but this was amply compensated for by the large surplus in revenues. However, as was now his custom, Smith could not refrain from noting that "there is no reason to expect that the causes that have brought about this surplus will continue to operate indefinitely, or to assume that the original programme of reform and economy is less urgent than it was when the Reconstruction Law was passed."[657] On the other hand, strikes made life more difficult for everyone. First it was the taxi drivers' strike in Budapest between December 30, 1924, and January 8, 1925, followed immediately by a strike in the coal mines in Pécs. Finally, work resumed four days later, because they were granted a 10% bonus.[658]

The real sensation, and really bad news, was that Smith got seriously ill. The pace at which he had been working started to take its toll. When he was about to start his journey to Hungary, he was characterized as "a man of abounding health and vigor."[659] The constant hard work that he had been doing so conscientiously attacked his health in the beginning of the New Year, and he simply "blew up."[660] On January 14th, Smith sent a telegram to his sister saying that he was not well, but he said it was nothing serious.[661] On the same day, however, the Commissioner-General had to move to a sanatorium in Budapest where the doctors predicted a two to three week period of rest.[662] Rumors started right away. *The New York Times*, for instance, referring to governmental circles, reported that there was no hope that Smith would carry on his work and after the required months of cure he would resign and return to the United States.[663] To counter such unfounded rumors, Tyler quickly had a statement issued through the Hungarian Telegraphic Agency that "Jeremiah Smith about whose health alarming reports have been circulated abroad, is in reality taking a short rest and will resume his work in

657 Smith's Ninth Report, LNJ, 6th Year, No. 4, April 1925, 545–53.
658 Brentano to Hughes, February 12, 1925, 864.00/616, Roll 7, M. 708, NARA.
659 *Boston Daily Globe*, April 8, 1924.
660 Smith to Niemeyer, May 25, 1925, OV9/437, BoE.
661 *The New York Times*, January 15, 1925.
662 *Magyarország*, January 15, 1925, XXXII/11.
663 *The New York Times*, January 15, 1925.

the course of a few days."[664] The breakdown of Smith's health was all the more unfortunate because he was facing heavy schedule. He was supposed to attend the meeting of the Committee of Control in Paris, but due to his illness he could not and the meeting was postponed to a later date. Also, in early February there was the League Council Meeting in Geneva, where Smith was expected to appear and give a report in person. In a few days' time Smith recovered to a satisfactory level and his Hungarian secretary György Királdi Lukács informed the press that Smith would be in Geneva on February 6th.[665] Despite such reassurance soon another article appeared in *The New York Times* predicting Smith's resignation "according to reliable information gathered in diplomatic circles."[666] James Speyer was worrying lest he lost such an invaluable link to Hungary, where he hoped to make more money in the future, and asked Smith to contradict reports about his early resignation.[667] Before Smith could reply, Speyer must have been happy to read that an unnamed British banker refuted the rumors about Smith's intention to resign his post in spite of his weakened health.[668] Finally, it was Smith who put an end the speculations and denied all the rumors and declared that from March 1st, he would again resume his post with full responsibility.[669]

Smith appeared before the Council in Geneva on February 6th. Here he mainly dealt with the issue of state officials and their salaries. Since 60% of the budget expenditure went to the salaries of these people, obviously anything touching upon their issue was of great importance. The idea was to increase the salary of a group of the state employees by 15%. It would have meant 34,000 people who made up, in the Commissioner-General's opinion, "an effective political machine."[670] It was obvious that to have such a high number of officials amounted to luxury under the present circumstances, but for political reasons the government was reluctant to part with many of them. Finally, Smith suggested that "the Hungarian Government should be authorised to make an advance to the officials of five months' salary upon an increased rate of 15 per cent" involving "an expenditure of 9 million gold crowns."[671] Salter would have

664 Tyler to Felkin, January 17, 1925, T. II. Incoming and outgoing telegrams, September 24–June 26, C. 120, Financial Reconstruction of Hungary, LNA; Press communiqué, January 17, 1925, P.III. Press communiqués, C. 117, Financial Reconstruction of Hungary, LNA.
665 *Magyarország*, January 28, 1925, XXXII/22.
666 *The New York Times*, February 6, 1925.
667 Speyer to Smith, February 6, 1925, T. II. Incoming and outgoing telegrams, September 2, 1924–June 30, 1926, C. 120, Financial Reconstruction of Hungary, LNA.
668 *Wall Street Journal*, February 10, 1925.
669 *The New York Times*, February 12, 1925.
670 Minutes of the Seventeenth Session, Second Meeting, February 6, 1925, F. /17th Session/P. V. 2(1), LNA.
671 Minutes of the Seventeenth Session, Eighth Meeting, February 10, 1925, F/17th Session/P.V. 8(1), LNA.

liked to see a bonus instead of an advance, but the Chairman of the Financial Committee thought it should fall under the decision of Smith which one to choose, but the sum was not to exceed 7.5 million gold crowns ($1.5 million) and was only for six months.[672] On the question of 15 million gold crowns ($3 million) for agricultural loan, upon Smith's suggestion, however, the Committee decided not in Hungary's favor. The ruling was that it was not possible to include such an amount of capital expenditure in the budget and could be only discussed if the Hungarian government provided a detailed plan as to its utilization.[673] Therefore, for the Hungarian government the February meetings in Geneva was a mixed success, but Bethlen still warmly praised Smith's work and emphasized that Hungary could thank a lot to the American Commissioner-General.[674]

Jeremiah Smith, Jr. did not return to Hungary right after the conclusion of the official agenda. He decided that he needed some more rest. He chose to spend two weeks at Territet, close to Geneva. He wrote a letter to Norman to inform him about the situation in Hungary. He said the Hungarian population was "already heavily taxed – if not overtaxed," and that he could not conceive of anyone lending the city of Budapest a loan at present.[675] The letter was the first he had written in a month and it was a very good testament how much he did need physical rest. The words he produced were misshapen, sometimes hardly decipherable, and they showed a severe strain on the author. Whatever the sickness might have been, Smith was still suffering from poor eyesight.[676] Toward the end of the month he had regained enough of his energy to go to Paris and take part in the postponed meeting of the Committee of Control. Only then did he return to Budapest on March 7th. Although improved in health, he worked less than formerly. He decided that the best thing for him would be a longer vacation in the United States and made preparations to leave for six weeks in early April.[677]

This period was the low point for Smith and not only from the state of his health. For the first time he was the subject of attack, a phenomenon so far unheard of. The incident took place on February 20th, at a district political banquet of the Democrats of Budapest, and the person criticizing Smith was Vilmos Vázsonyi of the National Democratic Party, also a member of the National Assembly. Although the speech was severely criticized by *Pester Lloyd*, it evoked no comment in other papers.[678] In addition, Smith was staying in Switzerland

672 Ibid.
673 Ibid.
674 *Pesti Hírlap*, February 14, 1925, XLVII/36.
675 Smith to Norman, February 15, 1925, OV33/73, BoE.
676 Ibid.
677 Brentano to Kellogg, April 10, 1925, 864.00/629, Roll 7, M. 708, NARA.
678 Brentano to Kellogg, March 11, 1925, 864.00/622, Ibid.

recovering, and had no chance to defend himself if he wanted to. To make things worse, shortly after his return to Hungary, Pál Sándor of the Liberal Citizens' Party attacked the Commissioner-General's work, accusing him of letting Hungary to be subjected to financial oppression.[679] His accusation appeared on the front page the next morning. He was quoted saying, "Jeremiah Smith is here to make sure that the sum that was given to Hungary would go to foreigners [...] He did not have the courage to say that he would not let the population to be racked [...] Smith is weak and has not done his duty."[680] Although other papers defended Smith, the attacks must have hurt him. He had done all he could for this country and still there were a few persons disparaging his work and saying he wanted not the best for the country. If anytime, this would have been an occasion to resign in fact. But Smith was made of stronger stock and with the worst of his health problem behind him, these attacks, if anything, only made him want to work more and achieve good results. Brentano, the American minister in Budapest reinforced in a message to the State Department that the resignation of Smith appeared to be "entirely unfounded."[681]

Among such circumstances Smith wrote his tenth report about the turbulent month of February. Here he started off with countering once more the charges that had surfaced. He emphatically denied that the program was impossible to carry out, that there was no sufficient cooperation between the Hungarian government, and that he would resign. In connection with the extra money to the state officials, he mentioned that in the end 95,000 of them will get relief from February through June. After deducting the 7 million gold crowns ($1.4 million) this action would consume, there would still remain a comfortable surplus. Smith dealt with the State Ironworks in this report. The earlier experienced phenomenon also held true here, that is, the expenses on the officials and pensioners were about twice as much compared to the pre-war period. Also, while in 1913 there was a surplus, now the industry could boast of a deficit five times the amount of the earlier surplus. In addition, Smith was of the opinion that there were too many people in active employment and the industry produced more than what could be realistically sold. Good news was also announced. The multiplier was further reduced to 14,600, and the prospects for a bountiful harvest were good, which in the case of Hungary was always very important. On the other hand, despite some decrease in the prices of textile, clothing, and some manufactured articles, these were still higher than in France, Italy, Austria, and often higher

679 Brentano to Kellogg, April 10, 1925, 864.00/629, Ibid; Barclay to Chamberlain, March 12, 1925, C3858/260/21, 10772, FO371, TNA.
680 *Magyarország*, March 12, 1925, XXXII/58.
681 Brentano to Kellogg, March 11, 1925, 864.00/622, Roll 7, M. 708, NARA.

than in Great Britain and the United States.[682] This was partly a result of the new decree according to which import duties were raised on 36 articles between 20 and 1,500%, including textile articles, plate-glass, iron and steel pipes, safety razor blades, razors, and cutlery.[683] This was evidence that things were still in need of improvement and the commercial treaties the League of Nations had put so much emphasis on, first and foremost with neighboring countries, were far from being concluded.

Part of the answer to Hungary's reluctance to conclude such trade agreements was the idea of economic nationalism, which was typical in Hungary, although this was not the exception in Central Europe in the 1920s, and later as well. Even though the League of Nations tried hard to press Hungary and other countries into this direction, it eventually failed to counter this trend. The idea behind this economic nationalism, namely that Hungary might be largely self-sufficient was not rooted in realistic ideas. That is one of the reasons why Hungary was slow in arriving at commercial treaties with various other European countries. Being an agricultural country, relatively backward in industry, Hungary, just like other Central European countries, would have needed more eagerly to join the circulation of free trade on the continent. Various hikes in tariffs over time did not help to create a healthier economic environment.

March was the last full month Smith had spent in Hungary before he left on vacation to the United States. His next report reflected a successful Hungary on the road to full financial maturity. True, for the first time since October a deficit was to be present in the monthly budget, to the extent of 1.6 million gold crowns ($320.000), but it was normal and was expected. There was also some decrease in the pledged revenues, but the sum alone in March was enough to cover 60% of one year's service of the loan. The state budget for the 1924/25 financial year showed a deficit of 99,930,500 million gold crowns ($20 million), a measure the National Assembly accepted on March 15th, and a figure that was just under the 100 million mark provided for by the Reconstruction Law. With all these good results, during the month Smith consented to certain money withdrawals by the government from the forced loan account. He allowed for 30 billion paper crowns ($411,000) as a loan for the purchase of livestock, 6.8 billion ($93,000) as a loan to the Pest Comitat Irrigation Company to bring wasteland under cultivation, and 8.5 billion ($116,000) to continue to build small lodging houses. Toward the end of March, the National Bank reduced the discount rate from 12 ½ to 11%. Semi-officially it was admitted that it was a somewhat experimental step and depending upon a positive reaction from the market, further reduction

682 All the information in the paragraph is from Smith's Tenth Report, LNJ, 6th Year, No. 5, May 1925, 661–72.
683 Brentano to Kellogg, March 11, 1925, 864.00/622, Roll 7, M. 708, NARA.

would take place. Also in the category of good news, a commercial treaty was signed with Poland on the most-favored-nation principle, the biggest advantage of which would be for Hungarian wine. It was also good news that both wholesale and retail prices showed a significant decrease in the first months of the year .[684] Despite his negative views earlier, the British adviser to the National Bank was also optimistic concerning the overall picture. In his memorandum he concluded the following:

> It is fairly safe to assume that nothing short of an international catastrophe can now shake the stability of the Hungarian Crown. If an odious comparison were permissible it might even be said that Hungarian currency is in fact – as it certainly is in the general opinion – more secure than Austrian currency.[685]

He also mentioned that "the weak spot of Hungarian public finance" was that 60% of the expenditure went for the payment of the personnel.[686] Another significant event was James Speyer's latest visit to Hungary. He timed it well just in time before Smith was leaving for a longer vacation. He stayed in Budapest for three days late March, and met with Smith among others.[687] He was again working on the preparation of another loan scheme for Hungary. Smith finally left Hungary for his long awaited holiday. Although he felt much better than during the winter, he was far from total recovery, and was looking forward to visiting his home.[688]

Smith arrived in the United States on April 15th. This was the first time he had traveled home since being appointed back in April 1924, so it was understandable that he craved the quiet of his home surroundings. While at home, he had to deal with his health issue as well. He saw a number of American doctors who agreed that he never had a hemorrhage of the brain at all. They claimed that the Hungarian diagnosis was wrong though the treatment prescribed was right. According to them, Smith had a "circulatory spasm," which meant that the circulation went wrong in certain parts of his body, as a result of advancing age and fatigue. His sight got bad and a blue spot appeared in each eye. The doctors

684 All the information in the paragraph is from Smith's Eleventh Report, LNJ, 6th Year, No. 6, June 1925, 813–21.
685 Siepmann's memorandum on the Hungarian situation, March 15, 1925, C4189/260/21, 10772, FO371, TNA.
686 Ibid.
687 Speyer to Smith, March 19 and March 23, 1925, T. II. Incoming and outgoing telegrams, September 2, 1924–June 30, 1926, C. 120, Financial Reconstruction of Hungary, LNA.
688 Smith to ter Meulen, March 23, 1925, C.III. (11) Correspondence - Mr. C. E. ter Meulen, C. 111, Financial Reconstruction of Hungary, LNA.

told him that he needed much more rest, which was bad news in light of the pace of the first eight months spent in Hungary.[689]

Also, he was target of some newspaper attention. One thing he was asked about was his refusal for compensation in the beginning of the job. He had this to say in connection with the topic: "I did it because I live simply and require little for my own needs. It hardly seemed fitting that I should urge sacrifice and economies upon the Hungarians and yet not show the same spirit myself."[690] He was also busy countering earlier accusations surfacing in the American press that he had problems with the Hungarian government. He praised the cooperation between the Bethlen government and himself and gave out optimistic vibrations about the Hungarian finances.[691] Coincidentally, an article of the Hungarian Prime Minister appeared also in the April issue of *Foreign Affairs*. Smith's interviews had been a great prelude to what Bethlen wrote. Aside from the political aspects that were phrased in a way to give the biggest possible legitimacy to the Hungarian government, Bethlen also played the financial card:

> I cannot sufficiently emphasize to my foreign readers the fact that even in her present form and structure Hungary offers the most favorable field conceivable for the investment of foreign capital. The industrial, commercial and agricultural possibilities open here to foreign capital and foreign enterprise are practically unlimited; all that is required is for them to be energetically seized and transformed. I am convinced that the financial world of America [...] will on this occasion too discover Hungary— which to a certain extent is perhaps still a terra incognita for American business men— is worthy of interest and study.[692]

As can be seen, he did everything possible in his power to induce American investors to look to Hungary as a lucrative spot, and Smith's widely quoted reports about the positive financial reconstruction had been preparing the ground for such plans.

No matter how apolitical Smith was and how much he wanted to avoid even the shadow of any charges that he was dealing with politics, sometimes he had to step up and say a few words in connection with such a subject. The incident that served such a situation was the Károlyi propaganda in the United States that Hungary should get no more loans because it would be spent on war intentions

689 As for Smith's health, the information came from Smith to Siepmann, in Siepmann to Norman, May 19, 1925, OV33/39, BoE.
690 *Boston Daily Globe*, April 15, 1925; *The New York Times*, April 16, 1925.
691 *Wall Street Journal*, April 16, 1925.
692 István Bethlen, "Hungary in the New Europe," *Foreign Affairs* 3 (April 1925): 455.

only.[693] He countered such charges with the logical assertion that only through him could the government have access to money to spend, but he would only provide money for the sensible financial and economic goals. He was quoted in *Time* magazine as saying: "The Government has no capital at its disposal which it could use without my knowledge for secret armaments and the rumors about preparation for war are nothing but naïve horror stories." [694] Smith defended the Bethlen government as well: "The Hungarian Government has risked even political unpopularity to cooperate with me, a fact of which I can speak only the greatest appreciation."[695] Whether he agreed with the Bethlen government politically is a different topic. But he certainly had found a cooperative partner in Bethlen and his government, a fact that he highly cherished, especially compared to what Alfred Zimmerman was subjected to in Vienna.

The report covering the month of April, when Smith was staying in the United States, showed further progress in the reconstruction program. Smith consented to further money withdrawal by the government from the forced loan account in April: 8.5 billion ($116,000) for small lodging houses and 12.8 billion ($175,000) to continue the building of a powder factory. Wholesale prices showed a further decrease, a continual occurrence since the start of the year. Although the revenues declined in a fashion Smith had warned about earlier, this phenomenon did not give reason to be alarmed, because the reasons were largely attributable to seasonal changes. Since the start of the reconstruction, the number of bankruptcies had been relatively low, 109, although so-called insolvencies had been abundant, 912. The big news was that Great Britain had reached gold parity again and it meant that Hungary, its crown pegged to the pound, got on gold value as well. This was naturally taken as good news. The crown had been stable for many months now and the debate had begun that how soon a new currency unit should be introduced.[696] So, when Smith returned to Hungary on May 15th, he had every reason to be "very cheerful and quite well."[697] His words that he was happy to be back in Budapest and was doing his

693 Count Mihály Károlyi was originally not granted visa to enter the United States, where his wife stayed ill, but later this was modified and he was permitted to visit but was not allowed to speak or write for publication while in the United States, a condition to which he agreed. When this sparked some debate in Congress, Hughes claimed that the action was taken under war legislation, which still survived. Finally, he was allowed to reply to attacks made against him on March 7, 1925, at a lunch given in his honor by the American Civil Liberties Union. His serious speech impediment made it unlikely for anyone to understand what he was going to say, anyway. Howard to Chamberlain, February 27, 1925, 3303/434/21, 10777, FO371, TNA.

694 *Time*, May 11, 1925.

695 Ibid.

696 All the information in the paragraph is from Smith's Twelfth Report, LNJ, 6th Year, No. 8, August 1925, 1095–1104.

697 Goode to Norman, May 19, 1925, OV33/73, BoE.

job with great pleasure pleased everyone reading front page news.[698] Smith also told Siepmann after his return that he had more will to learn about Hungary and to take an interest in forms of investment, a feature not present a year earlier.[699]

In his report for the month of May, Smith wrote that due to a falling-off in customs receipts, the smallest amount of pledged revenues was realized since last September. Still, owing to the good overall picture and realistic optimism about the future, Smith consented to an advance of 24 million gold crowns ($4.8 million) to certain towns, counties, and drainage societies for such work. Wholesale prices had been decreasing continually since the start of the year and deposits in the banks kept growing. As a sign of more healthy circumstances prevailing, on May 28th, the Bank's discount rate was reduced from 11% to 9%. Behind the step was a clear initiation by the National Bank to induce the other Budapest banks to follow suit and lower their interest rates in order to help enterprises to get easier access to credit. Unfortunately, such interbank cooperation brought no encouraging results.[700] Smith confirmed the overall good results in a personal letter to Otto Niemeyer, but complained that prices, despite a 15% decrease since last July, were sometimes still higher than in New York.[701] He added that the Hungarian government had provided "every evidence of goodwill and support [...] and they have really done very well up till now."[702] The foreign adviser, however, started to formulate negative criticism again. In a letter to Norman, Siepmann wrote his mentor that he was beginning to be afraid of what he called "the free lance campaign of borrowing" by Hungary.[703] He had a point. Just as the Bethlen article was a good indication of such initiatives, Hungary did indeed offer itself for foreign capital, mostly American, without paying too much heed for possible future consequences. What helped such a course was partly the opinion held by the banker segment in the United States. As an analyzing company concluded, of the foreign loans raised in the United States four were entitled to a preferred rating (the Austrian, the Hungarian, the German, and the Czech issues), but "the most attractive" was the Hungarian bond.[704] One of the reasons on which they based this conclusion was that the Hungarian reconstruction was under the supervision of Smith.

---

698 *Magyarország*, May 19, 1925, XXXII/112.
699 Siepmann to Norman, May 19, 1925, OV33/39, BoE.
700 All the information in the paragraph is from Smith's Thirteenth Report, LNJ, 6th Year, No. 8, August 1925, 1105–16.
701 Smith to Niemeyer, May 25, 1925, OV9/437, BoE.
702 Ibid.
703 Siepmann to Norman, May 19, 1925, OV33/39, BoE.
704 W. A. Harriman & Co. Analyses, June 5, 1925, L.V. (2) May 1925–Dec 1927, C. 114, Financial Reconstruction of Hungary, LNA.

Speaking of American capital, Speyer was as active as ever. He wanted to confer with Smith in person while the latter was still in the United States, but he missed him by one day and the banker had to rely on letters again. The subject was a possible agricultural loan for Hungary, which earlier the League refused to advance from the loan money. Speyer asserted that William Goode's plan to raise the money in London was impractical, since the London market was closed for the season, and concluded that "it naturally follows that our market here is the principal one to rely on for this and similar foreign businesses during this period."[705] He reiterated in the same letter that it was "an essential condition for us that you approve of the plan."[706] Speyer gave the bankers' responsibility toward the League as a natural reference to the approval of the League Commissioner. Smith in his answer, however, categorically objected to his name being used in connection with loans falling outside the League. He was quite afraid that his name referred to in that fashion "would be misunderstood by people who ought not to draw erroneous conclusions but who probably would do so."[707] Finally, Speyer had to settle for the municipal loan for Hungarian cities, which was good business for the American banking house.

Although Smith did not respond to Speyer's inquiry about his health, in a personal letter to Elliot Felkin, member of the Financial Committee, he wrote about his health condition. His answer was revealing: "I am a good deal better than I was, but I am not entirely recovered yet and don't expect to be for a good while. I have my ups and downs and some days think that it is quite impossible to continue with the work, and other days think quite differently about it."[708] This was the closest that Smith had ever come to expressing doubts about his physical capability to go on with the League job. It can be attributed only to his dogged persistence and his high sense of responsibility that he kept on working with the same amount of zeal and optimism. Naturally, he had Tyler and Charron to rely on. He also confided in Siepmann concerning his health, and the Briton duly sent the information to Norman. According to Siepmann, Smith would not be "quite his old self," would take more care of himself, would work less, and was already planning to go back to the United States in the middle of November for two months.[709] With lingering problems about his health put on the sideline, he started to look after the state finances of Hungary with renewed vigor and was preparing for the next League Assembly

705 Speyer to Smith, May 15, 1925, A. IV. a. Agricultural credits, mortgage bonds, land reforms, C. 106, Financial Reconstruction of Hungary, LNA.

706 Ibid.

707 Smith to Speyer, May 30, 1925, Ibid.

708 Smith to Felkin, May 22, 1925, C.III (6) Correspondence - M. A. E. Felkin, C. 111, Financial Reconstruction of Hungary, LNA.

709 Siepmann to Norman, May 19, 1925, OV33/39, BoE.

meeting in early June in Geneva, which Tyler predicted would be "a critical juncture."[710]

Smith was a feature of the second League Assembly of the year and he appeared before the Council on June 9th. This was the official platform to summarize the first year of reconstruction for everybody interested. Naturally, the figures were known thanks to the monthly reports of Smith; still, such a gathering offered a more prominent stage to highlight the most important achievements and to introduce the results of the first year to the world at large. The most spectacular element without any doubt was the fact that the 100 million gold crowns estimated for the deficit for the first year had not been drawn upon and there would be a surplus of 63 million gold crowns ($12.6 million) instead.[711] The Financial Committee decided that this surplus and a further 30 million gold crowns ($6 million) could be used for productive purposes, subject to the agreement of the Commissioner-General.[712] The Council approved that for about 95,000 state officials the increase in salaries of 15% in February should be permanent to the amount of 20 million gold crowns, even if it meant a 15 million ($ 3 million) extra burden on the budget annually.[713] The low point of the report was the tax question. It remained very substantial, 75 gold crowns ($15) per head, which was extremely high for Hungary and meant 135% of the pre-war level. As Smith put it in Geneva, "the taxation in Hungary has reached the limit of possibility and capacity."[714] It was obvious that sooner rather than later some tax reduction was necessary and the government started to work on it.

In addition to the Council resolutions, Smith mentioned the following points in his report for June. The results of the 1924/1925 financial year altogether, and somewhat surprisingly, made Smith conclude that "it is certain that there will be a substantial surplus—a result far beyond the most sanguine expectations entertained by anyone a year ago." In the first year of the reconstruction program retail price index decreased by 14%, while whole-sale prices fell by 8%. The average wages reached the prewar level, but in terms of purchasing powers they still lagged behind. The estimate for the financial year of 1925/26 showed a budget surplus of 27.5 million gold crowns ($5.5 million), the government using a multiplier of 14.500. Commercial treaties were concluded with Greece and Spain, on June 3rd June 17th, respectively, with the most-favored-nation clause. Deposits in the banks grew further, which was a clear indication of the trust

710 Tyler to Mildred Bliss, April 15, 1925, Tyler Papers.
711 LNJ, 6th Year, No. 7, July 1925, 859.
712 Report of the Committee, June 11, 1925, C. 335 (I). M. 116. 1925, LNA.
713 LNJ, 6th Year, No. 9, September 1925, 1243–1244.
714 *Pesti Hírlap*, June 6, 1925, XLVII/125.

was for twenty years and carried a 7.5% interest.[720] Speyer bought the bonds at 82% and sold them for 89%, thus realizing a comfortable profit.[721] Therefore, it can be safely concluded that Speyer & Co. filled an important segment in the investors' camp providing loans for Hungary.

Despite its conspicuous role, the relationship between Speyer & Co. and the Hungarian government was not always harmonious, however. Sometimes there were serious frictions on account of business. For instance, Speyer was hurt because his offer for the upcoming Counties Loan, after the reconstruction program was successfully finished, was better than that of Rothschild's, still the Hungarian government chose the London house. This happened despite Speyer's repeated protests to the contrary and the promise of privileges earlier promised by Finance Minister Bud. In fact, according to Bud, the problem arose from Speyer's noncommittal attitude. Already during the Cities Loan, Speyer & Co. was willing to negotiate about the price of issue on the very last day only. This time around, the American company did not go farther than verbal declarations despite several urgings from the Hungarian Finance Minister, who,

720 One year later, Speyer & Co. was also the agent in floating a second series of the same type of loan, the Second Hungarian Consolidated Municipal Loan, which was issued September 1, 1926. This loan was for $6,000,0000, for twenty years and with 7% interest.

721 The sum provided by the loan, however, did not prove sufficient for most of the cities involved, and new cities wanted to apply for a similar loan. So, the government raised the sum with 34,470 gold crowns. Inántsy-Pap, *A magyar városok Speyer-kölcsönei*, 12. Originally, the cities wanted much more, and the option was "offered to Speyer, without a time limit." Siepmann to Norman, May 31, 1926, OV33/42, BoE. It meant a further $6 million from Speyer & Co., which meant 30 million gold crowns. According to Article 6 of the first contract, the cities had to make an offer for Speyer & Co. first, and in case of identical offers Speyer & Co. was the house to conclude business with. This was basically a contractual repeat of the promise earlier made by the Hungarian Finance Minister. Thus Speyer & Co. was also the agent in floating the second series of the same type of loan, the Second Hungarian Consolidated Municipal Loan of $6,000,0000, also for twenty years. This contract was signed on October 27, 1926, and the offer was quite decent. The interest rate went down to 7%, the price of bonds Speyer & Co. paid was raised to 89% and the price of issue was 93.5%, a spectacular difference compared to the first installment. From the second loan, less than 10% was allowed to be spent on nonproductive investments, while in the case of the first loan, this number was 25%. Inántsy-Pap, *A magyar városok Speyer-kölcsönei*, 16. Out of the total $16 million, the cities received a net sum of 74,349.659 gold crowns (almost $15 million). In the end, out of the 74,349.659 gold crowns, 13,350.126 were spent on nonproductive investments, and 60,999.533 on productive investments. Ibid., 20, 26. The cities did not always spend the money in a wise way. A typical example was that of the city of Miskolc, which after the two Speyer loans in 1925 and 1926, from which the city tried to finance too many things, was forced to take up a third loan to the amount of $800,000, under strict conditions, in order to be able to repay the Speyer loans and keep financing the construction works under way and other various projects. Still, by 1931 the city defaulted and was unable to pay. In detail, see István Dobrossy. "Miskolc infrastruktúrájának modernizálása és a 'Speyer' bankkölcsön felhasználása (1925–1950) [The Modernization of the Infrastructure of Miskolc and Using the Speyer Loans]," In. *Yearbook of the Herman Ottó Museums*, XXXIII–XXXIV (Miskolc: 1996), 423–51.

in the end, chose the Rothschild-Baring-Schröder group, which made a slightly worse offer.[722] But the American banking house was way too important for the Hungarian government, Speyer's origins notwithstanding. William Goode, the British adviser on the Hungarian government's payroll, warned earlier, too, that "It is, of course, important to retain Speyers' goodwill."[723] For Hungary, it was simply very important to have a bank in the United States they could count on. Racial views were forgotten in such cases. Those only had place within the borders of the country.

Aside from the Speyer Loan, not much happened in July. The final statistics for the 1924/25 fiscal year showed a budget surplus of roughly 63 million gold crowns ($12.6 million). This information in itself was not very telling. Obviously, just the pure fact that there was a significant surplus on hand made Smith, the Hungarian government, and the League all satisfied, because it gave clear evidence that the program was on the right track. Further boost emanated from the fact that foreign credit had started to come, mostly in short-term form, with a few long-term ones, chiefly from the United States. Even more importantly, so far Hungary had avoided overborrowing. The National Bank's metal reserves had doubled since its opening and this made Smith conclude: "It is safe to say that the Hungarian crown is now secure not only in fact but also in the confidence of the public." Commercial treaties had been concluded with Poland, Greece, Spain, and Italy. In terms of foreign trade though, the most important partners were Austria and Czechoslovakia, Germany being a distant third, countries with which there were no treaties concluded yet. Wholesale prices showed a further decrease, while deposits in the banks grew and reached an amount five times more than a year before. All these data and symptoms meant that Hungary was "far in advance of the Reconstruction Plan," which made Smith look to the future with "confidence and great hope."[724] The multiplier was officially reduced from 17,000 to 14,500 for the payment of taxes, public dues, and rentals, and as of July 1st, 2,000 more officials were retired.[725]

In a confidential memorandum, Smith also made account of the expenses of the commissariat. It was about $37,000, and as far as his own expenses were concerned, he wrote this: "The Commission-General has been furnished

722 Bud to Goode, August 5, 1926, 1/22/1926/91–92, K 276, Bud Papers, HNA. The loan issued in London by the Rothschild group was successful and was oversubscribed twenty times. There was another British consortium, the British Overseas Bank and Helbert Wagg & Co., which complained of not receiving the contract despite of offering a higher bid than the Rothschild group. However, the prestige of the Jewish banking house seemed to be overwhelming for Hungarian officials. Goode to Bud, July 30, 1926, /87–89, Ibid.

723 Goode to Bud, November 20, 1925, 1/7/1925/8, Ibid.

724 All the information in the paragraph is from Smith's Fifteenth Report, LNJ, 6th Year, No. 11, November 1925, 1637–46.

725 Brentano to Kellogg, July 31, 1925, 864.00/656, Roll 7, M. 708, NARA.

by the Hungarian Government with a residence and a motor car, but has not drawn from the Government the full amount of $18,000 per year to which he is entitled, having taken only his living expenses in Budapest, which are at the rate of substantially $200 a month."[726] This summary showed well that Smith indeed tried to save as much money as possible and make a good example by not accepting his salary. Almost as a symbolic close for the 1924/25 fiscal year, once again a small commemoration was held at the George Washington statute on account of July 4, where both Brentano and Smith appeared. It was a rare occasion where photos were actually taken of Smith and later they also appeared in newspapers.[727]

The August report shed some light on the revenues in term of taxes. In the 1924/25 fiscal year, out of the whole revenues, direct taxes were responsible for about one fifth, whereas turnover taxes produced about a quarter of the total. This was somewhat surprising and not necessarily welcomed news. The direct taxes had been expected to produce a larger percentage and it was not clear why the 36% planned in the reconstruction plan achieved only 20% of all revenues from various taxes. As part of this result and of the overtaxation of the population Smith had already complained about, the turnover tax was reduced from 3% to 2% as of August 1st. The other surprisingly large proportion of such revenues was the customs, which produced more than twice as much as planned. This was not necessarily good news because of its negative effects on the domestic trade of the country. The Council had agreed that the Hungarian government could make capital investments for 70 million gold crowns ($14 million). In his sixteenth report, Smith listed under thirteen headings the planned program for the first half of the 1925/26 fiscal year.[728] As Smith notified Finance Minister Bud, he accepted every suggestion of the government, except the 68,000 gold crowns ($13,600) for exploration purposes, which he did not accept as capital investment.[729] The rest of the August report made also mention of negotiations with France and Turkey for commercial treaties that had been concluded, and about the now standard feature of the reconstruction program, namely that wholesale prices showed a further decrease and deposits in the banks grew anew.[730] In addition, since last September, the number of unemployed had been the lowest in August,

726 Smith to Salter, September 24, 1925, E.I.–1. Expenses, July 1, 1925–June 30, 1926, C. 113, Financial Reconstruction of Hungary, LNA.
727 *Pesti Hírlap*, July 7, 1925, XLVII/149; *The New York Times*, August 9, 1925.
728 All the information in the paragraph is from Smith's Sixteenth Report, LNJ, 6th Year, No. 11, November 1925, 1647–57.
729 Smith to Bud, August 25, 1925, B.V. (3) Budget Surplus Account, 1924–25, C. 109, Financial Reconstruction of Hungary, LNA.
730 Smith's Sixteenth Report.

but this was largely thanks to the harvest season, when many unemployed people found temporary job.[731]

In August, not only Smith wrote about the Hungarian financial landscape. Prominent experts came to study the financial situation in Hungary. Professor Allyn Young of Harvard and a Belgian financial expert, Maurice Frère, spent a little bit over three weeks in Hungary going over all the possible details of the present financial and economic life in Hungary before traveling to Geneva to give verbal summary of their report.[732] The report was not intended to be as fully detailed as the Layton-Rist report in the case of Austria, which was the basis for this study to be carried out, but rather to inform the Hungarian Commissioner-General. It is worth mentioning the main conclusions of the report, which was finished on August 24th.[733] As far as population was concerned, the authors claimed that the ratio of urban population was too high and this would lead to such results as a relatively low level of real wages, a relatively low industrial output per capita, a wasteful multiplication of middlemen, and a tendency to rely upon state aid rather than upon productive efforts. The report emphasized that agriculture should receive four times as much weight as industry. Light was also shed on the well-known fact that "the present level of money wages in Budapest [wa]s extremely low [...] In most of the industrial countries of Europe they [we]re distinctly higher." In the realm of taxation, the report echoed Smith in the assertion that the country was heavily taxed. The suggestion was a new tax form along new lines in place of the present and much discredited income tax. The most important point was, especially in hindsight, that Hungary needed foreign capital to complete the economic recovery. The following observation was made: "The danger lies, not in borrowing, but in over-borrowing or in borrowing for non-productive purposes [...] The real danger is from such borrowing as might be undertaken, not in order to reap business profits, but to 'better the situation.'" As can be seen, the report did not provide much new information; it rather confirmed earlier observations by others, Smith among them. Since the overall outcome of the report was optimistic and the dangers it listed seemed not present at the moment, it boosted the already successful reconstruction program.

September was again the time for the usual pilgrimage to Geneva, where Smith was to give a summary of the past year in Hungarian finances. In front of the Council he claimed, "there is every reason to believe that the permanent

731 Ibid.

732 Smith to Slater, August 19, 1925, T. II. Incoming and outgoing telegrams, September, 1924–June, 1926, C. 120, Financial Reconstruction of Hungary, LNA.

733 The whole report can be found in 3/1921–1928 B/2. 570/925, K 468, Bethlen Papers, HNA. If not mentioned otherwise, the information discussed in the paragraph is from this source.

equilibrium of the Hungarian State finances will be maintained."[734] The next day he appeared at the Financial Committee to give a more detailed report. Smith informed the Committee about the main results of the first year, which were "far beyond what anyone could have foreseen."[735] As he explained, all this was achieved by the immense increase in revenues, 40–50% more than the estimates, which was attributable to the stabilization of the crown, despite the 10% increase in expenditure.[736] He once again hammered at the heavy taxation in Hungary. Although the total taxation in Hungary amounted to 75 gold crowns ($15) per head, much lighter than in Western European countries, when computed in percentage of the national income, the taxes proved high.[737] The future also seemed promising. The harvest had been the best since the war, the economic conditions showed a slow but steady improvement, the estimates showed a balanced budget for the 1925/26 fiscal year, and all these fragments made Smith believe that the satisfactory condition at present was going to be permanent.[738] The American again emphasized the cooperation he had received from the government, and praised the international effort brought on by the initiative of the League of Nations.[739] Smith's statement was very favorably received not only by the League but also by Hungary as well. He was especially praised for the act when he countered the Little Entente delegate's charges that there was any secret item in the expenditures.[740]

The Commissioner-General's report for September, as had been done on various earlier occasions, put a topic in the center. This time it was the question of taxation in Hungary. Based upon his calculations, the estimated per capita tax burden for the 1925/1926 financial year (60 gold crowns) was by and large the same as in the pre-war years. When compared to other European countries, the Hungarian tax burden seemed lightly. In Germany it was more than twice, in France two and a half times as much, the case was similar in Great Britain, and in Austria it was almost twice as much as in Hungary. However, it must be noted that the prewar taxes in the Austro-Hungarian Monarchy were higher than in most European countries, and Hungary being a chiefly agricultural country was not in a position to extract more money from its subjects. Moreover, in addition to state taxes, people were to pay local taxes as well, which meant, on an average, a further 12 gold crowns from the taxpayers. The rest of the

734 LNJ, 6th Year, No. 10, October 1925, 1355.
735 Statement of Smith, September 11, 1925, Financial Reconstruction of Hungary, Discussions at the 6th Assembly, 1925. Doc. No. 46255, Registry Files, R. 301, LNA.
736 Ibid.
737 Ibid.
738 Ibid.
739 Ibid.
740 *Pesti Napló*, September 11, 1925, 76/203.

report contained good news: For the first time since the war, August had showed a favorable trade balance (+8.3 million gold crowns) thanks to the excellent harvest, which had been the best since the war; deposits in the banks grew and since last September, the number of unemployed had been the lowest, although due to seasonal works.[741] To boost further confidence in what seemed a healthy business environment at work, the shares of the National Bank were issued on the Budapest stock exchange on September 21, 1925.[742] All segments seemed to ensure that the second part of the reconstruction would be business as usual.

October was a dull month compared to some preceding ones. That was actually good news because it was further proof that the program was running smoothly and no unexpected obstacles arose. In his report pertaining to this month, Smith had only the usual good news to tell about wholesale prices, the number of unemployed, and deposits in the banks. The only really significant event was also good news. The National Bank's discount rate was further reduced, this time from 9 to 7%. Behind this step the Commissioner-General surmised was the intention to keep the short-time foreign credits away as much as possible, and to induce Hungarians more to borrow money from the National Bank.[743] Smith, who had a really amicable relationship with the government, tried to use his practical American mind and convince them to make the most of the idle money of the loan that was not needed because of the good budget figures. He explained to Speyer, when the latter had information according to which Smith had refused to give consent for using the said money, that he had been for some time urging the Hungarians to utilize some part of the reconstruction money mainly for temporary investment, but they were not willing to do so.[744] As Smith calculated, the Hungarian government might have been afraid that doing so would be illegal, so he thought of using the money only with the consent of the League of Nations. The sole purpose would have been to gain some money and not to boost the price of the Hungarian Bonds, although that was a possible consequence as well.[745] Henry Strakosch absolutely resented the idea, because he saw in it only jobbing purposes.[746]

In the last week of October, as he had planned back in spring, Jeremiah Smith, Jr. once more traveled home to the United States. He was planning to spend two

741 Smith's Seventeenth Report, LNJ, 6th Year, No. 12, December 1925, 1759–1769.
742 Tamás Bácskai, ed., A Magyar Nemzeti Bank története [The History of the Hungarian National Bank] vol. 1. (Budapest: Közgazdasági és Jogi Kiadó, 1993), 549.
743 All the information in the paragraph is from Smith's Eighteenth Report, LNJ, 7th Year, No. 2, February 1926, 241–48.
744 Speyer to Smith and Smith to Speyer, September 12, 1925, L. V. c–1, June 24–30, 1924, C. 114, Financial Reconstruction of Hungary, LNA.
745 Smith to Norton, October 17, 1925, OV9/438, BoE.
746 Strakosch to Niemeyer, October 21, 1925, Ibid.

months on vacation, a period that his battered health was in great need of. Before setting sail, he stayed a few days in London to confer with the principal actors. He had long talks with Montagu Norman, for example. Smith asserted that state of Hungary was such "as to justify and demand the termination of League control by the end of June 1926."[747] The main points of these talks were the future of the *Geldinstituteszentrale* (a financial institution where public funds were kept outside the control of the National Bank) and the position of the Bank Adviser. In the former, the unanimous idea was that its role must be suppressed, while in the case of the Bank Adviser, the conclusion was that although the National Bank would be happy to have the Adviser for a prolonged time, the League had no right to renew the post.[748] The question would come up at spring session of the League of Nations.

Smith's homecoming was inadvertently set up by a Hungarian. Gustav Gratz, former finance minister of Hungary, was the principal speaker at the annual meeting of the Academy of Political Science on October 28th, where he praised Smith and his work in Hungary.[749] So, when Smith set on foot on his home soil after more than half a year again on November 6th, the ground was prepared. The main points and figures of his reports had been quoted in the leading newspapers, but since nothing special had happened in Hungary, only the continual good results, attention was somewhat lacking. With his relatively longer stay, Smith got again in the limelight, something he did not enjoy. He was seen by many as the ruler of Hungary in terms of monetary issues, which was true in many ways. However, when a leading paper asked what it was like to be the "financial czar of all the Magyars," he answered, "It is all very interesting. Undoubtedly I have great powers, but I see no chance of using them. All my work is done in collaboration with my Hungarian colleagues, and we have never yet had a single difference of opinion."[750] This was once again a typical Smith interview: succinct, modest, and going out of his way to praise the efforts of the Hungarian government. After the first barrage of interviews, Smith kept a low profile and spent most of his time with his sister and rested. Only occasionally did he take on public appearances. One was the prestigious annual dinner of the Alumni Association of Boston, in which he took part.[751]

While he was in the United States in November and December, life did not cease in Hungary, although no groundbreaking events took place. The reduction

747 Notes of conversation between the Governor, Mr. Jeremiah Smith, Commissioner General for Hungary, and Mr. Siepmann, November 6, 1925, OV33/40, BoE.

748 Ibid.; Norman to Salter, November 5, 1925, Norman to Niemeyer, December 11, 1925, and Niemeyer to Norman, December 12, 1925, all in OV33/40, BoE.

749 *Boston Daily Globe*, October 29, 1295.

750 *The New York Times*, July 11, 1926.

751 *Boston Daily Globe*, December 10, 1925.

in the National Bank's interest rate had not affected the ruling customs as far as interest rates went. In Budapest, the average was 12-13%, while in the provinces, three-month loans tended to charge 20% per year. In mid-October, control and restriction of foreign exchange was repealed. The most momentous event took place on November 6, 1925, when the National Assembly passed the bill providing for the introduction of the *Pengő* from January 1, 1927, based on gold. It would be equivalent of 12.500 paper crowns and its ration to the two leading foreign currency would be as follows: 1£=27.825 gold crowns and 1$=5.7176 gold crowns.[752] Upon Smith's and the League's prodding, the Hungarian government, in a meeting held on November 27th, decided that state money could be only held at the National Bank or at the Royal Hungarian Postal Savings Bank.[753] Although it was not carried out in absolute measures, it was an important step to break with older traditions, and a few months later a further decision now named the National Bank as the sole place where state moneys could be stored.[754] Faith in the National bank was strong outside Hungary, especially in the most important place, London. As Norman wrote to his apprentice in Budapest, "so long as M. Popovics is President, the interests of the National Bank will I am sure be in safe hands."[755]

Smith's latest and prolonged absence gave ground to various conjectures. One of the papers went as far as claiming that the financial control might cease before the originally planned date and the American commissioner would not even come back to Hungary.[756] Although such rumors reflected wishes rather than reality, their timing was not coincidental. In a few days' time, Geneva hosted the winter session and it was possible that very important decisions would be made in connection with Hungary.

This was the only occasion when Smith could not be present at the Assembly meeting and in front of the Financial Committee. Such task fell on his deputy, Royall Tyler, who "enjoyed it after the first emotion was over."[757] The Financial Committee congratulated Hungary and Smith, agreed to the release of $50 million gold crowns ($10 million) for productive purposes, but called attention to further commercial treaties and centralization of state funds.[758] The Hungarian sub-Committee also stated that the overall results of the reconstruction program

752 All the information in the paragraph is from Smith's Nineteenth Report, LNJ, 7th Year, No. 3, March 1926, 466–74.
753 November 27, 1925, 10–11R/46. 7th daily item. K 27, Records of Cabinet Council Meetings, HNA.
754 March 12, 1926, 18–19R/46. 11th daily item. Ibid.
755 Norman to Siepmann, December 10, 1925, OV33/40, BoE.
756 *Pesti Hírlap*, December 1, 1925, XLVII/272.
757 Tyler to Mildred Bliss, December 31, 1925, Tyler Papers.
758 LNJ, 7th Year, No. 2, February 1926, 131.

so far were commendable. Based upon Smith's earlier report, the Committee listed all the achievements but called attention to what in its opinion was still missing: further liberalization of the tariff policy, although it was a question of closer cooperation with neighboring states, and further decrease in taxes, especially in indirect taxes.[759] Incidentally, the money given to Hungary for productive purposes was a compromise. Despite the fact that the representative of the Little Entente wanted the question of the 50 million gold crowns to be postponed, the Council agreed to grant it, but at the same time it refused the Hungarian request for the release of the remainder of the loan, (132 million gold crowns, $26.5 million) for capital investments over a period of three years.[760] The decision was obviously a political one. On the one hand, the Little Entente with French backing did not want to see Hungary prospering beyond a certain limit if they could help it. On the other hand, Hungary was clearly on the way of recovery and the more it could spend on productive purposes, the sooner it would achieve a fully rehabilitated status, which was the primary goal of the whole reconstruction program. In addition, the overall European goal was that as many countries as possible should prosper and cooperate fully. The Council's decision was a classic political compromise that neither side could really challenge.

The Commissioner-General's report for December did not contain any significant news aside from the League Council's decision. He listed the usual pleasing data: the National Bank's metal reserves had been gradually rising overall and were very satisfactory; the past few months showed a slight favorable trade balance; retail prices had been the lowest since the reconstruction law was passed; and deposits in the banks further grew.[761] Despite the favorable results, Smith warned against increasing expenditure, because the past few months had been the best and they might be misleading in the long run. Still, he concluded with his now trademark optimism that "the possibility of the permanent equilibrium of the Budget can be looked to with confidence."[762] As the year of 1926 began, all concerned were aware that the financial reconstruction of Hungary had been on the right track and unless unexpected disaster struck, the planned conclusion to the work in six months' time would be a reality.

The two months Smith spent home were enough to recharge his batteries. The quiet surroundings of New England, the getaway from the daily strain of

759 Meeting of the Committee of the Council for Hungary, December 7, 1925, Financial Reconstruction of Hungary, Provisional minutes of the 9th Session: December 1925. Doc. No. 48287, Registry Files, R. 301, LNA.

760 Ibid.; LNJ, 7th Year, No. 2, February 1926, 231–32. In addition, Hungary was warned once more to conclude more commercial treaties and further suppress the number of officials. Ibid.

761 Smith's Twentieth Report, LNJ, 7th Year, No. 3, March 1926, 475–83.

762 Ibid.

work, and the positive results so far all made Smith look forward to the next and hopefully closing period. He sailed back to the old continent on January 1st and, after a few days in London and Geneva, he arrived on the Orient Express back in Budapest in mid-January.[763] The Hungarian newspapers reported the event as a major one. Giving weight to the return of the Commissioner-General, even photographs appeared in some of the papers.[764] A conspicuous feature was his returned vigor. As one paper described, "he returned to Hungary with great joy and wishes with renewed energy to work, in cooperation with the government, on the economic reconstruction of the country."[765] Just as an echo to this news, right after his arrival, Smith met with Bethlen and Bud and conferred with them about the past two months and the next period. In a special interview given to a paper the same evening, Smith had good news to tell.

> I am happy to state that the foreign circles concerned with Hungary all share the same opinion that today the success of the reconstruction is a fact [...] They see that Hungary has managed to own all the tools that can guarantee the confident progress of the economic improvement [...] Based upon my impressions elsewhere, foreigners look upon the Hungarian economy with the biggest trust.[766]

This was confirmed by the Hungarian legation in Washington. In its January report it emphasized that the favorable opinion in the United States was attributable to Smith's reports that always got place among the news, and the American population heavily relied on them in formulating its opinion about the Hungarian economic and financial situation.[767] When Smith was asked about the recently uncovered franc forgery, he quickly demonstrated his apolitical nature again and tersely replied, "I do not deal with this question."[768]

---

763 *Boston Daily Globe*, December 31, 1925; Brentano to Kellogg, January 30, 1926, 864.00/669, Roll 7, M. 708, NARA.
764 *Magyarország*, January 15, 1926, XXXIII/11; *Pesti Napló*, January 15, 1926, 77/11.
765 *Budapesti Hírlap*, January 15, 1926, XLVI/11.
766 *Pesti Napló*, January 15, 1926, 77/11.
767 53/1926 I–5. Washington I/57, K 66, Press and Cultural Department, HNA.
768 *Pesti Napló*, January 15, 1926, 77/11. On December 14, 1925, a Hungarian officer, Aristid Jankovich was arrested in the Netherlands when trying to pay with forged 1,000 French franc note. From the end of January, Bethlen was also compromised, but Horthy, Apponyi, Great Britain, and Italy were backing him. First, some officials in the French foreign political establishment wanted to make use of the scandal and cause a government crisis or change in Hungary, but nothing came of it and during the League session in March, the franc forgery was not dealt with officially. Finally, the alleged perpetrators got their not too heavy sentences in the summer. More about the scandal in detail, see Ignác Romsics, "Franciaország, Bethlen és a frankhamisítás," [France, Bethlen, and the Franc Forgery] *Történelmi Szemle* 26 (1983): 67–86.

Back in harness, Smith focused with all his energy on the reconstruction. He was in an easier situation compared to when he had started, because the past year and a half had been ample proof that the goal would be reached comfortably by the planned deadline, June 30, 1926. The *Geldinstituteszentrale* remained on the agenda. The British axis, Norman and Siepmann, was of the opinion that President of the National Bank Popovics was the key person, who should have put more pressure into restricting the functions of the institution. Norman simply said that the institution "should be suppressed," although he did not question its sometimes useful role in the unusual Hungarian circumstances.[769] Niemeyer urged Smith that this question be solved as soon as possible, especially in light of the franc forgery scandal.[770] Smith replied that the government had seemingly made up its mind that all state moneys should be concentrated at the National Bank, but in order to avoid it without aggravating the local opinion any further in this question, the *Geldinstituteszentrale* should be "bought off."[771] He also laid pressure on finance minister Bud in this question. He managed to get a personal guarantee from him that by the end of June 1926, the problem would be settled "beyond any possibility of cavil," even if there were voices against this move.[772] The Center would be reorganized to its original function, that is, to provide help in exceptionally difficult times. Strangely, the nagging and unsettled question of this institution had been on the agenda basically all through the reconstruction period and never seemed to go away. Once again it was evidence that old traditions died a very slow death in this part of the world.

In January the National Assembly accepted the State budget for the 1925/26 fiscal year. 20 million gold crowns ($4 million) were temporarily released from the loan for buying silver and other metals necessary for coinage of the new currency. The sum would be repaid as soon as coins had been minted and were ready to be put into circulation. Right after the franc forgery scandal began, speculators started to take advantage of the situation, but the Bank was able to offer unlimited amount of foreign currency and thus saved the stability of the Hungarian currency. £1,000,000 of the 7% Land Mortgage Bonds of the Hungarian Land Mortgage Institute (*Magyar Földhitel Intézet*) was issued in London with success. The bankers paid 86.5 and it was offered at 93 to the public. Although food prices were on a similar or lower level compared to other countries, some manufactured articles were two to ten times as expensive as in Paris, London, or New York. The question of how to spend the surplus and the

769 Lojkó, *Meddling in Middle Europe*, 125–26.
770 Niemeyer to Smith, January 11, 1926, OV9/439, BoE.
771 Smith to Niemeyer, January 22, 1926, Ibid.
772 Siepmann to Norman, February 3, 1926, OV33/41, BoE; *Magyarország*, April 9, 1926, XXXIII/79.

released money by the League for capital investments came to the fore again. The list included twenty-one different items on which the 73 million gold crowns ($14.6 million) were going to be spent. Among the many items such various recipients were named as municipal public hospitals, schools, development of the public road, short-term agricultural loans, tobacco planters, the previously mentioned *Geldinstituteszentrale*, State Ironworks, Port of Budapest, and Drainage Societies.[773] Smith later approved a further increase of 55,000 gold crowns ($11,000) for the Komló State coal mines and 2 million gold crowns ($400,000) for the Central Credit Association for Agriculture.[774] But Smith did not consent to the inclusion of establishing branches of the State vine cellars in Vienna, Warsaw, and Germany, simply because he did not think that it would be the kind of capital investment the League of Nations had in mind.[775] Smith thus was not giving a blank check for Hungary so that they could spend the surplus on whatever they thought. If they wanted to include something in the investment program that did not fit Smith's ideas, he would stubbornly refuse it.

7.3. The Closing Accords of the Great Work

The next few months brought a calm prelude to the grand finale. No major events took place in February and March, and Smith had only good news to tell once more. In 1925, unfavorable trade balance was only minus 5.4% but the total volume of trade had been growing. On February 21st, the commercial treaty with France entered into force, but most importantly, after a year of negotiation agreement had been reached with Austria on commercial convention. The convention signed on February 27th was the highlight of the discussed period and the first concluded with a really important country as far as trade went. Obviously, this was a very important agreement since Austria was Hungary's most important trade partner and had taken so far one-third of Hungary's total export. The agreement was first and foremost lucrative to the flour and wine industries. With the new regulations, these products could enter the Austrian market with an approximately 50% reduction in duties.[776] What Smith could add

773 All the information in the paragraph is from Smith's Twenty-first Report, LNJ, 7th Year, No. 5, May 1926, 678–88. On the Land Mortgage Bonds, see Péteri, *Revolutionary Twenties*, 191–97.
774 Smith to Bud, February 22, 1926, and April 1, 1926, B.V. (3) Budget Surplus Account, 1924–25, C. 109, Financial Reconstruction of Hungary, LNA.
775 Smith to Bud, April 19, 1926, C.III (7) Correspondence - Hungarian Ministers, 1926, C. 111, Financial Reconstruction of Hungary, LNA.
776 All the information in the paragraph is from Smith's Twenty-second Report, LNJ, 7th Year, No. 5, May 1926, 689–97.

in his March report was that thanks to improved conditions and better method of collection, there had been a gradual and steady increase in the direct taxes, which almost doubled, while in the case of the turnover taxes a similar decrease had taken place.[777] This was judged by Smith to be a step in the right and healthy direction. He was also satisfied in reporting that both retail prices and wholesale prices had reached the lowest point since the start of the reconstruction period, though the latter was still 123% compared to the prewar level.[778] In the true fashion of "the good news is if there is no news," the financial reconstruction of Hungary was advancing at a nice pace without any major obstacles. The work done so far only portended the successful conclusion in a short time.

By April the state debt to the National Bank had been reduced by a large margin and there was a new agreement between the two sides for further reduction of such debt. It was a welcomed further step in the direction of currency reform and reaching Article 83 of the Statutes of the Bank, which declared that the government debt must be reduced to 30 million gold crowns ($6 million). The concentration of government balances at the National Bank had been carried out for the most part in the past month. A beginning was the transfer of *Postsparkassa* monies from the *Geldinstitutszentrale* to the National Bank. Those government balances remaining at the *Geldinstitutszentrale* would be concentrated at the National Bank by the end of June 1926, as had been promised earlier. All this indicated that the path planned and thought best was and would be traveled by the Hungarian government. The news that a commercial treaty with Spain entered into force on April 18th also bore some significance. Both retail prices and wholesale prices had reached another record low point and deposits in the banks kept growing.[779]

The most momentous episode was not mentioned in the monthly report. It was Smith's letter to the League of Nations in which he forwarded Bethlen's request that he expected "to raise the question of the termination of the control of Hungarian finances, under the Geneva Protocol No. 2, at the June Meeting of the Council."[780] In the December meeting of the Hungarian Committee, the representative of the Little Entente was against the release of 50 million gold crowns ($10 million) from the loan because, as they stated, they had not had enough time to study the question. As the letter disclosed, the reason why the Hungarian Prime Minister was already thinking about this sensitive issue was "that all interested parties may have time to prepare themselves for the

777 Smith's Twenty-third Report, LNJ, 7th Year, No. 6, June 1926, 778–86.

778 Ibid.

779 All the information in the paragraph is from Smith's Twenty-fourth Report, LNJ, 7th Year, No. 6, June 1926, 787–96.

780 Smith to the Secretary General, April 24, 1926, Financial Reconstruction of Hungary, Cessation of the control of Hungarian finances. Doc. No. 51126, Registry Files, R. 301, LNA.

discussion of this matter."[781] Bethlen's move was well-founded. He knew that he could not expect anything favorable from the Little Entente. The mutual dislike between Hungary and these countries, burdened with the problem of the franc forgery, which the Little Entente wished to use as a possible card against Hungary, made Bethlen play it safe. And since the question was that of the termination of direct control, he was well aware that he had to act ahead of time, so that the Little Entente would have fewer possibilities to cause trouble. Lukewarm May was only a prelude for the climax in June, that is, the anticipated termination of financial control.

In early June during the summer Assembly of the League of Nations, the main point was the termination of the control of finances both in Austria and Hungary. The franc forgery was a serious issue, because France and the Czechs might have wanted to use it as a weapon not to let the control be lifted. This, in turn, could have meant Bethlen's fall, which Britain did not want to see. As a Foreign Office minute put it, "If there is a danger of their [the French] doing this it may be advisable for us to make representations to the French Govt. before the meeting of the Council [in June] so as to convince them of the error of their ways."[782] In fact, it was no secret that the French were planning to ask for postponement of the termination of control exactly due to the forgery scandal.[783] The British were determined not to let the French have their way and put off the decision about lifting the control in Hungary till September.[784] The British were angry and with good reason. The Protocol said that control should cease if the financial stability of Hungary was achieved, but for such a declaration unanimous decision was needed. If the French or the Little Entente wanted to play hardball, there was a danger that such a decision might not be reached.

The representatives of France and the Little Entente on the Financial Committee acted as expected. Vilem Pospisil, the Czechoslovak representative eon the Financial Committee, thought the decision about decontrol should be postponed, but Strakosch, Niemeyer, Wallenberg, and ter Meulen defended the end of control by June 30th, since, the main aim, that is, financial stability had been achieved. Even the French chairman, Dubois thought that since the post of the Commissioner-General was coming to an end in Austria, then in Hungary,

---

781 Ibid.
782 Minute by unknown FO official, May 21, 1926, FO371 11369 C5795/443/21. See also Goode to Niemeyer about the position of Bethlen, Goode to Niemeyer, May 11, 1926, Ibid.
783 Ross to Niemeyer, June 3, 1926, C6375/443/21, 11369, FO371, TNA. Still, according to Siepmann, who based his information on Charron, the French man on Smith's team, the French minister in Budapest wrote to Paris that he favored the complete abolition of control at the end of June. Siepmann to Norman, May 31, 1926, OV33/42, BoE.
784 Crewe to Chamberlain, June 2, 1926, C6443/433/21 and Niemeyer to Lampson, June 4, 1926, C6392/443/21, 11370, FO371, TNA.

which seemed to be in a stronger position financially, it should also come to an end. Maybe more importantly, it would be a loss of prestige for the League if decontrol was deferred, in addition to which, Smith had himself asked to be relieved from his post.[785] There was unanimous agreement that the post of the bank adviser should cease, but as for the reliquat, the decision was, after a close vote, that at the moment nothing should be said about it.[786] Smith thought the Financial Committee should show signs of resolve and not allow politics to dictate their decision.[787] Finally, in its report to the Council, the Committee stated that in its examination of the financial position of Hungary it "considered the financial and economic data furnished to it [and] it does not consider that such circumstances as the franc forgeries (entirely deplorable as they were) have affected the financial position of the country."[788] In Salter's opinion, "the knowledge of the Council's ultimate right was effective in securing unanimity in the Committee."[789] A few days later the Financial Committee officially agreed to the termination of the office of the Commissioner-General.[790] According to British memorandums, it was wholly attributable to Chamberlain's efforts, and Bethlen's position was more secure than ever.[791] In any event, the main objective of lifting direct control was achieved. The next day Smith thanked the Hungarian government and people for their continual cooperation, for the Financial Committee for its work, and for the Council for entrusting him with the job and giving support all throughout the reconstruction period.[792] It is important to note that the termination of the post of the Commissioner-General did not mean the end of control of Hungarian finances. Control over the revenues from the assets assigned for the service of the loan and over the balance of the loan remained in place after June 30th. The key person to act as the bridge between the League of Nations, the Trustees, and the Hungarian government would be Royall Tyler, the

785 Actually, Siepmann believed that Smith's sickness may have been a major factor why control was brought to an end by the end of June. He characterized Smith as "tired and ill. He looks to me at the moment like a sick man." Siepmann to Norman, May 31, 1926, OV33/42, BoE.

786 Financial Committee, Twenty-second Session, Minutes of the Fourth Meeting, June 4, 1926, OV9/340, BoE.

787 Siepmann to Norman, May 31, 1926, OV33/42, BoE.

788 Report of the Financial Committee to the Council, June 6, 1926, Financial Reconstruction of Hungary, Deliberations at the 40th Session of the Council, June 1926. Doc. No. 52083, Registry Files, R. 302, LNA.

789 Salter, *The United States of Europe*, 68.

790 Work of the Financial Committee during Its Twenty-second Session, June 3-9, 1926, C. 359. M. 127. 1926. II, LNA.

791 Selby's Memorandum, June 10, 1926, C6695/443/21 and Chamberlain's memo in Chamberlain to Tyrrell, June 9, 1926, C7619/443/21, 11370, FO371, TNA; Barclay's minute, June 16, 1926, C7059, 11368, FO 371, TNA.

792 LNJ, 7th Year, No. 7, July 1926, 876–77.

deputy of Smith, also an American, who enjoyed the backing of both the League and Bethlen.[793]

Smith was highly praised by all sides. One League representative was of the opinion that "Mr. Smith's personality, the breadth of his views, his tact, his indefatigable energy and, his rare kindness, had been among the principal factors in the success of this difficult work."[794] Bethlen, who besides praising the Hungarian people, the League of Nations, and the Financial Committee said that "Hungary owed a particularly large debt of gratitude to the Commissioner-General and his collaborators [who showed] wide understanding and sympathy towards the Hungarian people."[795] In its resolution of the same day, the Council declared that Smith's functions would end on June 30, 1926, since the financial stability of Hungary was assured. It also expressed its "deep appreciation of his work," and concluded that "the rapid completion of his task at the date contemplated in the original programme is due in no small measure to the personal qualities he has shown—to his disinterested devotion and his sound judgment."[796] Eric Drummond thanked Smith in a personal letter and emphasized the personal relations as a key to the success achieved.[797] Smith obviously felt the same, since it was his worldview to move issues onto the personal level where it would be much easier to solve them diffused from political content. However cordial his relationships were to Geneva, Smith used to call the League Secretariat a "Madhouse."[798]

Smith was also in high esteem in Hungary. Apponyi, the grand old man of the country, lavishly commended Smith's work and spoke of the puritan gentleman thinking that characterized the American commissioner.[799] As a reply to this, another Member of Parliament said that "Smith, during his work, cared for the interests of the country to such an extent that in case he should leave us, we ought to line up at his departure to express our appreciation his work is worth."[800] In the National Assembly, Prime Minister Bethlen spoke highly of Smith's work

793 Ter Meulen to Salter and Strakosch to Salter, June 18, 1926, and Bethlen to Salter, July 5, 1926, Financial Reconstruction of Hungary, Services and expenses of Mr. Tyler, a representative of the Trustees in Budapest. Doc. No. 52197, Registry Files, R. 302, LNA.

794 Extract from the Minutes of the Council, June 10, 1926, Financial Reconstruction of Hungary, Deliberations at the 40th Session of the Council, June 1926. Doc. No. 52083, Registry Files, R. 302, LNA.

795 Ibid.

796 Ibid.

797 Drummond to Smith, June 15th, 1926, Financial Reconstruction of Hungary, Appointment of a Commissioner General by the League. Doc. No. 33315, Registry Files, R. 298, LNA.

798 Tyler to Mildred Bliss, May 2, 1933, Box 3, Tyler Papers.

799 *Budapesti Hírlap*, May 22, 1926, XLVI/114.

800 Ibid.

in Hungary. This part of his speech was underscored with the outlook for further American loans. Bethlen thanked Smith for the fact that he had

> worked in the reconstruction of the country upon objective points of view, with love and sympathy for this fallen Hungarian nation, and helped to save us from the morass, from the difficulties, and strenuous past from which only by the League of Nations and his help have we been able to get out. I thank him, the American citizen, who had proven that if an American citizen undertakes a task, he will carry out true to the tradition of that great nation; he has done this in the post he represented in Hungary.[801]

Indeed, Smith's consequent apolitical manner all throughout his tenure as Commissioner-General appealed to basically everyone. Naturally, the ruling general feeling in the country concerning the close departure of the Commissioner-General was that of relief. After all, the country would regain its financial independence, which was no small issue. In this relation, few people minded Smith's leaving. As for Bethlen, the main point about lifting the control was, for both domestic and foreign policy reasons, that "the end is in sight."[802] Finance Minister Bud may actually have been the only one not happy to see Smith leave. He was afraid about the pressure for money that now he would be experiencing from the various departments.[803] Another exception was the Public Servants National Union, which was specifically sad that Smith's time was winding up, because they had so much hope in the American as far as the question of pensions were concerned.[804]

Hungarians were grateful for their American Commissioner-General with good reason. The financial reconstruction of Hungary was not only successfully concluded but exceeded the most optimistic expectations. In his final report covering both May and June, which was completed afterward, as was usual in the case of each month, Smith did not deal too much with the specific numbers for the months, but instead put the emphasis on overall significant figures and conclusions. For one, total receipts from the pledged revenues in the 1925/26 fiscal year was 258 million gold crowns ($51.5 million), eight times the annual service charge, which was 33 million gold crowns ($6.5 million). In light of this it was no big surprise that budget surplus for the same fiscal year was 62 million gold crowns ($12.5 million), a large sum indeed. From the almost 253 million loan,

801 National Assembly Diary, 1922–27, 25:42.
802 Siepmann to Norman, May 31, 1926, OV33/42, BoE.
803 Ibid.
804 Public Servants National Union to Smith, June 20, 1926, K. I. – K. A. N. Sz., C. 113, Financial Reconstruction of Hungary, LNA.

only 70 million had to be spent on budget deficits and back debts to June 30, 1924. 100 million gold crowns ($20 million) had been authorized by the League Council for capital investments, and there was 81 million ($16.2 million) left as available from the original amount. Not only had the originally required reforms been carried out, but in addition those suggested by the Financial Committee had also been executed. These latter ones were state money centralization at the National Bank, laws requiring annual publication of all expenditures and receipts of the Government not included in the ordinary budget, and monthly statements of estimated expenditures and receipts. On the whole, during Smith's tenure there had been a continual increase in banks deposits and both retail and wholesale prices had seriously decreased. Smith, as always, praised the assistance and support he had been given all along. As he phrased it, "without the co-operation of both the Government and the people, it would have been impossible to make any satisfactory progress with the reconstruction plan, and this has been completely given at every stage of the work."[805]

Smith proudly declared that the League of Nations had met the challenge and performed its duty and the responsibility expected of the international organization:

> The League has now done all that it undertook to do—*i. e.*, to create a sound budgetary and financial position, which is necessary to establish a firm foundation for the future upon which the complete economic recovery of Hungary can take place. Economic conditions have slowly and steadily improved since the plan became effective, and if the present position is maintained by Hungary itself, the economic conditions should continue to improve until they reach at least the normal pre-war conditions.[806]

This last statement is important, because it clearly shows that regardless of the euphoria felt by the successful conclusion of the reconstruction program, the comparison with pre-war Hungary in economic terms still lagged behind. This was not the fault of the program. Rather, this proved how low Hungary had stood at the end of the war and the social and political disturbances shortly after the war not only from a financial but also, and mainly, from an economic point of view.

Smith also had a slight warning to give. Despite the rosy numbers at the moment, he warned against imprudent fiscal policy in the future. One of the problems had been the high taxation, which was new to Hungarians and made

805 All the information in the paragraph is from Smith's Twenty-fifth Report, League of Nations, *Financial Reconstruction of Hungary*, 164–87.
806 Ibid., 169.

a lot of sacrifice on the population. Smith wrote that if there appeared an unbalanced budget once more, the only recourse for the government would be to raise taxes, obviously a risky choice from every aspect. The solution was conservative fiscal policy and to avoid raising expenditures. He listed the long-term loans issued during the time of the reconstruction. These were issued on 7.5% and meant about 51 million gold crowns ($10.2 million) annuity. In addition to the long-term loans, there was a considerable amount of short-term foreign credits outstanding. The total amount of these was very difficult to calculate since they showed significant fluctuation. But from the information available, it was not believed that it was excessive "or likely to throw an undue strain upon the financial situation of Hungary."[807] In hindsight, it can be easily stated that the ever-optimistic American was wrong in predicting the future in his final report, but the fault did not lie with him, but rather with the unstrained borrowing of the Hungarian government in the next few years. But he also said that something would go wrong. Siepmann was already starting to be afraid of what he termed "the free-lance borrowing" practiced by Hungary.[808] He had not shared the optimism of Smith almost all throughout the reconstruction period, and toward the end he drew a different conclusion. His sharp observation to Norman deserves to be quoted: "I hope, and on the whole I believe, that the League will have the wisdom to get out of this undertaking while it still looks something like a success."[809] Indeed, in five years time, the debt of Hungary reached a very high numbers and there was no chance to repay them.

With Smith's departure on July 1st, the financial control did not cease altogether, although it became much looser. As was mentioned, Smith's deputy, Royall Tyler, who did a very useful job, was entrusted with the nominal control of the Hungarian finances. Tyler enjoyed sympathy from all sides and had no trouble keeping up the cordial relation that Smith had established. His reports, drawn up in a similar fashion to Smith's, and opinion were important. It was his agreement with the government's plan that made the League authorize a further 50 million gold crowns ($10 million) from the loan in March 1927.[810] It was again his consent that needed a few months later for the remaining sum of 33.9 million gold crowns ($6.8 million) to be given to the Hungarian government.[811] Finally, Tyler's mission

807 Ibid.

808 Siepmann to Norman, May 19, 1925, OV33/39, BoE.

809 Siepmann to Norman, May 31, 1926, OV33/42, BoE, also quoted in Péteri, *Revolutionary Twenties*, 202.

810 Work of the Financial Committee during Its Twenty-Sixth Session, C. 152. M. 44. 1927. II, LNA. The 1927/28 fiscal year was also a success. Both revenues and expenditure grew, although budgetary surplus was 97 million pengős compared to 121.5 in the preceding fiscal year. Eugene Havas, *Hungary's Finance and Trade 1928* (London: London General Press, 1929), 7.

811 LNJ, 9th Year, No. 2, February 1928, 127.

came to an end in June 1929 and less than one year later the function of the Committee of Control was terminated as well.[812] With these final steps Hungary absolutely regained its financial freedom. Unfortunately, the government did not heed the good advice and Hungary used more and more loans. While in 1926 it was a reasonable $29.51 million, it almost doubled in the next few years, and tripled in 1931, reaching $87.57 million.[813] Another interesting feature was the ration between British and American investments in Hungary. While at the start of the reconstruction, British investments were totaling at $38,487 million, more than four times larger than the American $9 million, in the next few years the trend reversed and in 1928 the American investments were almost double of the British ones.[814] To give a testimony to the leading character of these two countries in terms of money coming to Hungary, of all the investments between 1924 and 1930, the United States had 44.5%, while Great Britain had 40%, of the total investments, thus these two countries were responsible for 84.5% of the total.[815]

The financial reconstruction of Hungary, parallel to the Austrian one, which came to an end on the same date, was a very successful achievement of the League of Nations. Austerity measures seemed to work. The organization, whose prestige was on the line, emerged as a body that was capable of organizing international cooperation on a large scale. Its reconstruction programs paved the way for the German reconstruction known as the Dawes Plan and further European reconstruction programs in Eastern and Southern Europe.

7.4. Balance Sheet

After all this it is worth concluding the balance sheet of the reconstruction period in Hungary. The international loan was used for the original plan, that is, to create a stable currency and achieve budget equilibrium instead of deficit, only in the first half year of the program. This, in turn, begs the question: why was so big a reconstruction loan needed in the first place? One reason is that League of Nations estimates for the period of the reconstruction were too conservative, or just too cautious, and they predicted substantially less money from the assigned revenues. But perhaps a more important reason lies in the thought behind the reconstruction of all Europe, which did not only

812 Tyler later returned to Hungary in 1932 as financial adviser to the government and remained in that capacity until 1938. He also mastered the Hungarian language during his protracted stay.
813 Péteri, *Global Monetary Regime*, 138.
814 Péteri, *Revolutionary Twenties*, 180.
815 Ibid.

mean economic-financial rehabilitation, but political stability as well. It was important for the Western powers that Hungary should have and be able to maintain a strong and stable government, even if the idea of democracy was seriously curbed. This was achieved and Hungary performed well. During the reconstruction period, state revenues of all kinds continuously rose, and the tax reductions introduced in 1925 did not alter this trend. The budget kept producing surplus. Even after the program was over, in the 1927/28 financial year the state budget could boast of a 97 million surplus, which was from all angles a great success.[816] On the other hand, Hungary started to find itself more and more in debt, which course speeded up after 1926, and by the summer of 1928 it reached 1778.9 million pengős ($311 million), a staggering amount compared to the size of the country.[817]

The reconstruction program, without a doubt, achieved the goals it set out to reach at the commencement. The Hungarian currency became very stable and inflation disappeared at the very beginning of the program. Budget deficit was a thing of the past from 1925, and even considerable surplus was realized. This was largely achieved by reducing expenditure and raising revenues by a large margin. A great asset in this was the new tax system, in the wake of which the population had to bear a high per capita taxation relative to Hungary. State moneys were concentrated at the National Bank, which was another important element of healthy fiscal and monetary policy. The Bank managed to reduce the interest rate, and from the 12.5% at the start it shrank all the way to 6% in August 1926. Parallel with all this, the reduction in the numbers of state employees was also carried out. The Hungarian government reached the promised number in the first year. The number of state officials decreased from 198,000 to 160,000, which was somewhat more than promised. The salaries of these officials rose too, although this hardly alleviated their pecuniary hardship. The expenses on personnel meant a huge burden on the state. 60% of the whole budget was spent on personnel alone, salaries and pensions, and by the end of the reconstruction period this number showed only a minimal decrease of 5%. Although this was still too high, it was a step in the right direction. The Hungarian state managed to conclude a series of trade agreements based on the principle of the most favored nation, and by the end of 1926, most of the neighboring countries were included in this circle.

816 The budget surplus showed the following picture (in million pengős): 1924–25: 131,7; 1925–26: 98,1; 1926–27: 143,6; 1927–28: 97; 1928–29: 2,5; 1929–30: 2,2. Magos, *Az angol és amerikai monopoltőke szerepe a Horthy-fasizmus megszilárdításában* (Budapest: Művelt Nép Könyvkiadó, 1953), 67.

817 "Dealing with Hungary's Finances," VII/5, Hungary's Financial and Economic Situation, K 284, Szabóky Papers, HNA.

With all the favorable results, the negative effects of the program also surfaced. The steps leading to the increased revenues, such as the higher taxes,[818] higher customs duties, or freeing the market, caused a general rise in prices and a lower standard of living for the population in general. The above mentioned rise in the salary of the officials still lagged far behind the desired level and could hardly ensure that these people would make ends meet, and compared to prewar salary levels, they represented only 50%. The number of bankruptcies and insolvencies together with the cases of suicides also showed an unfavorable picture.

Naturally, the political opposition in Hungary was not very enthusiastic with the results. Many of them found fault with the fact that the government succeeded in achieving the outcome only by squeezing money from the citizens. Basically it was the clash of ideas in favor of austerity and giving up some freedom versus more political independence at the possible price of facing protracted recession. The opposition also attacked Bethlen because the remainder of the loan, about 82 million gold crowns ($16.4 million), was not freed at the end of the reconstruction program, and that Smith's departure only meant the on-the-ground supervision, but control was not wholly demolished. Behind this the opposition suspected was the issue of the franc forgery.[819] Bethlen in his answer tried to refute the charges in a curt way, then said the following, which in hindsight was very important. "We need to take great care, despite the hard conditions, not to make this country deep in debt. And believe me, my fellow representative, it is hardly sufficient to create investment plans for the next year, or for the next two to three years. We will have to make such plans for decades in case we want this country to recover to some degree, and this will not be possible without further credits and loans from abroad."[820] With this the prime minister basically projected the course Hungary should not have followed, but what in fact the country did pursue in the next few years. By 1930, Hungary found itself in a devastating amount of debt, and by that time the favorable results of the reconstruction period were also long gone.

---

818 The tax burdens rose in a substantial way compared to the prewar years, although various sources give different data. According to one, the per capita tax rose from 59 pengős in 1913 to 91 pengős in 1925–27, while another source gave 140 pengős for 1927. A third work on the subject concluded that the net per capita burden in Hungary was 128 gold crowns, which, together with Great Britain, meant the biggest proportion between taxing and GDP with 22%. Zsuzsa Demény, *Századok statisztikája. Statisztikai érdekességek a magyar történelemből* [Statistics of Centuries. Interesting Statistics of Hungarian History] (Központi Statisztikai Hivatal, Budapest, 2001), 170; "Hungary's Economic Conditions," Financial Reconstruction of Hungary, C. 118, R. III. Reconstruction – Economic and Financial Situation, LNA; and Csizik Béla, "Államháztartás és közteher", [State Finances and Public Taxes] *Közgazdasági Szemle* 75 (January 1930) 584–85.

819 National Assembly Diary, 1922-1927, 45:43–91.

820 Ibid., 99.

Mention must be made about the reparations as well. Bethlen and his advisors for a long time hoped that they would somehow manage to avoid having to pay this money. Although in this they were frustrated, the finally declared amount of 200 million gold crowns ($40 million) and the twenty-year duration did not mean unbearable burden on the state. To get a much clearer picture as to what this reparation meant, a point of comparison can be provided with the reparations Hungary had to pay after World War II.

Similarly to what happened after World War I, Hungary in 1945 was yet again among the defeated countries. The Paris Peace Treaty in 1947 punished Hungary for this fact. The country had to pay reparations anew, the amount of which this time was $300 million. This was already a somewhat reduced figure thanks to the efforts of the United States to lessen the original Soviet plan of $400 million. The $300 million was due to three countries: the Soviet Union ($200 million), Yugoslavia ($70 million), and Czechoslovakia ($30 million). The payment of this amount had to be done in eight years mainly in goods since Hungary had basically no financial resource. The figure, however, is misleading. This amount in 1947 was worth $242 million compared to a U.S. dollar in 1924. Only this factor alone means that after World War II Hungary was forced to pay six times as much reparation as in the 1920s. Obviously further variants complicate the picture. One such element was the conduct of Soviet occupation in Hungary, which practically robbed the country blind in the span of a few years' time, and Hungary paid to the Soviet Union about five times the original $200 million.

Hungary paid only 30 million gold crowns ($6 million) of the set reparations of 200 million gold crowns ($40 million) in the second half of the 1920s. Then, in light of the failed policies in Europe and the Great Depression, the Western powers decided to cancel such payments. After World War II, however, the picture was dramatically different. This time Hungary was made to pay many times more than the required amount of $300 million. The multiplier between the two figures that Hungary paid is about 180, that is, Hungary lost 180 times as much money, or material translated into money, in the period between 1945 and 1953 than between 1927 and 1931. If one also takes into consideration the loss of population and the difference between the productive capacity of Hungary in 1927 and 1945, when the reparations payments started, respectively, the 200-million gold crown reparations in 1927 can be said to have been lenient.

of the public. Balance available from the loan on June 30, 1925, amounted to 182,652,607.41 gold crowns ($36.5 million).[715] With the end of the first financial year of the reconstruction period, all expectations had been exceeded by the results and the optimism that, for example, Jeremiah Smith, Jr. had shown all along, seemed to be paying off and materialize. A significant intergovernmental agreement was the Treaty of Friendship, Commerce, and Consular Rights, signed at Washington, June 24, 1925.[716]

As for Speyer, he did not give up and now made inquiries at the League of Nations as to how the Commissioners-General could be involved in advertising new loans. Since Smith wanted to avoid appearing in the prospectus of any possible loan for fear of controversy, Speyer hoped the League would ease such worries. Although Alfred Zimmerman would have gone further, Smith, whose position was obviously more complicated in terms of American loans, consented only to a short private letter to the issuing house that could be attached to the prospectus: "We are authorized to state that from the point of view of the League of Nations reconstruction plan for Austria/Hungary there is no objection to this loan."[717] He was adamant that for American issues this formula would be sufficient. So Speyer had achieved some progress, but he wanted the best insurance for any business. In light of the State Department's somewhat strict attitude about foreign loans, he asked Smith to issue a statement that he encouraged the pending city loans for Hungarian cities by Speyer & Co. He basically begged for Smith's help. "We fear we shall have to abandon this business unless we get from you some such statement as above. Please help all you can."[718] Smith in the end did not provide more what he thought was moral and legal, but Speyer did not need to fear failure. On July 1, 1925, the $10,000,000 Hungarian Consolidated Municipal Loan by Speyer & Co. was signed and advertised in New York Papers.[719] The loan

715 All the information in the paragraph is from Smith's Fourteenth Report, LNJ, 6th Year, No. 9, September 1925, 1242–53.

716 For the text of the treaty, see FRUS, 1925: 2:341–54. Right after the signing of the treaty, however, Kellogg signaled that the Senate will add certain reservations concerning Hungarian immigration to the United States and how long the treaty will remain in force. Hungary accepted such reservations. Kellogg to Széchényi and Széchényi to Kellogg, June 24, 1925, and Brentano to Walkó and Walkó to Brentano, September 4, 1926, Ibid., 354–57.

717 Niemeyer to Norman, June 10, 1925, OV33/73, BoE.

718 Speyer to Smith, June 10, 1925, T. II. Incoming and outgoing telegrams, September 2, 1924–June 30, 1926, C. 120, Financial Reconstruction of Hungary, LNA.

719 *The New York Times*, July 5, 1925. The different papers relating to the loan can be found in 332 and 334–38, K 269, Finance Ministry, General Papers, HNA. The cities, altogether 48 of them, applied for 139,904 gold crowns initially, of which amount 104,166 was planned to be spent on constructive investments. The government finally allowed an application for a loan of 75,865 gold crowns. Elemér Inántsy-Pap, *A magyar városok Speyer-kölcsönei* [The Hungarian Cities' Speyer Loans] (Budapest: Home Printing House of Budapest, 1938), 5, 10.

Chapter 8

The Personal Side of the Hungarian Reconstruction

8.1. The Human Side at Work

Aside from the technical aspects that had been discussed above there is another dimension that must be introduced. And that is the personal attitude and investment that Jeremiah Smith, Jr. provided. The private character of the Commissioner-General played a large role and was as much the reason for the success as any financial consideration. It is worth introducing Jeremiah Smith, Jr. the private citizen, the man who stayed in Hungary, and who became Hungary's friend.

Smith had a post with wide powers as was stipulated in the second Protocol. With these powers relating to control came duties, of which maybe none was more important than the human responsibility. Right from the outset it was clear that an American would be the best official from the political point of view. Also, if an American citizen was to fill the post of Commissioner-General, there was a good chance that the American money market would be more interested in Hungary. This was not only in the best interest of Hungary, which had been looking for foreign capital, but that of the League of Nations as well, for the reason that Europe was weak in transferable capital and London alone was in a position to offer more substantial sums. Thus, when finally an American was chosen after a few months of desperate search, everybody was confident that this person would not only guarantee the flow of American capital, but his nationality would also ensure that possible political ruffles would be ironed out. Naturally, much more was needed for the successful completion of the task. Both the League and Hungary were very lucky to have the services of a man whose personality was in many ways the key to the triumphant conclusion of the financial reconstruction of Hungary.

As was mentioned earlier, Smith was a restrained man, one who tried to be out of the limelight as much as possible. He was a bachelor too, never married, and never had children. He was content to have his sister, Elizabeth, as his family. This fact, on the other hand, makes it more difficult to unwrap the man's inner sphere. All that is available are the memories of others and a few articles. Smith is not known to have kept a diary or have been a man of correspondence. Outside his official duties, he rarely took up the pen to write, and although he was at the crossroads of great events for almost fifteen years, he did not publish memoirs or a regular column in a newspaper. There were only a few pieces written by him, but these dealt with technical issues mainly relating to his work. Thus, at best, the impression one forms must be cautionary before jumping to conclusions. Still, through the haze of time and second-hand memories, a fair picture can be drawn about Jeremiah Smith, Jr. the man.

As a start it is worth remembering those memories by other contemporaries that refer to Smith. Sir Arthur Salter described him "shy, inexpressive" but with a well-hidden "shrewd judgement and a firm will."[821] Lord Cecil called him "a nice, straight fellow," and Bethlen came to know the man whom he called a friend.[822] The Prime Minister and other officials of Hungary also witnessed firsthand what the leading paper of Smith's hometown characterized as a "capacity to come down to brass tacks on a complicated situation, stick to the issue and win his point, and still keep the confidence and good will of the other fellow."[823] A Hungarian diplomat remembered that Hungary "could not have gotten a better, more honest, and more puritan commissioner," who was like "a bonus *pater familias* who carried out his task with conscience and a sense of responsibility."[824] Boyden also spoke of Smith's characters in the best possible manner.[825] Eric Drummond, the Secretary-General of the League of Nations, said that Smith was "the perfect example of an American gentleman."[826] The man most close to Smith was in all probability Thomas Lamont, his old schoolmate and the person that helped Smith's international career. He wrote that "Jerry, as everybody called him, was the most entertaining man I think that I ever met. [...] He was intensely patriotic [...] a man whose simplicity carries him through all barriers."[827] His deputy, Royall Tyler, described his compatriot as "exceedingly attractive" and "dear, and the perfect man for the job."[828] Arthur Sipemann, who credited his decision to go to Hungary to Smith, remembered "the clear blue eyes of this Bostonian and his innocent manner, which gave the impression of a helpless child."[829] With all these descriptions it was no wonder that when Smith started to speak in his "frank, vigorous and open" voice, people listened and trusted him.[830]

821 Salter, *Personality in Politics*, 168.

822 Hevesy to Daruváry, April 5, 1924, 209/123, 10–1390/1399, K 69, Economic Policy Department, HNA.

823 *Boston Daily Globe*, April 13, 1924.

824 György, Barcza, *Diplomata emlékeim, 1911-1945* [My Diplomatic Memoirs] vol. 1-2., (Budapest: Európa História, 1994), 1:189.

825 Boyden to Széchenyi, April 9, 1924, 1924, 264/113, 50052–50263/929, K 69, Economic Policy Department, HNA.

826 *The New York Times*, October 11, 1925.

827 Lamont, *Across World Frontiers*, 82.

828 Tyler to Mildred Bliss, April 26, 1924, and September 3, 1924, Box 2, Tyler Papers.

829 Siepmann's *Memoir*, 35, Siepmann Papers.

830 Rácz to the Press Department of the Foreign Ministry, May 13, 1924, 209/123, 10–1390/1229-30, K 69, Economic Policy Department, HNA.

Throughout the time he served as Commissioner-General, Jeremiah Smith, Jr. did everything in his capacity to earn the friendship and respect of the Hungarian people and government. A few small episodes will be a good indication why that was the case, and how Smith functioned in personal relations.

A feature that was characteristic of Smith was his apolitical manner. He had made up his mind that the position that he was going to fill would not allow him to express political opinion. Naturally, he was well aware of the political situation both inside and outside of Hungary with the understanding that his status as an American supervisor was too important in itself. His job would have suffered in the long run had he voiced any political point of view. Right after he had set foot on Hungarian soil, he made it clear that his duties were "financial, not political."[831] Early during his stay, for example, the representatives of the Kossuth Party visited him at his office. This provided him with yet another platform to emphatically formulate his stance of being free of politics. He said from behind the desk that once had belonged to Kossuth, "I am independent from everyone and, in spite of having contact with all the parties, I will defend my absolute impartiality."[832] Obviously, there were elements who would have liked to see a commanding commitment from Smith to Hungary once he was the controller. Alternatively, the majority knew that the American had extenuating powers and his goodwill would be necessary in order to be able to achieve the objectives of the reconstruction program. So, the majority of both the population and politicians overlooked the fact that Smith avoided taking sides in politics.

Smith's impartial personality ensured others' trust in him. On many occasions he was visited in person or asked in letters for help. Not much after the reconstruction program began in earnest, Smith received the delegation of the building industry, which was led by Ignác Alpár, the renowned architect. They asked the American controller if he could try to help that the amount appropriated for public works be raised.[833] Smith could only promise that he would do all he could, but Alajos Szabóky rejected the request of the delegation. A week later it was another delegation that called on Smith. This time the teachers of the University of Pécs were represented by a small group to put forward their wishes. The government was angry because such an action lay outside their legal possibilities; even an inquiry was initiated with a goal to hold the organizers of the action accountable.[834] As can be seen, the trust coming from the people was not absolutely welcomed by the government. It seemed that everybody would

831 Smith's press release in Budapest, May 2, 1924, P.III. Press communiqués, C. 117, Financial Reconstruction of Hungary, LNA.
832 *Pesti Napló*, June 6, 1924, 75/110.
833 *Magyarország*, August 1, 1924, XXXI/156.
834 9-10R/39, August 8, 1924, K 27, Records of the Cabinet Council, HNA.

have had the Commissioner-General for their own interest. However, Smith had made it clear that he wanted to focus solely on the financial issues of Hungary as he was responsible for the execution of the reconstruction program drawn up by the League of Nations.

One thing was nonetheless indisputable: Jeremiah Smith, Jr. had unusually great powers over the financial life of Hungary. For a time, this caught the attention of the foreign press, especially the distant American newspapers. *The New York Times* said that Smith was "for all practical purposes the financial czar of Hungary."[835] Another American influential paper called him "the real monarch of this land."[836] *Time* referred to him as "financial king—a Yankee at the Court of the Habsburgs or, in the parlance of jazz, a Yankee-doodle doing it."[837] Originating from his personal composition, Smith refused such titles and always thought of himself more of a friendly adviser than someone ruling over a country. The former foreign minister of Hungary also thought that the Hungarians "should be grateful to Mr. Smith for not interfering too much with Hungary's finances," for his "quiet way of working," and for the fact that "he exercises his power not in an extensive, but rather restrictive manner."[838] Smith always consistently emphasized that he was receiving immense help from the Hungarian government.[839] This was basically true and no surprise. It was the elementary interest of the Bethlen government to cooperate fully with the Commissioner-General. They knew exactly how much depended on his goodwill. They were also aware that the country should faithfully carry out the program in order to have a real chance to lure some capital, first and foremost American capital, to Hungary.

Thanks to Smith, Hungary earned a somewhat more prominent status in the American public consciousness. One must not think that the large majority of Americans knew where Hungary was or what kind of political problems the country was facing, but the simple fact that an American citizen was the financial controller of the small European country made the average reading public increasingly aware of Hungary. In addition, his monthly reports were always summarized in the leading papers and the usually positive data he provided further increased his and Hungary's good standing back in the United States.

Aside from the news his reports made every month, Smith himself contributed within his capacity for Hungary to be better known. When the Hungary Society of America asked him to write an article about Hungary, his experience there, and the chances of economic recovery for the first issue of a new quarterly, *The*

835 *The New York Times*, August 3, 1924.
836 *The Washington Post*, September 28, 1924.
837 *Time*, February 3, 1925.
838 Hungary and the Commissioner of the League of Nations by dr. Gustav Gratz, March 19, 1925, R. III, C. 118, Financial Reconstruction of Hungary, LNA.
839 *Wall Street Journal*, October 16, 1924.

Hungarian Review of America, Smith sent a short article, which was a shorter version he had already submitted to a Swiss paper, the *L'Europe Nouvelle*.[840] In this article, he reiterated his positive impression about Hungary and how the people there conducted themselves toward him.

> I must take this occasion to express my gratitude for the very cordial reception I received and for the courtesy, consideration and support I have since met with from everyone with whom I have come in contact. It would not be surprising if the presence of a foreigner with the powers of the Commissioner-General under the reconstruction plan aroused some opposition and provoked some evidences of resentment, but I have encountered nothing of that kind and am only too grateful to the Hungarian people for the welcome I have received.[841]

In the same month he got a request for an article from the American Bankers Association's Journal.[842] He responded with another article a month later, which appeared in the December issue. In this he summarized the short history of the financial reconstruction of Hungary so far. Smith identified the main problems as the lack of capital, especially in the form of long-term loans from the United States, the restrictive tariff duties that prevailed in and around Hungary, and the question of state officials. In his conclusion, he reiterated his high regard for the international cooperation that was the most striking feature of the plan, the cordial reception in Hungary he had been the subject of, and his optimism for the success of the plan.[843] This article was important from the point of view that the *Journal of the American Bankers Association* was read by about 80% of the American banking society. Jeremiah Smith, Jr. did everything in his power to help the country through any channel that opened up to him.

The cordial reception by average Hungarians and the honest cooperation of the government he had written about on several occasions was really true. Smith was looked upon not as a foreigner who would work against the country, but rather as a man who could provide help for the poor country in need. Aside from the initial distrust that was naturally present for a very short time, Hungary had taken Smith in. His straight style accompanied with modest manners was extremely popular and for most people he embodied the well-

840 Piváњy to Smith, September 16, 1924, and Smith to Pivány, September 30, 1924, R. III. d, C. 118, Financial Reconstruction of Hungary, LNA.
841 Smith to Pivány, September 30, 1924, Ibid.
842 Clark to Smith, September 16, 1294, Ibid.
843 The article can be found in Smith to Clark, October 24, 1924, Ibid.

intentioned Yankee that many Hungarians would have liked to see in a person in his position. The articles, often written by American newspapers living in Europe, emphasized Smith's popularity, placing the stress on his human quality.[844] According to personal sources, the Hungarian vocabulary quickly became richer with the idiom "why not be more Smithy?" instead of "why not be more frank or modest?"[845] His good friend Thomas Lamont recalled years later in his memoirs that Smith had given "a word to the Hungarian tongue, perhaps also an idea. When a bright new scheme was proposed, purportedly bereft of the usual flim-flam of bargaining, the doubtful would ask, 'Come now, is this absolutely *Jerry*?'"[846] These accounts, although not verified, point to a very important fact, namely that Jeremiah Smith, Jr. was in high esteem in Hungary, genuinely liked for his straightforwardness and honesty. Brentano also shared the opinion that Smith's popularity lay in his being an American and leaving a modest life.[847]

Smith phrased best the Hungarian situation and his role in it after a good year had passed in the reconstruction period. In an interview given to one of the leading dailies in the United States on his return for a longer vacation in the fall of 1925, he summed up the past seventeen months in this fashion:

> Without their [Hungarians] sincerity, their ardent resolve to balance their budget, I could have done nothing. As it was, I was just sent down there to see that the League plan was carried out. And I sat and watched it being done. That's every bit there is to it. [...] The great trouble with all Governments is that there is too much politics and not enough business about them. [...] Well, in Hungary we cut out a bit of politics and introduced a bit of business—and a lot of honest good-will and determination and grit.[848]

He also spoke of the political value of the League of Nations as he saw it: "The League is slowly creating a new international public opinion that will insist on many things; among them the suppression of the old secret diplomacy and the introduction of morality more on a par with the modern individual standard."[849] Here one can already foresee Jeremiah Smith, Jr.'s political views that he would later express on higher forums.

844 See, for example, the article in *The Washington Post*, September 28, 1924.
845 *Boston Daily Globe*, October 5, 1924.
846 Lamont, *Across World Frontiers*, 84.
847 *Budapesti Hírlap*, April 29, 1925, XLV/96.
848 *The New York Times*, October 11, 1925.
849 Ibid.

8.2. Smith's Great Magnanimity

The largest and most famous showcase of Smith's magnanimity came at the conclusion of his tenure in Hungary. The National Assembly wished to express the gratitude of the country toward Smith. Soon a decision was born and on June 22nd the Assembly unanimously accepted the proposal to "record our people's gratitude to the departing Commissioner-General in our Proceedings, and [...] to hand to him an extract from the proceedings of National Assembly."[850] When deputy of the Assembly, Béla Kenéz, praised Smith, he also emphasized the American card:

> And although he kept himself far from politics, his faith in the Government made it possible to settle all questions in full accord. He acted before the League of Nations not only as a controller who fulfills his duty, but also as an intercessor of great weight and authority in the interests of the Hungarian Nation. His reports [...] won the confidence of foreign countries for us, and opened up the resources of foreign capitalists. [...] All his efforts were centered in the wish to regain our sequestered financial and economic freedom and to assure the conditions of our economic prosperity. The activity of the Commissioner General reminded us of all the historic ties, which existed between the United States of America and Hungary since the beginning. [...] He takes with himself not only the consciousness of a well performed task, but also the gratitude of the Hungarian nation, as well as its demand to keep us in his memory.[851]

His answer was read in the Assembly on June 24th. In this he thanked the Hungarian people for their good will, said he would look back on his time in Hungary "with the greatest pleasure," and wished the country "the greatest good fortune in the future."[852] Horthy said goodbye to Smith, "a reliable friend of our country," in a private meeting, where he gave Smith a photo of himself as a parting gift.[853] It is hard to tell what the American thought of this farewell gift, but he used his chance to ask for a present. Smith said he wished to see St. Stephen's Crown. The request somewhat surprised Horthy, but naturally such a friend could not be refused. As Horthy remembered, "Mr. Smith stood speechless before this product of a Byzantine goldsmith's art [...] called on me again and

850 Extract from the proceedings of the Hungarian National Assembly of June 22, 1926, JSAA.
851 Speech of deputy Béla Kenéz, given in the Hungarian National Assembly, June 22, 1926, Ibid.
852 Typescript of Mr. Smith's letter of response to Dr. Béla Scitovszky, Budapest, dated June 23, 1926, Ibid.
853 Horthy, *Memoirs*, 158; *Pesti Napló*, June 29, 1926, 77/144.

declared: 'I understand now. That wasn't the crown. Saint Stephen's Crown is Hungary herself.'"[854]

On June 26th, the government held a farewell dinner in honor to Jeremiah Smith, Jr. in Hotel Hungaria. The guest list of approximately 150 people included all the names that counted. Present were the ambassadors of Spain, Austria, Italy, Great Britain, Poland, France, Germany, and Greece, as well as the ministers of the United States, Bulgaria, Czechoslovakia, and Serbia. In addition to William Goode, important newspapers were represented, such as the *Chicago Tribune*, the *Christian Science Monitor*, the *Chicago Daily News*, and other leading European papers.[855] Bethlen praised Smith anew:

> We venture to hope that his friendship will outlast his two years' stay in our country. [...His part] has been inspired by and has been in complete accordance with those noble and friendly traditions which have always marked the relations of the United States of America towards this country of ours. And indeed the expression of thanks and gratitude offered to Mr. Jeremiah Smith must of necessity be extended to the whole of the United States of America, and may I be permitted to express the hope of the Hungarian nation that the sympathies of your great Democracy will not be withdrawn from our sorely visited country.[856]

Smith in his speech showed once again the modest style everybody loved him for: "We have had the privilege and the honor to assist [...] we have only been assistants and we cannot claim the credit for the results. No progress could have been made in this work without the co-operation not only of the Hungarian Government but of the whole Hungarian people." He concluded that although "we came here as strangers [...] in leaving it we find that we are leaving behind us friends."[857] Brentano read aloud the State Department's warm words for Smith and its satisfaction that it was an American who helped the Hungarian reconstruction:

> I hope you will express the satisfaction of the Government of the United States and of the people of this country at the successful termination of Mr. Smith's work. Americans who have followed it are glad that it should have been an American citizen who has been able to give this important aid to the Hungarian Government and people.[858]

854 Horthy, *Memoirs*, 159.
855 *Budapesti Hírlap*, June 27, 1926, XLVI/143.
856 Barclay to Chamberlain, June 28, 1926, C7497/443/21, 11370, FO371, TNA.
857 Speech to be Delivered by Commissioner-General Jeremiah Smith at the Dinner Given in His Honour by the Hungarian Government, Junen26, 1926, JSAA.
858 Quoted in Mark Imre Major, *American Hungarian Relations 1918-1944* (Astor, Fl: Danubian Press, 1974), 182–183; Brentano to Kellogg, June 30, 1926, 864.00/675, M. 708, Roll 7, NARA.

Somewhat interestingly, despite Goode's prodding and the role the British had had in the program, the British minister did not read out any official speech of thanks or praise, which Goode thought to be a shame and was angry about.[859] Smith was clearly the hero of the day, and, without his deliberately adding to it, he earned new vocabulary of gratitude and fame.

The story that propelled Smith into a short spell of real fame was the fate of his salary. At the conclusion of his more than two years in Hungary, the Hungarian government wanted to present him with a check for $100,000, his salary up to his departure, but the American refused it. This happened on June 29th and the very next day everybody learned who Jeremiah Smith, Jr. was. On June 30th, all the leading American dailies spread the story of the magnanimous act of Smith. *The New York Times* quoted Smith as saying on refusing the check: "Give it to charity. Your poor need it more than I do. The only compensation I desire for my work is the appreciation and friendship of the Hungarian people."[860] When Bethlen protested that "the vouchers already have been issued by the State and their entry cannot be altered in the Treasury books," Smith allegedly answered, "Then re-enter it in your books as a gift from the American people to the people of Hungary."[861] To top it all, when the Hungarian Prime Minister wanted to give at least a high decoration in honor of Smith, the American was appalled and replied, "If you do, then I shall never forgive you. Your friendship and gratitude are more precious to me than any decoration."[862] With this generous act, Smith's name became a household celebrity overnight both in Hungary and the United States.

Jeremiah Smith, Jr. left Hungary in the early morning of July 1st, on the board of the Orient Express. He bid a final farewell for the Hungarian nation through the press. In this message he said thanks for Hungary for the kindness with

---

859 Barclay to Lampson, July 7, 1926, C7829/210/21, 11368, FO371, TNA. Barclay added: "Between ourselves, I think the mixed drinks had been too much for him!" Ibid. Siepmann spoke also of his compatriot in a negative vein. He said Goode "has had a finger, as usual, in every pie." Siepmann to Norman, May 31, 1926, OV33/42, BoE. If anyone, the British had won with the financial reconstruction of Hungary, and not only in the political sense. Both the British share of the import trade of Hungary and the visible balance in favor of Great Britain more than doubled during the period, and the total imports of British goods showed an increase of 54%. *The Times*, July 29, 1926.

860 *The New York Times*, June 30, 1926; *The Washington Post*, June 30, 1926; *Christian Science Monitor*, June 30, 1926.

861 Ibid.

862 Ibid. On the other hand, James Speyer, whose status was assured in Hungary and was even acknowledged as a friend of Hungary, was not so modest. The Cabinet agreed that Speyer should be awarded a medal as recognition for his services to Hungary. Accordingly, he was decorated with the Hungarian Order of Merit with Stars, Class II, which he received in the United States from the Hungarian Minister, Count László Széchenyi. Records of Cabinet Meetings, September 14, 1928, 32–33R/56, K 27, Records of Cabinet Council Meetings, HNA; *The New York Times*, November 1, 1941.

which he had been received, and for the Hungarian press for the understanding it had showed to him and the support it had provided.[863] As he formulated his good bye, he said, "I will always think back to my stay in Hungary with the greatest pleasure. I will always watch the future of the country with the greatest interest."[864] Only three days after his departure, tributes were paid to Smith on the 4th of July celebration at the statue of Washington, where he twice had been a participator.[865] Smith's gesture of giving his remaining salary to the Hungarian government "has increased his popularity, already great in this country."[866] But the sudden star status was not restricted to Hungary only.

The news that Smith had given his salary to the Hungarian people evoked positive feedback in his home country. Malcolm Donald, a partner of Smith in their law firm, said of Smith's act, "There is little that can be said to indicate our admiration of the act itself. It must, however, be said by those who know Smith very well, it is exactly like him to have done this."[867] Frederic H. Curtiss, Chairman of the Federal Reserve Bank in Boston, drew a broader conclusion: "If we had more Mr. Smiths who could go to Europe and lend such able assistance in the solution of critical problems there the more speedily would the great questions of the world sympathy and understanding be clarified and settled."[868] Another influential business man who had known Smith's father was happy with the son's act, because it countered the European claim that Americans were selfish.[869] As the Hungarian minister reported, "there had never been so many articles written about Hungary since the existence of the legation," and the "real torrent of articles" were about the conclusion of Smith's work especially touching on the story of the $100,000.[870] An American newspaper also noted that the "widespread publicity [...] focused interest more full on Hungary and its bonds through Mr. Smith's generous action that probably could have been accomplished in any other way."[871] In honor of Smith, the *American Hungarian People's Voice* brought out a special edition, dressed in Hungarian national colors. They also cabled to Smith, "Your generosity is a symbol of the great American spirit which is a natural instinct of America's great sons of which you

863 *Budapesti Hírlap*, July 1, 1926, XLVI/145.
864 Ibid.
865 *The New York Times*, July 4, 1926.
866 Barclay to Chamberlain, July 7, 1926, C7772/443/21, 11370, FO371, TNA.
867 *Christian Science Monitor*, June 30, 1926.
868 Ibid.
869 Ibid.
870 53/1926 I–5. Washington I/368, K 66, Press and Cultural Department, HNA. In addition to the three newspapers already mentioned, the following papers reported on Smith: *Public Ledger, Pittsburgh Post, Evening Star, New York Herald Tribune*, and *New York World*. Ibid.
871 *Wall Street Journal*, July 21, 1926.

are one of the foremost."[872] Scores of praising letters were delivered to the editor of *The New York Times*, and the paper was proud to print some of them.[873] A reader even compared Smith to George Washington.[874] James Speyer was among the large group of those congratulating Smith. "We all [are] here delighted to learn of your generous action on terminating your successful work. You have not only rendered Hungary but also our own country distinguished service. We will all welcome you back home."[875] Smith's act even boosted the standing of the Hungarian reconstruction bonds at the New York Stock Exchange with a new price of 102 on June 28th.[876] Tyler, his deputy, who stayed behind as the link between the trustees and Hungary, claimed, "Smith did a magnificent job in Hungary, and his name will live long there. The U.S.A. couldn't have had a better representative there – though of course he didn't represent the U.S.A. except in a purely extra-official way."[877] Jeremiah Smith, Jr.'s popularity was at its height both in Hungary and in the United States.

This indeed great story of generosity suffered a minor drawback when Smith admitted that he had already declined drawing his salary at the start of his work. It is worth quoting at length his interview given to *The New York Times* upon his arrival back to the United States:

> As a matter of fact, I don't know exactly how much I did refuse, and actually the refusal was made two years ago. The League of Nations, from which came my appointment as Commissioner General, and the Hungarian Government had agreed on $5,000 a month to cover all the costs, and I was there a little over two years. I stipulated at the start that I would take no salary, for when you are going to work blue-penciling other people's salaries you can't very well take a big one yourself. I did accept my living expenses. That wasn't much, for the Government provided my quarters. When this and the cost of maintaining my staff was deducted there might have remained $60,000. According to the European way of doing things, they sent a messenger to my first assistant, Mr. Royall Tyler, who also comes from Boston, and suggested him that he suggest to me that I take the $60,000, or whatever it was. In fact, they suggested it twice. I had told them I wasn't going to take anything, and I honestly believe it helped my work. Then they asked me what they should do with it and I told them it was their money, the first they had to spend, so they

872 *The New York Times*, July 4, 1926.
873 Ibid., July 3 and 8, 1926.
874 Ibid., July 18, 1926.
875 Speyer to Smith, July 1, 1926, T. II. Incoming and outgoing telegrams, Sep 24–June 26, C. 120, Financial Reconstruction of Hungary, LNA.
876 *Wall Street Journal*, July 21, 1926.
877 Tyler to Mildred Bliss, July 21, 1926, Box 2, Tyler Papers.

> might as well do as they liked. They asked if there was any objection to using it as a scholarship fund to send students to the United States. I said there was not, so they did. I don't know how the $100,000 story started. The first I knew of it was in London, when I bought an American paper. I was caught in a traffic jam so I opened it and found myself all over the front page. I was somewhat embarrassed then and even more when I landed from the Laconia here today and found an accumulation of letters from everywhere, praising me, condemning me and asking for a piece of the $100,000. I don't believe there was that much money, and anyway I never saw a check for it. I had a great time over there. I am glad to get back and 'join the army of employed,' but of course I wouldn't have left if the work wasn't all done.[878]

However, this information coming three weeks later made no difference and the glory was forever sealed. It is interesting to note that in the United States the money that Smith had given to Hungary came under scrutiny from the tax authorities. There was some debate whether it was a sum after which Smith should pay taxes. In the end, the officials said that probably the $100,000 gift would be tax exempted because of a new provision inserted in February.[879] The Hungarian government decided to use the money for a good cause. They set up a "Jeremiah Smith Scholarship Fund," which was to send two Hungarian students for an academic year to the United States every year. The initiative had been brewing for some time. Already during April, the American minister had informed the State Department about such an idea.[880] With the scholarship, Smith's name and nimbus remained unbroken in Hungary.

The American Commissioner-General not only helped Hungary and Hungarians in his official status and through occasional articles, but he also weighed in if he thought that his personal influence might tip the balance in favor of someone. Such a story was when the League of Nations was looking for a man suitable for the post of Internal Control Officer in the Secretariat. Smith was also asked if he knew anyone who could fill the position, but he first informed the League that, in his view, he knew no one who would qualify.[881] Later, however, he changed his mind and came to the conclusion that a certain young Hungarian, Pál Makay, a secretary at the Finance Ministry, would be best for the job, even if he had

878 *The New York Times*, July 20, 1926. According to a contemporary, it was György Lukács's, Smith's Hungarian secretary, idea that the $60,000 should be turned into a foundation under Smith's name. Barcza, *Diplomata emlékeim*, 1911-1945, 1:189.
879 *The New York Times*, July 2, 1926.
880 Brentano to Kellogg, April 22, 1926, 864.00/677, Roll 7, M. 708, NARA.
881 Smith to Ames, May 28, 1925, C.III (5) Correspondence - League of Nations, C. 111, Financial Reconstruction of Hungary, LNA.

not reached the age of 35, which was a prerequisite.[882] His opinion carried enough weight for Makay to become attached to the Secretariat under Herbert Ames. Makay was not the only one on whose behalf he tried to intervene. At the conclusion of his post in Hungary, he tried to arrange a post for his Hungarian secretary, György Lukács, at the League of Nations. He wrote to Eric Drummond that in case the League wanted another Hungarian in addition to Makay, he would take "great pleasure in recommending very strongly George Lukács," who spoke English, French, and German fluently and had visited Genoa along Smith twice.[883]

Finally, it is worth mentioning two small episodes that shed light on Smith from another angle. Obviously, Smith had no financial problems. He had been close enough to the nerve of the financial center of the world and he had accumulated a handsome fortune. The post in Hungary was indeed a challenge for him not from the pecuniary side but from the lofty international aspect he represented as an American. Still, he preached thriftiness, and he tried to live up to it. He lived modestly and did not take part in grandiose events if he could avoid it. He even refused his salary, because he thought it would not be right to accept it when the country that would pay it was in financial trouble. Sometimes he seems to have carried it to the extreme though. After returning from the fall Assembly in Geneva in 1924, Smith felt he was cheated on the train back by the railway company. As he informed the company, he had had to pay extra fare on the Orient Express due to wrong information he had received in Zürich and he requested a refund for this expense.[884] The sum was negligible, but for Smith it was a question of principle that not an extra crown should be paid from the budget of the League Secretariat in Budapest unnecessarily. Another story a year later, which is humorous, involved Smith also with the same problem but on a very different level. It is the best to quote the whole in original to get the taste of it and enjoy Smith's humor:

> On my return here, I find that the butler has quarreled with the cook and locked her out of the kitchen, on the ground that she is cheating in the purchase of food. Both parties have appealed to me, but as I am unable to communicate with them in any language they can understand I have adopted

882 Smith to Ames, August 13, 1925, Ibid. Also, Cabinet Meeting, September 25, 1925, 15–19R/43, K 27, Records of Cabinet Council Meetings, HNA.

883 Smith to Drummond, June 30, 1926, Ibid. However, Lukács was not employed by the League in the end. In December 1926 he was appointed by the Hungarian government to lead the press relations office in Vienna. Cabinet Meeting, December 10, 1926, 43–44R/45, K 27, Records of Cabinet Council Meetings, HNA. Later he worked as a government employee in Paris and London.

884 Smith to Cook & Son, September 15, 1924, E. I. May 1924–June 30, 1925, C. 113, Financial Reconstruction of Hungary, LNA.

> the line of least resistance, which is to postpone the matter until the arrival of Excellency Tyler on Thursday night, when he will be greeted with this problem. The Austrian, Turkish and Greek questions are nothing to it![885]

As can be demonstrated through these small episodes, Smith was a real human being. Often, through the official reports and contacts this side of him hardly appeared. He was a man of principles and he would fight to the very end of those principles. Also, as others referred to it, his personality had a lighter side that promised a man of occasional jokes and a worldview that contained not only the serious, but also the jolly.

All of this must be assessed in the light of Smith's continuous sickness since the start of 1925. Despite the handicap, about which the stays in the United States could help little, it was a nagging phenomenon making life difficult for the Commissioner-General. Although he tried to handle it in a light manner, his sickness was staying with him throughout. That is exactly why it is additionally appreciable that he was able to continually show the positive side of his personality, which earned him the friendship of Hungarians.

8.3. Difference of Personalities

A comparison can and must be drawn between the two Commissioners-General. This is required due to the fact that they held identical positions in neighboring countries under the aegis of the League of Nations during the same timeframe, and they were entrusted with the same task: to oversee the financial reconstruction and control the finances of their host countries, Austria and Hungary. They both held a wide range of equal powers concerning such a job and they followed the almost identical reconstruction plan to be executed drawn up by the League of Nations. In light of such antecedents, it should be logical to expect that things happened in a very similar fashion in the two countries. Although, form an overall point of view this may be more or less accurate, on the personal level nothing is further from the truth.

In the earlier chapters, it was analyzed what kind of personality Alfred Zimmerman and Jeremiah Smith, Jr. were. While the Dutchman was severe, rigid, somewhat haughty, and not at all friendly toward his host nation, Smith was almost everything his Dutch counterpart was not: he was friendly, modest, flexible, and helpful. If one compares the descriptions in contemporary opinions and later recollections, the two sets of memories could not be more strikingly

885 Smith to Felkin, September 15, 1925, C.III (6) Correspondence – M. A. E. Felkin, C. 111, Financial Reconstruction of Hungary, LNA.

different. That is definitely not to say that Zimmerman was not a good organizer or was not an expert at what he was doing, or that Smith had no disagreements with the Hungarian government during his tenure. However, the general view was that they were strikingly different. Owing to the difference between the two men, they tackled the problems they were facing in a conspicuously dissimilar manner. Zimmerman was "by the book" almost all of the time and was adamant that his views should prevail, which, only to be fair, were often the same as those of the League of Nations. In contrast, Smith was capable of smoothing the occasional differences in opinion between him and the Hungarian government. Due to his personality, he was indeed able to reconcile the other party to his view without either committing offense or preventing the possibility of revising the decision at a later time. Smith too, nonetheless, followed the League agenda closely in the reconstruction period; hence the significance of the differing approaches of the two men.

Smith had a no-nonsense approach and attitude despite "the very difficult and delicate task which you and your staff had to perform."[886] This practical outlook met the will of cooperation on the part of the Hungarian government, which Smith never missed to mention and commend; on the other hand, he mitigated his own role at the same time. Although these statements were so typical of him, Smith worked excessively while in Hungary, for which he paid with his health. He never recovered after going through so much strain and for the rest of his life he was often tormented with a weakened state. Perhaps, had he turned out to be an almost totalitarian supervisor similarly to Zimmerman, he might have escaped such ailment. That would not have been him though. He gave all he had.

Another striking difference was between the two men's attitudes toward money. Zimmerman was bargaining for more, right from the beginning, and lived in luxurious style in Vienna, much to the resentment of the Viennese people. Smith, on the other hand, not only lived in modest circumstances while in Budapest, but he also forwent his salary right at the time of his nomination. He said he refused compensation "because I live simply and require little for my own needs. It hardly seemed fitting that I should urge sacrifice and economies upon the Hungarians and yet not show the same spirit myself."[887] He accepted only enough to cover his expenses. The spectacular refusal of his salary at the end of his tenure was not a sudden idea, despite being turned into a media event, but was the manifestation of the deep worldview of Smith.

As a further proof of Zimmerman's being perceived as out of touch and not meriting the highest praise, it is worth quoting his compatriot in connection with

886 Drummond to Smith, June 15, 1926, Appointment of a Commissioner General by the League. Doc. No. 33315, Financial Reconstruction of Hungary, Registry Files, R. 298, LNA.
887 *The New York Times*, April 16, 1925.

him and Smith. Colijn, who was talked out of coming to Hungary by Zimmerman in order that the latter could enjoy his services, said to the American Minister at Budapest in 1926, "Zimmerman undoubtedly accomplished very useful work as financial adviser to the Austrian Government. But your compatriot has made his name even more illustrious than my countryman."[888] This coming from Zimmerman's compatriot and colleague speaks volumes for the personalities involved.

Ironically perhaps, today in Rotterdam there is a street named after Alfred Zimmerman, *Zimmermanweg*. This is not for his work in Austria, but his earlier reign as the mayor of that city. No similar memory is preserving Smith's name either in his home town or in Hungary despite the fact that, allegedly, a movement was started by OMKE (Hungarian National Trade Association) to have a street named after Smith and a monument erected in his honor.[889] Still, Smith got his reward of recognition in the end in another form. Thanks to a grant from the Ford Foundation, Harvard Law School established two professorships in International Law. The second of these was voted to be in the memory of Smith in recognition of his "distinguished services to his country and to this University" in 1958.[890]

888 Major, *American Hungarian Relations*, 183.

889 *Magyarország*, March 17, 1935, XLII/63.

890 Kristin M. Flower (Franklin D. Roosevelt Presidential Library and Museum), email message to author, November 25, 2008.

Chapter 9

Post-Reconstruction Relations between an American and Europe

9.1. Smith and Hungary

With Jeremiah Smith, Jr.'s departure, the ties between the country and the man who had done so much for it were not broken. Although the actual work of financial reconstruction had been accomplished, Hungary was still very much interested in fostering good relations with the United States. This was a normal wish from both political and economical points of view. Hungary expected further American capital to come to the country, and the rapport between the two countries since 1920 had been excellent although not on a very high level. This good relationship was further enhanced by Smith's two-year stay in Hungary and the positive result he and Hungary achieved. In addition, there was the Jeremiah Smith Scholarship Fund, which was to send two Hungarian students each year to the United States. Since the initiative was named after Smith, it was only natural that his affiliation to Hungary would be strengthened by the outcome of that program.

Smith, who many regarded as the savior of Hungary, after returning to his home in the United States, resumed his lawyer career in Herrick, Smith, Donald & Farley. Naturally, his sudden fame was a welcomed asset to the firm. Whether Smith thought that now his international career was over or he hoped that new challenges would come his way is unknown. Whatever Smith thought, it was evident that his quiet work in the law firm wasted his international expertise – and, from the Hungarian standpoint, his potential influence as an ally. They did not want to lose such a liaison, because they knew that even his informal connections and name alone could open new doors for Hungary in the New World.

Hungarian high-level state officials did everything in their capacity to strengthen the impression that Hungary was closely connected to Smith, which was true in many ways. In October, two instances of such character happened, when both Bethlen and Finance Minister Bud used an American media outlet to praise Smith's services to Hungary.[891] Bud even requested the reporter "to report Hungary's gratitude to the American citizen who had shown this country the way to financial prosperity."[892] Being sure of Smith's goodwill toward Hungary,

891 *The New York Times*, October 28 and 31, 1926.
892 *The New York Times*, October 28, 1926.

Bethlen had no qualms about asking him for information concerning a certain American financial group that showed some interest in the economic life of Hungary.[893] Naturally, there was nothing immoral or illegal in these steps on part of the highest Hungarian political circle. It was rather a proof that the leadership of Hungary was well aware of how to maintain a crucial relationship. At the end of the year, Bethlen's good wishes for the new year were another incentive for Smith to thank everyone in Hungary by reiterating that he was not going to forget Hungary.[894] Hungary's appreciation was also expressed in the beautiful set of Herend porcelain foreign minister Walkó sent to Smith for Christmas.[895]

Smith indeed continued to be identified with Hungary after his departure, on account of his name. What is more, even before he left his post in Hungary, he had become the prominent sought after person for an organization. The American-Hungarian Society was formed in 1923 and the next year it was incorporated as the American-Hungarian Foundation in Michigan, Ill. Its main aims were to establish an agency for the interchange of knowledge, to establish an American-Hungarian institution in the University of Budapest, to establish a periodical for the education of Hungarian immigrants in America, and to publish American literature in Hungary and Hungarian literature in America.[896] Széchenyi, the Hungarian minister in Washington, had started the preliminary work in May. He suggested Victor James Dowling, a long-time Justice in the 1st District and of the Appellate Division of the New York Supreme Court, that he should compose a letter to Smith in which the history of the Society should be made familiar to the New Englander and his attention should be drawn to the fact that "he would be the best asset for the Society."[897] Dowling acted in this fashion and wrote to Smith, but the latter refused to be associated with the organization because he felt it might compromise the impartiality that he wanted to keep at all cost.[898]

The idea of securing a household name in America stemmed from a pecuniary objective. Lacking financial support, the budget of the organization was basically empty; the American members were of the opinion that they would only be willing to give money if the American-Hungarians showed a larger interest and financial sacrifice.[899] It was a scarcely hidden factor that with the name of Smith on the banner, the Foundation should have a much easier time finding more

893 Bethlen to Smith, November 4, 1926, 7, 1922–1931 B/4. 706/926/27, K 468, Bethlen Papers, HNA.
894 Smith to Bethlen, January 4, 1927, 3, 1921–1928 B/2. Files relating to foreign policy. 148/927/28, K 468, Bethlen Papers, HNA.
895 Smith to Walkó, January 4, 1927, /23, Ibid.
896 89/94–95, K 106, Papers of the Washington Embassy, HNA.
897 Széchenyi to Dowling, May 12, 1926, 90/143–144, Ibid.
898 Pelényi to Deák, September 27, 1926, 89/64, Ibid.
899 Ballenbegger to Széchenyi, June 19, 1926, 89/30, Ibid.

money. Stephen P. Duggan, Director of the Institute of International Education, and the person who organized Apponyi's lecture tour in the United States in 1923, thought that Smith becoming the President of the organization would smooth all such problems and traveling expenses of students coming from Budapest to American colleges would not be an obstacle.[900] So, on the very brink of Smith leaving Hungary, without his knowledge, he was already singled out for a new role.

Smith, who had his share of health problems during his extended stay in Hungary, chose a quiet place to rest after returning to the United States, and went to Canada for a vacation before resuming his active career as a lawyer. Since he was indeed a conscientious man, he wanted to follow the fate of the scholarship named after him. Already during his physical and mental recuperation in the north, he wrote that when he had come back to Cambridge, MA, he wanted to hear about the scholarships.[901] In early October he met with an official from the Hungarian legation, and he was confronted again with the idea of becoming the main man of the society. Although he first seemed bent on not joining the organization, because it would take up a lot of time, toward the end of the conversation he became mollified and willing. He gave assurances in terms of his good will and said that "naturally, I shall always do my share whenever I could help Hungary."[902] Smith, on his part, suggested a comprehensive reform of the society in order to make sure that it could function more efficiently. He also thought desirable that the Hungarian government should participate in the form of paying the expenses of the Hungarian professors that might come over to the United States.[903]

On November 6th, a prominent group of people came together for tea in Boston to discuss the problems of the society. The illustrious gathering comprised Roscoe Pound, Dean of the Harvard Law School; Jeremiah Smith, Jr.; Professor James of International Law, a certain Professor Joseph Redlich, a historian from Vienna; Professor Gilbert Murray of Oxford University, who represented the League of Nations' Committee of Intellectual Cooperation; Robert Dodge, director of the Massachusetts branch of the American Bar Association and member of the Massachusetts Judicial Council, and the younger brother of the king of Siam and heir apparent to the throne. The problems of the society were, however, not solved with Smith, especially with his health making it impossible for him to take on a new challenge in the winter of 1926. The next year, when he felt better again, he was already planning to come back to Europe for a more ambitious position.

900 Duggan to Deák, July 26, 1926, 89/73, Ibid.
901 Deák to Pelényi, August 16, 1926, 89/70–71, Ibid.
902 Deák to Pelényi, October 5, 1926, 89/59–60, Ibid.
903 Butterfield to Pelényi, October 23, 1926, 89/26, Ibid.

In the meantime, there was the question of the scholarships. In 1925, an exchange program had already begun between the United States and Hungary, when six Hungarian students went to the United States on fellowship opportunities provided through the efforts of the Hungarian Ministry of Education in Budapest and the Institute of International Education in New York.[904] The Jeremiah Smith Scholarship Fund was integrated into this already existing program. Although the program was soon full-fledged and every year a small number of Hungarians, typically three, were given the means to travel to the United States. However, by 1928 the program was plagued with financial problems. Upon the suggestion of the Finance Ministry, the program was launched with about 240,000 golden crowns ($48,000) in 1926 and was invested in bank stocks to guarantee some yield.[905] With time though, the proper care needed was not taken and the amount was dwindling. The Hungarian government was neglectful of ensuring that the students, once in the United States, should get their money, and often they were left without any help. The money was to be delivered quarterly through the Hungarian legation in Washington, but the money did not always arrive, and the legation was not informed about the students' arrival.[906] Unfortunately, the situation did not improve much in the following years. The bulk of the scholarship money was paid to the students back in Budapest, but it was almost totally consumed by traveling expenses. Széchenyi regularly pleaded with the Foreign Ministry to pay more heed to this issue.[907]

The students themselves were also responsible for the problems, although unintentionally. Since most of the applicants were coming from poor families, the Ministry of Religion and Education almost always paid their half-priced ship ticket and the expenses from Budapest to Fiume.[908] The idea of giving $10 as pocket money to each student on a monthly basis did not appeal to the Ministry, but any such requirement that the students contribute with a smaller amount would have made the number of applicants shrink to basically zero.[909] The situation was very awkward and the Institute of International Education was forced to ask for a refund of $500, which the Hungarian Relief Society paid.[910]

---

904 Pelényi to Palmer, November 1, 1928, 161/811, Ibid.

905 January 21, 1927, 6 and 11R/28, 10th daily item. K 27, Records of Cabinet Council Meetings, HNA. See also, János Botos, A Magyar Nemzeti Bank története. [The History of the Hungarian National Bank] vol. 2. Az önálló magyar jegybank, 1924–1948. [The Independent Hungarian Bank of Issue, 1924–1948] (Budapest: Presscon Kiadó, 1999), 90.

906 Magyary to Walkó, December 22, 1928, 160/832, K 106, Papers of the Washington Embassy, HNA.

907 Széchenyi to Walkó, January 21, 25, 1932, 161/789–90, 792–93, Ibid.

908 Jánossy to Pelényi, April 8, 1929, /801, Ibid.

909 Ibid.

910 Palmer to Pelényi, December 19, 1928, and Pelényi to Magyari, January 23, 1929, /803–04, Ibid.

Such was the state of affairs of the Hungarian students going to study in the United States.

Sometimes the best intentions are not enough and the obviously positive initiative of the Jeremiah Smith Scholarship Fund kept losing much of its original momentum. In the fall of 1932, for example, it was possible for only one new student to commence her studies.[911] The situation improved only a fraction when, on account of Széchenyi's services coming to an end in Washington, Georgetown University paid him tribute in a generous fashion. They decided "that a Hungarian student of His Excellency's choice be granted a tuition Scholarship for four years in either the College of Arts and Sciences, or the School of Law, or the Foreign Service School."[912] With this school added, an impressive list can be given of the various institutions where Hungarian students could spend some time in American educational environment. For example, they visited College of St. Catherine, Michigan College of Mining, City Hospital, Welfare Island, Harvard Law School, Clark University, Vassar College, Carleton College, Rollins College, Elmira College, New York, Eastman School of Music, University of Rochester, Cornell University, University of Pittsburgh, University of Chicago, Northwestern University, and Rutgers University.[913]

It can be concluded that the Hungarian government did not live up to its side of the bargain. The resolution to establish a foundation named after Smith had been born well before the $100,000 story started.[914] The decision to use Smith's money for this purpose was prudent, pleasing Smith as well. Although Smith tried to be involved somehow in further helping Hungary within the United States, he could not render as much service as Hungarian officials had hoped. The good relation nevertheless remained intact. In 1928, Széchenyi presented Smith with the embossed copy of the thanks passed by the Hungarian Assembly back in June 1926, at a dinner at the Ritz-Carlton Hotel.[915] Smith's reply of thanks to the National Assembly was read out in that body as well.[916] A few weeks later Béla Alapi, Managing Director of the City Savings Bank Company, Ltd., went to New York to promote closer financial relations between the two countries. He praised Smith lavishly and said that there was one statue of an American, that of George Washington's statue erected in 1906, but "if we put up another, it will be that of Jeremiah Smith's."[917] The Hungarian-American Commercial Chamber

911 Douglass to Széchenyi, November 22, 1932, 162/25, Ibid.
912 Nevils to Széchenyi, February 21, 1933, /121, Ibid.
913 Archie Palmer to Pelenyi, November 19, 1928, 161/121, and Jessie Douglass to Szechenyi, November 22, 1932, 162/121, Ibid.
914 Brentano to Kellogg, April 22, 1926, 864.00/677, Roll 7, M. 708, NARA.
915 *The New York Times*, January 11, 1928.
916 National Assembly Diary, 1927–1932, 11:137.
917 *The New York Times*, February 12, 1928.

gave a dinner in honor of Lóránt Hegedűs, former finance minister of Hungary, at Waldorf Astoria, in March 1928. Among the roughly five hundred guests many represented the financial and commercial elite of New York, such as James Speyer or Marshall Brown, and a score of reporters, while President Coolidge and Vice President Dawes sent congratulating telegrams. The speakers emphasized the traditional friendship of Hungary and the United States, and urged closer ties along commercial and financial lines. When Hegedűs uttered Smith's name, those present commenced a stormy applause.[918] When a few weeks later Hungarian pilgrims visited the United States, they wanted to pay respect to Smith in person. Unfortunately, Smith was outside the country, but in his letter sent to Zsigmond Perényi, he thanked for the pilgrims' intention and apologized that he could not meet them. He once again reiterated that he enjoyed his stay in Hungary and wished all the best for Hungary and Hungarians.[919] Despite the rapport between the country and the man, by the turn of the decade, the momentum was gone and seemingly beyond repair.

9.2. Smith and the League of Nations

At the successful conclusion of his stay in Hungary as Commissioner-General of the League of Nations, Smith wanted nothing more than to go home to New England again. The extensive work, even if with interludes, had shaken his health and he knew he needed to retire for a period. In this semi-retirement, as was shown above, he did not lose contact with the outside world and tried to use his enhanced status as a possible tool for further help for Hungary. However, at the end of the year, his physical condition once again took the better of him, and he had to stay away from any challenge that might have gotten in the way of recovery. Smith's health and outlook in the United States were not only of concern to Hungary. The League of Nations was following its distinguished servant's future as well.[920]

The League was grateful for Smith. In 1924, he quickly said yes when the organization offered him the job and thus the League, already with heavy time deficit on hand, was not forced to go courting another person. Naturally, the League found in Smith exactly what it had been looking for in the sense that the American was representing, even in a private capacity, his country under

918 Daily News, Daily Reports (1920-1944), March 19, 1928, K. 428. a, HNA.

919 May 12, 1928, Ibid.

920 Felkin to Smith, December 20, 1926, No. 12. Correspondence Letter-Book. 1923–1930, No. 3. 26. Correspondence 1926, S. 115, Salter Papers, LNA; Salter to Smith, February 15, 1927, No. 12. General Correspondence. Sir Arthur Salter's Correspondence, 1927, S. 116, Salter Papers, LNA.

the League banner. Moreover, he had excellent contacts in the banking world, although his Morgan card did not pay off concerning the American tranche. Besides, Smith was a Democrat believing in the League of Nations and he very much wanted the scheme to succeed. In this success he had a substantial part, because his manner, style, and convincing power made it possible that he and the Hungarian government managed to cooperate smoothly throughout the reconstruction period. Taking into account the load of problems Zimmerman caused and faced in Vienna, it is understandable why the League was thankful that in Hungary it was not subject to the same score of trouble.

Smith, for his part, based upon his experiences, became absolutely convinced that the League of Nations was not a mere paper dragon, but had the potential to become a really strong and well-organized body with an immense effect on the world. His international outlook, strongly meshed with his New England traditions, made him a firm believer of the League. The fame he achieved in Hungary made him an even more household name in the United States, not in the closed circles of law and finance alone, but nationwide. Already during his stay in Hungary, mainly on Lamont's prodding, he accepted the position of President General Exeter Alumni Association from July 1926. Probably Lamont's experience in the same position about "duties only nominal" and "even speechmaking unnecessary" must have been a winning point for Smith.[921] As a sign of how well-known his name had become, it is enough to mention that he was a regular feature in intercollegiate events.[922] Smith was also elected to be successor of Dr. Henry Pickering Walcott as a member of the Harvard Corporation.[923] His now clearly prominent status gave him the chance to try to make waves for his political belief in his own country.

The most spectacular moment of showing his faith in the League of Nations came at the dinner of the Phi Beta Kappa Society of Harvard University in the summer of 1927. To counter any possible future charges of his un-Americanism, he started off with the assertion, "I am neither a pacifist nor an internationalist."[924] In this speech, Smith gave a description of the international situation as he saw it and shared his view with the high-standing audience. He thought if things did not change, another war would be in store, and the only remedy against such a course would be public opinion. "There must be an international public opinion which will insist on higher standards of international morality in international dealings."[925] This is where the League came in the picture as

921 Lamont to Smith, March 5, 1926, T. II. Incoming and outgoing telegrams, Sep 1924–June 1926, C. 120, Financial Reconstruction of Hungary, LNA.
922 *The New York Times*, May 23, 1926, May 1, 8, 15, 22, June 5, 1927.
923 *The New York Times*, May 18, 1927.
924 Smith, *The Preservation of the Peace*, 1.
925 Ibid., 5.

the only international body significant and powerful enough to form such an opinion. "I am a strong believer in what the League of Nations is trying to do, provided it is done properly, that they confine themselves to public discussion of questions and do not undertake to coerce people."[926] After gently criticizing the conduct of foreign affairs in the United States and in general, Smith gave a precise description of the present situation in America and a farsighted picture of the not-so-distant future:

> All I hope to accomplish is to induce some of you to think on this question. It cannot be settled except by public opinion. It is not politically possible for the United States to do anything to-day in regard to entering into the League of Nations. Rightly or wrongly one of the great political parties succeeded in convincing the average man [...] that there is a sort of conspiracy on the part of old wicked Europe to get the United States involved in matters which are none of its affair. As long as that opinion continues it is politically impossible to do anything. [...] There must be a radical change in the method in which international affairs are conducted. If there is not, we shall all be back where we were in 1914, and the last state of this world will be worse than the first.[927]

Here was then a man, who had achieved quite some fame through diligent work both home and abroad, and who felt the time had come to presage a grim future and warn those who were willing to listen to try to make changes. He must not have had any illusions as to what such a speech could achieve, but his conscience would have plagued him had he not done what he could.

It is little wonder that the League of Nations felt positive about Smith. After fulfilling the job faithfully in Hungary, he kept advocating the League as the possible key to the future and preserving the peace. The League of Nations did still not give up on luring the United States into its ranks, and was of the opinion that the more Americans served in the organization, the better future chances there would be to achieve such a goal. This aim suffered a setback when the United States government decided not to continue the unofficial representative on the Reparation Commission, which took effect from 1927.[928] In light of such events and hopes, it was natural that when there was an unfulfilled seat on the Financial Committee, the wheels were set in motion to secure an American citizen. Basically, it was an unsaid conclusion that the League wanted to enjoy Smith's services again, now as a member of that Committee.

926 Ibid., 11.
927 Ibid., 14.
928 For the correspondence on this subject, see FRUS: 1926, 1:120–25.

Once again, the principal man overseas was Benjamin Strong. First and foremost, he was sought out to give advice on a possible candidate, and Salter wrote frankly what the League expected. "It is essential that the member should be someone enjoying the confidence both of the Federal Reserve and the principal private banks, and that we should have and continue to have the necessary backing from both."[929] The response arrived the very next day that Strong duly suggested Smith, and Owen Young agreed with that proposal.[930] Strong had very positive opinions about Smith. "I have the utmost confidence in his judgment and good sense and in his general knowledge," he said.[931] On the European continent the usual suspects all welcomed the idea of Smith joining them.[932] Montagu Norman was also joyful. As he wrote to Niemeyer, "I think J. S. would be a wonderfully good member, that you will be lucky if you can get him, and that Strong is a perfect conjuror."[933] Smith was willing to accept the honor, but there was some difficulty to straighten out. This was to do with another pleasant engagement.

Smith's old friendship with Lamont meant another opportunity to get close to the thick of things, which he did not want to miss. In September, the two men traveled to Japan to prepare the ground for new American loans through J. P. Morgan & Co. Smith accompanied Lamont as his legal advisor. Since the American-Japanese relations were satisfactory at the time, Secretary of State Kellogg assured Lamont that the government would support their work, only to withdraw such support in the end.[934] This was the reason why Smith had some reservation about the League appointment in September when he would not be on hand. In addition, Strong wanted a very quiet nomination, because he feared that there would be outcries due to Smith's connections to the Federal Reserve Bank in New York.[935]

Smith was appointed as additional member to the Financial Committee as of September 1, 1927. The official reasoning of the League was that "the work of the Committee has arrived at a stage at which the presence of an American member would be of the greatest value, and the Committee has reason to believe that Mr. Smith's appointment would be very acceptable to those concerned in America, and that he would be free to accept, if invited."[936] Thus Smith became a member of a small body that he had been officially connected to while he was in Hungary in 1924–26. The announcement was discreet just as Strong

929 Salter to Young, July 20, 1927, OV9/257, BoE.
930 Young to Salter, July 21, 1927, Ibid.
931 Strong to Norman, September, 23, 1927, G35/7, BoE.
932 Niemeyer to Salter, July 29, 1927, OV9/257, BoE.
933 Norman to Niemeyer, August 19, 1927, Ibid.
934 E. Lamont, *The Ambassador from Wall Street*, 231. In more detail about the trip, see Ibid., 231–37, and *The New York Times*, October 4, 9, 1927.
935 Strong to Norman, August 31, 1927, G35/7, BoE.
936 LNJ, 8th Year, No. 10, October 1927, 1101.

had hoped. The expectation was quite high, but Norman was confident that Smith's presence would "mark a very important stage in the development of the Financial Committee and its work."[937] In mid-November, Smith was one of the chief speakers at the annual dinner meeting of the Academy of Political Sciences at the Hotel Astor. Smith here emphasized anew that the League of Nations was the most effective agency to solve international problems and create peace.[938] With being an official member of the organization, the assertion might have seemed a little bit strange, but Smith did not worry on that account because he had earlier already said the same thing. If anything, he felt more assured about his belief. The very day after the prestigious dinner, he sailed to Europe to start his tenure in the Financial Committee, and shortly after arriving in Geneva he took part in the deliberations of the Committee for the first time.

Smith's work in the Financial Committee was not characterized by any large impact in the life of that body. In fact, Salter thought if an American was brought into the League, perhaps American banking would be more drawn into possible League loans.[939] This wish was not fulfilled. It soon was clear that his post would not mean a deluge of further American loans. If anything, Smith tried to counter British efforts to further strengthen the gold-exchange standard.[940] As had been the case earlier, Smith was doing his work out of the limelight. When his expertise and advice was sought, he was more than ready to provide it. His experience gave him the basis to draw up a plan concerning the control of an international loan that was issued on behalf of a country attacked or threatened with war. Perhaps the biggest news was when he, together with C. E. ter Meulen and Marcus Wallenberg, was appointed to the advisory committee on the investment of the League's $1,000,000 library fund, which had been given by the Rockefeller Foundation.[941] The stay in Europe did Smith good beyond doubt. When he visited the Tylers in France and spent a little time with his former deputy in Hungary, he made the following impression on Tyler's wife:

> We have had Jeremiah Smith to stay here with us. He was more delightful than I could have believed he could be. Everything pleased and interested him. He was quite boyish and happy, and said his few days here had done him a world of good. There is a man whose European experiences have broadened and deepened, and who has become more conscious of his own great power and resources, by contact with the accumulated forces of centuries. He is so sensitive and so responsive, under his New England granite![942]

937 Norman to Strong, September 14, 1927, G35/7, BoE.
938 *The New York Times*, November 18, 1927.
939 Orde, *British Policy and European Reconstruction*, 313–14.
940 Ibid., 314.
941 *The New York Times*, January 26, 1930.
942 Elisina Tyler to Mildred Bliss, September 16, 1928, Box 2, Tyler Papers.

The only period when he was in the limelight to some degree was in the first half of 1929. His name appeared first on account of the Kellogg-Briand Pact, or officially, the Treaty for the Renunciation of War.[943] When the treaty was under the ratification debate in the upper house of Congress, Smith's letter to Massachusetts Senator Walsh was read out in the Senate as a positive argument for the ratification. In this letter he reiterated his belief about the importance of some kind of public opinion. He considered the treaty that was awaiting confirmation from the Senate was "one more step in building up an international public opinion of the right sort," and "a very important instrument in maintaining the peace."[944] The treaty was ratified by the United States on January 15, 1929, and signed by the president two days later.[945] Not much later Smith was chosen to be a member of the American delegation that was to serve on the international committee for revision of German reparations. He was in an elite group of compatriots in early 1929, such as Owen D. Young, after whom the comprehensive plan was named, J. P. Morgan, and Thomas Lamont.[946] In preparing the Young Plan, Smith served in an advisory post to the "big guns," with his usual modesty and useful expertise on Central European relations. Young, after returning from four months of negotiations in Europe concerning the plan for Germany, said that Smith and other assistant experts rendered "most helpful service."[947] The plan was hailed at the time as the remedy for the wrecked situation, so Smith was entitled to feel proud having taken part in the momentous undertaking.

Smith's health, however, forced him once again to take a rest. This time, with the somewhat advanced age of over 60, he made the decision to retire from the Financial Committee. He was reluctant to take this step, but in early 1931 he finally resigned. Arthur Slater's resignation as head of the Economic and Financial Section might have had something to do with his decision. In any case, the trend he had started continued and the Financial Committee invited another American, Norman Davies, to take his place.[948] This was the end of Smith's international career spanning 15 years and three continents.

943 The text of the Treaty and the list of the original fifteen signatories that signed it on August 27, 1928, can be read in FRUS: 1928, 1:153–56.
944 Congressional Record, 70th Congress, 2nd Session, 1568, January 11, 1929.
945 Congressional Record, 70th Congress, 2nd Session, 1731, January 15, 1929, and 1774, January 17, 1929.
946 *The New York Times*, February 2, 1929.
947 *The New York Times*, June 15, 1929.
948 *The New York Times*, July 23, 1931.

9.3. The Last Years

While a member of the Financial Committee, just like in the case of his Hungarian post, Smith often traveled home to the United States. Much as he was fascinated with the League of Nations and was very proud of having been an active member of it for years in different capacities, he was always yearning to spend the most time possible back at home. He needed good rest, because his health was never satisfactory for long cycles. When he was home, he usually spent his time with his sister, Elizabeth, or went fishing with his good friend Lamont, or visited his law firm.[949]

However, he was still active in other capacities. He was first sought out for legal help in the Sacco and Vanzetti case. This happened before he was selected as a member of the Financial Committee. Even before Governor Fuller asked Abbott Lawrence Lowell, President of Harvard University, to preside over the panel to decide over the case, Smith was asked to serve in that capacity. According to Charles E. Wyzanski, who was Senior District Judge of the U. S. District Court in Boston for 45 years, and was Harvard Law School professor and later Supreme Court Judge Felix Frankfurter's student, "Jerry conducted his doctor who told him that he must not serve because at any moment he might die [...] he felt so badly at declining [...] that he privately undertook to read the entire record, and concluded that both Nicola Sacco and Bartolomeo Vanzetti were guilty and had not been denied a constitutionally adequate trial."[950] Therefore, it can be said that Smith applied his legal knowledge in a positive way, considering the fact that neither the guilt nor the innocence of the two men has ever been conclusively proven. Naturally, he might have been reluctant to serve in a case, even in an advisory capacity, which would have required much more energy that his health could have allowed. In less stressful options, he opted for service.

Aside from his long held trusteeship at Exeter, his home school, he filled other high posts. In the summer of 1928, for example, the Chairman of the American Telephone and Telegraph Company resigned. The post was discontinued, but a new director was needed to carry on the work of the ex-president. The board elected Smith to fill that post in August.[951] Two years later, he was elected to the Board of Trustees of the Carnegie Endowment for International Peace. Also, he often appeared at distinguished events. After returning to the United States for good, he was a guest at various prestigious dinners. In addition to the principal speaker Lamont, Smith also spoke at the fiftieth annual dinner of the Academy

949 E. Lamont, *The Ambassador from Wall Street*, 248.
950 Wyzanski to Russel, March 31, 1986, Scrapbook and miscellaneous papers relating to the Sacco-Vanzetti case and trial, 1962–1988, Francis Russell Papers, Boston Athenaeum, Boston.
951 *The New York Times*, August 16, 1928.

of Political Sciences at the Hotel Astor.[952] He remained faithful to the League of Nations and grabbed every opportunity to promote the possible cooperation between the organization and the United States. Smith was also among those 100 signatories that signed an open letter to President Hoover urging him to submit the protocols of the World Court to the Senate and calling for a prompt ratification. Other famous persons were John J. Pershing, Averell Harriman, Henry Morgenthau, Frances Perkins, Norman H. Davies, Roland Boyden, Thomas Lamont, Frank Polk, Paul Warburg, and Walter Lippmann.[953]

The posts and rare activities did not demand a very large amount of time and energy, but unfortunately for Smith, these were the two things he had little of. His waning vigor was becoming a constant obstacle for him to act in any capacity. After resigning from the Financial Committee, he became nearly blind and doctors just could not find out the reason.[954] Soon after, his sight got better, but only for short spells. Nonetheless, he carried on for some time with his posts in the United States, but before long he had to admit that even these were too much for him. Due to ill health, first he resigned from his post as director at AT&T in February 1932.[955] Not even with reduced work was he able to compete and after a happy moment at the polls in November 1932, when Franklin Delano Roosevelt was elected president, Smith resigned from the Harvard Corporation after five years of service.[956] The remaining time of his life was free of work or excitement, but that was a further problem. He had been a diligent man all his life devoted to his ideals, and, since not a man of many words, he had always been quick to step in and deliver. These opportunities had disappeared from his life by the early 1930s. Although there was a cause to fight for, he had no physical resources left to take part in any such fight. He was at peace with the world, and the more international approach emanating from the Roosevelt White House filled him with hope. In his last years, he was compelled to remain at home on account of "the advance of a mysterious malady" and he had to spend most of his time in bed.[957] The fast waning light turned to darkness sooner than it should have and on March 12, 1935, Jeremiah Smith, Jr. passed away.

His death did not create any waves in the United States. The funeral was attended only by the family, which meant his sister and a few distant relatives.[958] Smith never married and neither did his sister. An ancient line of New England Yankee family came to an end. Just as during his life he shunned publicity, he

952 *The New York Times*, November 15, 1930.
953 *The New York Times*, November 24, 1930.
954 Tyler to Mildred Bliss, May 1, 1931, Box 3, Tyler Papers.
955 *The New York Times*, February 18, 1932.
956 *The New York Times*, November 22, 1932.
957 Beale, "*Jeremiah Smith, Jr.,*" 549.
958 *The New York Times*, March 13, 1935.

would have been content to know that the news of his death was not a major heading in any newspapers. Naturally, papers reported his death in a few lines, but now the world was living the dangerous years of the mid-1930s and the 1920s already seemed a distant dream. The obituary of *The New York Times* falsely wrote that Smith had been offered the post of Secretary of Treasury; no documents support such a claim.[959]

In understandable contrast, most of the Hungarian newspapers commemorated Smith's death and recalled his work in Hungary. One editorial had the title, "A Good Friend of Ours Is Dead," and emphasized Smith's role in securing the league loan.[960] Another paper claimed that the American had "wanted to help and help he did as far as his authority allowed," and "the name of Jeremiah Smith had become indelibly the part of our nation's history."[961] *Pesti Napló* recalled the story on how he had refused to accept his salary and said that Smith's name "should be put on the pedestal of the anonym Hungarian taxpayer."[962] *Magyarország* reported that both Bud and Bethlen praised Smith and, allegedly, a movement was started by OMKE (Hungarian National Trade Association) to have a street named after Smith and a monument erected in his honor.[963] This news echoed Béla Alapi's earlier assertion that the next statue of an American would be that of Smith's. In the end, the ambition to keep his memory alive did not bear fruit. The next statue in Budapest of an American was erected the following year, but it was not that of Smith's but General Harry Hill Bandholtz's, whose brave confrontation with the Romanian soldiers in 1919 led to saving the treasures of the National Museum. No matter how much Jeremiah Smith, Jr. deserves a prominent place in the twentieth century history of Hungary, by the end of the Second World War his name was largely forgotten and, for political reasons, left untouched. Not much difference took place in this after the change of the political system in Hungary, and in the new millennium, hardly anybody in Hungary knows who Jeremiah Smith, Jr. was.

959 *The New York Times*, March 13, 1935. Bob Clark, e-mail message to author, November 8 and December 3, 2008.
960 *Budapesti Hírlap*, March 14, 1935, LV/61.
961 *Pesti Hírlap*, March 14, 1935, LVII/61.
962 *Pesti Napló*, March 14, 1935, 86/61.
963 *Magyarország*, March 17, 1935, XLII/63.

Chapter 10

The Financial Reconstructions in Europe

10.1. Two Schemes, One Aim: The Comparison of the Austrian and Hungarian Reconstructions

The Austrian and Hungarian financial reconstructions were the first of a score of similar plans drawn up by the League of Nations and carried out under its watchful eyes. These first two attempts, as we have seen, were successful in the short run. These triumphs had several important consequences. First, the League's prestige grew immensely in Central Europe and elsewhere. Secondly, the success paved the way for further initiatives in this field, and other countries applied for the same remedy that had worked in the case of Austria and Hungary. Thirdly, the know-how of technical details that had been worked out and put into practice in Central Europe provided the blueprint for the following attempts at restoring fiscal stability in other Eastern and Southern European countries. Fourthly, and in many ways the most important, the initial success achieved in these two countries, helped enormously the German reconstruction attempt that came to be known as the Dawes Plan in late 1924. Although the first two programs shared much in common, there were many smaller or sometimes more significant discrepancies.

A comparison of these first two reconstructions programs is warranted. Since both schemes were claimed to have achieved the same goal, namely to create a stable currency, to stop the budget deficit, and to have an independent national bank, they were almost identical. At first glance indeed both programs showed the same features, but there were several differences, most of them not major, but significant enough to call attention to them. It is logical to first list what was conformable between the two rehabilitation efforts.[964]

The most important feature of both cases was that it was undertaken by the League of Nations. This fact alone defined certain aspects. Its role was crucial in creating the international collaboration necessary for the reconstruction efforts to occur. Neither Austria nor Hungary was in a situation to seriously initiate such an effort—without a benevolent supporter these countries had no real hope to bring their financial chaos to a halt. Both tried to achieve it through private channels first, but both failed. In the political landscape of

964 Since most of the data in this section is from earlier chapters of the dissertation, only those sources will be given that contain new information.

Europe in the early 1920s, an ex-enemy country had no real expectation of being treated in a friendly or fair manner by its neighbors or the big powers of the continent. The one exception, the United States, showed no inclination to take responsibility for Europe. So, without the League of Nations no such plan could have been carried out. Therefore, it was a necessity that in both cases the League of Nations draw up the plan, thus giving credence to both reconstruction schemes.

Some further elements that were basically identical sprang from the League's fathering of the plans. The Protocols that were signed by the involved countries in both cases defined the major characteristics of the schemes: to set up a new central bank that was independent of the government; to stabilize the currency; to offer certain revenues as pledge for an international long-term loan; with the help of that loan to begin to carry out certain reforms and to achieve a balanced budget that would last; and to have a Commissioner-General take up his post in the given country to supervise and control the reforms being carried out and to function as a link between the host country and the League of Nations. In conformity with the Protocols, the two reconstruction plans could not be very different. All the points mentioned were closely followed and this defined the major similarity between the two programs. Even the countries that were willing to issue the long-term loan were almost the same in the two cases. Moreover, it was Montagu Norman's lead that ensured that the money conceived as essential was available. In addition, in both instances, the United States took a smaller-than-hoped part of the whole, signifying that American capital was interested in European financial issues only to a certain degree, Germany excluded. Naturally, the most important similarity was the triumphant accomplishment of both the Austrian and Hungarian reconstruction programs.

Although it is true that the aforementioned similarities outweigh the differences of both schemes, still, it is worth shedding light on some features that were different in these cases and try to answer why they were possible or necessary. A difference in the beginning was that Austria first applied to the Allied Powers and only after finding refusal there did it knock on the door of the League of Nations. The answer for that is that in 1921 and 1922 the League had not been able to assume the necessary prestige and leadership it wished to play. In many ways, it was the Austrian financial reconstruction that earned the organization the needed reputation, and in the case of Hungary it was almost evident that the help of the League was sought after attempts to secure private loans had failed. The first real significant difference was the question of reparations. This issue was the most sensitive and responsible for many bitter arguments among winners and losers, but also among the victorious countries. The new smaller countries of Central and Eastern Europe had Hungary and Austria as their main targets in this aspect. Finally, in the case of Austria, the reparation payment was put off for twenty years.[965] It meant that during the whole term of the loan, Austria was freed from a heavy financial obligation. The reason for this was political. Austria was in really dire straits, so much so, that, with Great Britain in the lead, the contemporary European community accepted that if Austria was to be saved, some sign of magnanimity was essential. Great Britain did not want to see Austria collapse because it feared such a scenario might spread to the whole region, which ran against British aims in Central Europe. With their prestige and influence in and out of the League of Nations, the British in the end successfully exempted Austria from reparations during the service of the loan.

As for Hungary, the picture was different in two ways. First, Hungary's overall situation in 1923 looked much better than that of Austria in the previous years. Being an agricultural country, Hungary was at least able to feed itself, so the rampant famine experienced in Vienna was not a real threat. On the other hand, one of their main political aims of the Little Entente was to squeeze out of Hungary as large reparations as possible. Since the peace treaty did not specify the amount to be paid, Hungary's hostile neighbors were not content to sit and watch idly as Hungary was getting international money without paying reparations to Czechoslovakia, Romania, Yugoslavia, or Italy. It took many rounds of bitter and fierce negotiations and often British blackmailing to achieve a compromise. Hungary did get the international loan but it had to pay reparations. The amount was an average of 10 million gold crowns ($2 million) a year for twenty years, which meant 1.25 gold crowns ($0.25) burden per annum per capita of the population, with the alleviation that payments had to start in earnest only from 1927, when the reconstruction program had supposedly ended, and the yearly sum showed a progressive scale starting with smaller amounts climbing toward bigger ones.[966] The idea was that with the help of the reconstruction program, Hungary would be in a position to be able to pay.

Another important difference was the amount of money the international loans provided for the two countries. This question also touched upon the assumption that Austria was in next to impossible conditions whereas Hungary was able to provide food for its own population. In line with this thought, Austria was received the net amount of 613 million gold crowns, roughly the equivalent of $125 million. True, out of this money, Austria had to pay back earlier financial commitment to Great Britain, France, Czechoslovakia, and Italy to the extent of 130 million gold crowns, which sum represented 25% of the loan.[967] Britain had given so much money prior to the League of Nations loan that it was essential

965 In the end, there was no reparations paid by Austria and after World War II the situation was the same, although for somewhat different reasons.
966 Royall Tyler, "The Eastern Reparations Settlement," *Foreign Affairs* 9 (October 1930): 111; League of Nations, *The Financial Reconstruction of Hungary*, 201–02.
967 League of Nations, *Financial Reconstruction of Austria*, 143–46.

to be reimbursed to some degree, while in the case of Czechoslovakia, it was a political deal that it should receive some of its money back in exchange for the Loan Protocols. It was decided that Hungary was to be given a much smaller amount despite the Hungarian government's efforts for a similar sum. In the end, Hungary received a net 253 million gold crowns, approximately $50 million, which was 40% of what Austria had been given. Although the terms of issue were not favorable for either country, Hungary came off better. While the Austrian rate of issue was 83%, the Hungarian was 88.5%; the rate of interest was 6.3% in Austria's case and 7.5% for Hungary, the figures representing the average. With hindsight, it can be easily concluded that the men behind the plan had sized up the conditions and possibilities well and both countries got the adequate amount. A further difference was how the two countries were allowed to redeem the loan. A major alteration was that in the case of Hungary any amount of money saved in terms of principal and interest, typically through purchase in the market, could be used for amortization, whereas in Austria's case it was only the principal that counted. The idea was that with this method the redemption of the loan was going to be quicker, a point on which the bankers insisted.[968]

Another reason why Austria was provided with a larger sum was the guarantee certain powers undertook on its behalf. The state of Austria was so devastated and the political circumstances showed a possibility of serious turmoil that the possibility of raising a loan was only possible with certain guarantees. In the end, the principal countries took responsibility for a long-term loan, which was guaranteed as follows: Great Britain, France, and Czechoslovakia 24.5% each, Italy 20.5%, Belgium and Sweden 2% each, Denmark and the Netherlands 1% each. In the case of Hungary, on account of the better financial conditions, and the successful execution of the Austrian long-term loan, the League of Nations was of the opinion that no state guarantees would be necessary, especially for a much smaller amount. The negotiations for the Hungarian loan showed that this was a somewhat optimistic view and the issue of the loan was far from easy. It cannot be, however, said that with state guarantees it would have been any easier.

Also, in many ways as a consequence of the previously listed differences, the Protocols showed several minor discrepancies. Although in their main lines they were very similar, the differences shed light on the divergent nature of the two reconstructions. In both cases, the first one was the so-called Political Protocol. These were almost identical, but Austria had to promise not to alienate its independence (a further insurance against the *Anschluss*). Hungary, on the other hand, had to pledge that it would carry out the obligations stipulated in the Treaty of Trianon, especially the military clauses. The Austrian case was in

968 Leese to Smith, June 21, 1924, OV33/76, BoE.

deference to Czechoslovakia and Italy, while the requirement for Hungary was obviously spelled out according to the wish of the successor states. As far as the Committee of Control was concerned, there were variations. In the case of Austria, the duties and powers of this body were detailed in a separate Protocol, whereas in the Hungarian Protocols this part was only an article of Protocol No. 2.[969] Naturally, in the first such undertaking, the emphasis was very large on control, and that is the reason why the League found it necessary to have it drawn up in a separate Protocol. By the time the Hungarian Protocols had to be completed, it was apparent that the control the Commissioner-General could exert was enough for the aims, and in the case of Hungary this feature was not emphasized as strongly. In the Hungarian Protocols, some of the powers of the Committee were also given over to the Commission-General. Moreover, in the Austrian Protocols no mention was made about Trustees and only in late 1925 did the Council set up a system of trustees, similarly to the case in Hungary, to control the assigned revenues.[970] Aside from these points, the two sets of Protocols and the means of control they set out were essentially identical, which was a further proof that the League of Nations wished to set up a workable system for financial reconstructions, because it knew that it had to deal with other countries on the continent.

In the field of control, the embodiment of extra control was the Bank Adviser in both cases. It was seen as essential that the new central banks, both independent of the governments, should be watched over exactly to help them retain that status and to forestall murky deals that would have endangered their independence in any way. The major difference, naturally, was at the end of both reconstructions. In the case of Austria, the League of Nations made the requirement that the Adviser should remain in office for three more years after Zimmerman's office was terminated. In Hungary no such extra safety regulation was needed. Article 127 of the Statutes of the Hungarian National Bank read as follows, "The functions of the Adviser shall terminate at the same date as those of the Commissioner-General of the League of Nations [...] A Bank Adviser will be re-appointed either when the control by a Commissioner-General is re-established (Article VII of Protocol II) or when Treaty charge transfers are discontinued for two years or more (Article XIII, para. 3)."[971] Arthur Siepmann's term as Adviser to the National Bank ended on the same day as that of Jeremiah Smith, Jr., June 30, 1926, and they left Budapest together.

---

969 League of Nations, *Financial Reconstruction of Austria*, 139–42.
970 Note to the members of the Financial Committee, May 9, 1926, Financial Reconstruction of Hungary, Memorandum on the technical and legal conditions for the eventual suspension of the control of the Commissioner-General in Hungary. Doc. No. 51442, Registry Files, R. 301, LNA.
971 Ibid.

An interesting divergence was the currency on which the Austrian and Hungarian crowns were stabilized. In the case of Austria, it was the US dollar that the Austrian crown was based on, a feature that did not meet Norman's expectations and support. In all likelihood, as the Austrian reconstruction was a first step and no one was sure about the rest, Norman did not push for a sterling-based Austrian currency, partially in deference to his American counterpart, Benjamin Strong. However, when the Hungarian loan was managed and about two-thirds of it was coming from London, Norman was adamant that the Hungarian currency should be pegged to the British pound sterling.[972] For Norman it was not only a question of prestige; this policy fell in line with his idea of European reconstruction, where London would be the leading player and the center of things.[973]

In both countries, a lot of attention was given to the conditions and numbers of state officials. This was a point on which reforms were absolutely necessary. In both countries a swollen staff of state officials worked, which prevented a well-oiled state machinery. Moreover, their salary ate up much of the expenditure of the budget. In Hungary, for example, Smith and others kept complaining that the salary of state officials was 60% of the yearly budget. Austria was to dismiss 100,000 officials during the reconstruction period out of 250,000. The League considered even this number inefficient, but social disturbance and outrage were two factors that they wanted to avoid. As was mentioned earlier, Austria never fully lived up to this expectation. In Hungary's case, the number of officials was significantly smaller, but it was proportionally still too large. A reason for this was that many state officials arrived from the ex-territories and the Bethlen government thought it only fair to let them retain their jobs. This gesture may have been politically right and from a human point of view admirable, but it put extra strain on a weak Hungarian economy, currency, and budget. As the Bank Adviser accurately prophesized it in the beginning of the reconstruction period, "the Beamtenfrage will be with us until the end of time."[974] Hungary played with the ratio of multiplier and, at the end of the day, the 15,000 state officials that Hungary was required to dismiss during the two and a half years of reconstruction was a much easier target to reach than in Austria. Despite the fact that the question was a sensitive one, since these officials earned very little money and they faced prolonged unemployed status once on the street, Hungary was actually able to top this number somewhat.[975]

972 Péteri, *Global Monetary Regime*, 92.

973 Lojkó, *Meddling in Middle Europe*, 11–12.

974 Siepmann to Strakosch, July 27, 1924, 1/1924. May–June, K 304, Siepmann Papers, HNA.

975 2/VIII/8, K 288, Papers of the Financial Delegation to Geneva, HNA.

The League put the emphasis on limiting expenditure in the case of Austria. This was thought to be the main cause of the financial woes, and the idea was that if Austrians learned how to economize, long-lasting results in the financial and economic domain might be achieved. In the case of Hungary, the League emphasized taxation. The League thought in Hungary there was "an inertia in trying to raise money and an unwillingness on the part of the people to contribute to the expenses of government."[976] Whereas Viennese in particular were willing to accept high taxation, the population in Hungary, especially in the country, was not. The measure of the taxes of the Hungarian population was a constant question during the time of reconstruction. The League estimate proved wrong in the case of Austria in the sense that the country never mastered saving on state level and the expenditure kept rising. Balanced budget was achieved through increased taxation rather than economies.

Last, but not least, it must be noted how the two countries fared after the reconstruction programs were concluded. In many ways, the real test of the League of Nations reconstruction programs came after they were concluded. As long as a League controller was in place, it was relatively easy to ensure that both countries would follow the guidance coming from Geneva. The real question was how they were going to act once their financial freedom was achieved again. Would they adhere to the introduced reforms and strict fiscal policies, or would they fritter away what they had gained in the previous period?

One of the initial intentions of the League of Nations programs, namely that once the financial conditions were put right, the foreign capital would start flowing in and the economy would become thriving, partially came true. In both countries, now declared financially stable, foreign investors saw a good market for their money. For a few years to come, both Austria and Hungary became relatively safe investments, and they became part of the loan boom so typical of the years between 1924 and1928. Both countries had some surplus remaining from the international loans. Austria, with the agreement with foreign creditors, spent most of the money on improving the railways and the telegraph system.[977] Hungary spent its remaining loan money on projects not strictly connected to reconstruction. Unfortunately, this trend was a characteristic of all loans coming to Hungary. Only 20% of the long-term loans in the 1920s were used for productive investments; 25% of it was used to expand the state bureaucracy, luxury building constructions, all in all, for consumption goals.[978] Still, the financial year ending on June 30, 1927, produced a large surplus, savings and

976 Alzada Comstock, "The Technique of Reconstruction as Applied to Hungary," *Political Science Quarterly* 40 (June 1925): 209.
977 Berger, "Rebuilding Economies after External Shocks," 70.
978 Berend and Szuhay, *A tőkés gazdaság*, 220.

the gold stock of the National Bank rose further, while the State debt to the Bank, the number of insolvencies and the unemployed declined significantly. As a real sign of short-time success, average real wages had doubled since the reconstruction program started in 1924.[979]

At this stage overborrowing seemed a remote possibility, although the first signs were there. Still, if someone saw it, in the end no mention was made of it, because everybody was interested in the successful conclusion of the work. But this characteristic proved very grave for both countries in the end. Short and long-term loans arrived in such big numbers that after a while the debt grew so large that newer loans were needed to pay off the old ones. On behalf of Hungary, for example, in the three years following the reconstruction 38 long-term loans were issued.[980] It is little wonder that the country was heavily indebted by the end of the decade. Still, in the second half of the twenties, both countries could boast of a balanced budget and a gold-based currency. By 1930, however, a sudden change had occurred. Both had a state budget with serious deficits and the central banks had lost most of their foreign currency reserves.[981] The main problem again was the inappropriate usage of loan moneys. As the British Royal Institute correctly summed up in the early 1930s, "Foreign loans that were used for the reconstruction of Europe were needed, but in the end, the sum was bigger, than the debtors could have hoped to be able to pay back."[982] One of the reasons leading to this sorry state of affairs was that on the European continent "a significant portion of the invested loans was mainly used for unproductive goals, which raised the level of standard of living in the given country, but did not create such improvement in the efficiency of these countries' exports that they could be able to fulfill their debt obligations."[983] With such mindset and short-term planning, it is no wonder that the League reforms were not able to create long-term prosperity.

The other fatal blow to both countries was the Great Depression out of which neither country really found a way. This crisis, which maimed economies and financial institutions all over the world, left neither county intact. Still, until the Credit-Anstalt crisis in Austria in 1931, in which the biggest bank of the region collapsed, both countries faithfully kept paying their loan annuities. Both countries asked for help from the League of Nations again, but despite some

979 Eugene Havas, Hungary's Finance and Trade, 1927 (London: General Press, 1928), 7, 25–27, 35–36.
980 Ibid., 218.
981 Ágnes Pogány, Párhuzamos történetek [Parallel Stories]. In. *Ötven éves a Budapesti Közgazdaságtudományi Egyetem* [Budapest University of Economic Sciences Is 50 Years Old]. vol. 2 (Budapest, 1998): 1214–28.
982 Quoted in Berend and Szuhay, *A tőkés gazdaság*, 221.
983 Ibid.

short-term credits and insignificant help, the problem could not be solved. All through the next few years, both Austria and Hungary were in shaky but manageable conditions. Default on foreign bonds became the norm rather than the exception. Though Hungary always paid its dues after the League of Nations loan, when it came to other loans, and American ones were a major part of them, the situation proved different. The Hungarian government put the United States Government Relief Loan second on its priority list, yet it did not undertake to meet the roughly $7,000,000 per annum annual service charge on other dollar bond issues.[984] Strange as it may seem, the only real way to reach some prosperity for these countries again was the coming of World War II, for which, though, both had to pay a dear price.

10.2. Other Schemes in Europe by the League

After the Austrian reconstruction had been launched and the first signs of success were manifest, the League of Nations wanted to spread its services in this field to further countries in great need of outside help to reach financial stabilization. It is worth taking a quick view of the other rehabilitation efforts in a chronological order. In two cases, namely in Greece and Bulgaria, the League stepped in twice years apart.

The situation in Greece was different than in Central Europe. The country was experiencing a huge wave of refugees. These were of Greek nationalities fleeing from Turkey and their number reached more than a million, which represented about 25% of the whole population. For some time, the American Red Cross had carried out relief work in Greece. Until June 30, 1923, it had spent $3 million, but wanted to get out because the problem seemed to be a permanent one requiring huge sums of money.[985] Greece turned to the League of Nations for help. Parallel, Norman gave £1 million advance to the Bank of Greece with the condition that the chair of the pending committee would be an American.[986] Indeed, the Refugee Settlement Commission was established and Henry Morgenthau of the United States became its Chairman, who was later succeeded by another American, Charles P. Howland.[987] The Protocols were signed in September 1923,

984 Allen W. Dulles, "The Protection of American Foreign Bondholders," *Foreign Affairs* 10 (April, 1932): 481.
985 Correspondence between Payne (Chairman of the American Red Cross) and Phillips (Under Secretary of State), February 19, February 28, and March 1, FRUS: 1923, 2:318–22.
986 The Chargé in France (Whitehouse) to the Secretary of State, August 25, 1923, Ibid., 371–72.
987 Marx Winkler, *The Investor and the League Loans* (New York: Foreign Policy Association, Volume 4, June 1928, Supplement No.2), 20.

and in November 1924, a loan of $60 million was issued, of which $11 million was offered in New York, £7,500,000 ($33 million) in London, and £2,500,000 ($11 million) in Athens.[988] The rate of interest was 7% and the issue price was 88.[989] Greece had to make every effort to balance its budget, and the Council had the right to supervise the Refugee Settlement Commission's work and to give decisions pertaining to that work.[990] The majority of the refugees were successfully settled by the end of the work.

The pledge on Greece's side to carry out a fiscal policy that would ensure a balanced budget remained merely rhetorical. Not surprisingly, soon enough Greece asked for the League's help again in securing another loan. In a new Protocol signed, Greece undertook to stabilize its currency, set up a new Bank of Issue, maintain a balanced budget, and pay off arrears of debt. Of the £9 million ($39.6 million), one third was spent to increase the liquid assets of the Bank, one third to pay off arrears of debt, and one third to continue the refugee settlement work. The second Greek loan was issued early in 1928. The amount was $36 million, of which $17 million was offered in the United States and £4,070,960 ($19.8 million) in London. The rate of interest was 6% and the price of issue was 91. The United States took so large a part, because according to an agreement with Greece, out of this loan Greece would be enabled to pay back war indebtedness to the US. There was no guarantee for the loan by other governments and no Commissioner-General was appointed. But as usual, a Bank Adviser was appointed for three years. It was a British citizen, H. C. F. Finlayson, whose office was twice renewed, all the way until 1934. In 1929, a further $12,000,000 was raised in the USA exclusively for refugee settlement work. Though Greece this time performed well, the Great Depression made those results soon disappear. In 1932 Greece unilaterally suspended the transfers for its foreign debt service and all through the 1930s it was unable to meet its payment commitments.[991]

Danzig was an extreme case of the various peace treaties. It became a so-called "free city," which was due to its unique position as the most important port city in the region. The League of Nations already in 1921 dealt with the question of Danzig, when the High Commissioner there proposed that the League should guarantee a loan. Nothing came of it. Then in January 1923, the Reparations Commission granted a one-year moratorium for Danzig on payments. In September 1923, the Danzig Senate decided to introduce a new

988 Ibid., 21.

989 League of Nations, *Reconstruction Schemes*, 60.

990 Ibid., 59.

991 The paragraph is based upon League of Nations, *Reconstruction Schemes*, 61, 68, and, 73; Winkler, 21. The issue of the American tranche was dependent upon Greece concluding the debt settlement with the United States, which finally, although a little bit later, took place. FRUS: 1927, 3:1–19, and FRUS: 1928, 3:1–13.

currency and set up a new bank of issue early next year with the financial help of the Bank of England, thus the new currency was based on sterling. The first loan was a municipal one issued successfully in London in the spring of 1925. Its interest rate was 7% and it was mainly used for development works. Then Danzig got in financial trouble and the League proposed in September 1926 that a long-term loan should be issued for balancing the budget and for certain productive purposes. Since requirements were slowly executed by the city, the loan was issued only in June 1927. The interest rate was 6.5%; the amount was £1.9 million ($9.2 million), of which the biggest part was used to pay off treaty charges. Danzig faithfully executed its annuities and stopped paying any further transfer only two months before it was incorporated into Germany.[992]

Bulgaria's case was different from other ex-enemy countries in the sense that it was the only country whose reparation obligation was spelled out in the Treaty of Neuilly in late 1919, to the amount exceeding $400 million. After Bulgaria asked for a three-year moratorium on this obligation, negotiations began, and in February 1923 the reparation was reduced to $100 million with favorable terms of payment.[993] The successful Austrian and Hungarian reconstructions persuaded Bulgaria to turn to the League of Nations for help. Though in 1925 the British Treasury opposed a League loan for Bulgaria because they thought it would rob the League of some of its prestige, in 1926 both the Treasury and the Bank of England approved of such a course, in which the positive behavior of Bulgaria in the conflict with Greece in the fall of 1925 might have played some role.[994] The high number of refugees further made Bulgaria's situation more difficult. There number was much lower than in Greece, still, it put a heavy burden on the government, which found itself in financial turmoil.

The League of Nations drew up a plan for Bulgaria and a protocol was signed in September 1926.[995] René Charron was appointed Commissioner, who had to submit quarterly reports. For the settlement of refugees, a loan of £2,250,000 ($11 million) was to be raised. Just like in Austria and Hungary, the loan was to be secured by specific revenues and was to have a first charge on any other revenues in case of need. In December, a long-term loan was issued in London ($8.3 million), in Italy, Switzerland, and the Netherlands ($3.2 million), and New York ($4,500,000). The price of issue was 92 and the rate of interest was 7%. Of the nominal amount of £3.3 million ($16 million), £625,889 ($3 million) was used to settle claims by France originating from before World War I. Another Protocol

---

992 The paragraph is based upon League of Nations, *Reconstruction Schemes*, 98-105, and Orde, *British Policy and European Reconstruction*, 279.

993 Orde, *British Policy and European Reconstruction*, 289.

994 Ibid., 289–90.

995 All the information in this paragraph is from League of Nations, *Reconstruction Schemes*, 80–97.

in March 1928 spelled out a scheme for a financial reconstruction with the help of a foreign loan of £4.5 million ($22 million) secured on customs revenue, later increased to £5 million because of the earthquakes. It was issued in November and December 1928, in London ($8.8 million), New York ($13 million), and Paris ($2.4 million). The prices of issue were 96, 97, and 93, respectively; the rate of interest was 7½ %. The number of state employees was to be reduced by at least 10,000 in two years. The Bank Statutes were very similar to those of Austria and Hungary, but a little bit stricter. In September 1928, Charron was also appointed Technical Adviser to the National Bank, and he held both positions until 1932. The work was practically finished in the fall of 1931. In 1932, Bulgaria first decided to partially and temporarily suspend transfer payments, which meant a 50% reduction, then in 1934, it unilaterally started to pay only 15% of the interest. Finally, in 1940, Bulgaria defaulted on its League loan.

Estonia, the new independent small state, arrested inflation and reached budget equilibrium on its own. In 1926, however, it turned to the League of Nations for advice. The League suggested the Estonians should set up a new bank of issue along modern lines. The Estonians accepted the recommendation and a protocol was signed on December 10, 1926. A financial adviser was appointed to the government. Walter J. F. Williamson became the adviser to the new bank from May 7, 1927, and remained in that position till September 1930. The long-term loan to be issued was to be spent mainly on the new bank and on a new mortgage institute. In June the British issue was £700,000 ($3.4 million), the American $4,000,000, the price of issue was the same in both countries, 94.5; the interest rate was 7%. Currency and banking reforms were carried out according to the protocol and Estonia was a real success story. Even the Great Depression caused a relatively small disturbance in the state's financial affairs. Up until Estonia was incorporated into the Soviet Union, the country maintained the full service of the loan.[996]

The abovementioned programs, together with the Austrian and Hungarian ones, can be said to have been successful as far as their original goal was concerned.[997] A new central bank was set up in each country, inflation was arrested, the budget was stabilized, and with the help of an outside loan, the financial means were at hand to accomplish far-reaching reforms. In wake of the early signs of stability, foreign capital started to come to these countries, which in the end led to overborrowing. It is very interesting that out of all these countries, the per capita foreign debt service was the highest in the two real success stories, Austria and

996 This paragraph is based on League of Nations, *Reconstruction Schemes*, 106–09.
997 There were plans and negotiations for a League loan for Albania and Portugal in 1924 and 1927–1928, respectively, but both came to naught in the end. In more detail about the two cases, see, League of Nations, *Reconstruction Schemes*, 110–24.

Hungary.[998] As Smith was said to have remarked frequently, "This scheme is doing altogether too well. I don't know what's going to happen. But something is sure to go wrong, somewhere."[999] Although the reconstruction schemes were successful from a financial point of view, economic soundness and large-scale cooperation among the other countries broke down. As a consequence, the mechanism that was to ensure a revitalized Europe in economic terms was not operating. This was destined to lead to trouble and in only a few years' time the region, together with the whole world, found itself in the deepest economic and financial crisis modern society had ever faced.

10.3. Reconstruction Programs outside the League

The problems mentioned in the above chapters were not unique to the Central, Eastern, and Southern European regions. In almost every country in Europe some kind of financial rehabilitation was necessary in order to create the basis of a new Europe in the financial and economic spheres in the 1920s. Some other countries that also needed to step on the path of financial recovery with outside help, however, chose a different course than that of the League of Nations. A short overview of these examples is all the more well-founded, because all these countries represented a different political problem. With the conspicuous exception of Germany and Poland, the countries that undertook financial overhaul did not carry the threat of political instability and the fear of spreading Bolshevik ideas. The chapter first deals with these countries, then turns to Germany and Poland.

The talks had been going on for the stabilization of the Belgian franc for more than a year before the final agreement was made in October 1926. The negotiations were basically handled by Norman and Strong, therefore, it was a genuine Anglo-Saxon undertaking. The currency was to be stabilized at a gold value, the Belgian government was to secure a long-term foreign loan of roughly $100 million, and the Belgian National Bank had to arrange for about $41 million credit form other central banks. Norman called this central bank cooperation "a miracle," especially because the central banks of both Germany and France took part, a unique cooperation between archenemies. As a sign of real central bank effort, even small countries such as Austria and Hungary participated with £500,000 ($2.4 million) each in the central bank credit. Since the major part

998 Ibid., 150.
999 Quoted in Ibid., 152.

of the loan was supposed to come from America, it was well within Belgium's interest to reach a debt settlement with the United States. This was duly done and according to plans, $50 million out of the total $100 million was issued in the US. The price of issue was 94, a high figure in European loans during the 1920s; the interest rate was 7%. No specific revenues were assigned as security for the loan. The Belgian case provided the first case when the League assistance was avoided and rather central bank cooperation was put in practice. A lot of elements were taken over from earlier League loan cases as might be expected. However, there was the conspicuous lack of foreign controller like Smith in Hungary, and no real control was set up. The closest manifestation of control was the Bank of England's request for periodic reports from the National Bank of Belgium about the progress, which it received.[1000]

Italy also wanted to get a share of the loan boom engulfing Europe and it needed some outside help. The debt settlement concluded with the United States in November 1925 helped Italy's case and, accordingly, J. P. Morgan & Co. floated the $100 million Italian stabilization loan within weeks. But the lira soon started to fall and other measures were needed in order to secure a stable currency. One of the main reasons was the lack of an independent central bank in Italy, where the Mussolini regime held sway over it. In December 1927, the Norman-Strong pair started the negotiations in earnest after some preparation work, and a week later an agreement was hammered out. The $75 million central bank credit by 15 central banks was carried out with the lead of London and New York, the two latter also securing $50 million private credit, but Austria and Hungary also participated with a smaller sum. The independence of the National Bank of Italy was not really restored, but the participants did not deem it as the most important aspect and no control similar to any of the League loans was set up. In 1929 the again stable lira started to lose its value and in the 1930s Italy stepped on the road leading to military expansion and fiscal policy was subordinated to such a course of action.[1001]

Romania was another country where the help of the League of Nations was avoided despite Norman's effort to secure it. Similarly to Poland, the Romanians did not want any League control and they were lucky to find an influential friend. France, who by this time had become financially strong, believed that Romania could be a place to oppose Norman's scheme for League action. In 1929, Charles Rist was appointed Technical Adviser to the National Bank, succeeded by another French man, Roger Auboin. In December a Protocol was signed. The

1000 This paragraph is based on Meyer, *Bankers' Diplomacy*, 16–41, and Chandler, *Benjamin Strong*, 351–53.

1001 The paragraph is based on Meyer, *Bankers' Diplomacy*, 42–57, and Chandler, *Benjamin Strong*, 388–89.

National Bank of Romania got a $25 million credit from 14 central banks, with the United States, Great Britain, and France each taking $4.5 million, while smaller countries such as Austria and Hungary had a share of $500,000. Romania also secured a $101 million long-term foreign loan, with the largest offering of $22 million coming from France. As a compromise, the Financial Adviser was to be in Romania only for 4 years instead of 5, but agreement between as to who that person should be never took place. The two British persons offered were not accepted by Romania. Rist, the Adviser, had even less power than in the Polish case. He did not have "authority even to control the use of the loan proceeds or the revenues pledged as security for the loan." He was there for three years as a figurehead and he stayed in Bucharest only in the first year of the program. Although Romania stabilized her currency, the world crisis hit her hard and the country asked for League help in 1932. The League drew up a scheme but in May 1934, Romania officially renounced the agreement and the financial plan was never used.[1002]

Germany was a much different case than all the other countries mentioned so far. This was the pivotal question in Europe: what to do with Germany? The Versailles Peace Treaty in 1919 said that Germany was responsible for World War I and was to pay interim reparation of 20 billion gold marks ($5 billion) before May 1, 1921, to other countries, and the Reparations Commission was supposed to fix the total sum by that date. Indeed, on April 27, 1921, the Commission announced the total money to be paid by Germany was 132 billion gold marks ($33 billion).[1003] The London Schedule of Payments of May 5, 1921, basically created a myth about this sum. On the one hand, the 132 billion was maintained as a set figure toward the public, but in reality the true amount was cut down to 50 billion gold marks ($12.5 billion).[1004] The Allies were well aware that Germany could not pay the originally set amount, but politically it was impossible for them to retreat. Soon enough Germany stopped paying the yearly installment due to weakened economic conditions. In large part this was due to the German plans to let the financial situation get worse in the hope that the reparation measures would be reduced with time, a tactic that paid off in the end.[1005] As a response to the lack of living up to the agreement on the German part, French and Belgian troops occupied the Ruhr Valley in January 1923, which was considered the most valuable asset of Germany. The United States felt it had to do something in order to create an escape route out of this chaos.

1002 This paragraph is based on Meyer, *Bankers' Diplomacy*, 101–35, Chandler, *Benjamin Strong*, 404–05, 422, and League of Nations, *Reconstruction Schemes*, 125–32.
1003 For text of the Reparation Commission decision, see FRUS, PPC, 13:433.
1004 Sally Marks, "The Myths of Reparations," *Central European History* 11 (September 1978): 233–37.
1005 Ibid., 239.

The United States had an enormous stake in Germany and it was in its best interest to arrive at an agreement with the other parties. Germany was seen as the center for both the political and economic problems. As Norman Davies warned Woodrow Wilson, "If Germany is not at work," it would be "in a chaotic condition and unprosperous," therefore it would be "impossible for the rest of Europe to get to work and be prosperous."[1006] Thomas Lamont later recalled that "the British and ourselves regarded Germany as the economic hub of the European universe. We feared that unless Germany were rebuilt and prospered all the surrounding countries of the Continent would likewise languish."[1007] Political and ideological points of view also played a role. The United States did not want to see a broken and very weak Germany in the heart of Europe, because that would have meant French hegemony on the continent and a possible German tendency toward Bolshevik sentiment. It meant responsibility, which America's first postwar ambassador to Germany, Alanson B. Houghton, well recognized, shared, and hoped to implement in practical actions. As he put it,

> The American people must understand their responsibility and their opportunity. God has given us the power to render a vast service to humanity. No such opportunity has ever come to any nation in two thousand years. The world has become an economic unit. The United States must recognize this and shape her policies in accord with this new fact in her history. The idea of isolationism must be dismissed. The sentiment and the sense of responsibility for building a better world civilization must be cultivated.[1008]

The largest debtors to the United States, Great Britain and France, paid their dues out of the reparation installments they managed to squeeze out of Germany. If Germany could not pay, the United States would not have received money from the Allies either. Therefore it was vital for America to find a solution for the intricate problem.

Although the US government systematically denied any relation between war debts and reparations, the highest political voices made it clear what the United States wished to see. Secretary of State Charles Hughes already in 1922 hinted that the United States would be interested in reaching a consensus as far as Germany was concerned:

1006 Quoted in Costigliola, *Awkward Dominion*, 37.

1007 Quoted in Chernow, *The House of Morgan*, 248. The British shared this view. As the foreign minister, Lord Curzon announced to the cabinet, Germany "is to us the most important country in Europe." Quoted in Ahamed, *Lords of Finance*, 116.

1008 Quoted in Jeffrey J. Matthews, *Alanson B. Houghton. Ambassador of the New Era* (Lanham, MD: Rowman and Littlefield, 2004), 47. Houghton was fluent in German and can be said to have had a Germanophile attitude.

> If statesmen cannot agree, and exigencies of public opinion make their course difficult, then there should be called to their aid those who can point the way to a solution. Why should they not invite men of the highest authority in finance in their respective countries—men of such prestige, experience and honor that their agreement upon the amount to be paid, and upon a financial plan for working out the payments, would be accepted throughout the world as the most authoritative expression obtainable? [...] I have no doubt that distinguished Americans would be willing to serve in such a commission.[1009]

Naturally, one of the reasons why the United States was willing to take a decisive role in the negotiations was the basic difference that unlike the previous Central European countries' loans, the German reconstruction would not be under the auspices of the League of Nations. In the cases of Austria and Hungary, American private capital took only a lukewarm albeit very important part. In the case of Germany, so much more money was needed that it seemed impossible to solve the financial question without Americans right from the very beginning. Therefore it was insured that whatever method would be agreed on, it needed to have American blessing. This was only possible outside the framework of the League of Nations. Not surprisingly, despite the large role the United States was sure to play in the German question, at least on the economic front, the administration did not assume any larger political liability than before.

The formative period of what came to be known as the Dawes Plan was a good occasion for American officials to express once again that they took no responsibility for any loans issued on the American market. President Coolidge was quick to declare that no American would go as a representative of the US government and the government did not participate officially in the German reconstruction.[1010] Economic Adviser of the Department of State Arthur N. Young's address repeated the same line of thought.[1011] But American experts playing a crucial part in the plan to resolve the German reparation question clearly added an American flavor to the whole settlement. The official White House statement said that "It is the desire of the Administration that the Dawes Plan should be put into effect as speedily as possible. This is the first and essential step to economic recovery abroad in which this country is vitally

1009 Hughes at the Annual Meeting of the American Historical Association at New haven, Connecticut, December 29, 1922. Hughes, *The Pathway of Peace*, 57.
1010 Quint and Ferrel, eds., *The Talkative President*, 178, 180.
1011 Text of address of Dr. Arthur N. Young, August 26, 1924. "The Department of State and Foreign Loans." No. 14. 21, S. 118, Salter Papers, LNA.

interested."[1012] It is clear that the main interest of the United States in Europe related to Germany. The rest of Europe was judged in relation to this country. To the east, it was essential to have stable governments, so the Bolshevik ideology could not spread to and fester the new states; to the west, the task was to ensure that Germany would be e able to climb back to the community of strong and prosperous states.

With American initiative then, an expert committee started serious work on how to fix the problem. The fruit of their labor was the so-called Dawes Plan, the name coming from the chairman of the committee, Charles Gates Dawes.[1013] There was another committee investigating German holdings abroad. The plan, in many ways, built upon the Austrian and Hungarian reconstruction programs, and thus can be seen as a continuation of the work started there. Moreover, from a political point of view, the two earlier Central European financial reconstructions must be seen as the prelude to this effort. However, in Germany, the stakes for many countries were much bigger than in tiny Austria and Hungary.

Dawes announced the committee's recommendations on April 9, 1924. The main points were as follows: the Ruhr Valley must be evacuated[1014]; the German central bank (*Reichsbank*) was to be reorganized; a loan of $200 million was to be issued, of which the largest part, $110 million, would be subscribed in the United States; currency stabilization and a new monetary unit, the *Reichsmark*, was introduced; no set figure for reparation was established, but rather a scale of payments based on financial prospects in Germany was set up, starting with two hundred and fifty million dollars (1 billion gold marks), and reaching six hundred and twenty-five million dollars (2.5 billion gold marks) four years later; it was insured that payments did not threaten the financial stability of Germany; largely to enforce this point, the appointment of an Agent General for Reparations Payments was a prerequisite.[1015]

The clear manifestation that the US government was committed to the success of the plan came from the highest authorities. President Coolidge spoke up for the German reconstruction with heavy American involvement:

1012 Hughes to Kellogg, June 25, 1924, FRUS: 1924, 2:32.

1013 Out of the ten members, Dawes and Owen Young represented the United States.

1014 French and Belgian troops occupied the region on January 1, 1923, on account of Germany defaulting on reparation payments. In accordance with the later agreement, the Ruhr Valley was evacuated by the foreign troops on August 31, 1924, prior to the start of the Dawes Plan.

1015 In more detail, see Harold G. Moulton, *The Reparation Plan* (New York: McGraw-Hill Book Company, 1924).

> I trust that private American capital will be willing to participate in advancing this loan. [...] We have determined to maintain, and can maintain, our own political independence, but our economic independence will be strengthened and increased when the economic stability of Europe is restored. [...] A final adjustment for the liquidation of reparations ought to be the beginning of a new era of peace and good will.[1016]

Secretary of State Hughes also gave a good hint of how the US government assessed the Dawes Plan and American involvement in it:

> You may count upon our interest and assistance in the necessary measures to assure the economic rehabilitation of Europe. It does not matter that this aid is not given by the government. Without wishing to say anything controversial on this occasion, I may give it as my conviction that had we attempted to make America's contribution to the recent plan of adjustment a governmental matter, we should have been involved in a hopeless debate, and there would have been no adequate action. We should have been beset with demands, objections, instructions. That is not the way to make an American contribution to economic revival. You have the Dawes plan and you have had the participation of American experts, with the liberty of constructive effort which was essential because it was undertaken in the only way in which success was possible. When you deal with economic rehabilitation, you doubtless have in mind such contribution as America may be able to give in disinterested advice, and later, in participation in the absolutely essential loan. [...] We appreciate the difficulties, but we believe that the Dawes plan opens up the path of confidence and prosperity. For that reason, we are deeply interested in its prompt execution.[1017]

Once more, the official expressions were trying to blur the lines between clear governmental commitment and pure business undertaking, the relation between reparation payments and intergovernmental debts, and between the depoliticized outside cover and the deep involvement of the US government.

1016 Speech delivered by Coolidge on April 22, 1924, at the Annual Luncheon of the Associated Press in New York, in Hughes to Herrick, April 23, 1924, FRUS: 1924, 2:14. The message was also sent to the American embassies in London, Rome, Berlin, and Brussels. His personal advice for the American delegation was the trademark short form, "Just remember you are Americans." Quoted in Jones, *U.S. Diplomats in Europe, 1919-1941* , 47.
1017 Hughes's speech at the Pilgrims' Dinner in London, July 21, 1924. Hughes, *The Pathway of Peace*, 108.

As another sign of American interest and influence, it was an American demand, and European acquiescence, that this post be filled by an American. Finally, Seymour Parker Gilbert was appointed, who, after a short interim filled by Owen Young, took over the post on October 30, 1924, and resigned six years later. The Agent General for Reparation Payments, as its name indicates, was of a little bit different kind than the controllers in either Austria or Hungary. The emphasis was on the reparation payments, and this key notion gave a bad name to European affairs in the 1920s; American investors, for instance, considered the Reparations Commission a "black beast."[1018] The experts who worked out the details thought that the solution, at least for the time being, was in some kind of reparation payments, if for nothing other than political necessity. France wanted payments, and without it neither Great Britain nor the United States could have been paid back to at least some extent. Benjamin Strong, who was not part of the team working out the details of the plan, thought that it was "a most ingenious plan, if not in fact a masterpiece of ingenuity."[1019]

The $200 million loan was to be issued in the fall and the circumstances in its issuance said as much about the American interests on the continent as anything else. As usual, the American tranche of $110 million was organized by J. P. Morgan & Co. Morgan naturally wanted governmental assurance anew for the whole business. Not surprisingly, the mammoth banking house had to face the rigid official line of non-involvement. Secretary of State Hughes only used general terms and gave nonbinding assurances to Dwight Morrow of J. P. Morgan & Co. in September, when the latter referred to "the heavy responsibility" in case America failed to go ahead with the plan and this fact would cause a breakdown.[1020] He informed the other partners that this was "as good as we can expect," and they had to make the most of it.[1021] Under the surface nonetheless, the American government encouraged the bankers to undertake the loan.[1022] But the active, albeit non-official, participation of the administration went farther than seeking business support at home. To make sure that parts of the loan would be floated in Europe, the State Department used its influence. When J. P. Morgan & Co. signaled that they were not willing to float the French loan unless France participated in the Dawes Plan, Hughes agreed with such a view. He further stated that France could count on US State Department support in the

---

1018 Jones, U.S. Diplomats in Europe, 1919-1941, 19. On the Dawes Plan, also see, Ahamed, *Lords of Finance*, 197-216.

1019 Quoted in Chandler, *Benjamin Strong*, 271.

1020 Clarke, *Central Bank Cooperation*, 55–56.

1021 Morrow to Morgan and Lamont, September 20, 1924, quoted in Costigliola, *Awkward Dominion*, 124.

1022 Hogan, *Informal Entente*, 71; Costigliola, "The United States and the Reconstruction of Germany in the 1920s," 493–94.

pending $100 million loan to France only if it agreed with proposed annuities under the Dawes Plan.[1023] J. P. Morgan & Co. also did its part in what was a clear case of blackmailing France. The company said that the loan France had been seeking would not be floated unless there was French cooperation.[1024] Morgan partners used scathing rhetoric when they put the question to France whether they wanted "a rehabilitated Germany" together with American money, or "a broken Germany and what has been called 'security.'"[1025]

The fact that $110 million of the total of $200 million was raised in America also underscored the fact that this time the United States, even if on unofficial and private level, played a part the importance of which could not be underestimated and misunderstood. Most of the remaining sum of the loan was floated in Great Britain. The two countries thus took 7/8th of the total, which was a further proof of the close Anglo-American cooperation. The loan proved to be a huge success and was heavily oversubscribed. The French got their reward for participating: in a few weeks' time, a $100 million twenty-five-year loan was floated in the United States.[1026]

The Dawes Plan became effective on September 1, 1924, and for some time it showed signs of success. Thanks to a great injection of American loans in the first place, Germany met its financial obligations almost fully. Next to the financial aspect, soon politically sensitive breakthroughs were attached. For example, In 1925 England, France, Italy, and Germany signed the Treaties of Locarno, which finally established the western borders of Germany and began the withdrawal of occupation forces along the Rhine. As a sign of political reconciliation, Germany was also admitted to the League of Nations in 1926. With the United States taking a huge part in the rebuilding of the German economy, it was finally concluded that America would not let Europe remain a spot of financial and economic chaos. Beyond the private initiative of J. P. Morgan & Co., there was substantial, albeit unspoken, government support for the scheme. As the Agent General Gilbert put it, the government was "committed [...] as much as it is humanly possible."[1027] The Dawes Plan and the American loan in connection with it was a landmark case in the relationship between the United States and Europe.

With time however, it became evident that the Dawes Plan could not provide the framework for a lasting solution. Initially money started to pour into Germany, first and foremost from private American sources. In the years following the

---

1023 Hughes to Herrick (for Logan), November 11, 1924, FRUS: 1924, 2:72–73.
1024 Clarke, *Central Bank Cooperation*, 68; Lamont, *The Ambassador from Wall Street*, 203; Marks, "The Myths of Reparations," 248–49.
1025 Quoted in Costigliola, *Awkward Dominion*, 122.
1026 E. Lamont, *The Ambassador from Wall Street*, 212.
1027 Gilbert to Morrow, November 26, 1924, quoted in Costigliola, *Awkward Dominion*, 122.

launch of the reconstruction program, American investors put up far the biggest part borrowed by German public credit institutions, local governments, and large corporation. Until the end of 1926, out of the 106 external loans 36 were offered in the United States, but in terms of money, out of the nearly $885 million, the share of the United States represented almost $581 million, or 65.6%.[1028] This fresh capital ensured that Germany was able to pay its reparation payment from which the Allies paid back some of their war debts to the United States. But the successful surface hid the harsh reality. The problem was that most of the loans raised for Germany were those of municipalities and states which did not use the money necessarily for productive purposes. The German government was against indiscriminate borrowing of the municipalities, but not having a clear majority in the *Reichstag*, it was quite powerless in this question. Gilbert and Hjalmar Schacht, president of the *Reichsbank*, also raised their voices against the indiscriminate borrowings with little avail.[1029] The German ambassador concluded the harsh reality already at the end of the first year of the Dawes Plan. He stated that "German industry, commerce, agriculture and finance are in a hopeless condition; reparations will never be paid; money loaned to Germany is thrown away [...] I have come to the conclusion that we can do no better service to Germany and to ourselves than to discourage the further placing of German municipal loans in America."[1030] Although the State Department agreed tacitly, it followed the path of official noninvolvement and assumed no responsibility.[1031] With almost everybody seeing the problem arising but doing nothing, it was just a question of time when reality had to be faced.

Indeed, once capital had stopped coming, which happened toward the end of the decade, the balance tipped and the payments ceased. The governments involved called for another round of experts' investigation into the problem, again with Americans in the lead. They thought this solution was the only possible remedy. The result was the Young Plan, named after the chairman Owen Young, who already played an influential role in the Dawes Plan.[1032] This new Plan, introduced in the summer of 1929, aimed at the following: it set the total

1028 Kuzynski, *American Loans*, 29.

1029 Gilbert concluded in 1927: "These tendencies [overspending and overborrowing], if allowed to continue unchecked, are almost certain [...] to lead to severe economic reaction and depression." Quoted in Mintz, *Deterioration in the Quality of Foreign Bonds*, 77. In general see, Policy of the Department of State regarding American Bankers' Loans to German Municipalities, FRUS: 1925, 2:172–87, FRUS: 1926, 2:201–04, and FRUS: 1927, 2:727–30. E. Rosenberg, *Financial Missionaries*, 171–72.

1030 Schurman to Kellogg, September 15, 1925, FRUS, 1925, Vol. 2, 174. See also his letters to the Secretary of State, September 23, 29, 1925, Ibid., 174–76.

1031 Kellogg to Schurman, October 17, 1925, Ibid., 177–78.

1032 On the efforts of revising the Dawes Plan and about the creation of the Young Plan, see Costigliola, *Awkward Dominion*, 205–17.

amount of reparations at 122 billion *Reichsmark* ($26 billion); it reduced the annual payment expected from Germany; it introduced a loosened form of Allied control over Germany's economy; and the Bank for International Settlement was set up to handle reparation payments. The Young Plan made the connection between war debts and reparations: any scaling down of the debts would bring about a corresponding reduction in reparations. The Plan, whatever its worth, worked for some time, but in 1931 the world crisis made its presence felt and drastic changes had to be introduced. Hoover's attempt to alleviate the problem in the form of a year-long moratorium on paying intergovernmental debts did not bear fruit.[1033] Finally, as a result of the Lausanne Conference in 1932, 90% of the reparations due under the Plan was cancelled. In addition, basically all reparation payments were cancelled, and Hungary also achieved a goal it set out to do earlier. But the joy, if any, over that achievement was short-lived, because the world crisis made life much more difficult for every country to get by.

Poland was in many ways in an exceptional situation. Soon after the end of World War I, it fought a short war against Soviet Russia in 1920. Its location signified the importance of the country. It was seen in the West as a defense line against Communism possibly spreading from its Bolshevik eastern neighbor. Therefore, the political, financial, and economic stability of the country was of immense importance. Although Poland did not have to pay reparations, by the end of 1923, the currency showed dangerous depreciation.[1034] In 1923, there were British advisers, but one of them, Frank Horsfall Nixon, made it clear that Poland would not accept a League intervention.[1035] The main reason for this was that Polish leaders did not wish to place their country under British influence. The Poles, similarly to other countries in the region, looked to the United States as the only possible country to bring peace and prosperity, and to ensure safety against either the Soviet or German threat. In turn, Benjamin Strong was of the opinion that in the case of Poland, some other plan should be found than the League of Nations scheme in Austria and Hungary.[1036]

Accordingly, the Poles secured Edwin Kemmerer for financial adviser, who spent a few days at the turn of 1925 and 1926 in Poland, and later returned for a longer period during the next summer. The coup led by the nationalist Jozef

1033 President Herbert Hoover's sudden proposal for a one-year moratorium commencing July 1, 1931, on all intergovernmental debts, can be found in FRUS: 1931 (Washington, DC: Government Printing Office, 1946), 1:33–35. The idea of the Hoover moratorium came from Russel Leffingwel, and it was largely due to Lamont's persuasion that Hoover accepted it. Lamont, *The Ambassador form Wall Street*, 294–96. On the Moratorium, which Hoover wrote of as his own idea, see Hoover, *Memoirs*, vo. 3, 67–72.

1034 Lojkó, *Meddling in Middle Europe*, 311.

1035 Orde, *British Policy and European Reconstruction*, 277.

1036 Meyer, *Bankers' Diplomacy*, 72.

Pilsudski in the spring of 1926 brought a halt to any negotiations, but finally, in the summer of 1927, based upon Kemmerer's second study, the Polish plan of stabilization was born, "a man size job and a perpetual one ."[1037] Poland would get a credit of $20 million for one year, in which 14 central banks took part with a conspicuous American lead. The Federal Reserve Bank of New York provided $5,250,000; Great Britain, Germany, and France each gave $3 million; while Austria and Hungary were on the list with $500,000 each.[1038] The heavy American involvement may have had a political underpinning as well. The American minister to Poland wrote that lack of American money threatened "the turning of the country to Bolshevism, thereby breaking down the wall between the [U]SSR and the rest of Europe."[1039] Poland was to secure a $60 million loan and accept that a foreign adviser should be appointed to the Bank of Poland.[1040] In October 1927, a loan of $72 million was finally raised in seven countries. More than half of it, $47 million was issued in New York, while £2 million ($9 million) was issued in London.[1041] It was the first case that Strong and not Norman had played the leading role in a European financial reconstruction. The interest rate was 7%; the price of issue was 92.[1042] Out of the $72 million, only 15 million was spent on currency stabilization, and the stabilization of Polish economy did not really take place.[1043] The 1929 crisis changed the whole landscape and Poland found itself in trouble like all the other countries. Still, it did not default on its loan and until 1936 it made full payment, later on only partial one.

The fierce antagonism on the part of Poland toward foreign control is a good example of a wider phenomenon. Poland embodied the majority of the countries in the sense that they did not want control. If anything, they were willing to subject themselves to a much looser kind of supervision under fellow central banks. In the beginning and in the most sensitive countries, the League of Nations, or the countries involved in a loan, was adamant on the point of control. In fact, it was one of the key issues. After the Austrian, Hungarian, and German stabilization efforts seemed to achieve the desired results, the political necessity was not there anymore to demand a strict supervision. It was thought instead

---

1037 Kemmerer to William Hard, April 28, 1926, Folder 8, Poland, Correspondence G-L, 1926-1927, Box 209, Kemmerer Papers; Meyer, *Bankers' Diplomacy*, 65.

1038 Ibid., 87.

1039 Stetson to Kellogg, May 10, 1926, Quoted in *U.S. Diplomats in Europe*, 67. Stetton was a sharp observer. He wrote to the Secretary of States that "All money which comes to Europe turns at once into political force [...] Therefore, whether we admit or not, we are participating in European politics." Stetson to Kellogg, May 10, 1926, quoted in Ibid., 68.

1040 Chandler, *Benjamin Strong*, 401-402.

1041 Meyer, *Bankers' Diplomacy*, 90.

1042 Meyer, *Bankers' Diplomacy*, 89.

1043 Frank Costigliola, "American Foreign Policy in the 'Nut Cracker': The United States and Poland in the 1920s," *The Pacific Historical Review* 48 (February 1979): 102.

that along pure financial lines, and the inherently built-in control through the usually newly set up central banks, the loan business would work more or less automatically. Although the Great Depression and the world crisis in its wake changed everything, it still looks debatable that the idea was inherently sound. These central and eastern European countries historically lacked what was the financial norm in the West and they could not function prosperously without the presence of strict control. But from a political point of view, exactly that kind of strict supervision was impossible to install. In a Catch-22, everyone was a loser, which fact loomed large in the many defaults and nervous attempts to arrange some kind of transfers from the early 1930s. Jeremiah Smith, Jr. was right: somewhere something surely went wrong,

10.4. The Three American Financial Controllers in Europe in the 1920s

The three American financial controllers, or advisers, show an interesting imprint in the United States' both official and unofficial attitude toward Central Europe. The persons in question, Jeremiah Smith, Jr., Seymour Parker Gilbert, and Charles Dewey, in chronological order, fulfilled very similar posts with similar functions. This statement is especially true for the first two of the trio, who both commenced their work in 1924, and in both cases the reconstruction schemes were similar. They were supposed to watch the investors' interests and in order to be able to function in such capacity they were entitled to control the finances of the target countries in order to insure that the planned reforms would be carried out and the governments would not use the monies for unproductive purposes. Obviously, to a differing extent, they were the means of broader political considerations. They showed what limited commitment the United States was willing to take in order to ensure the financial stabilization of the Central European region. Beyond this well-hidden interest lied an immense stake for the United States in Germany. No wonder that out of the three countries, this was the place where the American involvement was the biggest. Despite the fact that an official coming from the United States enjoyed immense prestige in the mentioned region, their statuses, however, were very different in each case.

The first of these three Americans, Jeremiah Smith, Jr., was in the "most comfortable" situation. He was the first chronologically, but most importantly, he was functioning under the League of Nations, which made a lot of difference. He was not chosen by the State Department, because the American government did not wish to be involved in a League undertaking, and, consequently, he did not serve direct US governmental interests. Still, it was well for the Coolidge administration that an American was selected, since an American citizen, even in his private capacity, did represent the United States and, in a fortunate case, managed to spread the values and philosophies of what America stood for. Also, by virtue of a loan under the strict rules by the League of Nations, it was basically guaranteed that the Hungarian government would cooperate with Smith. It was in their best interest to do so: they viewed the loan as the ticket into the international financial arena where the conspicuous strength of private American investors was impossible to miss. Performing well under an American was thought to give the green light for future American investments. It is obvious that it was not the nationality of the person that made the difference whether American capital would come or not but the financial situation and performance of the country. Still, it is undeniable that the good news coming from a compatriot made the American bankers more willing when it came to deciding about a Hungarian loan. The great hope of American capital also started to materialize and between 1924 and 1928 it was a total of $115,150,000, therefore the expectations of having.[1044] In addition, Smith's personality was perfect for cooperation, understanding, and pragmatic flexibility. His status as a friendly adviser, as he liked to see himself, bore fruit in the relation between him and both the Hungarian government and the population at large. Therefore, it is safe to say that an American controller paid off. It managed to qualm political whims, it worked in the practical and professional American style, it functioned as a smooth conduit between Hungary and the League of Nations, and the American capital started to come into the country as well. The farewell from Jeremiah Smith, Jr. meant for Hungary the end of the explicit League control, and it was all up to Hungary how it managed its household

Contrary to Smith, Seymour Parker Gilbert was the epitome of the postwar American attitude toward Europe. Only a few months after Smith began his work in Budapest, Gilbert was chosen for the most influential financial post in postwar Europe. His selection as the Agent General for Reparations Payments showed certain important features.[1045] First of all, the person had to be an American, since most of the money was coming from the United States.[1046] Secondly, the very fact that Gilbert was a consensus choice of the government and big business shows that in the case of Germany the United States went farther than

1044 Péteri, *Revolutionary Twenties*, 180.

1045 The first candidate was Logan, but J. P. Morgan & Co. was against him and wanted Dwight W. Morrow for the job. The administration was not enthusiastic about him and he refused on personal grounds. Finally, Gilbert was selected. In more detail about the problems surrounding his nomination, see FRUS: 1924, 2:135–39; Kenneth Paul Jones, "Discord and Collaboration: Choosing an Agent General for Reparations," *Diplomatic History* 1 (Spring 1977): 118–39.

1046 "There was unanimous desire, with Governments also agreeing, for appointment of an American as Agent General." C Myron T. Herrick (Logan) to Hughes, July 2, 1924, FRUS: 1924, 2:136.

in any other country toward making sure that events would unfold according to its taste. This was the most spectacular example of how important Germany was for the US government. Since the Dawes Plan was not a League effort but cooperation with American leadership, the Coolidge administration had a very large interest in having the Agent General represent the American interests well. This was also the goal of J. P. Morgan & Co. from the investment point of view. They needed a person to watch over the Germans in case they did not play by the rules. Moreover, the Agent General had to be strong to resist possible outside pressure from Great Britain, but most importantly from France. Finally, the choice of Gilbert shows the governmental efforts: he stepped down in the fall of 1923 as Under Secretary of the Treasury. The unofficial representation by a former government employee cannot be read differently than unsaid commitment on the part of the US government. Consequently, through his filling the post in Germany, the Coolidge administration did manage to send its own man. Naturally, the US government wanted to remain officially aloof and the official line was as uncommitted as ever. As the Secretary of State put it to the President, "there is no objection here to this appointment provided the suggestion comes in the proper way from the Governments represented on the Reparations Commission and has the approval of Germany."[1047] This was vintage US postwar attitude toward the European problem: to depoliticize the issue, not to take responsibility, though still wishing to take the lead and dictate conditions. Despite Gilbert's unofficial status, nobody could doubt that he had relations to the administration, which he indeed did.

Obviously, it was of crucial significance who filled the all-important post. The main problem with Gilbert was that of his age, a tender 32. Although he was appointed under secretary at the age of 28, ran the department in the absence of Secretary Mellon, and was called a "thinking machine," the hosts were not very much keen on him.[1048] The Germans in particular were of the opinion that such a young man would not be able to carry out the task at hand. He had to try to keep a balance between what Germany was able to pay and a scenario that lead to no danger of financial instability. The whiz kid did try his best but the whole plan, with the office and the performance of the Agent General, was not promising right from the start. In addition, Gilbert was not an easy person and he stayed aloof from Germany in general. He did not learn to speak German in six years, nor did he socialize with Germans. This in itself would have been not a real problem. But owing to his mumbling way of speaking, he was oftentimes not understandable even to his own countrymen.[1049]

1047 Hughes to Coolidge, August 16, 1924, FRUS: 1924, 2:138.
1048 Chernow, *The House of Morgan*, 253.
1049 Ibid.

Despite his best efforts, Gilbert's work did not amount to a success story. With time, it became evident that the Dawes Plan could not provide the framework for a lasting solution. Notwithstanding a massive injection of money in the shape of loans, the German economy could not climb out of its hole and indiscriminate borrowing was a pastime among German municipalities. Gilbert raised his voice against the indiscriminate borrowings with little avail.[1050] Therefore, on both accounts, professionally and humanly, Gilbert did not measure up to Smith.

In the case of Poland, any financial adviser would have found himself in no easy situation. The last example of an American adviser to a Central European country in the 1920s was a strange mixture at best in the end. It was a political necessity for Poland to try to rehabilitate the country with American help and not through the League of Nations, so the financial adviser also had to be an American. However, the high nationalistic feeling and pride of the country made it impossible for a strict control of the finances. Edwin Kemmerer, who paid two well-paid visits to Poland as an adviser in his famous "money doctor" glory, informed Strong that "the prospects look good that we may be able to accomplish something worth while."[1051] But for the actual post of advising the Poles, Charles Schuveldt Dewey was selected, also a former banker and Assistant Secretary of the US Treasury, by the effective involvement of Strong.[1052] Dewey asked for Kemmerer's help in getting information about a place the "doctor" had visited, and was also looking for any suggestion as to whom he should take with him as an assistant.[1053] Dewey was not as warmly received as Kemmerer. While the Polish government was happy to pay Kemmerer $10,000 and expenses for his services, in the case of Dewey, they expected him to pay his assistant from his own salary.[1054]

Dewey had relatively a wide circle of powers to protect the bond holders, but as far as general control over the monetary issues of Poland were concerned, his powers were much more limited than those of either Smith's or Gilbert's. The

1050 Gilbert concluded in 1927: "These tendencies [overspending and overborrowing], if allowed to continue unchecked, are almost certain... to lead to severe economic reaction and depression." Quoted in Mintz, *Deterioration in the Quality of Foreign Bonds*, 77. In general, see, Policy of the Department of State regarding American Bankers' Loans to German Municipalities, FRUS: 1925, 2:172–87, FRUS: 1926, 2:201–04, and FRUS: 1927, 2:727–30; E. Rosenberg, *Financial Missionaries*, 171–72.

1051 Kemmerer to Strong, July 14, 1926, Folder 5, Strong, Benjamin, 1916-1928, Box 16, Kemmerer Papers.

1052 Chandler, *Benjamin Strong*, 402.

1053 Dewey to Kemmerer, October 3, 1927, Folder 4, Correspondence, 1927 October – 1928 January, A – D, Box 40, Kemmerer Papers.

1054 Diary entry, December 17, 1925, Folder 2, Diaries of Edwin Kemmerer – Poland, April 30, 1925 - September 18, 1926, Box 293, Kemmerer Papers; Dewey to Kemmerer, October 3, 1927, Folder 4, Correspondence, October 1927 – January 1928, A – D, Box 40, Kemmerer Papers.

main reason for this was that there was no international body behind him as in the case of Zimmerman or Smith.[1055] In contrast to his peers in Austria, Hungary, and Germany, he had little real power over how the Polish finance ministry was working. The British were angry at the lack of real control. Frederick Leith-Ross of the Reparations Commission said it was like "trying to reform a harlot by providing her with funds against a promise of chastity."[1056] His role was rather to insure that further loans would come to Poland.

The similarity between his and Gilbert's posts cannot be missed. He claimed later in his life that it was Secretary of Treasury Mellon who appointed him for the post, which seems to refute the suggestion that he was a pick by the bankers.[1057] Poland was a sensitive country for the United States, if for nothing else but for its close geographical proximity to the Soviet Union. However, in this case the US government never worried about the fact that the Poles viewed Dewey only as the key to further American loans, and they made no secret about it. As excerpts from two letters make it clear, the Adviser was a paper tiger at best:

> I express my wish that the Adviser should abstain from reading Polish and German newspapers [...] In this way, the Adviser would avoid poor and erroneous information, the correction of which would take all of the government's time without leaving it a minute of rest after its work. Furthermore, I desire that the Adviser should endeavor to avoid mixing in any manner whatever in the internal affairs of the State by undertaking to defend any party or group, and that he should be careful, in the economic and financial area, never to put himself in opposition to the Minister of Finance and the President of the Cabinet.[1058]

Ciechanoswski, Polish Minister to the US, also informed the Adviser-designate Dewey about such wishes. He informed him that "whatever analogy may actually exist between your work as Adviser in Poland and such activities as those of Mr. S Parker Gilbert in Germany, or Jeremiah Smith in Hungary, I consider it is important for you to avoid stressing any such analogy."[1059] Possibly, his only tool of control would have been his reports on the financial and economic situation due every three months. These, however, were means of a pseudo control. If he painted a negative picture, the credit of Poland would have suffered, and consequently, the

---

1055 Meyer, *Bankers' Diplomacy*, 83.
1056 Leith-Ross to Niemeyer, June 7, 1927, quoted in Costigliola, "American Foreign Policy," 104.
1057 E. Rosenberg, *Financial Missionaries*, 181.
1058 Letter to the bankers signed by Pilsudski, October 13, 1927, quoted in Meyer, *Bankers' Diplomacy*, 90–91.
1059 Ciechanowski to Dewey, November 5, 1927, quoted in Ibid., 91.

goal toward which Dewey was working, that is, the stabilization of the country, would have been endangered. Therefore, Dewey tried to create an optimistic impression in his reports, which behavior also spared him confrontations with the Polish officials and the public in general. His low status in Poland, in a sharp contrast to his nationality and connections to the government, was well tangible in his nickname by his host country. He was called *Dawaj* (hand it over!), which indicated that the only role he really was thought of playing was to make sure that foreign capital would come to Poland.[1060] When soon after the initial success, the Polish bonds showed a sharp decline and Poland could not secure much more money, the reputation and integrity of Dewey experienced a similar drop.

Unlike Jeremiah Smith, Jr., neither Gilbert nor Dewey managed to strike an honestly friendly chord with their host countries. Both latter persons were looked at suspicion and impatience, while they too did not make every effort on their part to be better understood and accepted either. Simply, they were inadequate to meet the social challenge inherent in their job. In a sharp contrast to both, Smith was a real favorite in Hungary. Although his job might have been facilitated by a more cooperative government that did not dare to challenge the League of Nations, which would have been very counterproductive from every point of view, the popularity he achieved cannot be explained by this mere fact. Aside from his luck that he served at the best time when overborrowing had not reared its ugly head yet, and the Austrian League scheme was serving as a very useful springboard, still, Smith's personality was a key factor in his work and success. He did not represent his government; he had no governmental connections. He did work for the League of Nations, an international body he had faith in for the political future of Europe and the world at large. But most importantly, he did everything in his capacity to serve Hungary and the Hungarian people, who were very grateful for such open and modest magnanimity.

1060 E. Rosenberg, *Financial Missionaries*, 182.

Conclusion

What was the goal of the Central European Reconstruction as initiated by the League of Nations? The major goal of these reconstruction schemes was obviously two-fold. On the one hand, the Western powers saw a huge market in the region with massive population. But without bringing them up to a certain level of prosperity, these countries could not have represented the spending power they were targeted for. Therefore, it was very much in the interests of the big powers to strengthen these states from a financial point of view. If the monetary situation was stable, this line of thought presumed, the economies of this region would also follow and the basis of big-time trade could commence. The free flow of trade was considered to be the main pillar of an economically healthy Europe, and the world at large. Due to political considerations and realities, such an undertaking was only imaginable under the auspices of the League of Nations. And this was the other important factor. The countries of Central Europe represented a politically volatile sphere in Europe. Thanks to World War I and the successive peace treaties, the Central and Eastern European region was a beehive of hostile feelings and jealous attention among the countries, and this was especially true for neighboring states. In addition to such unstable conditions, of which the clearest manifestation was the short-lived Bolshevik regimes in Bavaria and Hungary, the threat of communism was also a decisive factor in the thinking of the western powers. So, it was only natural that they tried to fight against a political anathema by financial means.

One of the main recommendations of the League of Nations was to build up trade between the countries of the region. This was the central motif in the resolutions of the two biggest conferences in the early 1920s, the Brussels Conference and the Genoa Conference in 1920 and 1922, respectively. Unfortunately, the semi-automatic answer to the problems from each country was to raise tariffs, which doomed any possibility of weathering the economic storm. The inadequate peace treaties continued to haunt. The redrawn map of Europe did not put into consideration the economic factors. In Royall Tyler's assessment, "The Danubian countries were tending to trade ever less with one another, and were striving, each and every one of them, to add economic self-sufficiency to political independence, indulging in a lively game of beggar-my-neighbor."[1061] It is hard to assess the programs in the long term, simply because the financial crisis starting from late 1929 and the Great Depression in its wake put an end to any possible healthy economic life in and outside Europe. Still, in Arthur Salter's words, "The first decade of post-war reconstruction, successful to all appearance in almost every sphere of effort [was] rebuilt on insecure foundations; and the whole structure, which had seemed only to need a coping stone, crumbled before us."[1062] Thus, it was not only the problem of the economic and financial crisis that was to play havoc.

The system itself was not reliable and well-founded enough. The main evil was overborrowing. The huge sums lent to the countries of the region were only partially used for productive purposes and even in that case, governments "borrowed too easily and spent too recklessly."[1063] By the early or mid-1930s, basically all of these countries found themselves in partial or total default. Still, the League efforts cannot be said to have been in vain and the idea of trying to strengthen these countries financially was one not without merit, even if behind the notion political interests were looming large.

Yet another aspect of this period must be studied, namely the United States' overall relation to the financial reconstruction efforts in the Central and Eastern European region in the examined period. It must be stressed that the successive Republican governments did not want to take responsibility for any region of the continent. They believed that whatever sort of help was coming from the United Stated, it should be a private undertaking, mainly in the form of capital.

Early in the armistice period, the United States made the biggest effort as far as relief work was concerned. On the one hand, this was understandable given the much more affluent and secure position America enjoyed compared to any European country. On the other hand, this was the period when it was not clear what future steps the US government under Woodrow Wilson could and would make. The sobering fact that the United States Senate finally voted against the Versailles Peace Treaty and together with it against American participation in the League of Nations made a few things inevitable: the United States would not become an integral part of postwar Europe in the political sense; the League of Nations would have to make do without the probably most influential country; as a consequence of both points, the European reconstruction would lack US governmental support; and as a logical result, the only chance for Europe to cooperate with the United States would be the private sphere. Moreover, this

1061 League of Nations, *Reconstruction Schemes*, 154.
1062 Salter, *World Trade and Its Future*, 50.
1063 Salter, *Political Aspects of the World Depression* (Oxford: Clarendon Press, 1932), 14.

private sphere was essential to the financial rebuilding of the old continent, because otherwise there would not have been enough money available to achieve certain monetary goals that were deemed crucial in order to reach an overall stable system in Europe.

The indifferent attitude of the successive Republican governments did not mean that they did not monitor very closely the events in Europe. On the contrary, the United States was following closely the unfolding situation, because even if it did not wish to take the responsibility, it was clear that for America a stable and friendly Europe was highly needed. While a stable Europe meant secure markets for American products and investments, there were ideological roots as well. The new political menace that appeared from the East in the form of Bolshevism made the US realize that this was the new enemy to fight against. The war-stricken countries of Central and Eastern Europe had to be stabilized in order to avoid a possible spread of the Bolshevik ideology, which reared its head for a short spell in Bavaria and Hungary. The common wisdom in America was the saying that "people with full bellies are not Bolsheviks."[1064] Therefore, the help that was coming from the United States had a dual purpose. It wanted to help the poorest nations, but there can be no denying that this effort was intertwined with the aim of making these countries economically and politically as stable as possible, which was seen as a first priority in avoiding a possible Bolshevik takeover. Herbert Hoover himself gave account for this American attitude:

> This fear [Famine and Pestilence] was strengthened by the possibility that the pressure of starvation would break down the weak revolutionary governments of Central and Eastern Europe into anarchy. After the Armistice, there began to loom up a greater fear from a more potent enemy of freedom than anarchy, which after all is an unorganized force. Communism, which had captured Russia, was a new form of organized destruction of Liberty. And it was vengeance itself. The Communists had captured the Czarist gold reserves. Their agents spread over Europe, subsidizing a new revolution. Soon we began to realize that its infectious poison was spreading alarmingly among all starving peoples. Here loomed up a defeat off all we had fought for—to establish liberty.[1065]

In accordance with this attitude, the United States was very active in its relief efforts concerning the region. In some of the cases, the United States provided 99% of the whole effort, but if there was some British or other involvement,

1064 Glant, "Herbert Hoover and Hungary," 103.
1065 Hoover, *Memoirs*, 1:283.

America was still responsible for about 75-80% of the total.[1066] Naturally, Hungary received a minor part of these supplies partly owing to the fact that it was an enemy country, partly because of the Bolshevik coup in the spring of 1919. This latter feature represented a challenge the United States wanted to resist.[1067] In light of this, it is understandable that although Austria was an enemy country as well, it received 16.6% of the total supplies distributed to the area, while Hungary was the recipient only to the extent of 1.3% of the total.[1068] Thus with smaller population, although in worse conditions, Austria was much more important to the United States in this period than Hungary, a feature that was to loom again after World War II.

When the first wave of relief work had been concluded and the various peace treaties had been signed, the vital region of Central and Eastern Europe did not show signs of much improvement. It was soon clear that significant outside help was needed in order to save these countries from bankruptcies, which, again, might have had carried the danger of their falling pray to radical ideology. The League of Nations undertook the first reconstruction efforts pertaining to financial matters in Central Europe, namely in the cases of Austria and Hungary. Since both were a League undertaking, the United States was a distant party and only took part to a limited extent. As was seen, in both cases the private sphere provided some money, which had a political message as well, namely that the region was important for America. In Hungary, Jeremiah Smith, Jr. represented officially the League of Nations, but being an American citizen, aside from the fact that he had neither official nor unofficial relation with the State Department, he was seen as a true representative of the United States. But these two countries were only the prelude to Germany.

The United States was willing to play a larger role only when the stakes were really high too, and for America the pivotal question of future Europe was Germany. Even if the American administrations did not wish to admit that there was a close relationship between reparations and interallied debts, they were nonetheless forced to accept schemes that were to alleviate the tension between the two. Furthermore, it was basically an American initiative in the case of Germany that finally led to the Dawes Plan in 1924. Germany was important both from the political and economic points of view. In order to create a politically stable Central Europe, and a Europe at large, Germany was the most significant piece. It was too important to be taken out of any context. The general belief was

1066 In more detail and specific numbers, see Ibid., 353–420.

1067 In more detail about the American relief provided for Hungary, see, Glant, "Herbert Hoover and Hungary," 95–109.

1068 Tibor Glant, "Herbert Hoover és Magyarország, 1918–1920" [Herbert Hoover and Hungary, 1918–1920] In. *Emlékkönyv L. Nagy Zsuzsa 70. születésnapjára,*. János Angi and János Barta, eds (Debrecen: Multiplex Media, 2000), 389.

that if Germany became prosperous again, there would be no fear of it wanting revenge for its defeat and humiliation. Economic considerations stemmed from the fact that the latent capability of the German industry was huge and its trade was significant. It was, therefore, an economic must for the United States to have a strong Germany that would integrate into a rehabilitated Europe, again, a similar feature to the post-World War II scenario. Accordingly, private American capital was very active in the period starting in 1924.

With the Austrian and Hungarian schemes providing the basis for the German financial reconstruction, with the launch of the Dawes Plan, American investment banks started to issue loan after loan for Germany. In the next two years, of the total of $885,063,600 the US participation was $580,797,500, that is, 65.65%, while Great Britain was a distant second with $125,721,277, which meant 14.2%.[1069] That is, the trend remained that Germany was an irresistible magnet for American investors, although it was soon clear that Germany, similarly to other countries in the region, was overborrowing and there was no guarantee that it would be able to pay back such huge sums. The cycle did not stop and the peak year was 1927. Despite such voices as Thomas Lamont's, who warned against "indiscriminate lending and indiscriminate borrowing" in an address before the International Chamber of Commerce at Washington in 1927, the picture changed only in 1929, when it was already too late.[1070] By this time, US involvement in the League of Nations efforts had also diminished, despite such rare counterexamples as Jeremiah Smith, Jr.'s becoming a member of the Financial Committee. The US government, for instance, successfully prevented the League to send its representatives to American conferences such as the Pan American conferences.[1071] The Coolidge administration decided also not to continue the post of unofficial representative on the Reparation Commission, which took effect from 1927.[1072] This latter move well represented the staunch American point of view that interallied debts and reparations did not have anything to do with each other. When it came to the economic and financial domain, the United States proved more cooperative. The US government in 1927 decided to take part officially in the International Economic Conference held at Genoa.[1073] The United States, naturally, pursued its own interests and did not want to become involved in the European affairs, only to the necessary extent. This attitude did not help full recovery.

1069 Kuczynski, *American Loans to Germany*, 29.
1070 Lewis, *America's Stake*, 380.
1071 FRUS: 1925, 1:302–04.
1072 For the correspondence on this subject, see FRUS:1926, 1:120–25.
1073 For correspondence, note of the President, and report of the American delegation, see FRUS: 1927, 1:238–46.

A comparison of the four countries of the region, Austria, Hungary, Germany, and Poland, in terms of incoming American capital in the period between 1924 and 1928 gives a fair picture of American private capital involvement there. Austria secured $54 million, Hungary $70.1 million, and Poland $116.2 million, which more or less fairly represents the size of the population of these countries. In Germany's case, however, the total incoming loans reached the staggering amount of $1,137.7 million, a disproportionately large number.[1074] This sum was also 41% of all loans issued in Europe, and more than one-fifth of all American loans issued around the whole globe.[1075] It can be safely concluded that Lamont's earlier quoted words about Germany, that it was seen "as the economic hub of the European universe," and without a prosperous Germany, "all the surrounding countries of the Continent would likewise languish," truly expressed the general sentiment in the Anglo-Saxon financial circles.

The crisis starting in late 1929 put an inevitable end to further loans from the United States to Europe, partly because the priorities had suddenly changed. Europe seemed more or less stable, Latin America was secured as a safe backyard both in the political and financial spheres, but first and foremost, America needed to concentrate on its own domestic affairs and try to put them in order. Since the Great Depression was a lasting one and it consumed most of the energies of the country, it is little wonder that the American presence dwindled to a negligible amount in Europe and the continent was left on its own. In the early 1930s, it became clear that European financial stability was not achieved permanently and the countries of the region defaulted on their loans one by one. The Young Plan could not solve the situation either; it only meant a couple of years' breathing room. The next few years the economic problems only added to the trouble that was menacingly brewing and the end result was widespread political instability and the pending catastrophe of World War II.

Only the devastation and the new political and ideological challenge immediately after World War II made sweeping changes in official American foreign policy thinking. The rhetoric changed because the political elite of the US, or, at least, a larger part of it, had realized that the dangers the US faced were very similar to those after World War I, except both the Bolshevik invasion and the economic distress were much larger and more tangible. Therefore, the US had to come up with a solution and part of it was that unless an economically stable Europe was not created, even if only in the Western part of the continent, the consequences would be incalculable and grave, and incalculably grave at that. Right after the conclusion of World War II, certain American memorandums emphasized the danger of destroying the remnant of the German industry, which

1074 The data are coming from Lewis, *America's Stake*, 619–22.
1075 Ibid., 628–29.

in turn could produce an "infection which might well destroy all hope we have of encouraging democratic thinking and practices in Europe."[1076] Already during the Potsdam Conference the idea was born that "a completely coordinated plan be adopted for the economic rehabilitation of Europe as a whole."[1077] Thus, the early manifestation of the Marshall Plan grew out of the concern of what Europe would face after the hostilities ended. Only free trade and free societies would ensure "an economically stable Europe," which, according to the same memo, "with the impetus it can give to free ideas, is one of the greatest assurances of security and peace we can hope to obtain."[1078] The political leaders in 1945 gave up and broke away from the notion that ruled the American foreign policy thinking in the 1920s, namely that the private sphere should take care of what seemed too burdensome for the administrations. It had become evident that the US government, irrespective of its party affiliation and timeframe, had to assume the responsibilities of Europe in order to be able to serve its own national security considerations.

And what was Hungary's place in all this? Hungary's situation was unique after World War I. Having been the part of the Austrian empire for so long made the country possess somewhat naïve notions about its safety in the sea of Slavic peoples in and around the empire. The Treaty of Trianon was a harsh reality check for Hungary as to how much weight it carried in the West including the United States. Still, when the circumstances were ripe for the launch of a reconstruction program, Hungary could only count on Western Europe, first and foremost on Great Britain and the new number one power the United States. Both in terms of political and financial power, these two countries dominated the post-war international scene. Hungary saw only in these two powerful actors the only way out as to a brighter future, first in the economic sense, then later hopefully in the political domain too. The fact that an American citizen, Jeremiah Smith, Jr. took up the League's Commissioner-General's post in Budapest in 1924 only strengthened the illusion that the country could count on the United States, even if Smith only carried out his task as a private citizen and under the aegis of the League of Nations. Still, his being here and helping the reconstruction program reach its successful end gave an enormous prestige to Hungary in the region, and made sure that further American capital would come.

With Smith's departure, however, the strict control was abolished and Hungary started to follow an unwise course. Financially, the country stepped on the path of overborrowing and despite a higher standard of living, the country's debt

1076 The Secretary of War (Stimson) to the President, July 16, 1945, FRUS: 1945, The Conference of Berlin, (the Potsdam Conference) (Washington, DC: Government Printing Office, 1960), 2:757.
1077 Stimson to Truman, July 22, 1945, Ibid., 809.
1078 Ibid.

skyrocketed with little possibility to pay it back. Only newer loans could keep Hungary afloat. With the 1929 crisis, even these channels came to a naught, and Hungary found itself in serious trouble, just like all the other countries in Europe and around the world. With worsening conditions and political impatience, Hungary was drifting toward Germany both in the political and economic sense. With the naïve hope that the Treaty of Trianon could be reversible, the Hungarian political leadership invested all its energies into the course of revisionism, which in the end led to a similarly big disaster during and after World War II. In the 1930s Hungary became an ally of fascist Italy and Nazi Germany, since this provided hope of getting lost territories. The blind fate and false hope of that aim drove Hungary ever closer to Berlin, which led the country down the path of declaring war on the Soviet Union. "Betting on the wrong horse" limited not only Hungary's already limited military capabilities, but also its independent foreign and economic policy, and caused the death of about a million of its population, including more than half a million Jews. After the war Hungary also became part of the Soviet sphere and for more than forty years it had no way of being reintegrated into Western Europe. Interestingly enough, when history finally provided the country with such a possibility, Hungary soon enough had to find the same recourse to help as eighty years earlier. In 2008, in face of the oncoming economic and financial crisis, Hungary applied for an International Monetary Fund relief loan, which step might be repeated four years later. Only the future can tell whether this time the country will use its resource and the financial help to create more stable conditions and lasting prosperity.

Index

Appendix 1.

The subscription of the Austrian State Loan, 1923.

Source: League of Nations, *The Financial Reconstruction of Austria*, 41-42, and League of Nations, *Reconstruction Schemes*, 157.

Country of Issue	Nominal total			Rate of interest %	Rate of issue %	Net yield		
	Original currency	£	Gold crowns			%	Original currency	Gold crowns
Great Britain	14,000,000	14,000,000	318,836,000	6	80	76.25	10,675,000	243,112,000
USA	25,000,000	5,417,361	123,375,000	7	90	85.625	21,406,000	105,640,000
Belgium	25,000,000	292,834	6,669,000	6	80	77	19,250,000	5,135,000
France	170,000,000	2,323,263	52,910,000	6.5	84	78	132,600,000	41,270,000
Italy	200,000,000	1,986,871	45,249,000	6.5*	93	87.8	175,600,000	39,729,000
Switzerland	25,000,000	972,512	22,148,000	6	80	76	19,000,000	16,832,000
Sweden	13,110,000	720,427	16,407,000	6	78	76.55	10,035,705	12,560,000
Holland	3,000,000	254,852	5,804,000	6	80	76.5	2,295,000	4,441,000
Spain	52,300,000	1,484,632	33,811,000	6	81	77	40,271,000	26,035,000
Czechoslovakia	544,267,000	3,512,778	80,000,000	6	75**	75	408,200,250	60,000,000
Austria (US dollars)	13,000,000	2,817,028	64,155,000	7	91-3	89.5 – 91.5	11,814,075	58,302,000
Totals		33,782,558	769,364,000					613,056,000

* There was a 15% coupon tax.

** Rate at which loan was taken over.

Appendix 2.

The timetable of the Hungarian reparation payments.

January 31, 1924 – December 31, 1926: Deliveries in kind or payment not exceeding the amount of 880 tons of coal per working day.

Source: League of Nations, *The Financial Reconstruction of Hungary*, 201-202.

June 30, 1927	2,500,000 gold crowns
December 31, 1927	2,500,000 gold crowns
June 30, 1928	2,500,000 gold crowns
December 31, 1928	2,500,000 gold crowns
June 30, 1929	3,000,000 gold crowns
December 31, 1929	3,000,000 gold crowns
June 30, 1930	3,500,000 gold crowns
December 31, 1930	3,500,000 gold crowns
June 30, 1931	4,000,000 gold crowns
December 31, 1931	4,000,000 gold crowns
June 30, 1932	4,500,000 gold crowns
December 31, 1932	4,500,000 gold crowns
June 30, 1933	5,000,000 gold crowns
December 31, 1933	5,000,000 gold crowns
June 30, 1934	5,500,000 gold crowns
December 31, 1934	5,500,000 gold crowns
June 30, 1935	6,000,000 gold crowns
December 31, 1935	6,000,000 gold crowns
June 30, 1936	6,500,000 gold crowns
December 31, 1936	6,500,000 gold crowns
June 30, 1937	6,500,000 gold crowns
December 31, 1937	6,500,000 gold crowns
June 30, 1938	6,500,000 gold crowns
December 31, 1938	6,500,000 gold crowns
June 30, 1939	6,500,000 gold crowns
December 31, 1939	6,500,000 gold crowns
June 30, 1940	6,500,000 gold crowns
December 31, 1940	6,500,000 gold crowns
June 30, 1941	6,500,000 gold crowns
December 31, 1941	6,500,000 gold crowns
June 30, 1942	7,000,000 gold crowns
December 31, 1942	7,000,000 gold crowns
June 30, 1943	7,000,000 gold crowns
December 31, 1943	7,000,000 gold crowns

Appendix 3.

The subscription of the Hungarian State Loan, 1924.

Source: League of Nations, *The Financial Reconstruction of Hungary*, 52-53.

Country of Issue	Nominal total			Rate of interest %	Rate of issue %	Banker's rate %	Tax %	Stamp %
	Original currency	£	Gold crowns					
Great Britain	7,902,700	7,902,700	168,722,645	7.5	88	84	–	2
USA	7,500,000	1,733,606	37,012,488	7.5	87.5	80	–	–
Italy	170,000,000	1,696,864	36,228,046	8.05*	92	88	–	1.2
Switzerland	30,000,000	1,226,996	26,196,364	7.5	89	85	1	1
Sweden	4,585,000	280,772	5,994,482	7.5	88	84	0.5	1
Holland	5,000,000	433,605	9,257,466	7.5	88	84	–	1
Czechoslovakia	83,620,000	568,845	12,144,840	7.5			–	2
Hungary (US dollars)	2,350,000	543,195	11,597,250	7.5	88	86		–
Totals		14,386,583	307,153,581					

* 7% interest plus a coupon tax of 15% of the interest, making together 8.05%.

Country of Issue	Net yield			
	%	Original currency	£	Gold crowns
Great Britain	82	6,480,214	6,480,214	138,352,569
USA	80	6,000,000	1,386,885	29,610,000
Italy	86.8	147,560,000	1,472,878	31,445,944
Switzerland	83	24,900,000	1,018,407	21,742,983
Sweden	82.5	3,782,625	231,647	4,945,448
Holland	83	4,150,000	359,892	7,683,697
Czechoslovakia	82.75	69,195,550	470,719	10,049,635
Hungary (US dollars)	86	2,021,000	467,148	9,973,635
Totals			11,887,780	253,804,131

Appendix 4.

Article VI. of Protocol No. II.

Source: League of Nations, *The Financial Reconstruction of Hungary*, 84-86.

The Commissioner-General.

(1) Hungary accepts the appointment by the Council of the League of Nations of a Commissioner-General who shall be responsible to the Council and removable by it.

(2) The Commissioner-General shall reside at Budapest. He may provide himself with the necessary technical staff. The expenses of the Commissioner-General and of his office shall be approved by the Council and defrayed by Hungary.

(3) It will be the duty of the Commissioner-General to supervise the execution of the whole programme of reform and to exercise the powers conferred upon him in this Protocol for the purpose of ensuring that the said programme is carried out and budgetary equilibrium as defined under Article II is attained or, in the event of his reappointment in accordance with Article VII, restored. It is anticipated that he will work, to this end, on the basis of monthly estimates (within the six-monthly limits of the general programme).

(4) The Hungarian Government will give him throughout the whole period of his control all the information he may require, and all the facilities for obtaining information which he may request, as to all items of the expenditure or revenue of the Hungarian State, whatever their source or nature may be, and as to the whole of the administrative system and operations connected with the State finances.

(5) Subject to the due execution of the preceding paragraph of this Article, and except in cases of military expenditure declared by the proper authority inconsistent with the provisions of Part V of the Treaty of Trianon (to which it will at all times be his duty to object), the Commissioner-General will not, so long as the progress of the reform scheme is up to or in advance of the programme drawn up in accordance with Article II, object to particular items of expense or require modifications of the taxation system except on the ground that the particular expense of feature in the taxation system is such (*e.g.* by involving serious later commitments) as in his opinion to compromise the later progress of the scheme; but if the progress of reform is at any time

behind what is prescribed for the six-monthly periods, or contemplated in the monthly estimates referred to in paragraph 3 above, he may, to such extents as he considers the situation demands, and in order that the six-monthly limits may be assured, object to any item of expense and may also, or alternatively, require the Hungarian Government to increase the yield of existing taxation or to impose new taxes. Should the Hungarian Government fail to satisfy his demands, the Commissioner-General shall, to such extent as he may decide, withhold authorisation for payments to the Hungarian Government out of the special accounts contemplated under Articles Xi and XII.

(6) The Hungarian Government undertakes, during the Commissioner-General's control, to grant no concessions and enter into no agreement which he may think such as top compromise the execution of the programme of reform.

(7) The Hungarian Government will not, during the Commissioner-General's control, negotiate or conclude any loans other than those contemplated in the programme to be drawn up in accordance with Article II, except with his assent.

If the Hungarian Government at any time considers itself to obliged to envisage the issue of loans not covered, in the opinion of the Commissioner-General, by the conditions of the porogramme contemplated under Article II, it will first submit such plans for the approval of the Commissioner-General.

(8) The Commissioner-General shall present monthly to the Council a report upon the progress made in executing the programme of reform contemplated under Article II. He shall communicate this report at the same time to the members of the Committee of Control whose function form the subject of Article VIII.

(9) If the Hungarian Government considers that the Commissioner-General has abused his authority it may appeal to the Council of the League of Nations. Before taking any decision on such an appeal, the Council will give to the Committee of Control the opportunity to make any such observations as it may think fit.

(10) Subject to the provisions of Article VII, the functions of the Commissioner-General shall be brought to an end by the decision of the Council of the League of Nations when the Council shall have ascertained that the financial stability of Hungary is assured.

Appendix 5.

Jeremiah Smith, Jr.'s First Report to the League of Nations.

Source: LNJ, 5th Year, No. 7, July 1924, 974–981.

To the Council of the League of Nations:

I have the honour to submit to the Council of the League of Nations the first of the monthly reports required by Section 8 of Article VI of the Geneva Protocol No. II upon the progress of the programme of reconstruction in Hungary.

On the first day of May I arrived in Budapest and entered upon the performance of my duties. This report therefore covers the month of May, and future reports will cover the period from the first to the last days of each calendar month.

I. Adoption of Laws.

The Reconstruction Law conferring full powers for the re-establishment of budgetary equilibrium and the Law creating the Bank of Issue were adopted by the National Assembly on April 17th and were promulgated on April 26th, becoming effective from that date.

In all substantial respects these Laws, as adopted, are identical with the draft laws agreed upon between the Hungarian Government and the Delegation of the Council of the League of Nations that visited Budapest in March last. The few amendments which were made in the course of their passage relate to minor matters and do not affect the execution of the plan in any material respect.

II. New Bank of Issue.

Immediately upon the adoption of these Laws, steps were taken to establish the Bank of Issue. The subscription list for the shares was opened on April 28th and closed May 7th.

The whole capital of the Bank, *i.e.* 30 million gold crowns, was subscribed. In order to accomplish this result it became necessary, as the Financial Committee had foreseen might be the case, for the State to intervene by underwriting the payment of subscriptions to shares amounting to 11.85 million gold crowns. Of this latter amount, 2.4 million gold crowns have already been sold, and sales are progressing which it is hoped will result in the early disposal of the entire amount underwritten by the State. The final result of the subscription is not at all unsatisfactory and compares favourably with the result of the first subscriptions to the shares of the Austrian Bank of Issue. Probably it would have been still more satisfactory had the time for reparation been longer and had not a printers' strike in Budapest (which ended May 6th) interfered with bringing the matter properly to the attention of the public.

The constituent assembly for the organisation of the Bank was held on May 24th.

The Minister of Finance reported that 50% of the subscriptions had been paid in gold or stable foreign currencies and deposited as follows:

			Gold crowns
National City Bank, New York	$	1,351,466.50	= 6,669,791.40
Anglo-Austrian Bank, London	£	100,000	= 2,162,162.16
Midland Bank, Ltd., London	£	124,837.18	= 2,699,198.56
Amsterdamsche Bank, Amsterdam	Gd.	41,987.87	= 77,470.92
Schweizerische Kreditanstalt, Zurich	S. frs.	1,282,839.90	= 1,126,048.34
Skandinaviska Kr., Stockholm	Sw. kr.	2,667.50	= 3,468.68
			15,092,614.99

M. Popovics (a former Governor of the Austro-Hungarian Bank and also formerly Minister of Finance) was nominated and appointed Governor of the Bank, and a Board of Directors was elected, of whom four represent banking interests, four represent agricultural interests, two represent industry, two commerce and one is the President of the present Noteninstitut. Under the law creating the Bank, it must open for business on or before June 24th.

III. Inflation.

The new Bank is entirely independent of Government control. Government officials and Members of the National Assembly cannot become directors.

Advances to the State, Municipalities and other similar public bodies are prohibited except against gold or stable foreign currencies, and discounts and loans of a commercial character are strictly regulated as provided in the report of the Financial Committee and the Delegation of the League.

As the Bank has the exclusive right to issue bank notes, inflation through further issues of unsecured bank notes by way of loans to the Government or otherwise automatically ceases when the new Bank commences business.

Pending the opening of the new Bank, inflation of the note issue has been limited to the issue of notes in payment of outstanding arrears due by the Government, and this amount has not exceeded the average of 30 milliards a week agreed upon with the Delegation.

IV. Loan Negotiations.

The Hungarian Government has appointed a delegation to conduct the negotiations for the Reconstruction Loan consisting of M. J. Teleszky (former Minister o Finance) and Mr. P. Bark, who took an active part in the negotiation of the Austrian Loan. The Delegation has visited London, Paris, Rome and Switzerland, and the negotiations are now (May 31st) being actively carried on.

V. Assigned Accounts and Treasury Operations.

A. *Pledged Revenues.*
The gross receipts of the Customs, the tobacco monopoly, the sugar tax, and the net receipts of the Salt Monopoly are pledged to secure the Reconstruction Loan and the short-term advances made in anticipation of it.

Receipts from these sources have been deposited in a special account under my control, which was opened April 25th, several days before my arrival in Budapest.

The receipts from these accounts from April 25th to May 31st inclusive were as follows:

	Millions of paper crowns		
	April 25-30	*May* 1-31	Total
Customs	752	24,410	25,162
Tobacco Monopoly	2,666	66,777	69,443
Sugar tax	16,526	9,551	26,077
Salt Monopoly	—	3,122	3,122
	19,944	103,860	123,804

Of this amount I have released, for purposes explained under the heading "Treasury Operations in May", 96 milliard paper crowns, leaving on hand June 1st 27,804 million paper crowns. I propose to retain during the month of June an amount sufficient to cover the interest on the loan in Swiss francs obtained from the Hungarian banks and industry which is due on June 30th; at the present rate of exchange this will be from 8 to 9 milliard paper crowns.

B. *Internal Banking and Industrial Loan.*
An advance of 20 million Swiss francs was negotiated in the month of April with the Hungarian Banks and certain industries, of which amount 19,110,158.65 francs have been paid in up to May 31st. Prior to my arrival, 3,287,671 francs had been drawn by the Treasury to cover deficits, and the remaining proceeds of this

account were put under my control May 8th. During the month of May I released 5,685,213.60 Swiss francs, leaving a balance on June 1st of 10,137,274.05 francs.

C. *Forced Loan.*
For the purpose for covering in part the Budget deficit to June 30th, the Hungarian Government has made a compulsory internal loan payable in paper crowns on the basis of the rate of exchange of the Sparkrone.

Up to June 1st, the total amount collected has been 378,488,777,555 paper crowns of which 368,300,000,000 have been used to cover in part the deficit in current expenses, leaving on June 1st a balance of 10,188,177,555 paper crowns.

Another instalment of this loan is payable June 4th and is expected to produce 100 milliards of paper crowns, which will be applied to cover the deficit in current expenses.

D. *Treasury Estimates for May and June.*
The Reconstruction Plan provides for monthly budgets with receipts and expenses estimated in detail under certain heads specified in the Budget Law. The method of preparing these monthly budgets for the approval of the Commissioner-General and of furnishing closed accounts is now being discussed with the Treasury. It is of the utmost importance that preliminary budgets should not be furnished at the last possible moment but should be submitted to the Commissioner-General a sufficient length of time in advance to permit careful examination of their details; that closed accounts for past months should be submitted as soon as possible after the close of each month in order to be of value; and that accurate statements of debts contracted and remaining unpaid should be furnished monthly, and the sources of the plan depends in no small degree upon establishing a practice which will insure these results. The details of the plan for payment of all receipts into and all expenditures from the central treasury are also under the discussion and the next report will set out the arrangements for effecting these reforms which are essential to a proper control of the budget and an exact knowledge of the Treasury position from month to month.

The methods which it is proposed to put into effect are not those followed by the Hungarian Treasury in the past, and consequently it has not been possible to prepare the estimates for May and June in this manner. The Government has, however, submitted estimates of its current receipts and current expenses for May and June.

To the deficit shown by these estimates must be added the amount necessary to pay arrears of indebtedness and the debts arising from taking over the *Devisenzentrale* by the new National Bank, and the total so ascertained must be met within the limits of the provisions made in the plan to cover the deficit to the end of the current fiscal year, June 30th, 1924, in order that the budget for the approaching fiscal year (July 1st, 1924, to June 30th, 1925) may not be burdened by having to make provision for payments for pre-existing debts.

The estimates of current receipts and expenses for May and June appear in Appendix I.

	Milliards of paper crowns
Expenses are estimated at	1,335
Receipts are estimated at	772
Deficit	563

The receipts estimated from the Tobacco and Salt Monopoly are not receipts and there have been deducted from the expenses incidental receipts of certain departments and also the railway traffic tax.

The estimates for the position of the Treasury from May 1st to the end of the fiscal year on June 30th are as follows:

Requirements	*Milliards of paper crowns*
(a) Deficit in current expenses	563
(b) Payment arrears of debt	766
(c) Debts incurred on abolition *Devisenzentrale*	500
(d) Repayment of advance obtained from the Banks and Industry (20 million Swiss francs at 16,000)	320
(e) Bills non-acceptable by the new bank	170
	2,319
Cover	
(a) Balance of Swiss franc advance (16.7 million at 16,000)	267
(b) Balance available from forced loan, including June payments	200
(c) Balance from State debt to Note Institute (inflation). (Total limited to 110 million gold crowns. Annex 4: Report of Delegation)	1,036
(d) 60 million gold crowns from Reconstruction Loan available for deficit to June 30th, 1924, as reported by the Delegation (1-18,000)	1,080
Total	2,583
Leaving a balance of	264

Provision must be made from this balance for the interest due June 30th on the banking and industrial loan and interest on any other advances received during June.

E. *Treasury Operations.*

During May the Treasury has furnished at the beginning of each week estimates of its requirements and, at the close of the week, statements of the payments actually made, so that it has been possible to follow closely the cash operations of the Treasury.

During the first two weeks of May, the Treasury was able to meet its deficit by recourse to the proceeds of the forced loan without asking for releases from the assigned revenues. For the third week, the balance available from the forced loan was insufficient, and the Commissioner-General released from the assigned revenues 67 milliards of paper crowns. In the fourth week, it was necessary to release 29 milliards from the assigned revenues and 90 milliards of paper crowns from the advance by the Banks and Industry.

The funds released were applied solely to cover the deficit in current expenses. Arrears of debt paid during May were provided for by inflation amounting to 110 milliards of paper crowns, the total amount of which has been kept within the limits fixed by agreement between the Government and the Delegation (Report of Delegation, paragraph 11 and Annex 4.)

The May operations with respect to current expense are as follows:

	Milliards of paper crowns	
Treasury requirements		373.5
Cover		
a) Brought forward from April 30th	20.3	
(b) Returns from Caisse d'Etat	106.9	
(c) Drawn from assigned revenues	96	
(d) Drawn from forced loan	87	
(e) Drawn from Swiss franc advance	90	400.2
Leaving balance of June 1st		26.7

On June 1st the balance available in the assigned revenue account was 27,804 millions of paper crowns and in the Swiss franc account obtained through the banking and industrial loan was 10,137,274.05 Swiss francs.

VI. Measures of Reform.

1. *Commerce.*

The Financial Committee of the Council recommended the abolition of the existing prohibitions on exports and advised a speedy reduction of the restrictions and prohibitions upon imports.

A. *Exports.*

Most of the restrictions upon export have been abolished since the departure of the Delegation from Budapest. Among the more important products the export of which is no longer prohibited are wheat, rye, hay, barley, flax, hemp, wool, sugar beets (dry), meat, cattle (when exported by rail or boat), butter, cheese and maize (the latter as from June 3rd). Wheat and rye are two of the chief exports of Hungary, and the prohibition of their export was abolished on May 18th. Their export is, however, subject to the payment of an export tax of 5%, which is imposed in order that the Hungarian flour mills, which are obliged to pay manufacturing and turnover taxes on the wheat and rye purchased by them, may not be handicapped in competition with foreign flour mills. The export of certain articles is still prohibited, such as sugar (which may be exported under licence) salt and tobacco (which are the subjects of a State monopoly) and beans (the free exportation of which is to be allowed within a few months), raw hides and various articles of minor importance. The export situation has been much improved by these measures.

B. *Imports.*

The importation of articles of luxury, most textile products and a great number of manufactured articles is still prohibited except under licence, which is granted only for limited quantities, and this is one of the causes of the high prices now prevailing for such articles in Hungary.

C. *Customs Tariffs.*

A new tariff bill has been introduced in Parliament and is now under discussion. The draft law provides generally for the imposition of high maximum duties and is designed to afford protection to Hungarian industries. It is understood that when this law becomes effective, most, if not all, of the restrictions on imports will be removed. The law contains provisions under which it will be possible to negotiate reciprocal commercial treaties, and after its passage the Government intends to commence definite negotiations for the conclusion of such treaties with various countries. In certain cases, active negotiations are already in progress.

Although this law should be an improvement on the existing condition of prohibitions and licences, it cannot in itself be said to follow the suggestions made by the Financial Committee toward creating a greater export trade.

1. *State Employees.*

The Government statistics show the number of permanent State officials as 140,955, excluding the Army. Of this number 51,658 constitute the personnel of the various State commercial enterprises. In addition to the Permanent State officials there are some 50,000 workmen employed by the State, and approximately 23,000 permanent officials in the comitats, communes and municipalities, not including those employed in commercial enterprises carried on by these communities.

Some progress has already been made with plans for reducing the number of State employees. The Food Ministry is being discontinued and 240 of its staff will have left the Government's service by August 31st.

The Refugees Office, the Office of the Coal Commissioner, the Office for the Regulation of Prices and several small departments are being discontinued, and 270 employees will be dismissed.

Before July 1st of this year, the Budapest Police are to be cut down by 2,300 dismissals.

A comprehensive plan is under preparation by the Government to bring the total number of dismissals up to 15,000 by June 30th, 1926, as recommended by the Financial Committee, and it is expected that the plan will be advanced far enough to permit notices of dismissal under it to be given during June.

VII. Financial.

A. *General Conditions.*

The circumstances of the moment at which the reconstruction programme in Hungary was first put into operation were, from the purely financial point of view, somewhat unfavourable. A crisis of which it was difficult to estimate the probable proportions, was rapidly developing in Vienna, and its reactions were certain to be felt in Budapest. By popular opinion the financial difficulties of Vienna were attributed largely to bear speculation in French francs, and there can be little doubt that although other, and perhaps more deep-seated, influences were at work, this was at least an important contributory cause. Hungary had not been to any serious extent committed to such speculations, but the financial links between Austria and Hungary are still strong, and the market in Budapest was exposed, during the month of May, to certain risks. As happens on every such occasions, rumour far outstripped the event, and a feeling of distrust was created which, precisely because it rested upon a foundation of mere conjecture, could not easily be dissipated. It became known that not only in Vienna but also in Holland and Germany important exchange losses had been suffered; and when the Allgemeine Depositenbank (of Vienna) closed its doors, the public and the press were in a mood to question the security of other institutions of still higher standing. Moreover, this shock of confidence was delivered at a time when the Bourse in Budapest had already endured a prolonged period of depression, and before any convincing proof could be given that the prospects of Hungary had really been improved by the launching of the reconstruction scheme. The natural consequence in a country which since the war has become accustomed to feel disillusioned was that the difficulties of the moment overshadowed everything else in the public estimation, and faith in the prospects of the reconstruction programme could only be won at the price of concrete evidence which it was not possible to furnish immediately.

Financial anxieties were further aggravated by the economic situation. Commodity prices continued in many cases to rise, and substantial increases (of from 30 to 50%) in railway freights and fares had to be decreed towards the middle of the month. The proposed new tariff had given rise to a vigorous controversy in which it was freely contended that further advances in the cost of living would inevitably follow. Even the first steps taken to restore economic freedom appeared to bring additional burdens rather than relief. For example, the withdrawal of the prohibition against the export of wheat and rye was immediately followed by a sharp advance of grain prices, and the proposal gradually to remove restrictions upon rent bore heavily on the professional and salaried classes. At this time, too, the prevailing discontent among Government employees had come to a head, and a strike which had broken out among the coal miners was lasting longer than had been generally expected.

For these and similar reasons the mentality of the country was not altogether favourable at the outset. It may be the financial disturbances originating from Vienna will continue for a while to embarrass Budapest. But the position of Hungary is, as these temporary troubles have themselves helped to demonstrate, financially sound; and there can be little doubt that when experience has shown that the scheme of reconstruction is proceeding without hindrance, there will be a rapid return of confidence, which will itself contribute further to financial security.

B. *Exchange.*

From the beginning of March until the Easter holidays (April 22nd) the rate of exchange for Hungarian crowns had been relatively stable. But after Easter, when trouble was developing on the Viennese Bourse, the market in Budapest resisted the downward tendency and maintained for arbitrage securities a consistently higher level of prices than that which prevailed at the same time in Vienna. The immediate consequence was that these securities were dumped in considerable quantities on Budapest, and it is to this movement of securities that the first lapse of exchange may be attributed. By the end of April, the rate of Hungarian crowns, which had been about 80 at the beginning of the month in terms of Swiss francs, had already fallen to 73, a fall of approximately 10%.

In the first week of May there was a further fall of 10%, and by the middle of the month the quotation given out from Zurich had been as low as 57 ½ , a fall of almost 30% since the middle of April. It became necessary, very soon after the régime of control had been instituted, to determine what attitude should be adopted towards this persistent decline in the exchange value of Hungarian currency.

On the one hand it was apparent that the whole reconstruction scheme depends, at the last resort, upon a successful stabilisation of the currency. The necessary conditions of such a stabilisation had been provided by setting a definite limit to inflation and covering, with foreign assistance, the deficit of the State Budget during the transitional period. But in the meantime, inflation, though limited, was still proceeding; and foreign assistance, though promised, had not yet been secured. If in this period of uncertainty the Hungarian crown were to lose a great part of its value in exchange, the consequence would certainly be serious, for the whole economic life of the country adapts itself with great rapidity to a new standard of currency values, with the result that, even when depreciation is due to temporary influences or is not economically justified at all, its reactions are immediate and so far-reaching that lost ground is difficult to recover.

On the other hand, it is one of the cardinal principles of reconstruction that economic forces must be left free to produce a natural stability, and that attempts (which are usually unsuccessful and expensive) to force an artificial equilibrium must be abandoned. Exchange depreciation had therefore to be allowed to run its course provided that it resulted from conditions which, in a free market, would have produced a genuine excess of supply over demand for Hungarian currency. Moreover, it was of the highest importance that the new National Bank should not have to take over a currency which depended for stability upon artificial supports that could not long be maintained.

The rate for dollars in the free market (Schleichhandel) in Budapest rose gradually from 89 ½ on May 5th to about 93 on the 22nd, and from that time onwards it advanced more sharply, reaching 100 before the end of the month. This rate, like that of the Sparkrone, is intimately affected by the course of security prices on the Bourses of Vienna and Budapest.

C. *The Sparkrone.*

The Sparkrone is a money of account introduced towards the end of February 1924. Its value in paper crowns is calculated daily by way of three component elements, of which two represent the value of exchange and notes in Vienna, and the third is based upon the prices of arbitrage securities in the two centres. The resultant is intended to represent a stable gold value. From about the Middle of May, the rate for Sparkronen was rising steeply as a direct consequence of the relation between security prices in Vienna and Budapest. This contributed appreciably to the general unsettlement of opinion with regard to the future prospects of the Hungarian crown. With the opening of the National Bank the Sparkrone will come to an end and all Sparkronen accounts will be liquidated in paper crowns.

D. *Future Exchange Policy.*

The policy to be pursued by the National Bank in regard to exchange has been the subject of discussions between the Commissioner-General and the Governor of the Bank. The Devisenzentrale will cease to exist when the National Bank opens its doors. But the process of releasing the exchange market from control will necessarily be gradual, and the successive steps of this process are now being elaborated in consultation with the Control Commission. The recommendation of the Financial Committee that the separate official rate of exchange should be abolished as soon as possible has been already carried out. The rate at which the Devisenzentrale pays in paper crowns for foreign currency corresponds with the effective market rate of the day.

VIII. General Observations.

Future reports will contain statistical tables showing the progress of reconstruction, but so much time has been spent during the first month in organization of the control and in becoming acquainted generally with the economic, financial and administrative conditions that it has not been possible to prepare statistical tables for the first report. Generally speaking, the conditions appear fundamentally sound. The prospects are good for a harvest which should be at least an average one and there should be an exportable surplus. The trade balance for the first three months of the calendar year, in which there is always an adverse balance, shows great improvement. In 1923 the excess of imports over exports for the first three months was 69.9 millions of gold crowns, while for the same period in 1924 this adverse balance has been reduced to 25.8 millions of gold crowns.

There is no reason apparent why the execution of the Reconstruction plan should not produce the expected results and instil in the Hungarian people that spirit of confidence and hope for the future which is one of the essential features of the plan.

Appendix I.

Treasury Estimates for May and June 1924. (1 gold crown = 18,000 paper crowns) (Millions)

	Gross expenditure	Net expenditure		1st stage of the reform scheme
		paper crowns	gold crowns	2/12 gold crowns
Service of the Loan	63,953.0	57,953.0	3.22	1.4
Changes resulting from the Treaty	51,467.7	51,267.7	2.84	1.2
Army Staff	39,222.0	39,222.0	2.17	1.5
Army Other Expenditure	60,326.0	60,226.0	3.34	7.2
Interior Staff	96,289.8	96,289.8	5.34	2.4
Interior Other Expenditure	25,341.6	24,082.0	1.33	1.3
Finances Staff	52,164.6	52,164.6	2.9	2.0
Finances Other Expenditure	90,976.8	52,364.1	2.9	1.6
Education Staff	60,312.4	60,312.4	3.35	1.9
Education Other Expenditure	53,218.1	51,004.4	2.83	1.3
Other Administration Staff	80,251.0	80,251.0	4.45	3.3
Other Administration Other Expenditure	160,995.5	145,480.6	8.07	3.2
Allowances in kind	163,891.0	163,891.0	9.1	6.8
Subsidies to independent administrations	35,876.0	35,876.0	2	2.5
Pensions	113,544.0	113,544.0	6.33	5.7
Investments	—	—	—	2.7
Deduct:	1,153,820.5			
Revenue not derived from taxation 35,705.5				
Working expenses of Salt and Tobacco Monopolies 34,196.4				
	69,901.9			
Net expenditure		1,083,918.6	60.2	46.0
Receipts from tax on railway traffic		74,000.0	4.1	2.1
		1,009,918.6	56.1	43.9
Deficit on State undertakings		326,001.4	18.1	12.7
		1,335,920.0	74.2	56.6
Receipts		772,910.1	42.9	27.3
Deficit		563,009.9	31.3	29.3

	Gross receipts	Net receipts		1st stage of the reform scheme
		paper crowns	gold crowns	2/12 gold crowns
Direct taxes	—	80,000.0	4.44	5.7
Tax on business turnover	—	320,000.0	17.77	10.9
Duties		80,000.0	4.44	1.3
Commodity taxes	—	60,000.0	3.33	3.8
Customs	—	100,000.0	5.55	1.7
Saccharine monopoly and lottery	—	506.5	0.02	0.08
Salt	26,600.0	5,087.0	0.28	0.9
Tobacco	140,000.0	127,316.6	7.07	3.0
Total		772,910.1	42.90	27.3

Appendix II.

Statistics

Index of the cost of living:
(Average for 1913-14 = 1)

April 30th, 1924:	Foodstuffs	17,612
	Clothing	17,870
	Lodging	576
	Light and fuel	16,820
	Miscellaneous expenses	15,840
	Average index	13,395
	Average index excluding lodging	17,223

Cost of living calculated on a gold basis:
(Average for 1913-14 = 1)

April 30th, 1924:	Foodstuffs	1.06
	Clothing	1.02
	Lodging	0.03
	Light and fuel	0.96
	Miscellaneous expenses	0.91
	Average index	0.76
	Average index excluding lodging	0.98

(June 30th, 1914 = 1)

Foreign trade (millions of gold crowns):

	Imports	*Exports*	*Excess of imports over exports*
January 1924	37.6	32.1	5.5
February 1924	43.9	30.7	13.2
March 1924	51.3	44.2	7.1
Total	132.8	107.0	25.8

Stock exchange index (calculated on the basis of the value of the 10 most important securities quoted on the Stock Exchange (gold values):

1914 = 100

End of May 1924 = 24.4

Savings deposited in the Post Office Saving Bank:
March 31st, 1924 2,834 millions (paper crowns)

Number of emigrants:
March 1924 212

Wholesale prices of cereal:

(1913 = 1)		Index No.
April 30th, 1924:	Wheat	14,664
	Rye	15,907
	Barley	17,155
	Oats	15,156
	Maize	15,858
Combined index number of wholesale prices of cereals:		15,655

Appendix 6.

Jeremiah Smith, Jr.'s Twenty-fifth (Final) Report by the Commissioner-General of the League of Nations for Hungary (May 1st – June 30th, 1926).

Source: League of Nations, *The Financial Reconstruction of Hungary*, 164-187.

To the Council of the League of Nations:

I have the honour to submit to the Council of the League of Nations my Twenty-fifth and final Report. Owing to my attendance at the meeting of the Council at Geneva during the period when the monthly report for May ordinarily would have been prepared, this report covers the months of both May and June 1926.

I. Termination of Budget Control and General Supervision.

The fiscal year of the Hungarian Government ended on June 30th, and provisional accounts show a budget surplus for the year of approximately 62 million gold crowns. Closed accounts may be expected to show a somewhat larger surplus.

Since the reconstruction plan came into operation on May 1st, 1924, the Hungarian Government has completed two full financial years, each with a substantial budget surplus. As this result had long been foreseen, the Council of the League of Nations, at this meeting held in Geneva on June 10th, after hearing the report of the Financial Committee of the Council, declared "that, the financial stability of Hungary being assured, the functions of the Commissioner-General shall be brought to an end on June 30th, 1926, in pursuance of para. 10 of Article VI of Protocol II."

As Article VI of Protocol II established the control of the budget and the general supervision of the execution of the reconstruction programme by a Commissioner-General, the termination of his duties puts an end to any such control and supervision, and Hungary now assumes full responsibility for the management of its own finances. While the level of the budget is somewhat higher than the contemplated in the original programme of reconstruction, there seems no substantial reason to doubt that it can be maintained permanently at the present level. Whether it is so maintained or not is merely a question of capable administration, and depends, under ordinary circumstances, upon two factors. One of these is the continuance of a sound and conservative policy by the National Bank in the maintenance of the currency; the other is reasonably prudent management of the budget.

The management of the Hungarian National Bank has been sound and prudent; it has ample reserves of foreign exchange, and there is every reason to believe that the present policy will be continued.

Undoubtedly great pressure will be brought to bear upon the Government to increase the level of expenditure for all sorts of purposes, but strong reasons of a practical nature exist which should prevent the budget from again becoming unbalanced. In case a deficit should be created through excessive expenditure, recourse cannot well be had to foreign borrowing to cover this deficit, for the practical reason that the Peace Treaty prevents Hungary from giving security for any foreign loan without the consent of the Reparation Commission, which is not likely to be obtained for such purpose, and, without security, foreign loans would be difficult, if not impossible, to obtain: recourse can no longer be had to inflation, because the National Bank has the sole monopoly of note issue, is divorced from Government control, and is forbidden by its Statutes to lend money to the Government except against adequate security. Under existing conditions, it would be difficult, if not impossible, to issue a domestic loan (which must rank after reparations as a charge on the assets of the Hungarian State) for the purpose of raising funds to cover a budget deficit. Possibly Treasury bills might be issued to local financial institutions, but this resource is extremely limited in extent. Therefore, if the budget should again become unbalanced, the only recourse open to the Government is to raise taxes, and the unpopularity of such a measure should prove as strong practical deterrent from engaging in unwise and excessive expenditure. While the control of the budget and the general supervision of the execution of the reconstruction plan are terminated by the discharge of the Commissioner-General, two questions still remained to be dealt with, the details of which were settled by the decision of the Council. One of these questions is the management of the revenues assigned as security for the Reconstruction Loan, which is governed by the terms of the original Protocol; the other question is not governed by the Protocol and concerns the disposition of the unexpended balance of the Reconstruction Loan. In these two cases the Council adopted the following procedure, which is the same as that previously established in the case of Austria:

(a) Under the terms of Protocol II (Art. XI, 1), the Trustees of the Reconstruction Loan succeed of the duties of the Commissioner-General in the control of the special account of the revenues pledged for the security of the Reconstruction Loan, and, after retaining the amounts necessary to meet the service of the Loan, are to transfer the balance to the Hungarian Government.

(b) The Reconstruction Loan issued in 1924 produced a net amount of approximately 253 million gold crowns, which was to be used for the purpose of meeting budget deficits during the period of two and a-half years, which it was contemplated might be necessary to balance the budget. About 70 million gold crowns was used for this purpose for the budget year ending June 30th, 1924, and none of the Reconstruction Loan has been used for a similar purpose since that date. From time to time, the expenditure of 100 million gold crowns additional from the Reconstruction Loan has been authorised by the Council of the League of Nations, on the recommendation of the Financial Committee, for capital investments by the Hungarian Government, of which 50 million gold crowns was to be spent during the budget year ended June 30th, 1926, and 50 million gold crowns was authorised in December 1925 for the budget year July 1st, 1926 - June 30th, 1927. The balance remaining – approximately 81 million gold crowns – is to be retained in liquid form in a separate account managed by a person to be appointed by the Financial Committee, except in so far as it is released for expenditure within the budget for such purposes as the Council, on the recommendation of the Financial Committee, may from time to time approve, and for this purpose the Financial Committee has appointed M. ter Meulen, who will have the assistance of an agent residing at Budapest. Inasmuch as the capital investment programme of the Hungarian Government has been fully provided for up to July 1st, 1927, it was deemed unnecessary at this stage to authorise any releases beyond that date.

On making his final report, the Commissioner-General takes this occasion to express his thanks to the Council of the League and its competent organisations, and especially the Financial Committee, for the support, advice and assistance which he has constantly received from them, and, further, to express his gratitude to the Hungarian Government and the Hungarian people for the uniform kindness and courtesy with which he has been treated by all with whom he has come in contact. Without the co-operation of both the government and the people, it would have been impossible to make any satisfactory progress with the reconstruction plan, and this has been completely given at every stage of the work.

II. Objects and Results of the Reconstruction Plan.

The causes which made it necessary for Hungary to ask the League of Nations for assistance in 1923 have been admirably stated in the preface to the documents relating to the reconstruction plan, which were issued by the League of Nations in April 1924. Briefly summarised, they are as follows:

Disorganisation caused by war and consequent loss of territory, political difficulties, internal and external, which followed the Armistice, the undetermined liability for reparations, and the difficulty of reorganising a political and commercial establishment designed for a much larger country presented obstacles which could not be overcome. The budget became unbalanced, current expense was met from note inflation, which produced a continually increasing depreciation of the currency, and the only means of arresting it became a foreign loan to meet the budget deficit during the period necessary for financial reorganisation. The League entrusted the preparation of a suitable plan to its Financial Committee. The entire success of this experiment depended upon the preparation of the plan, and too much praise cannot be given to the Financial Committee of the League for the ability shown in this task. The Committee had the wisdom and courage to prepare a plan based upon sound financial principles which had been tested under normal conditions. Many people doubted the efficacity of such a plan under the abnormal conditions which prevailed at that time in Hungary, but the Committee rejected many of the theories which were then being put forward as necessary to correct abnormal conditions and preferred to rely upon principles which had stood the test of time. The result has vindicated the judgment of the Committee.

The principal features of the plan were:

(1) Definite settlement of the reparation liability for 20 years, which was obtained through a decision of the Reparation Commission, fixing annual payments on account of reparations until 1944, at an average rate of 10 million gold crowns a year.

(2) The stoppage of inflation through the creation of a central bank of issue, with the exclusive privilege of issuing banknotes, divorced from political control and forbidden to loan money to the State or any of its subdivisions without adequate security. The ultimate adoption of the free exchange of notes for gold is contemplated by this plan.

(3) The issue of an international loan, secured on some of the most productive revenues of the State, for the purpose of covering budget deficits until June 30th, 1926, when it was expected that the budget would be in a state of permanent equilibrium.

(4) The preparation of a budget covering the period up to June 30th, 1926, and the appointment of a Commissioner-General to supervise the execution of the whole programme and to control the expenditure of the proceeds of the Loan as well as the revenues pledged to secure the service of the Loan, with power to regulate expenditure and revenue in case the Government should fall behind the reconstruction programme.

(5) The adoption of a centralised system of Treasury receipts and disbursements, which would give exact knowledge of the cash position of the Treasury at all times.

The execution of the plan has proved even more successful than anticipated. As was expected, there was a large deficit for the financial year ending June 30th, 1924, which was met from the proceeds of the Reconstruction Loan. Since July 1st, 1924, the budget has been in a state of equilibrium, and it has been unnecessary to expend any of the proceeds of the Reconstruction Loan for budgetary deficits. This surprising result is not due to reductions in expenditure – for none was contemplated by the plan – but to unexpected increases in the estimated revenue of the State over the conservative estimates of the plan due to the stabilisation of the currency and the increased confidence which followed it. The currency has been stable since the National Bank was opened on June 24th, 1924, and the Bank has ample reserves for the maintenance of the currency.

It should not be forgotten that the Financial Committee of the League, in its original report, pointed out that the problem which confronted Hungary was a double one: financial and budgetary on the one hand and economic on the other. It further pointed out that the responsibility of the League should be expressly limited to remedying the budgetary and financial position. "The necessary economic adaptation must be effected by Hungary itself; the essential contribution (of the League) is to give a stable basis on which this adaptation can take place." The League has now done all that it undertook to do – *i. e.*, to create a sound budgetary and financial position, which is necessary to establish a firm foundation for the future upon which the complete economic recovery of Hungary can take place. Economic conditions have slowly and steadily improved since the plan became effective, and if the present position is maintained by Hungary itself, the economic conditions should continue to improve until they reach at least the normal pre-war conditions.

III. Statement of the Reconstruction Loan.

The following table gives a statement of the Reconstruction Loan on June 30th, 1926:

Receipts	Gold Crowns
Net proceeds of loan (value June 26th, 1924)	253,803,555.13
Net exchange profits to June 30th, 1926	13,080,656.50
	266,884,211.63
Expenditure	Gold Crowns
Expenses of issue	524,583.95
Budget deficits and back debts to June 30th, 10924	69,551,482.07
Special reserve (General Bond, Clause XI)	15,618,753.57
Capital investments 1925-26 (approved by Council of League, June and December 1925)	50,000,000.00
Advances for silver purchases and Mint expenses (to be refunded)	11,729,546.90
Total expenditure	147,424,366.49
Balance	119,459,845.14
	266,884,211.63

Of the balance shown in this statement, an expenditure of 50 million gold crowns was authorised by the League in December 1925 for capital expenditure during the budget year 1926-27, leaving a balance available after this expenditure of 69,459,845.14 gold crowns. To this balance must be added the amount of the advances to the Hungarian Government for purchases of silver for the new coinage and minting expenses appearing in the above table, as this amount will be refunded to the Loan Account, making a total unappropriated balance ultimately available of 81,189,392.04 gold crowns.

As pointed out above under Section I, the balance of the Loan is to be managed, as in the case of Austria, in accordance with the decisions taken by the Council of the League of Nations at Geneva on June 12th.

Annex II contains a full statement of the balance of the Loan available on June 30th, 1926, in different currencies and gives the places where it is on deposit.

IV. Revenues and Treasury Operations.

A. *Pledged Revenues.*

May. – The receipts during May from the revenues pledged as security for the Reconstruction Loan were as follows, the receipts for the preceding month and for May 1925 being given for purposes of comparison:

	April 1926	May 1926	May 1925
		Millions of paper crowns	
Customs	125,077	119,417	98,644
Tobacco Monopoly	133,142	138,103	117,321
Sugar Tax	28,987	31,678	26,059
Salt Monopoly	11,504	9,571	8,953
	298,712	298,771	250,978

Converted into gold crowns at the fixed rate of 14,500 used in the budget, the receipts for May amount to 20.6 million gold crowns – the same as those for the month of April and approximately 17 per cent higher than those for May 1925. In addition to the amounts given above, the equivalent of 10,918 gold crowns has been received during May in payment of Customs dues.

June. – The receipts during June from the pledged revenues were as follows, May receipts and those for June 1925 being given for purposes of comparison:

	May 1926	June 1926	June 1925
		Millions of paper crowns	
Customs	119,417	114,163	83,537
Tobacco Monopoly	138,103	131,180	116,715
Sugar Tax	31,678	31,335	40,240
Salt Monopoly	9,571	12,903	10,087
	298,771	289,583	250,579

Converted into gold crowns at the fixed rate of 14,500, the June receipts for May amount to 19.9 million gold crowns, as compared with 20.6 million gold crowns for May and 17.3 million gold crowns for June 1925. Further, the equivalent of 14,426 gold crowns has been received in June in discharge of Customs dues.

Total Pledged Revenues, Fiscal Year 1925-26. – The provisional results show that the total receipts from the revenues pledged to secure the Reconstruction Loan during the fiscal year July 1st, 1925 – June 30th, 1926, have amounted to 258 million gold crowns.

The annual service charge of the Reconstruction Loan is slightly under 33 million gold crowns, and the annual receipts, which appear to be on a substantially permanent basis, are therefore approximately eight times the annual service charge.

B. *Total May Revenues.*

Gros revenues during May were as follows, the receipts for May 1925 being given for purposes of comparison:

	May 1926	May 1925	Difference
		Milliards of paper crowns	
Pledged revenues	298.7	250.9	+ 47.8
Other revenues	643.5	548.2	+ 95.3
	942.2	799.1	+ 143.1

Converted into gold crowns at the budgetary rate of 14,500, the gross receipts for May amount to 64.9 million gold crowns, against 55.1 million gold crowns for May 1925 – an increase of approximately 17.5 per cent.

The May estimates contemplated gross receipts of 57.8 million gold crowns and a surplus of 3.4 million gold crowns, but receipts were considerably larger than the estimates, and the actual surplus for May is 10.5 million gold crowns.

C. *June Budget.*

The budget for June appears in Annex I and estimates:

	Gold crowns
Gross expenditure	50,038,170
Gross revenue	50,111,912
Surplus	73,742

The following tale gives a comparison of the June estimates with the monthly average of the Reconstruction Budget:

	June Budget	Reconstruction Plan Gold crowns	Difference
Expenses (net)	39,529,355	34,125,000	+ 5,404,355
Receipts (net)	39,603,097	30,825,000	+ 8,778,097
Surplus	73,742	—	3,373,742
Deficit	—	3,300,000	—

D. *Total June Revenues.*

Gross revenues during June were as follows, receipts for June 1925 being given for purposes of comparison:

Pledged revenues	289.5	250.5	+ 39.0
Other revenues	398.3	393.9	+ 4.4
	687.8	644.4	+ 43.4

Converted into gold crowns at the fixed rate of 14,500, gross receipts for June amount to 47.4 million gold crowns, as against 44.4 million gold crowns, at the same rate, in June 1925. The June budget estimated a surplus of 73,742 gold crowns. As the June receipts, however, are 2.6 million gold crowns less than the estimated receipts, the month of June shows a deficit of 2.5 million gold crowns.

E. *Revenue for Entire Fiscal Year.*

The fiscal year ends on June 30th, and provisional accounts for the entire fiscal year 1925-26 are available, which show for the whole year a surplus of approximately

62 million gold crowns, after deducting from the actual receipts amounts which have been advanced or expended for various purposes during the year from this surplus with the approval of the Commissioner-General. Closed accounts should show a larger surplus than that given by the provisional accounts, as was the case last year.

These results are very encouraging, especially in view of the fact that very substantial reductions in taxation have been made during the course of this year, the principal among which are: reduction of the turnover tax from 3 to 2 per cent; reduction of the sugar tax by 22 per cent; and complete abolition of the participation of the State in house rents.

F. *Capital Expenditure*, 1926-27.

At the meeting of the Financial Committee of the Council of the League of Nations held December 1925, authority was granted for the expenditure of 50 million gold crowns by the Hungarian Government on capital investments for the budget year July 1st, 1926 – June 30th, 1927, the programme for expenditure to be approved by the Commissioner-General (see Twentieth Report, page 1). During May, the following programme was submitted to the Commissioner-General and has been approved by him.

	Million gold crowns
1. Continuation of construction of the commercial and industrial harbour of Budapest	4.9
2. Loan to drainage societies	10.0
3. Construction of public roads and bridges	9.0
4. Completion of the underground telephone cable to Vienna	6.6
5. Investments of the Posts and Telegraphs	5.8
6. Loans to persons receiving building plots under the Land Reform Law	5.0
7. Investments of the State Railways	3.1
8. Loans to promote building	3.0
9. Loans to communes for the purchase of breeding animals	2.0
10. Promotion of dairy co-operatives	0.6
	50.0

Many of the objects contained in this programme have been commented upon in previous reports under the heading of capital expenditure, and further comment on them is unnecessary at the present time.

V. Financial Conditions.

A. *National Bank.*

The Hungarian National Bank was one of the most important elements in the reconstruction plan, the success of which depended in no slight degree on the manner in which the Bank carried out its very important duty of maintaining the stability of the currency. It is now two years since the Bank opened its doors, and its position to-day is much stronger than anyone then expected. Commencing with limited resources, but under wise and prudent management, ample reserves have been accumulated sufficient to meet any contingency which can reasonably be foreseen. The currency has been established on a sound basis, and there is no reason to doubt that it can and will be maintained on this basis, while the Bank has been able to reduce its discount rate from 12 ½ to 7 per cent.

Under the statutes of the National Bank, the duties of the foreign Adviser – H. A. Siepmann, Esq. – terminate on the same day as those of the Commissioner-General, who takes this opportunity to express his appreciation of the ability and energy of which the Adviser has shown in the performance of his duties, which qualities have contributed in no small degree to the establishment of the Bank upon a sound basis.

As this is the final report upon the period governed by the reconstruction plan, it may not be out of place to review some of the more important events which have occurred during the last few months in connection with the position of the Bank.

The changes which have taken place in the position of the National Bank, as shown by the weekly returns, are chiefly due to the concentration of Government balances at the Bank. This concentration was planned to take place by stages and has now been completed without disturbance. It has involved some expansion of the discount portfolio of the National Bank, to compensate for the withdrawal of monies hitherto placed at the disposal of the market through the Geldinstitutszentrale. It also seems to have accentuated the tendency of temporary requirements to be concentrated at the end of the month, so the comparison of the figures in the Bank return from week to week is scarcely significant.

The preparations for the issue of the new currency are now well advanced, an there s no reason to think that there will be difficulty in carrying out the full programme, under which banknotes and coin should be ready for issue on January 1st, 1927, when the *Pengő* becomes the obligatory unit of account in

Hungary. The notes are being prepared and printed in the establishment which the National Bank purchased last year. The paper is being manufactured in Hungary, and deliveries to the National Bank are now in progress. The greater part of the silver required for the first issue of coin has already bought on a falling market at very satisfactory prices. In the transitional period before coins are issued to the public a certain proportion of the existing circulation of notes – increasing gradually to perhaps 50 per cent by the end of the year – will be over-stamped, so as to familiarise the public with the new currency values. Postage stamps in *Pengő* dominations are already in use.

The amount of notes in circulation is considerably greater than at this season last year, but it is still below what was estimated in these reports some months ago to be a reasonable and normal level. It should be possible to meet all the currency requirements of what promises to be a heavy season, without any fear that the expansion will be excessive. The reserve position has not suffered as much as might have been expected during the first six months of the year, when the visible balance of payments is adverse. It will probably be further strengthened during the coming months, and there can now be no question that exchange stability is secured. The National Bank has continued gradually to accumulate reserves in actual gold, and it is satisfactory that the Bank should already be in such a strong business position as to be able to afford the considerable loss of interest involved. The shares of the National Bank now stand on the Bourse at a price equivalent to about 112 and do not suffer the market fluctuations to which other shares are subject.

B. *Foreign Payments.*

The amount of long-term obligations, the service charges of which must be paid in foreign currency, has an important bearing on Hungary's international balance of payments. The following table shows the total amount necessary to meet the service charge on the long-term foreign obligations now outstanding:

	National amount	Annual service charge
	Gold crowns	
I. Loans since Reconstruction Period (May 1st, 1924).		
1. State Loan, Kingdom of Hungary, 1924 (Reconstruction Loan), issued Aug. 1st, 1924, in various countries and currencies; interest: 7 ½ % (in Italy only 7%)	320,556,421	32,907,810
2. Rimamuranyi Steel Co. Loan, issued in dollars, Feb. 1st, 1925; interest: 7%	14,805,000	1,184,400
3. Hungarian Consolidated Municipal Loan, issued July 1st, 1925, in dollars; interest: 7 ½ %	49,350,000	4,802,693

4. Hungarian Land Mortgage Institute (Magyar Földhitel Intézet): sterling issue, Jan. 5th, 1926 – £ 1 million; dollar issue, June 1st, 1926 – $ 3 million; interest 7 ½ %	38,822,300	3,237,362
5. Hungarian Banks' Co-operative Society Agri-Cultural Credit, issued April 30th, 1926; interest: 7 ½ %	24,675,000	2,009,045
II. Treaty Charges and Similar Obligations.		
1. Guarantee of interest on the Südbahn		3,604,292
2. British Clearing-House Payments[1]		12,017,518
3. French Clearing-House Payments		1,832,618
		216,792
4. Italian Clearing-House Payments (provisional)		108,590
5. Reparation Payments[2]		5,000,000
6. Relief Bonds, dated 1921; interest: 5%, except U.S.A. Bonds at 3%	12,782,854	1,269,071
III. Pre-War Obligations.		
1. State Loans:		
(a) Gold *Rente*[3] 1880, 1881, 1887, 1888, 1892; interest: 4%	578,229,219	13,249,419
(b) *Rente* of 1910[4]; interest: 4%	32,516,960	541,407
(c) *Rente* of 1913[5]; interest: 4 ½ %	16,013,580	352,654
(d) *Rente* of 1913[6]; interest: 4 ½ %	98,344,781	2,174,034
(e) Bonds of the "Steg"[7] issued at various times; interest: 3%	85,055,081	1,218,355
(f) Rent of the "Steg"		164,643
(g) Consolidated French Francs Treasury Bonds, Jan. 31st, 1922; interest: 6%	14,654,430	879,266
2. City of Budapest Loan[8], issued 1910, 1911, 1914; interest: 4% and 4 ½ %	199,135,768	7,013,052
Total		93,783,021

[1]This charge will be extinguished in approximately six years.

[2]These payments increase gradually until 1942, averaging 10 million gold crowns per year. (See schedule decision of Reparation Commission, February 21st, 1924.)

[3] These amounts are paid pursuant to the terms of the Innsbruck Agreement with pre-war creditors and are subject to revision in 1935

[4] Same as footnote 3.

[5]Same as footnote 3.

[6]Same as footnote 3.

[7]Same as footnote 3.

[8]Amounts fixed by the Ostend Agreement will be gradually increased according to the schedule appearing in the Seventeenth Report, page 5. In 1931-33, approximate payment will be 10,300,000 gold crowns; in 1934-55, 11,500,000 gold crowns.

While excessive borrowing abroad might become dangerous to the maintenance of the stability of the currency, there is no reason to suppose that the amounts contained in the table given above can have any effect upon the currency situation. In addition to the long-term loans, there is a considerable amount of short-term foreign credits outstanding, which is fluctuating and difficult to calculate at any given period. From such information as is available, it is not believed that they are excessive in amount or likely to throw an undue strain upon the financial situation of Hungary.

VI. Commerce and Reform.

A. *Foreign Commerce.*

The provisional returns of the foreign trade of Hungary for the first five months of the current calendar year are as follows:

	1925			1926		
	Imports	Exports	Difference	Imports	Exports	Difference
	Millions of gold crowns					
January	63.4	35.2	– 28.2	53.3	53.5	+ 0.2
February	58.8	39.9	– 18.9	62.7	50.3	– 12.4
March	57.7	52.2	– 5.5	70.5	49.1	– 21.4
April	52.6	46.6	– 6.0	61.9	43.6	– 18.3
May	52.8	52.6	– 0.2	58.4	49.7	– 8.7
Total	285.3	226.5	– 58.8	306.8	246.2	– 60.6

The volume of visible foreign trade for the period between January 1st and May 31st, 1926, is larger than it was for the first five months of 1925, exports having increased by 8.6 per cent and imports by 7.5 per cent. The unfavourable has increased by 3 per cent. It is possible that exports from Hungary to Austria have been delayed in expectation of the entry into force of the Commercial Convention, the negotiation of which was reported in the Twenty-second Report, III.B.

B. *Reforms.*

All reforms required by the reconstruction programme have been carried out. In addition there were certain reforms not included in the original programme but suggested by the Financial Committee as the result of developments which occurred during the progress of the plan. These have also been executed. The chief among them are the laws providing for the deposit of *Postsparkassa* monies and other State balances in the National Bank instead of in the Geldinstitutszentrale, and the adoption of laws requiring annual publication of all expenditure and receipts of the Government not included in the ordinary budget, as well as monthly statements of estimated receipts and expenditures and actual receipts for the preceding month.

C. *Miscellaneous.*

Harvest Prospects. – A report published by the Department of Agriculture on June 26th estimated the yield of the two chief cereal crops as follows, the actual yield in 1925 being also given for purposes of comparison:

	Estimate for 1926	Actual yield 1925
	Millions of metric centners	
Wheat	18.60	19.50
Rye	7.68	8.26

The average wheat crop from 1920 to 1924 inclusive was 13.87 million metric centners. Hungary's internal requirements for consumption and seed, in wheat and rye together, being about 18 million centners per annum, there should be a considerable export surplus.

The state of the autumn crops is very satisfactory.

Insolvencies. – Since the beginning of the year, the number of insolvencies coming before the courts has been as follows:

	Bankruptcies	Zwangsausgleiche	Total number of insolvencies coming before the court
		1926	
January	67	292	359
February	67	280	347
March	51	227	278
April	81	183	264
May	73	166	239
June	58	131	189

Annex I.

Preliminary Budget for June 1926. (Gold crowns)

1	2	3	4	5
	Expenditure		One-twelfth part of net estimates for 1925-26	Difference between columns 3 and 4
	Gross	Net		
Service of Government Debts	7,110,936	1,885,491	4,697,591	– 2,812,100
Charges under the Peace Treaty	608,386	608,386	666,666	– 58,280
Army personnel	3,024,723	3,024,723	3,383,461	– 358,738
Army other expenditure	1,682,620	1,668,759	2,083,806	– 415,047
Interior personnel	2,131,170	2,131,170	3,913,305	– 1,782,135
Interior other expenditure	1,681,270	1,586,083	757,541	+ 828,542
Finance personnel	2,264,246	2,177,703	2,176,167	+ 1,536
Finance other expenditure	3,009,496	1,462,779	914,107	+ 548,672
Education personnel	2,674,874	2,674,874	2,520,586	+ 154,288
Education other expenditure	1,783,021	747,677	801,527	– 53,850
Other Administrations personnel	3,782,169	3,782,169	3,981,562	– 199,393
Other Administrations other expenditure	7,237,773	5,628,607	2,623,819	+ 3,004,788
Subsidies to independent administrations	2,517,627	2,517,627	2,632,794	– 115,167
Pensions	5,579,203	5,579,203	6,105,633	– 526,430
Investments	1,150,656	1,150,656	1,000,000	+ 150,656
Total gross expenditure	46,238,170			
Deduct:				
Revenue not derived from taxation 8,358,256				
Working expenses of Tobacco Monopoly 1,254,007	9,612,263			
Net expenditure		36,625,907	38,258,565	– 1,632,658
Deduct:				
Receipts from tax on railway traffic		896,552	775,000	+ 121,552
Add:		35,729,355	37,483,565	– 1,754,210
Deficit on State undertakings		3,800,000	833,333	+ 2,966,667
Total net expenditure		39,529,355	38,316,898	+ 1,212,457
Revenue		39,603,097	40,616,666	– 1,013,569
Deficit				– 2,226,026
Surplus		+ 73,742	+ 2,299,768	

1	2	3	4	5
	Revenue		One-twelfth part of net estimates for 1925-26	Difference between columns 3 and 4
	Gross([9])	Net		
Direct taxes	4,413,793	4,413,793	10,641,666	– 6,227,873
Tax on business turnover	9,103,448	9,103,448	8,633,333	+ 470,115
Stamp and similar taxes	5,379,310	5,379,310	4,375,000	+ 1,004,310
Taxes on commodities	4,413,793	4,413,793	4,600,000	– 186,207
Customs	7,935,517	7,935,517	7,150,000	+ 785,517
Saccharine and Lottery Monopolies	59,310	59,310	50,000	+ 9,310
Salt Monopoly	631,035	586,416	933,333	– 346,917
Tobacco Monopoly	8,965,517	7,711,510	4,233,334	+ 3,478,176
Total	40,901,723	39,603,097	40,616,666	– 1,013,569

[9] The total gross revenue of the State is the amount given here, less the working expenses of the Salt Monopoly (44,619 for June), which are not paid directly by the State Treasury, plus "Revenue not derived from taxation" and "Receipts from tax on railway traffic", which have been deducted in columns 2 and 3 of the table of expenditure in order to ascertain "Net expenditure".

Particulars of Other Administrations

	Personnel	Other expenditure	
		Gross	Net
The Regent's Offices	73,926	34,222	33,160
National Assembly	54,152	139,478	139,478
State Court of Accounts	23,815	2,036	2,036
Court of Administration	37,746	3,872	3,872
Court of Land Reform	32,759	21,637	21,637
Prime Minister's Office	18,153	172,827	162,482
Ministry for Foreign Affairs	303,011	411,885	233,168
Ministry of Commerce	592,696	598,378	167,234
Ministry of Agriculture	560,474	751,178	374,311
Ministry of Public Welfare and Labour	354,449	4,268,416	3,780,106
Ministry of Justice	1,730,988	833,844	711,123
Total	3,782,169	7,237,773	5,628,607

Annex II.

Loan Account at June 30th, 1926.

		Net Proceeds		
		In original currencies	In gold crowns at rates on June 26th, 1924	In gold crowns at rates on June 30th, 1926
British tranche	£	6,480,214	138,352,568.90	155,648,260.06
U.S.A. tranche	$	6,000,000	29,610,000	29,610,000
Italian tranche	It. lire	147,560,000	31,449,275.36	26,265,680
Swiss tranche	Swiss francs	24,900,000	21,742,680	23,789,460
Swedish tranche	Swed. kr.	3,782,625	4,943,890.87	5,011,978.12
Dutch tranche	Dutch flor.	4,150,000	7,681,650	8,225,300
Czechoslovak tranhce	C. kr.	69,195,550	10,049,855	10,116,389.41
Hungarian tranche	$	2,021,000	9,973,635	9,973,635
			253,803,555.13	268,640,702.59

Releases		Balances available in gold crowns on June 30th, 1926	Where deposited
In original currencies	In gold crowns at the rates on dates of release		
£ 3,527,191 13s. 7d.	77,617,021.59	70,928,643.10	Bank of England
$ 3,743,982.02	18,476,551.26	6,198,447.74	Messrs. J. Speyer & Co., New York
		4,935,000	National City Bank, New York
Lire 93,688,057.08	20,128,457.15	9,677,928.15	Banca d'Italia, Rome
Sw. fr. 16,881,790	15,757,647.99	7,675,107.11	Union Financière, Geneva
Kr. 3,014,965.53	3,962,147.14	1,011,995.48	Enskilda Bank, Stockholm
Flor. 2,650,474.98	5,111,043.04	2,949,024.15	Messrs. Hope &Co., Amsterdam
C. kr. 69,195,550	10,175,263.44	—	
$ 2,021,000	9,973,635	—	
	161,201,766.61[10]	103,376,145.73	
Hung. kr. 2,190,105,496 at rate of June 30th at 14.481 151,239.93			National Bank of Hungary
	£377,344 3s. 9d. at 24.019 9,062,430.03		National Bank of Hungary
	$917,320 at 4.935 4,526,974.20		National Bank of Hungary
Swiss francs 1,954,100	at 0.9554 1,866,947.14		National Bank of Hungary
Dutch florins 240,216	at 1.982 476,108.11		National Bank of Hungary
Balance available	119,459,845.14		

[10] This amount includes releases made from the Loan Account as temporary advances for various purposes, most of which has been repaid. There is now outstanding an advance of £402,383 12s. and Hung. kr. 30 milliards for purchases of silver and other expenses in connection with the new coinage, which is to be repaid to the Loan Account when the new coins have been issued. All other advances have been repaid to the Loan Account, and the balance remaining available from these repayments appears in the list of different currencies shown at the bottom of the above table. The purposes for which these advances were originally made appear in detail in the different reports.

Annex III.

Comparative Table of the Balance-sheets of the National Bank of Hungary, May 1926.

	Pengő[11]			
	May 7th	May 15th	May 23rd	May 31st
Assets:				
Metal Reserve:				
Gold coin and bullion	93,734,310.78	102,095,073.46	108,402,064.47	110,545,870.57
Foreign exchange included under Art. 85 of the Statutes	146,512,266.50	131,246,084.36	121,164,810.74	128,547,117.88
Silver	900,226.59	907,749.80	903,988.18	903,988.18
Inland bills, warrants and securities	241,146,803.87	234,248,907.62	230,470,863.39	239,996,976.63
Advances on movable securities	162,110,623.71	150,760,664.46	147,889,229.38	174,946,837.72
Advances to the Treasury	21,174.08	21,174.08	21,174.08	20,374.08
Premises and equipment	151,788,790.24	151,788,790.24	151,788,790.24	151,788,790.24
Other assets	6,718,193.09	6,718,193.09	6,718,193.09	6,718,193.09
Total Assets	252,959,436.77	248,684,519.83	249,672,816.29	245,735,860.13
Liabilities:	814,745,021.76	792,222,249.32	786,561,066.47	819,207,031.89
Share capital (30,000,000 gold crowns)	34,756,095	34,756,095	34,756,095	34,756,095
Reserve Fund	1,588,951.56	1,588,951.56	1,588,951.56	1,588,951.56
Notes in circulation	392,964,562.71	371,718,808.12	347,519,005.48	387,503,780.54
Current accounts, deposits and other liabilities payable on demand	193,825,794.42	199,656,820.73	214,689,065.68	204,334,693.95
Other liabilities	191,609,618.07	184,501,573.91	188,007,948.75	191,023,510.84
Total Liabilities	814,745,021.76	792,222,249.32	786,561,066.47	819,207,031.89
Bank Cover (the cover required by Statutes must be equal 20% of note circulation plus sight liabilities minus State debt)	55.42%	55.82%	56.16%	54.52%
Bank rate	7%	7%	7%	7%

[11] 3,794 pengő = 1 kilogramme fine gold; 12,500 paper crowns = 1 pengő.

Annex III. a.

Comparative Table of the Balance-sheets of the National Bank of Hungary, June 1926.

	Pengő[12]			
	May 7th	May 15th	May 23rd	May 31st
Assets:				
Metal Reserve:				
Gold coin and bullion	110,606,099.20	115,512,529.98	119,039,023.27	121,142,678.69
Foreign exchange included under Art. 85 of the Statutes	128,307,979.07	121,820,713.53	111,701,450.23	107,125,613.27
Silver	907,749.80	909,630.59	907,749.80	907,749.80
Inland bills, warrants and securities	239,821,828.07	238,242,874.10	231,648,223.30	229,176,041.76
Advances on movable securities	160,798,034.98	155,955,411.57	147,197,101.54	165,097,858.16
Advances to the Treasury	20,374.08	20,374.08	20,374.08	20,374.08
Premises and equipment	151,726,497.52	151,726,497.52	151,726,497.52	151,726,497.52
Other assets	6,718,193.09	6,718,193.09	6,718,193.09	6,718,193.09
Total Assets	248,747,025.20	247,705,918.41	244,884,476.08	245,210,474.00
Liabilities:	807,831,952.95	795,369,268.77	782,194,865.61	797,949,438.61
Share capital (30,000,000 gold crowns)	34,756,095	34,756,095	34,756,095	34,756,095
Reserve Fund	1,588,951.56	1,588,951.56	1,588,951.56	1,588,951.56
Notes in circulation	373,889,147.80	361,667,665.57	354,359,075.10	395,419,001.42
Current accounts, deposits and other liabilities payable on demand	206,899,142.74	207,329,274.18	204,293,896.79	175,538,357.19
Other liabilities	190,698,615.85	190,027,282.46	187,196,847.16	190,647,033.44
Total Liabilities	807,831,952.95	795,369,268.77	782,194,865.61	797,949,438.61
Bank Cover (the cover required by Statutes must be equal 20% of note circulation plus sight liabilities minus State debt)	55.89%	57.09%	56.91%	54.65%
Bank rate	7%	7%	7%	7%

[12] 3,794 pengő = 1 kilogramme fine gold; 12,500 paper crowns = 1 pengő.

Annex IV.

Statistics.

Figures refer to the end of each month.

1. Retail Price Index (from the *Pester Lloyd*) (July 1914 = 1)

1924			1925		1926			
June	July	December	June	December	March	April	May	June
21,817	22,018	20,884	18,776	17,750	17,237	17,224	17,024	16,820

2. Wholesale Price Index (issued by Hungarian Statistical Office) (1913 = 1)

	Price Index	Change over preceding month	Comparison with 1913 gold prices
1924			
June	22,078	–2.7%	1.33
December	23,466	+1.6%	1.60
1925			
June	20,326	+0.3%	1.41
December	18,832	+1.1%	1.30
1926			
March	17,788	–1.3%	1.23
April	17,683	–0.6%	1.23
May	17,628	–0.3%	1.22
June	17,612	–0.09%	1.22

3. Stock Exchange Index (Ten important securities quoted on the Stock Exchange) (1914 = 100)

1924		1925		1926			
June	December	June	December	March	April	May	June
21.7	25.4	18.5	16.5	16.2	16.6	14.4	17.0

4. Deposits in the Postal Savings Banks and in Thirteen of the Most Important Banks in Budapest (Current Accounts and Savings Deposits)

	1924		1925		1926			
	June	December	June	December	March	April	May	June
	(In millions of gold crowns)							
Savings deposits:								
(a) In paper crowns	2.6	23.8	68.1	119.2	125.6	129.7	139.41	146.4
(b) In foreign currency	0.4	2.5	3.4	4.2	8.4	9.5	11.4	11.7
Current accounts:								
(a) In paper crowns	55.3	160.6	211.4	243.9	240.5	241.5	426.2	265.3
(b) In foreign currency	18.2	44.3	50.3	82.6	88.0	99.5	98.2	92.9
Total deposits:	76.7	231.3	333.2	449.9	462.5	480.2	495.2	516.3

5. Unemployed

(Figures relate only to members of the Union of Socialist Workers)

1924		1925			1926			
June	December	March	June	December	March	April	May	June
24,598	33,095	36,873	34,015	26,711	29,218	28,776	27,598	25,558

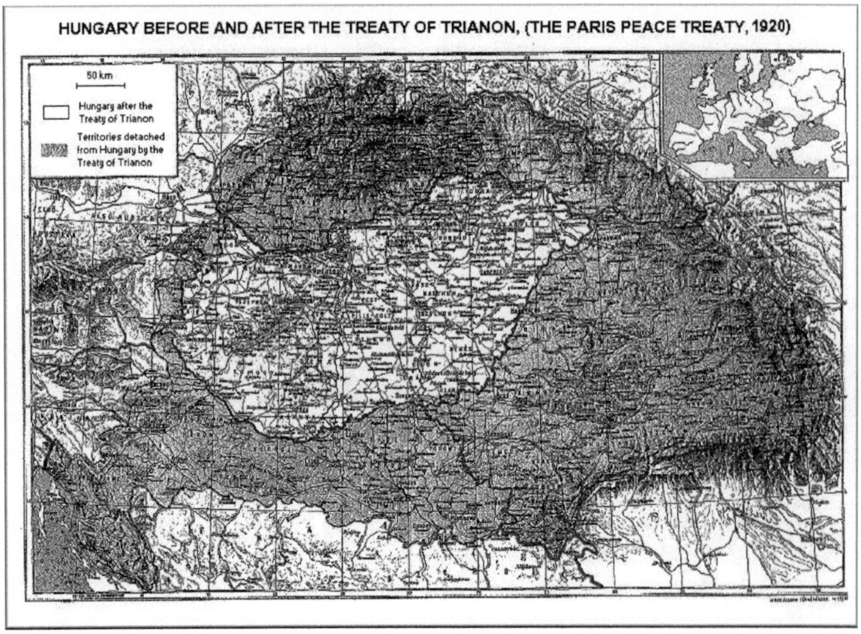

Map 1. Hungary before and after the Treaty of Trianon, (The Paris Peace Treaty, 1920). Copyright: András Szeitz.1920). Copyright: András Szeitz.

Picture 1. The Cotelle Gallery, where the Hungarian delegation signed the Treaty of Trianon on June 4, 1920. Author's own photo.

Picture 2. Miklós Horthy. Regent of Hungary, 1920–1944. Copyright: Enciklopédia Humana Association, Budapest.

Picture 3. István Bethlen. Prime Minister of Hungary, 1921–1931. Copyright: Babits Publishing House, Szekszárd.

Picture 4. Sir Arthur Salter. Director of the Economic and Financial Section of the League of Nations, 1922–1931. Copyright: League of Nations Photo collection, United Nations Library at Geneva.

Picture 5. Ignaz Seipel. Chancellor of Austria, 1922–124, 1926–1929. Copyright: League of Nations Photo collection, United Nations Library at Geneva.

Picture 6. Alfred Zimmerman. Commissioner-General of the League of Nations for Austria, 1922–1926. Copyright: League of Nations Photo collection, United Nations Library at Geneva.

Picture 7. Jeremiah Smith, Jr. Commissioner-General of the League of Nations for Hungary, 1924–1926. Copyright: League of Nations Photo collection, United Nations Library at Geneva.

Picture 8. Eduard Beneš. Foreign Minister of Czechoslovakia, 1918–1935. Copyright: League of Nations Photo collection, United Nations Library at Geneva.

Picture 9. Benjamin Strong. Governor of the Federal Reserve Bank of New York, 1914–1928. Copyright: Federal Reserve Bank of New York.

Picture 10. Jeremiah Smith, Jr. The picture was taken at a class reunion at Exeter. Photograph Courtesy of Phillips Exeter Academy.

Picture 11. Jeremiah Smith, Jr. Photograph Courtesy of Phillips Exeter Academy.

Works Cited

Primary Unprinted Sources:

Magyar Országos Levéltár [Hungarian National Archives] (HNA). Budapest, Hungary.
K 27, Records of Cabinet Council Meetings.
K 58, The Cabinet of the Minister.
K 66, Press and Cultural Department.
K 69, Economic Policy Department.
K 78, Collection of League of Nations Publications.
K 106, Papers of the Washington Embassy.
K 269, Finance Ministry, General Papers.
K 275. The Semi-official Papers of Finance Minister Kállay Tibor, 1901-1941.
K 276, Bud Papers.
K 304, Siepmann Papers.
K 428.a, Daily Reports.
K 468, Bethlen Papers.

League of Nations Archives (LNA). Geneva, Switzerland.
Economic and Financial Section.
Registry Files, 1919-1927.
Financial Reconstruction of Austria.
Financial Reconstruction of Hungary.
F. /17th Session/P. V; C. 267, 1924. II; C. 335 (I). M. 116. 1925; C. 440(1). M. 362(1). 1925. II; C. 359. M. 127. 1926. II; C. 152. M. 44. 1927. II.

Bank of England Archives (BoE). London, Great Britain.
ADM34, Diary of Montagu Collet Norman.
G3, Governor's Diaries, Duplicate Letters, etc.
G14, Committee of Treasury Files/Hungary.
G35, Strong-Norman Correspondence.
OV9, Sir Otto Niemeyer's Papers.

OV28, Overseas Files: Austria.
OV33, Overseas Files: Hungary.
OV112, Overseas Files: Czechoslovakia.

The National Archives of Great Britain (TNA). London, Great Britain.
Foreign Office Files, 371.
Treasury Files, 160.

National Archives and Records Administration (NARA). Washington, D. C., USA. Microfilm Publications, Records of the Department of State Relating to Internal Affairs of Austria-Hungary and Hungary, 1912–1929. Microcopy No. 708, Roll 6, Roll 7; Microcopy No. 709, Roll 1.

Jeremiah Smith Academy Archives (JSAA). Class of1945 Library, Phillips Exeter Academy, New Hampshire, USA.

Papers of Royall Tyler (1902–1967), Harvard University Archives, Cambridge, Massachusetts, USA.

James Speyer Papers, Rare Books and Manuscript Division, New York Public Library, New York, USA.

Siepmann's Memoir. Siepmann Family Archive of Private Papers of H. A. Siepmann, Bexhill, Great Britain.

Allen W. Dulles Papers, Princeton University Library, Princeton, New Jersey.

Francis Russell Papers, Boston Athenaeum, Boston, Massachusetts, USA.

Primary Printed Sources:

United States. Congressional Record. Washington, D. C.: Government Printing Office, 57th Congress, 1st Session; 63rd Congress, 2nd Session; 65th Congress, 2nd Session; 67th Congress, 1st Session; 68th Congress, 1st Session; 70th Congress, 2nd Session; 71st Congress, 1st Session,

Foreign Relations of the United States (FRUS). Washington, D. C.: Government Printing Office, 1919, Vol. 2; The Paris Peace Conference, Vol.12, 1920, Vol. 1; 1921, Vol. 2; 1922, Vol. 1, Vol. 2; 1924, Vol. 2;1925, Vol. 1; 1926, Vol. 1, Vol. 2; 1927, Vol. 1; 1928, Vol. 1, 1931. vol. 1.

Documents on British Foreign Policy (DBFP), First Series, vol. VI, Woodward, E. L. and Butler, Rohan, eds.London, 1956; vol. XII, Butler, Rohan, Bury, J. T., and

Lambert, M. E., eds.1962; DBFP, Vol. XXIV, ed. by by Medlicott, W. W. and Dakin, Douglas, 1983; vol. XXVI. Medlicott, W. W. and Dakin, Douglas, eds. London, 1985.

League of Nations. *The Financial Reconstruction of Austria. General Survey and Principal Documents.* Geneva, 1926.

League of Nations. *The Financial Reconstruction of Hungary. General Survey and Principal Documents.* Geneva, 1926.

League of Nations. *The League of Nations Reconstruction Schemes in the Inter-War Period.* Geneva: Economic, Financial and Transit Department, 1944.

League of Nations. Official Journal. 4th Year, No. 11, November 1923; 5th Year, No. 7, July 1924, No. 9, September 1924, No. 10, October 1924, No. 11, November 1924, No. 12, December 1924; 6th Year, No. 3, March 1925, No. 4, April 1925, No. 5, May 1925, No. 6, June 1925, No. 7, July 1925, No. 8, August 1925, No. 9, September 1925, No. 10, October 1925, No. 11, November 1925, No. 12, December 1925; 7th Year, No. 2, February 1926, No. 3, March 1926, No. 5, May 1926, No. 6, June 1926, No. 7, July 1926; 8th Year, No. 10, October 1927; 9th Year, No. 2, February 1928; 14th year, No. 4, April 1933.

Országgyűlés Képviselőházának Naplója [National Assembly Diary].1922–27, vol. XXII, XXIII, XLV. Budapest: Athenaeum nyomda, 1924, 1926. 1927–1932, vol XI. Budapest: Athenaeum nyomda, 1929.

H. W. V. Temperley, ed. *A History of the Peace Conference of Paris*, vol. 5, London: Henry Frowde and Hodder & Stoughton, 1921.

Magyar Törvénytár, 1920. évi törvénycikkek [Hungarian Law Collection, Law Bills of 1920] Budapest, 1921.

Autobiographies, Memoirs:

Apponyi, Count Albert. *Élmények és emlékek* [Experiences and Memories] Budapest: Atheaneum, [1933].

Bandholtz, Harry Hill. *An Undiplomatic Diary.* Safety Harbor, FL: Simon Publications, 2000.

Barcza, György. *Diplomata emlékeim, 1911-1945* [My Diplomatic Memoirs]. vol. 1-2., Budapest: Európa História, 1994.

Coolidge, Calvin. *The Autobiography of Calvin Coolidge.* New York: Cosmopolitan Book Corporation, 1929.

Hoover, Herbert Clark. *The Memoirs of Herbert Hoover.* vol. 1–3. New York: The Macmillan Company, 1951–1952.

Horthy, Nicholas. *Memoirs.* Safety Harbor, FL: Simon Publications, 2000.

Hughes, Charles E. *The Pathway of Peace.* New York: Harper and Brothers, 1925.

Lamont, Thomas W. *Across World Frontiers.* New York: Harcourt, Brace and Company, 1951.

Salter, Sir Arthur. *Memoirs of a Public Servant.* London: Faber and Faber, 1961.

Secondary Sources:

Books:

Ádám, Magda. *A Kisantant és Európa, 1920–1929*. Budapest: Akadémiai Kiadó, 1989

Ahamed, Liaquat. *Lords of Finance. The Bankers Who Broke the World*. New York: Penguin Books, 2009.

Aldcroft, Derek H. *From Versailles to Wall Street, 1919-1929*. London: Allen Lane, Penguin Books Ltd. 1977.

Aldcroft, Derek H. *The European Economy 1914-2000*. 4th ed. London and New York: Routledge, 2002.

Bácskai, Tamás, ed. *A Magyar Nemzeti Bank története*. [The History of the Hungarian National Bank]. vol. 1. Budapest: Közgazdasági és Jogi Könyvkiadó, 1993.

Berend, T. Iván, and Szuhay, Miklós. *A tőkés gazdaság története Magyarországon, 1848–1944* [The History of Capitalist Economy in Hingary, 1848–1944]. Budapest: Kossuth Kiadó, 1973.

Berend, T. Iván, and Ránki, György. *Magyarország gazdasága az első világháború után, 1919–1929* [Hungary's Economy after the First World War, 1919–1929]. Budapest: Akadémiai Kiadó, 1966.

Bethlen, István. Bethlen beszédei és irásai [Bethlen's Speeches and Writings]. vol. 1. Budapest: Genius Ltd., 1933.

Cartledge, Bryan. *Mihály Károlyi & István Bethlen: Hungary*. London: Haus Publishing Ltd., 2009.

Chandler, Lester V. *Benjamin Strong, Central banker*. Washington, D. C.: The Brookings Institution, 1958.

Chernow, Ron. *The House of Morgan*. New York: Atlantic Monthly Press, 1990.

Clarke, Stephen V. O. *Central Bank Cooperation: 1924–1931*. New York: Federal Reserve Bank of New York, 1967.

Clay, Sir Henry. *Lord Norman*. London: Macmillan & Co. Ltd., 1957.

Costigliola, Frank. *Awkward Dominion. American Political, Economic, and Cultural Relations with Europe, 1919–1933*. Ithaca, NY: Cornell University Press, 1984.

Cottrell, Philip L. *Rebuilding the Financial System in Central and Eastern Europe, 1918–1944*. Aldershot: Scolar Press, 1997.

Culberstone, William Smith. *International Economic Policies*. New York: D. Appleton and Company, 1925.

Deák, Francis. *Hungary at the Paris Peace Conference. The Diplomatic History of the Treaty of Trianon*. New York: Columbia University Press, 1942.

Demény, Zsuzsa. *Századok statisztikája. Statisztikai érdekességek a magyar történelemből* [Statistics of Centuries. Interesting Statistics of Hugarian History]. Központi Statisztikai Hivatal, Budapest, 2001.

Dennis, Alfred Pearce. *The Romance of World Trade*. New York: Henry Holt and Company, 1926.

Dinnerstein, Leonard. *Anti-Semitism in America.* New York/Oxford: Oxford University Press, 1994.

Eichengreen, Barry. *Golden Fetters: The Gold Standard and the Great Depression, 1919–1939.* New York: Oxford University Press, 1992.

Fink, Carole. *The Genoa Conference: European Diplomacy, 1921–1922.* Chapel Hill: University of North Carolina Press, 1984.

Foreign Policy Association Information Service. Volume III. Special Supplement No. 3. America. *The World's Banker.* New York: Foreign Policy Association, June 1927.

George, Lloyd. *The Truth about Reparations and War-debts.* London: William Heinemann Ltd., 1932.

Harper, John Lamberton. *American Visions of Europe. Cambridge*: Cambridge University Press, 1994.

Havas, Eugene. *Hungary's Finance and Trade, 1927.* London: London General Press, 1928.

Havas, Eugene. *Hungary's Finance and Trade 1928.* London: London General Press, 1929.

Heinrichs, Waldo H. *American Ambassador. Joseph C. Grew and the Development of the United States Diplomatic Tradition.* Boston and Toronto: Little Brown and Company, 1966.

Hogan, Michael J. *Informal Entente. The Private Structure of Cooperation in Anglo-American Economic Diplomacy, 1918-1928.* Chicago: Imprint Publications, 1991.

Holmes, Colin. *Anti-Semitism in British Society, 1876-1939.* London: Edward Arnold, Ltd., 1979.

Hornyák, Árpád. *Magyar-jugoszláv diplomáciai kapcsolatok, 1918–1927.* [Hungarian-Yugoslav Diplomatic Relations, 1918–1927] Újvidék: Forum Könyvkiadó, 2004.

Ináritsy-Pap, Elemér. *A magyar városok Speyer-kölcsönei* [The Hungarian Cities' Speyer Loans] Budapest: Home Printing House of Budapest, 1938.

In Memory of Roland William Boyden. Boston: Commonwealth of Massachusetts, 1933.

Isaacson, Walter, and Thomas, Evan. *The Wise Men. Six Friends and the World They Made.* New York: Simon & Schuster Inc., 1986.

Kaser, M. C. and Radice, E. A., eds. *The Economic History of Eastern Europe, 1919-1975.* vol. 1. Oxford: Clarendon Press, 1985.

Katzburg, Nathaniel. *Hungary and the Jews. Policy and Legislation 1920-1943.* Ramat-Gan: Bar-Ilan University, 1981.

Kerekes, Lajos. *Ausztria története, 1918–1955.* [The History of Austria, 1918–1955] Budapest: Akadémiai Kiadó, 1966.

Keynes, John Maynard. *The Economic Consequences of the Peace.* New York: Harcourt, Brace and Howe, 1920.

Keynes, John Maynard. "Scheme for the Rehabilitation of European Credit and for Financing Relief and Reconstruction," In. *The Collected Writings of John Maynard Keynes*, Vol. XVI. *Activities 1914-1919. The Treasury and Versailles.* Elizabeth Jonson ed. London: Macmillan, 1971.

Kuczynski, Robert R. *American Loans to Germany.* New York: The Macmillan Company, 1927.

Lamont, Edward M. *The Ambassador from Wall Street. The Story of Thomas W. Lamont, J. P. Morgan's Chief Executive.* Lanham, Maryland: Madison Books, 1994.

Lebzelter, C. Gisela. *Political Anti-Semitism in England, 1918-1939.* Oxford: Macmillan, in association with St. Anthony's College, 1978.

Leffler, Melvyn P. *The Elusive Quest: America's Pursuit of European Stability and French Security, 1919–1933.* Chapel Hill, NC: University of North Carolina Press, 1979.

Lewis, Cleona. *America's Stake in International Investments.* Washington, D. C.: The Brookings Institution, 1938.

Lojkó, Miklós. *Meddling in Middle Europe.* Budapest: Central European University Press, 2006.

MacMillan, Margaret. *Peacemakers: The Paris Peace Conference of 1919 and Its Attempt to End War.* New York: Random House, 2002.

Magos, György. *Az amerikai imperialisták szerepe a Horthy fasizmus stabilizásában, 1924–1929.* [The Role of the American Imperialists in the Stabilization of the Horthy Fascism] Budapest: Akadémiai Kiadó, 1952.

Major, Mark Imre. *American Hungarian Relations 1918-1944.* Astor, Fl: Danubian Press, 1974.

Masaryk, Thomas Garrigue. *The Making of a State. Memories and Observations, 1914– 1918.* New York: Frederick A. Stokes Co., 1927.

Matthews, Jeffrey J. *Alanson B. Houghton. Ambassador of the New Era.* Lanham, MD: Rowman and Littlefield, 2004.

McCartney, C. A. *Hungary and Her Successors. The Treaty of Trianon and Its Consequences, 1919–1937.* London: Oxford University Press, 1937.

Mendelsohn, Ezra. *The Jews of East Central Europe between the World Wars.* Bloomington: University of Indiana, 1983.

Meyer, Richard Hemmig. *Bankers' Diplomacy. Monetary Stabilization in the Twenties.* New York: Columbia University Press, 1970.

Mintz, Ilse. *Deterioration in the Quality of Foreign Bonds Issued in the United States 1920–1930.* New York: National Bureau of Economic Research, Inc., 1951.

Moulton, Harold G. *The Reparation Plan.* New York: McGraw-Hill Book Company, 1924.

Nagy, Zsuzsa L., "Amerikai diplomaták Horthy Miklósról, 1920-1944," [American Diplomats on Miklós Horthy] *Történelmi Szemle* 33, nos 3-4, (1990): 173-196.

Nemes, Dezső. ed., *Iratok az ellenforradalom történetéhez.* [Papers on the History of the Counterrevolution] vol. 3, 1921–24. Budapest: Kossuth Könyvkiadó, 1959.

Nicolson, Harold. *Curzon: The Last Phase*, London: Constable & Co., 1934.
Orde, Anne. *British Policy and European Reconstruction after the First World War.* Cambridge: Cambridge University Press, 1990.
Ormos, Mária. *Az 1924. évi magyar államkölcsön megszerzése.* [Raising the Hungarian State Loan of 1924] Budapest: Akadémiai Kiadó, 1964.
Parrini, Carl. *Heir to Empire: United States Economic Diplomacy, 1916-1923* Pittsburgh: University of Pittsburgh, 1969.
Pease, Neal. *Poland, the United States, and the Stabilization of Europe, 1919–1933.* New York: Oxford University Press, 1986.
Péteri, György. *Global Monetary Regime and National Central Banking. The Case of Hungary, 1921–1929.* Boulder, Colorado: Social Science Monographs, 2002.
Péteri, György. *Revolutionary Twenties. Essays on International Monetary and Financial Relations after World War I.* Trondheim: University of Trondheim, 1995.
Porter Kirk H. and Johnson, Donald Bruce, eds. *National Party Platforms, 1840–1968.* Urbana: University of Illinois Press, 1972.
Pressburger, Siegfried. *Oesterreichische Notenbank, 1816–1966* [The Austrian Bank of Issue]. Wien: Oesterreichische Nationalbank Hausdruckerei, 1966.
Quint, Howard H. and Ferrel, Robert H., eds. *The Talkative President. The Off-the-Record Press Conferences of Calvin Coolidge.* Amherst: The University of Massachusetts Press, 1964.
Ránki, György. *Gazdaság és Külpolitika. A nagyhatalmak harca a délkelet-európai gazdasági hegemóniáért (1919–1939)* [Economy and Foreign Policy. The Fight of the Great Power for Economic Hegemony in South-Central Europe, 1919–1936]. Budapest: Magvető Kiadó, 1981.
Romsics, Ignác. *István Bethlen: A Great Conservative Statesman of Hungary, 1874–1946.* Boulder, Colorado: Social Science Monographs, 1995.
Rosenberg, Emily S. *Financial Missionaries to the World. The Politics and Culture of Dollar Diplomacy, 1900–1930.* Durham and London: Duke University Press, 2003.
Rothbard, Murray N. *America's Great Depression.* Auburn: The Ludwig von Mises Institute, 2000.
Rothschild, Kurt Wilhelm. *Austria's Economic Development between the Two Wars.* London: Frederick Muller Ltd., 1947.
Rothschild, Joseph. *East Central Europe between the Two World Wars.* Seattle: University of Washington Press, 1974.
Salter, Sir Arthur. *Political Aspects of the World Depression.* Oxford: Clarendon Press, 1932.
Salter, Arthur. *The United States of Europe and Other Papers.* London: George Allen & Unwin Ltd., 1933.
Salter, Sir Arthur. *World Trade and Its Future.* London: Oxford University Press, 1936.

Salter, Arthur, *Security. Can We Retrieve it?* London: MacMillan and Co., Ltd, 1939.

Salter, Sir Arthur. *Personality in Politics.* London: Faber and Faber, 1947.

Sammons, Robert L. "Capital Movements." In *The United States in the World Economy,* ed. Hal. B. Lary and Associates Washington, D. C.: Government Printing Office, 1943.

Sayers, R. S. *The Bank of England, 1891–1944.* vol. 1. Cambridge: Cambridge University Press, 1976.

Siepmann, Harry. *Echo fo Guns. Recollections of an Artillery Officer, 1914-18.* London: Robert Hale, 1987.

Smith, Jeremiah. *The Preservation of the Peace.* Cambridge, MA: Harvard Law School, 1927.

Smith, Rixey, and Beasley, Norman. *Carter Glass: A Biography.* New York: Longmans, Green and Co., 1939.

Soule, George. *Prosperity Decade. A Chapter from American Economic History, 1917–1929.* London: The Pilot Press Limited, 1947.

Steel, Ronald. *Walter Lippmann and the American Century.* Boston Toronto: Little, Brown and Company, 1970.

Taraszovics, Sándor. "American Peace Preparations during World War I and the Shaping of the New Hungary." In Ignác Romsics, ed. *20th Century Hungary and the Great Powers.* Boulder, Colorado: Social Science Monographs, Atlantic Research and Publications Inc., 1994, 73-97.

Wilson, Joan Hoff. *American Business & Foreign Policy, 1920–1933.* Lexington, KY: The University Press of Kentucky, 1971.

Wilson, Joan Hoff. *Ideology and Economics: U.S. Relations with the Soviet Union, 1918–1933.* Columbia, Mo., 1974.

Winkler, Marx. *The Investor and the League Loans.* New York: Foreign Policy Association, Volume 4, June 1928, Supplement No.2.

Wueschner, Silvano A. *Charting Twentieth-Century Monetary Policy. Herbert Hoover and Benjamin Strong, 1917–1927.* Westport, Connecticut: Greenwood Press, 1999.

Zebel, Sydney Henry. *Balfour: A Political Biography.* Cambridge: Cambridge University Press, 1973.

Zöllner, Erich. *Ausztria története.* [The History of Austria] Budapest: Osiris Kiadó, 1998.

Articles:

Abrahams, Paul P. "American Bankers and the Economic Tactics of Peace: 1919." *Journal of American History* 56, no. 3 (December 1969): 572–583.

Adlgasser, Franz. "The Roots of Communist Containment: American Food Aid in Austria and Hungary after World War I." in *Austria in the Nineteen Fifties, Contemporary Austrian Studies* 3 (1995): 171–88.

Buchsbaum, Tamar. "A Note on Antisemitism in Admissions at Dartmouth," *Jewish Social Studies* 49, no. 1 (Winter, 1987): 79-84.

Beale, Joseph H. "Jeremiah Smith." *Harvard Law Review* 35, no. 1 (November 1921): 1–8.

Beale, Joseph H. "Jeremiah Smith, Jr. (1870–1935)." *Proceedings of the American Academy of Arts and Sciences* 71, no. 10 (Mar., 1937): 549–550.

Beneš, Eduard. "The Little Entente." *Foreign Affairs* 1, no. 1 (September 1922): 66–72.

Berdahl, Clarence A. "The United States and the League of Nations." *Michigan Law Review* 27, no. 6 (April 1929): 607–636.

Berger, Peter. "Rebuilding Economies after External Shocks." *Development and Finance* 1, no. 2 (2003): 64–74.

Bethlen, István. "Hungary in the New Europe." *Foreign Affairs* 3, no. 2 (April 1925): 445–458.

Burks, David D. "The United States and the Geneva Protocol of 1924: 'A New Holy Alliance'?" *The American Historical Review* 64, no. 4 (July 1959): 891–905.

Calderon, Garcia F. "Latin America, Europe and the United States." *Foreign Affairs* 7, no. 2 (January 1929): 183–197.

Comstock, Alzada. "The Technique of Reconstruction as Applied to Hungary." *Political Science Quarterly* 40, no. 2 (June 1925): 201–206.

Costigliola, Frank. "The United States and the Reconstruction of Germany in the 1920s." *The Business History Review* 50, no. 4 (Winter 1976): 477–502.

Costigliola, Frank. "American Foreign Policy in the 'Nut Cracker': The United States and Poland in the 1920s." *The Pacific Historical Review,* 48, no. 1 (February 1979), 85–105.

Béla, "Csizik Államháztartás és közteher", [State Finances and Public Taxes] *Közgazdasági Szemle,* 1930 January, 75/1, 569-616.

Dobrossy, István. "Miskolc infrastruktúrájának modernizálása és a 'Speyer' bankkölcsön felhasználása (1925–1950) [The Modernization of the Infrastructure of Miskolc and Using the Speyer Loans]," In. *Yearbook of the Herman Ottó Museums,* XXXIII- XXXIV, Miskolc: 1996, 423–451.

Dulles, Allen W. "The Protection of American Foreign Bondholders." *Foreign Affairs* 10, no. 3 (April, 1932): 474–484.

Egressy, Gergely. "A Statistical Overview of the Hungarian Numerus Clausus Law of 1920—A Historical Necessity or the First Step Toward the Holocaust?" *Eastern European Quarterly* 34, no. 4 (January 2001): 447–464.

Glant, Tibor. "Apponyi Albert és Jászi Oszkár amerikai vitája a népszövetségi kölcsönről 1923 őszén." [The American Debate of Albert Apponyi and Oszkár Jászi over the League Loan in the Fall of 1923] *Vasváry Collection Newsletter* 17, no. 1 (1997): 3-5.

Glant, Tibor. "Herbert Hoover and Hungary, 1918–1923." *Hungarian Journal of English and American Studies* 8, no. 2 (2002): 95–109.

Glant, Tibor. "Herbert Hoover és Magyarország, 1918–1920." [Herbert Hoover and Hungary, 1918–1920] In. *Emlékkönyv L. Nagy Zsusza 70. születésnapjára*, eds. János Angi and János Barta, Debrecen: Multiplex Media, 2000, 381–399.

Gratz, Gustav. "Business Combinations and Economic Conditions in Hungary and Neighboring States." *Proceedings of the Academy of Political Sciences in the City of New York*. vol. 11, no. 4 (January 1926): 174–180.

Hogan, Michael J. "The United States and the Problem of International Economic Control: American Attitudes toward European Reconstruction, 1918–1920." *The Pacific Historical Review* 44, no. 1 (February 1975): 84–103.

Jones, Kenneth Paul. "Discord and Collaboration: Choosing an Agent General for Reparations." *Diplomatic History* 1 (Spring 1977): 118–139.

Kane, N. Stephen. "Bankers and Diplomats: The Diplomacy of the Dollar in Mexico, 1921–1924." *The Business History Review* 47, no. 3 (Autumn 1973): 335–352.

Kemmerer, Edwin W. "Economic Advisory Work for Governments." *The American Economic Review* 17, no. 1 (March 1927): 1–12.

L. Nagy Zsusza, "Amerikai diplomaták Horthy Miklósról, 1920-1944." [American Diplomats on Miklós Horthy] *Történelmi Szemle* 33, nos 3-4, (1990): 173-196.

Leffler, Melvyn P. "American Policy Making and European Stability, 1921–1933." *The Pacific Historical Review* 46, no. 2 (May 1977): 207–228.

Magos, György. "The Role of the British and American Imperialists in the Stabilisation of Horthy Fascism." *Acta Historica. Academiae Scientarium*, 2, no. 1–2, ed. E. Nadics. Budapest: Magyar Tudományos Akadémia, (1953): 161–213.

Magyarics, Tamás: "Count Teleky's and Count Albert Apponyi's Missions in the USA in the First Half of the 1920s." In: *Americana and Hungarica*. ed. Charlotte Kretzoi. Budapest: (1989): 69–77.

Marks, Sally. "The Myths of Reparations." *Central European History* 11, no. 3 (September 1978): 231–255.

Martin, Percy Alvin. "Latin America and the League of Nations." *The American Political Science Review* 20, no. 1 (February 1926): 14–30.

Ormos, Mária. „Magyarország belépése a Nemzetek Szövetségébe." [Hungary's Entry to the League of Nations] *Századok* 91, no. 1 (1957): 227–269.

O. W. B. P. "Morison's Life of Smith." *The Christian Examiner and Religious Miscellany* 39 (July, September, November, 1845): 170–180.

Pogány, Ágnes. Párhuzamos történetek [Parallel Stories]. In. *Ötven eves a Budapesti Közgazdaságtudományi Egyetem* [Budapest University of Economic Sciences Is 50 Years Old]. vol. 2 (Budapest, 1998): 1214–1228.

Pollak, Oliver B. "Antisemitism, the Harvard Plan, and the Roots of Reverse Discrimination," *Jewish Social Studies* 45, no. 2 (Spring, 1983): 113-122.

Ribuffo, Leo P. "Henry Ford and 'The International Jew," American Jewish History 69, no. 4 (June 1980): 437-477.

Roberts, Priscilla. "Benjamin Strong, the Federal Reserve, and the Limits to Interwar American Nationalism." *Economic Quarterly* 86, no. 2 (Spring 2000): 62–98.

Romsics, Ignác. "Franciaország, Bethlen és a frankhamisítás." [France, Bethlen, and the Franc Forgery] *Történelmi Szemle* 26, no. 1 (1983): 67–86.
Romsics, Ignác. "Changing Images of Miklós Horthy." In *Cultic Revelations:* Studies in Modern Historical Cult Personalities and Phenomena. Ed. By Anssi Halmesvirta. Helsinki: The Finnish Literature Society, 2008), 127-148.
Rosenberg, Norman L. "From Colonialism to Professionalism: The Public-Private Dynamic in United States Foreign Financial Advising, 1898–1929." *The Journal of American History* 74, no. 1 (June 1987): 59–82.
Schuker, Stephen A. "American Policy Toward Debts and Reconstruction at Genoa, 1922." In *Genoa, Rapallo, and European reconstruction in 1922.* Carole Fink, Axel Frohn, and Jürgen Heideking, editors, Cambridge: Cambridge University Press, 2002, 95–130.
Seidel, Robert N. "American Reformers Abroad: The Kemmerer Missions in South America, 1923–1931." *The Journal of Economic History* 32, no. 2 (June 1972): 520–545.
Sipos, Péter. "Teleki Pál párizsi és londoni útja 1921-ben és a magyar külpolitikai orientáció." [Pál Teleki's Journey to Paris and London] In. *A hosszú tizenkilencedik és a rövid huszadik század.* [The long nineteenth and the short twentieth centuries] Ed. Gergely Jenő. Budapest: ELTE BTK, 2000), 496–97.
Speyer, James. "America's Cooperation in European Rehabilitation Primarily Dependent on Europe." A*nnals of the American Academy of Political and Social Science* 102, (July 1922): 175–77.
Topik, Steven C. "When Mexico Had the Blues: A Transatlantic Tale of Bonds, Bankers, and Nationalists, 1862–1910." *The American Historical Review* 105, no. 3 (June 2000): 714–738.
Tyler, Royall. "The Eastern Reparations Settlement." *Foreign Affairs* 9, no. 1 (October 1930): 106–117.
Williams, William Appleman. "The Legend of Isolationism in the 1920s," *Science & Society* 18, no. 1 (Winter 1954): 1–20.

Periodicals:

Time
The New York Times
Boston Daily Globe
Christian Science Monitor
Wall Street Journal
The Times
Az Est
Budapesti Hírlap
Magyarország
Pesti Hírlap
Pesti Napló

Bei Fragen zur Produktsicherheit wenden Sie sich bitte an:
If you have any questions regarding product safety,
please contact:

Walter de Gruyter GmbH
Genthiner Straße 13
10785 Berlin
productsafety@degruyterbrill.com